Advanced FileMaker® Pro 6 Web Development

Bob Bowers and Steve Lane

Wordware Publishing, Inc.

Library of Congress Cataloging-in-Publication Data

Bowers, Bob, 1969-
Advanced filemaker pro 6 web development / by Bob Bowers and Steve Lane.
p. cm.
ISBN 1-55622-860-0
1. FileMaker pro. 2. Database management. 3. World Wide Web.
I. Lane, Steve, 1965- II. Title.
QA76.9.D3B6739 2003
005.75'65--dc21 2003005386
CIP

2320 Los Rios Boulevard
Plano, Texas 75074

Printed in the United States of America

ISBN 1-55622-860-0

10 9 8 7 6 5 4 3 2 1
0303

All inquiries for volume purchases of this book should be addressed to Wordware Publishing, Inc., at the above address. Telephone inquiries may be made by calling:

(972) 423-0090

Dedication

To my parents, who paved the way.

Steve Lane

For my soon-to-be-born, yet unnamed son. You'll get your name in the next one.

Bob Bowers

Contents

Acknowledgments

We'd like to heartily thank all of the people whose help and support made this book possible. To start, Jim Hill, Wes Beckwith, Heather Hill, and Beth Kohler at Wordware Publishing were exceedingly patient with us, even as deadlines came and went. Thanks to Bill Bennett and Greg Lane for reading and commenting on chapters in spite of their own busy schedules. Aaron Holdsworth helped write the Web Server Connector section of Chapter 3. Thanks to Chris Moyer, Scott Love, and the rest of the Moyer Group team for keeping our business moving ahead and allowing us free time for writing.

Writing a book, I've come to discover, has a way of affecting the lives of everyone around you. Coworkers, clients, friends, and family can't help but get caught up in the stress and strain. Thanks to my in-laws, MaryAnn and Tom Moore, for the use of their cottage as a hideaway. Thanks to John Overton and Molly Thorsen for being such good friends and advisors. And thanks to Kim Fenn, Adam Christofferson, and Bethany Albertson for prescribing reality TV and cheese fondue as stress relief medication. I'd also like to thank Steve Lane for being such a great co-author, co-worker, friend, and all-around good guy.

Finally, thanks to my wife, Rebecca Moore. She's pregnant now with our first child, and nonetheless has been a constant source of love and support. She has given up many evenings and weekends and part of a vacation so that this book could be finished. The next major project is turning the guest room into a nursery—I promise.

Bob Bowers

No one writes a book alone. It's just the opposite: The more we lock ourselves away to pound the keyboard, the more we rely on those around us to keep us sane and healthy (or, in the worst case, fed and dressed!). And, especially with a technical topic, we also rely on constant recourse to the people who can answer the hard questions. Thanks to Jay Welshofer for straightening me out on the points of FileMaker's XML implementation and to Greg Lane and Andrew Nash for their rigorous "usability testing" on a number of chapters. Any errors or omissions that remain are my own. Bob Bowers has been a great partner—not just in this book, but in all of our work together over the last few years. Writing a book is never the easiest thing, but Bob's good humor, sound technical judgment, and determination made it much easier. Two are better than one, as they say, and Bob's always been there with a hand.

Steve Lane

Introduction

This is the second in a series of books on advanced FileMaker Pro development techniques. The first book, *Advanced FileMaker Pro 5.5 Techniques for Developers*, focused on programming techniques for pure FileMaker Pro solutions. These days, however, many powerful FileMaker solutions are not just pure FileMaker but hybrid solutions, where FileMaker is tied to other data sources and interfaces, including prepress workflows, SQL databases, legacy data from mainframes, and, of course, the ever-present web.

This book focuses on the last of these rich integration possibilities—publishing your FileMaker data to the World Wide Web. Over six years ago, we first used FileMaker to export HTML to build static web pages. Since then, we've watched as FileMaker has steadily added support for a wide variety of web standards. As the product has grown, third-party and open-source offerings have grown along with it. Today, a FileMaker developer charged with "putting our database on the web" has an almost bewildering variety of options, ranging from the built-in capabilities of FileMaker itself to commercial tools such as Lasso and open-source tools such as PHP and XML. Our goals in writing this book have been both to introduce you to the major web technologies that you can use with FileMaker and give you a decent footing in the general principles of designing data-driven web applications.

Whether you're a proficient FileMaker developer looking to make the leap to the web or you've already worked with one or more of the major FileMaker web tools and want to hone your skills, you should find something of value in this book. We're going to assume that you have intermediate-level FileMaker skills. To us, this means knowing how to create a FileMaker database, how to work with related databases, and how to work with basic calculations. We also assume that you have a basic familiarity with HTML.

You'll get the most out of this book if you follow along with our demo files, which are available for download at http://www.moyergroup.com/webbook/ and www.wordware.com/files/fmweb. Errata, if any, and other notes are available at these sites as well.

About the Authors

Bob Bowers is president of the Moyer Group, a FileMaker consulting and training firm with offices in Chicago, Atlanta, and San Francisco. He has been a columnist and contributing editor for *FileMaker Advisor* magazine since the publication's inception and is the co-author (with Chris Moyer) of *Advanced FileMaker Pro 5.5 Techniques for Developers*. At the 2002 FileMaker Developer's Conference, he was awarded the FileMaker Fellowship Award "for developing outstanding technical and educational resources for FileMaker." Bob holds a master's degree in musicology from the University of Chicago and enjoys playing guitar, singing, woodworking, and biking in his off hours.

Steve Lane is vice president for the Moyer Group, where he's involved in all phases of the application development process, from sales to development and deployment. His chief focus is on advanced web technologies as they relate to FileMaker Pro. He's worked with relational databases for over a dozen years. In his previous life he was a medieval historian.

Chapter 1

The Dynamic Web

So you want to put your data on the web? Join the crowd. Few 21st-century web sites consist of nothing but static HTML pages. Most web sites have at least some amount of dynamic content—meaning content that changes automatically (or at least according to some programmed schedule). More often than not, this content is fetched from some type of database in response to user inputs or preferences. This book shows you how to build dynamic web sites that use FileMaker Pro as a data source. In this chapter, we look at some reasons that you might want to do this and explore the ways in which accessing a database over the web differs from the regular FileMaker model you're probably used to.

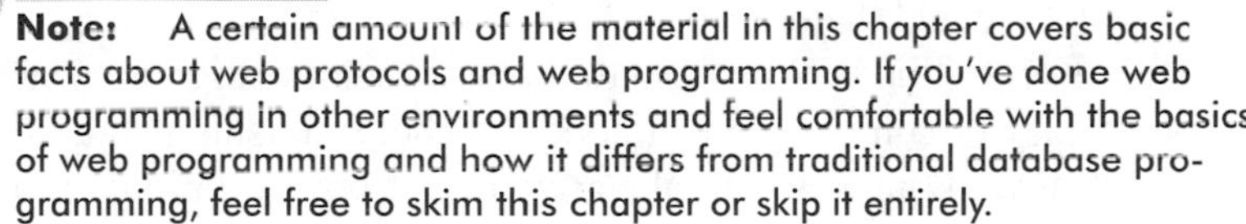

Note: A certain amount of the material in this chapter covers basic facts about web protocols and web programming. If you've done web programming in other environments and feel comfortable with the basics of web programming and how it differs from traditional database programming, feel free to skim this chapter or skip it entirely.

A Case Study

Let's take a hypothetical example. Blue Horizon Bison Breeders is a nonprofit organization dedicated to reintroducing the American Bison into the Great Plains. They run a web site explaining their mission and sell bison-watching "safaris" as well as the occasional buffalo sirloin to help pay the costs of their enterprise. (The fine print at the front of the book may already say this, but it's worth saying again—Blue Horizon, like all the examples in this book, is a fictitious organization. So, no, we can't give you their web address.) The Blue Horizon online store is a simple web page that lists all of the items that Blue Horizon sells, along with the price for each, and a phone number that visitors can call to place a phone order. Additionally, three to five items each week are featured as "specials" and shown prominently at the top of the store's web page with price reductions.

Karen Thornapple is vice president, buffalo breeder, and Blue Horizon's web site administrator. Each week Karen edits the Blue Horizon store web page, manually removing last week's specials and adding this week's. Blue Horizon actually tracks all of their sales to the public using a FileMaker database that Karen helped to write. (They track all of their breeding and herd statistics in FileMaker also, but that's a story for another chapter.) In any case, Karen is frustrated with having to edit the store page manually every week. Wouldn't it be easier, she reasons, if the store page could somehow pull data directly from her FileMaker system? Then all she'd have to do is check the Special box in FileMaker, and the list of specials would automatically be updated on the web page. Then she thinks what if customers could order products online and have their orders flow straight into the same FileMaker database that Blue Horizon's phone operators use to take phone orders?

Soon Karen starts to obsess about the possibilities (in a good way, of course). What if all the breeding data in their FileMaker system could be made available online for other breeders and researchers? What if veterinarians could query their herd medical statistics to learn about disease incidences in the Blue Horizon herds?

How hard could that be?

Well, Karen, this book is here to answer that question for you. It can be as easy or complex as you need it to be. Publishing data from FileMaker Pro to the web can take anywhere from five minutes to five weeks, or even five months. It can be as simple as clicking a few buttons or as complicated as building an entire application framework in a web-based scripting language like PHP or Lasso.

First, though, you need to know something about what the web is and how it operates. If you're used to the way your users interact with data in the world of FileMaker, you'll learn that there are some important differences when it comes to making that same data available through a web interface.

The Web as a Database Client

The web wasn't originally intended as an interface to any kind of database. It was conceived as a simple means to publish documents that would a) integrate different types of content, such as text and pictures, and b) provide a ready means to link these documents together using electronic cross-references called hyperlinks. This idea was sensational enough for its time, but like most good ideas, it has since far exceeded what its creators had in mind (all the way back in 1989 or so).

Let's look first at how the web works in its simplest, original form. Like FileMaker itself, the web follows a client-server model: A computer called a web server contains a repository of hypertext documents, and many users, usually physically distant from that machine, use a piece of client software called a web browser to query the server and request documents. You've probably seen references to HTTP (Hypertext Transfer Protocol); this is the language used by the web server and the web browser to communicate back and forth. A simple exchange might go something like this:

Web browser: "Hello, www.sasquatch.com, send me your main home page so I can look at it."

Web server: "Okay, here's the page."

Web browser (when user clicks a link): "That article about Bigfoot in Patagonia looks cool. Send it my way."

Web server: "Okay, here it comes. It has a bunch of pictures too."

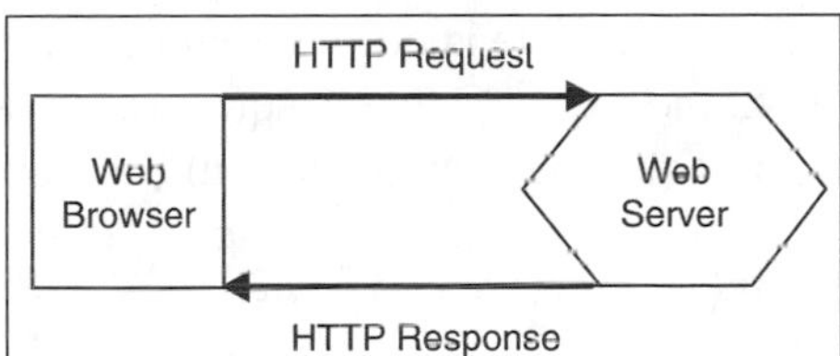

Figure 1.1

HTTP is a very simple request-response protocol; the client (web browser) makes a request for some resource, and if the web server has what's requested, it sends it back or reports an error if no such resource can be found. (If you've ever received a "404 Page Not Found" error, you've heard this reply from a web server.) The same transaction looks like this when expressed in the underlying HTTP protocol:

```
Browser Request:

GET / HTTP/1.1
Accept: image/gif, image/jpeg, */*
Accept-Language: en-us
Accept-Encoding: gzip, deflate
User Agent: Mozilla/4.0 (compatible; MSIE 5.5; Windows NT)
```

```
Host: www.sasquatch.com
Connection: Keep-Alive

Server Response:

HTTP/1.1 200 OK
Date: Mon, 25 Apr 2002 12:11:10 GMT
Server: Apache/1.3.24 (Unix)
Last-Modified: Sat, 04 Dec 2001 11:01:00 GMT
ETag: "6f8ab-132-312c4be5"
Accept-Ranges: bytes
Content-length: 367
Connection: close
Content-type: text/html

<html> <head>
<title>Welcome to the Sasquatch Watchers' Home Page</title>
</head><body>
<img src="/images/bigfoot.jpg">
<h1>Big Footprint Country</h1>
Dear Sasquatch fancier:
This page is still under construction. Don't you hate that? But in
the meantime click <a href=patagoniasighting.html>here</a> for a
breaking story on a sighting way down in Tierra del Fuego ...
</body>
```

As you can see, the request-response cycle is quite straightforward. The client asks for the default home page at www.sasquatch.com and also tells the web server what image types, languages, and compression schemes it can handle. The server sends back a message that says "okay, I have that" and follows with the actual text of the requested page, along with a link to an embedded image.

So much for HTTP. The pages sent down by the web server are written in another standard web language called HTML (Hypertext Markup Language), which describes the contents of the page and often contains instructions for how to display portions of the page as well. (Although features such as font size, margins, and color were not part of the original intention of the web, they have since been added to the web standards due to public demand.) For the purpose of this book, we're going to assume that you have basic familiarity with HTML and are comfortable writing and troubleshooting basic HTML code. We'll touch on details of constructing certain types of HTML from time to time, but a full tutorial is beyond the scope of this book.

This static model works well if you, as a web author, want to sit down, write a bunch of pages or an entire site in HTML, upload the files to a server, and sit back and watch the world beat a path to your door. But if you want users to come to your site and search for the latest specials on lamps from Bactria or see the ten most frequently viewed photos from your Aunt Cleo's retirement barbecue, you're going to need more than what a simple, static HTML page can give you. Your user now needs to interact not just with a web server but also with a database that contains the dynamic, changing content of your web site.

Hmm. Well, a web server by itself has no particular facilities for talking to a database. This is not actually a limitation of the web server but an example of an important software design principle called *loose coupling* (better known as "You Do Your Job, I'll Do Mine"). There are dozens of different database products in circulation. If I'm building a piece of web server software (such as WebSTAR, Apache, Zeus, or Internet Information Server), which database should my web server be able to talk to? Do I choose just one? Do I try to talk to a dozen different ones? Suddenly my web server is much, much more complicated than it was before. Worse—it's now tightly coupled to one or more database products; every time those products change, I may have to revise my web server product as well.

We don't need a web server that knows about databases or a database that can talk directly to a web server; we need a third type of software that can talk to both at once. The generic name for this kind of software is middleware. Middleware takes many forms. Some middleware is designed to attach to a web server and extend its capabilities (a web server plug-in or module). Other middleware can take the form of a stand-alone application that specializes in talking to databases but also provides some web serving capabilities (FileMaker's Web Companion falls into this category). In this book, we'll look at FileMaker-oriented middleware choices that fall into both of these categories.

So how does middleware actually work? Well, in the plug-in model that we just mentioned, the middleware is installed and configured alongside the web server software. The web server is aware of the existence of the middleware, and it knows that the middleware can handle certain special types of content. When a web server receives a request for a file with a name that ends in .html, it knows to simply fetch the page from disk and send it straight back to whoever requested it. But when the same server, appropriately configured, receives a request for a page ending in .php or .lasso, it may instead hand that page off to the PHP engine or the Lasso engine for processing. The middleware will read the page, execute any database commands that it contains, and return a page of plain HTML, which the server will then send down to the client as it would for a plain static HTML page.

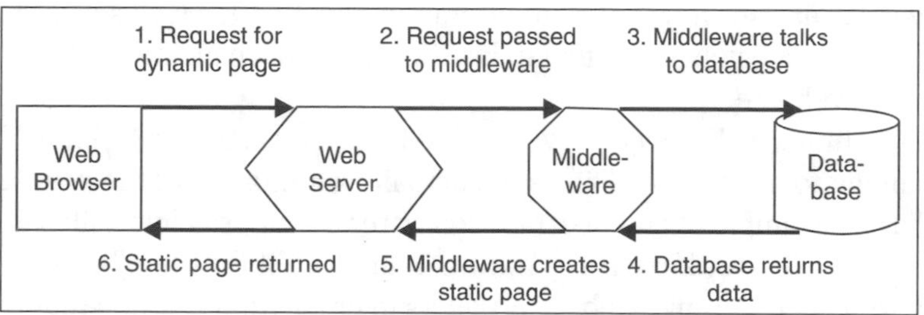

Figure 1.2

Well, that makes things more complicated. Instead of having to worry about two pieces of software (web browser and web server), we now have to worry about as many as four (adding in the middleware and the database). Not to worry. In the chapters that follow, we give you all the details that you need to get these different software components up and running in a FileMaker-based environment.

FileMaker on the Web

So how does all of this relate to FileMaker Pro? What, for that matter, does it mean to "put your FileMaker database on the web"? Do users see exactly the same interface as the users who access the files using regular FileMaker? Do scripts and buttons work the same way? Well, no, not quite. The snazzy interfaces that we're accustomed to building in FileMaker don't necessarily translate directly to a web environment. Even when they do, we often have to make concessions to the differences between the web environment and the regular client-server world of FileMaker. In general, the more full-featured and script-heavy your FileMaker application is, the more additional work you'll have to do to bring that functionality to the web.

To understand why this is so, we need to take a closer look at how regular FileMaker does things and then compare this to the web model. In regular FileMaker, the user's FileMaker software (the client) makes a connection to a FileMaker server of some kind (possibly just another copy of regular FileMaker but hopefully an instance of the more heavy-duty FileMaker Server software). The server registers the connection and remains aware of the client as long as the user is connected. The FileMaker client software, for its part, is responsible for reading all the layouts that the developer has created and turning those into the pleasing user interfaces that we associate with FileMaker.

Neither of these things happen this way in a web environment. HTTP is often referred to as a connectionless protocol. This means that once the web server has serviced a request (say, by sending a page back to a web browser), it promptly forgets that the particular browser has connected to it. This makes it more difficult to have a sustained interaction (often called a *session*) in which the server remembers important information about the client from one mouse click to the next. This is very easy to do in regular FileMaker (usually by using global fields). It takes a bit more work on the web.

FileMaker interfaces also don't translate directly to the web. Web interfaces are built by using the HTML language (often augmented by other technologies such as Cascading Style Sheets and JavaScript—though support for these varies widely from browser to browser). HTML was actually never designed with page layout in mind. Originally, HTML was simply intended to describe the structure of a document (this piece is a level one heading, this one is a blockquote, this one represents an ordered list). It was supposed to be up to the user to decide how she wanted those different kinds of structures to display. Almost immediately, though, there was a demand for HTML extensions that would provide control over fonts, colors, and the like. Though these are now in the process of being standardized and work fairly well, it's still relatively cumbersome to design a rich, complex layout for the web. In FileMaker, you drag fields onto layouts and position them accurately with the mouse. In HTML, you need to type out text codes that contain all of the graphical and positioning information for each element. There is no tool that can translate a FileMaker layout directly into accurate HTML (well, Filemaker Instant Web Publishing does—we discuss it later in Chapter 5).

Wait a minute, you say. I thought there were all kinds of great graphical editors for the web that would let me make web layouts the same way I make FileMaker layouts. Well, yes, there are many very good graphical tools for doing web work. The problem is that, sooner or later, you will need to add special middleware code to those pages, which means editing the raw HTML. Some modern tools are designed to work with different flavors of middleware, which can lessen the amount of time you spend typing actual text pages. But you're still a programmer; you'll need to troubleshoot when things don't quite work, and at that point the visual interface won't help you too much. In this book, we adopt a purist's stance—we think it's best to learn web programming and HTML by sitting down and typing. You'll need that level of control, and if you later find a visual tool that you really like, you should be able to figure out how to make the transition. If you start off in the visual tool, you'll learn how to point and click up a storm, but you're less likely to master the underlying web languages fully. When something breaks or doesn't work quite right, you'll need to know how things work under the hood.

The bottom line is this: There are a variety of ways to make the web closely mimic the feel and flavor of your FileMaker system, but there is no transparent, seamless translator available yet. You'll probably need to do some additional work to bring over your FileMaker functionality.

So, to sum up, the two principal differences between "regular" FileMaker and FileMaker on the web are: The web server does not remember from click to click and page to page who is connected to it, and secondly, it can be harder to construct a pleasing user interface with a FileMaker-like level of richness.

With these caveats in mind, let's learn more about how FileMaker data can be made available on the web. It's time to introduce you to the Web Companion.

The Web Companion

FileMaker, like other database systems, needs some additional help to serve its information to the web. Like other database products, it needs some type of middleware in order to pass database information out to the web. In FileMaker's case, the essential middleware is the Web Companion, which is not part of the FileMaker software itself but is a FileMaker plug-in.

Usually, to serve database content to the web, you need three pieces of software: database, middleware, and web server. In FileMaker's case, the rules are bent a bit for several reasons. In the first place, the "database" component of the equation in FileMaker's case can actually be as many as three pieces of software: FileMaker client, the Web Companion, and possibly a copy of the FileMaker Server as well. To further complicate things though, the Web Companion itself can actually act as a web server in its own right!

To make things a bit clearer, let's consider two examples for our friends at Blue Horizon. In the case that we talked about earlier, the products database for the Blue Horizon store is a simple FileMaker file that lives on a single machine in the BHBB store. Only one person inside BHBB needs to use the file, and when she does, she works at that machine. In this configuration, a single client copy of FileMaker has the served files open from a local hard drive, and the Web Companion is responsible for allowing requests for data to come in over the web. (This is not a great setup: The incoming web requests will interfere with anyone using the machine. It will work well enough if no one actually needs to use the machine much, and it just sits aside as a stand-alone machine.) The following diagram illustrates such a configuration. All incoming web requests are directed to a single computer (and specifically to the Web Companion plug-in running alongside FileMaker on that computer). The Web Companion communicates with FileMaker to service these incoming requests. All of this occurs on a single computer.

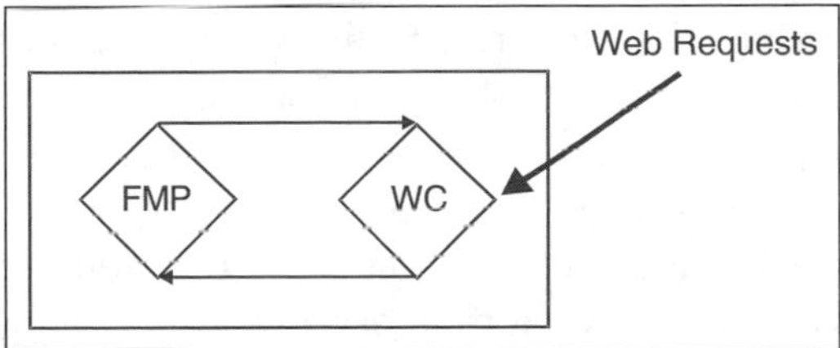

Figure 1.3

Now let's consider BHBB's large database system that tracks herd statistics, breeding, and disease in their population. This system is used by many people at different places inside the grounds of BHBB, so the files are run under FileMaker Server, with everyone connecting to them via the FileMaker client. Web Companion is a plug-in for the FileMaker client. It can't talk directly to the server, so this is now a three-link chain: The FileMaker client connects to FileMaker Server to request data, and the Web Companion connects to the FileMaker client in order to serve that data out to the web. In this instance, you would want to set aside a workstation that is dedicated to the FileMaker client/Web Companion setup; it's actually very disruptive to have your copy of FileMaker involved in web-serving while you're trying to get work done. Here's how this would look. All incoming web requests, as above, come to a single computer running FileMaker Pro and the Web Companion. (Technically, this computer should be running FileMaker Pro Unlimited, which we'll discuss in detail later on.) That single computer, in turn, is connected to a FileMaker Server machine where the files of interest are actually located. In this way, the web-serving machine is just one of several different clients using the served files.

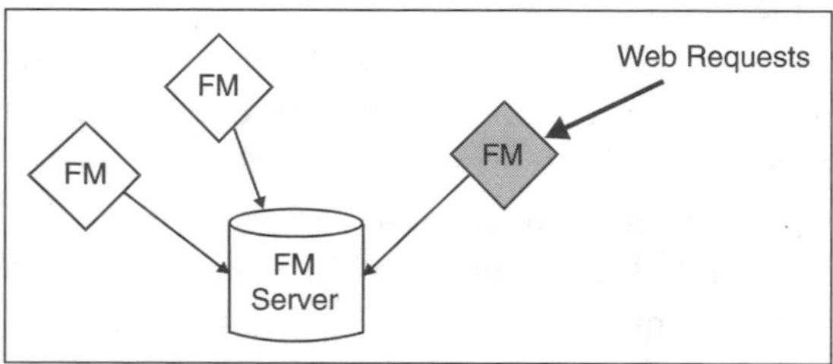

Figure 1.4

If you're thinking that this still sounds short on detail, don't worry. We document all of the setups in considerable detail for you later on. For now, though, just understand that the primary link between FileMaker data and the web is a plug-in known as the Web Companion, and that plug-in must always be paired with a client copy of FileMaker, even when the databases are being hosted by FileMaker Server.

There's one more important thing to know about the Web Companion, and it involves a bit of FileMaker history. FileMaker, Inc. introduced the plug-in architecture for FileMaker in version 4.0 of the software. At that time, the Web Companion was distributed with every copy of the regular FileMaker Pro client. Since a single copy of the Web Companion could be used to distribute FileMaker data to dozens or even hundreds of users, this was a pretty good deal. It was a good enough deal, in fact, that as of FileMaker version 5, the standard version of FileMaker comes with a Web Companion that no longer has unlimited web-serving capabilities. The off-the-shelf Web Companion is now limited to answering requests from a maximum of ten different Internet addresses in any 12-hour period. This is barely enough for some light testing and certainly not likely to be enough for any serious distribution of your data. If you want more than ten computers to be able to see your data in any 12-hour period, you'll need to get your hands on FileMaker Pro Unlimited. This is a copy of the FileMaker client software that is more or less the same as the regular client—the only difference being that the Web Companion included with Unlimited can serve to any number of Internet addresses (well, any number within reason). It is more expensive than the regular FileMaker client to reflect the fact that Unlimited can open your data to many other users, none of which need FileMaker to access your data.

Available Technologies

Once you've decided that you want to web-enable your FileMaker databases, you face a choice or rather, a wide range of choices. There are many possibilities here; this section gives you an overview of those possibilities, and subsequent chapters examine each one in greater (often much greater) depth.

Static Publishing: You can create web pages simply by exporting data from FileMaker Pro. It used to be that you'd have to create calculations inside FileMaker that would wrap your FileMaker data in HTML to display it nicely. You'd then export that HTML to static files and move those to your web directory. These days, with FileMaker 6 and its new XML Export capabilities, it makes more sense to write some XSL stylesheets to generate that HTML for you. XSL stylesheets are a technology that we spend more time on later.

Regardless of which export technology you choose, calculated HTML or XML/XSL, this technique is most suitable for web sites that draw on data that doesn't change by the minute. A database of press releases or other relatively slow-changing content could easily be published in this way.

Instant Web Publishing: FileMaker's built-in Instant Web Publishing, or IWP, is one of the easiest ways to publish a FileMaker Pro database on the web. With just a few mouse clicks, your system can be available to other users in a very attractive web interface. Though it's probably the easiest way to present a web interface to FileMaker, it does have some drawbacks.

IWP doesn't give you quite the level of control over the look and feel of your pages that you might need. It tries to provide a standard web appearance for FileMaker. It's excellent at reproducing the look and feel of your layouts, but it wraps them in a standard web appearance that you may or may not want. If you want to customize that appearance, you're pretty much out of luck.

IWP also doesn't let you override the pages that it builds. If you have complicated functionality in your system, there's no way to add it to the pages that IWP generates. If that functionality lives in FileMaker scripts, it won't do you much good. Only a few of the FileMaker script steps are currently compatible with IWP.

IWP is a great way to get a FileMaker database on the web quickly. If you don't need much look-and-feel customization or complex, scripted functionality, it's a great way to get a good-looking web interface for your files with minimum hassle.

Once you get beyond static web export and IWP, the difficulty curve begins to steepen a little bit. Your other choices all involve learning some kind of new programming language, which will allow you to express the same rich constructs on the web that you can create by using ScriptMaker inside of FileMaker. Each of these languages is different, and each has its strengths and weaknesses.

Custom Web Publishing: This is FileMaker's own "advanced" solution. Using Custom Web Publishing (CWP), you can create your web pages by hand in a text editor or similar tool. Each page contains programming instructions in a language called CDML (which actually stands for Claris Dynamic Markup Language, harking back to the days when FileMaker was produced by Claris Corp.). CDML instructions are intercepted by the Web Companion and used to insert dynamic FileMaker data into your page before it's sent to the user.

Though FileMaker uses the term "Custom Web Publishing" to refer specifically to CDML, we'll use it more generically to refer to any of the advanced programming technologies that are the next step up from Instant Web Publishing.

Lasso: Like CDML, Lasso is a markup language, meaning that it consists of commands that are inserted into web pages in order to populate them with dynamic data. Lasso is a commercial product made by BlueWorld Communications, Inc., that has long been a popular choice for web-enabling complex FileMaker systems. Its language is much richer than that of CDML and boasts many additional capabilities. In addition, Lasso can talk to many other database systems besides FileMaker Pro and thus offers the opportunity to integrate FileMaker data with data from, say, Sybase, more or less seamlessly in a single web application.

The Lasso environment is covered extensively in Duncan Cameron's *Lasso Professional 5 Developer's Guide* from Wordware Publishing, so we won't spend as much time on Lasso in this book as we might otherwise. We introduce you to the basic concepts and compare it with the other technologies that we discuss, but we refer you to Cameron's book for more extensive examples.

PHP: PHP is another markup language that can work with FileMaker. Unlike Lasso, it's not a commercial product but an *open-source* tool, meaning it can be downloaded and installed for free. This might seem like a huge advantage, but it also means that there is no telephone help hotline. We'll discuss the pros and cons of open source later. PHP is a hugely popular language for web application development. A quick check of your favorite physical or virtual bookstore should turn up dozens of books on this burgeoning language. Like Lasso, PHP can work with many other databases in addition to FileMaker, and its range of extra libraries and modules allow an intrepid developer to add everything from dynamically generated Flash content and PDFs to live graphs and charts to their web application. We think PHP is a language that deserves a fuller introduction to the FileMaker community, and we'll spend quite a bit of time with it in this book.

Java Server Pages: Like PHP, Java Server Pages (JSPs) are an extremely popular web technology with dozens of books on your local shelves. Using the FileMaker-supplied JDBC driver, FilerMaker can actually be accessed by any Java-based application—be it a web-based application that uses JSPs or servlets or a full-fledged graphical client written in Java.

JSPs are a powerful web technology, but using them presumes a solid foundation in the Java programming language. It's our guess that not too many FileMaker developers are also Java whizzes (we know that there are some of you, though!), so we decided it would not be appropriate to spend much time on JSPs in this book.

ODBC: Using FileMaker's ODBC drivers, it is technically possible to hook up other web development environments, such as the popular ASP language, to FileMaker. FileMaker's ODBC implementation, though, is not terribly fast, and this is probably not a great choice for web connectivity technologies, unless you're building an application that needs data from FileMaker infrequently and in small amounts.

XML/XSL: We mentioned XML's use in the static model of data serving. It also has intriguing possibilities for building a fully dynamic web site. Although XSL's limitations probably make it a bit cumbersome for large-scale sites, it can be a very effective publishing technology under the right circumstances.

So there's your menu. In the pages ahead, our greatest focus will be on XML/XSL, CDML, Lasso, and PHP. XML/XSL is an important part of FileMaker's stated strategic direction, and every web developer will need to be familiar with it. PHP is a very powerful tool for building web applications, from the modest to the very large, so we want to explore it thoroughly here. In between, we'll give some attention to Lasso and provide thorough coverage of FileMaker's built-in CDML technology.

Chapter 2

Preparing Your Databases for the Web

The transition from FileMaker jockey to web monkey won't be instantaneous, and it will require a modest investment of time and effort on your part. At the outset of your journey, you'll find yourself faced with a dizzying array of options and tools, and at times you may experience some anxiety over whether you're up for the challenge. That's a natural feeling when learning any new technology, and it's especially hard to be patient and start at the beginning if you're already skilled with other programming tools.

In Chapter 1, we discussed various scenarios where web publishing makes sense, and we talked broadly about some of the different tools available for web-enabling FileMaker Pro databases. Before looking more closely at these tools, we're going to discuss some larger issues about preparing your databases for the web. Whether you are retro-fitting an already existing solution or designing from scratch, we hope that by following our advice, you'll avoid some potential bear traps down the road. The main topics that we address in this chapter are:

- Planning the project
- Naming conventions
- Use of global fields, calculations, and summary fields
- Use of scripts
- Relationships, portals, and related fields
- Layouts

Preparing your databases is also about optimizing them for peak performance. Usually if a web application isn't performing up to snuff, the hardware, the software, or the network is the scapegoat. Many times, however, the application design itself is as big a determination of performance as those other factors.

Planning the Project

We find that most FileMaker web projects fall into one of four categories. Determining which category best fits your project can help you decide what tools you should use to put your database on the web. Mind you, these categories have nothing whatsoever to do with what business you're in or how you're going to use the databases. Rather, they're concerned with the state of your existing FileMaker databases and the role that the web will play in your organization. Each of the categories offers its own challenges, so knowing what you're up against before you start can help you anticipate roadblocks.

The Piecemeal Project

Piecemeal projects are the most common and often the easiest FileMaker web projects. They involve web-enabling a small portion of an established FileMaker solution that's untenable as a traditional FileMaker client-server application. For instance, you might want your outside salespeople to be able to look up contact or project information when they're on the road. You've tried to have them connect back to the FileMaker server directly (as the internal salespeople do) but have found that it's too slow. You don't need to web-enable the whole system—just a few components. Another example of this type of project is an art gallery that manages its entire business using FileMaker and now wants to put their catalog online. Here, it's not a question of speed, but it is rather simply that the catalog needs to be accessible from a web browser instead of a FileMaker Pro client.

Instant Web Publishing is a good place to start with these projects. It may not be robust enough for complex tasks, but it's so easy to try that you'd be remiss not to. Even if it's not up to the challenge, Intstant Web Publishing can still give you a good starting point for planning your custom web development.

You'll face a serious challenge in piecemeal projects if you don't have your own high-speed Internet connection. It's not that it's difficult these days to find a FileMaker-friendly hosting provider. The problem is that in a typical hosting situation, you'll need to place a copy of your database on a shared server provided by the hosting company. Now you have to worry about synchronizing two copies of your database, and this has the potential to be a nightmare. We suggest that you start by defining very rigorous business rules. For instance, maybe you make the copy at the hosting company a "read-only" file, and you refresh the data once a day.

Even if you do have a high-speed Internet connection, you might not want the responsibility or expense of hosting your own web server. In these cases, PHP can be a compelling solution. Most every ISP will have machines configured with Apache and PHP, and you can have PHP talk to a FileMaker Pro Unlimited machine in your office. There are two benefits to this configuration. The first is that you only need a very vanilla (inexpensive, ubiquitous) hosting arrangement. The second is that you avoid synchronization issues; web users access your live FileMaker system in real-time.

The Wholesale Migration Project

These projects are probably the hardest and riskiest of the bunch. They involve taking an existing FileMaker solution and replacing or replicating all of its functionality over the web. These projects often come about as an organization grows from a single location to multiple locations. The entire solution that worked great over the local area network now needs to be used by people in one or more remote offices. Instant Web Publishing is almost certainly not able to fulfill the needs of this type of project.

The risk here is that it can be very difficult, if not impossible, to faithfully replicate a FileMaker interface and FileMaker functionality in a web browser. We strongly suggest you don't even try. Instead, force yourself to think about it as a new system and design it from scratch. As a user interface, the web behaves much differently than FileMaker. For instance, you can't just jump into Find mode anywhere you want. You need to build search screens and search results screens. You'll also find that printing, importing, and exporting all require much more effort and a much different user interface on the web.

The temptation will be great to make the web interface as similar as possible to the FileMaker interface. You'll rationalize that it's a good thing because it won't require users to be retrained on the new system. However, as long as the business logic doesn't change, users will easily adapt to a new interface, and having the interfaces significantly distinct from one another will avoid confusion over the minor differences that will inevitably occur.

Be sure you also consider in advance what you plan to do with your existing FileMaker users. Do you still want them to use the FileMaker interface, or will they use the web interface as well?

There's no simple answer for this one. It really depends on your business and your users. If you have FileMaker veterans who move around the system with keyboard shortcuts and like to tweak layouts from time to time, you'll get strong resistance about moving to a web-only interface. If you have one interface for people in one location and another for people in every other location, that means you have to keep two interfaces up to date. Any new feature needs to be implemented twice. Invariably, there will be some functionality that's easier for people using FileMaker, and you'll run the risk of your other locations feeling like second-class citizens. They may even use the system differences as justification for not getting things done.

We're not trying to scare you. These projects can be quite successful. Just go into it knowing that you face some hard decisions, and it may feel like you're moving backward at times. You should probably also consider Citrix MetaFrame as an alternative. There are some hefty upfront hardware and software costs, but all of the risks associated with web development are eliminated.

Wholesale migration projects generally require that you have a high-speed Internet connection and are willing to host the web solution yourself. Because these projects typically have a complex business logic and often need to interact with the file system or other applications, PHP and Lasso are probably the tools that you should consider using. You'll likely need the power of a full service web server and the flexibility that these tools provide.

Whereas the first two project types described web-enabling existing solutions, the next two deal with new projects.

The Web-only Project

A web-only project, as its name hopefully suggests, is one in which the primary goal of the project is to create a brand new web application. You'll have a slew of technology decisions to make at the outset of such a project, including platform, operating system, middleware, and database. Should you use FileMaker or some other web-friendly database, like MySQL, PostgreSQL, or SQL Server? If you choose FileMaker, it's likely for one of a few reasons. Maybe you're using FileMaker for other applications and are loyal to the product. Or perhaps you'll need a few administrative screens or need easy access to the data collected over the web and are comfortable doing this yourself in FileMaker.

If you're undertaking one of these projects, go ahead and architect your solution as you would if you were creating a pure FileMaker solution, but don't spend much time on the database interface. Keep reminding yourself that the databases are just buckets of raw data. As we'll discuss later, you probably don't need scripts, relationships, calculation fields, or summary fields.

If you don't have your own high-speed Internet connection and a dedicated machine, you'll again need to consider finding a hosting company. You probably won't have the same hosting headaches with a web-only project that you do with piecemeal projects. You should consider the files located at the hosting company as the master set and then import or export data as necessary.

The Hybrid Project

We'll use the term "hybrid project" to describe a new project that's destined to be deployed as a part web, part FileMaker application. In the end, it will probably end up resembling either a piecemeal project or a wholesale migration project. Similarly, web-only projects often evolve into hybrid projects as the need arises for additional behind-the-scenes functionality.

The advice we have for hybrid projects is that you do the web portion first. Start out as if it's going to be a web-only project. Once you get the web interface done, then work on designing a FileMaker interface that's similar. It's much easier to make a FileMaker interface look and act like a web interface than it is to make a web interface look and act like a FileMaker interface.

Now that you've had a glimpse at some of the tasks that await you, we'll turn to the general preparation that you'll want to do no matter which type of project you're facing.

Naming Conventions

One of the most important considerations when preparing your databases for the web is what to call things. By "things," we mean any or all of the following:

- Field names
- Layout names
- Script names
- Relationship names

- Value list names
- Database names

Most FileMaker developers have their own habits for naming these things, and it's our distinct desire to stay clear of the debate over the relative merits of different habits. Rather, we'd prefer to discuss some broad "dos and don'ts" that you'll be able to incorporate into your particular set of habits. The reason for our reticence is simple. Many of you have systems that have hundreds or thousands of named objects, and it's folly to suggest that you should rename everything. In what follows, then, we offer some "best practice" conventions you should consider for future projects, but we also let you know of a few showstoppers that you need to scour from your existing files.

Spaces

Many web developers will glibly tell you that you should *never* use spaces in any of your names for *any* object. In truth, there's only one pitfall to be aware of, and it's easily handled. You've probably noticed when typing URLs into a web browser that you never see any spaces. That's the pitfall: A URL can't contain a space. If you had a field called "Last Name" and you were using CDML for Custom Web Publishing, the danger is that you could end up with a link like this:

```
http://10.10.10.10/FMPro?-db=contact.fp5&-layout=main&-format=
  test.htm&Last Name=Flintstone&-find
```

The space in the field name may cause this URL to fail. You would receive similar results if there were spaces in the database name or layout name. The "fix" for this, if for some reason you can't simply rename the offending object, is to encode the spaces. That is, you need to replace them either with %20 (the hexadecimal code for a space) or a + sign. The fixed URL might then appear like this:

```
http://10.10.10.10/FMPro?-db=contact.fp5&-layout=main&-format=
  test.htm&Last+Name=Flintstone&-find
```

If you're using Instant Web Publishing, this is done for you behind the scenes, and you don't need to worry about spaces at all. With Custom Web Publishing, we recommend avoiding spaces when possible and encoding as appropriate if you can't. Script names are where we usually draw the line. Most scripts you write will never be called from a browser. For those few that might, you can either name without spaces or encode. If you're worried about keeping things readable, you might consider using underscores in your names (e.g., First_Name, Last_Name).

Case

People often wonder whether it matters (for web publishing) if they name a field FirstName, firstName, or firstname. Some database systems are extremely case sensitive, but FileMaker is not one of them. The Web Companion, which handles all web requests, doesn't care at all whether you use uppercase, lowercase, or any combination of the two. For instance, these two requests will yield identical results:

```
http://10.10.10.10/FMpro?-db=CONTACT.fp5&-format=
  test.htm&-lay=MAIN&last+name=flintstone&-find

http://10.10.10.10/FMpro?-db=contact.fp5&-format=
  test.htm&-lay=main&Last+Name=Flintstone&-find
```

We recommend that you use whatever makes the most intuitive sense to you and stick to it. Consistency is a good thing.

Special Characters

The use of certain "special characters" is the one place where you need to be more disciplined in your naming. By special characters we mean things like punctuation symbols, math operators, and high ASCII characters. FileMaker itself places few restrictions on the use of these characters, and some of them can cause headaches on the web because they are defined to mean certain things to a web browser. The key things to avoid are symbols like &, <, >, /, \, #, @, -, ?, =, and ". For instance, an ampersand is used to separate name-value pairs passed as parameters in a URL. If you named one of your layouts Entry&Editing and then referenced that layout from the web (-lay=Entry&Editing), FileMaker would look for a layout named Entry and think there was some other parameter called Editing. You'd end up with a "Layout not found" error.

FileMaker itself protects against certain evil characters in field names and relationship names. You've probably experienced the following warning that pops up when you try to use one of FileMaker's own reserved symbols.

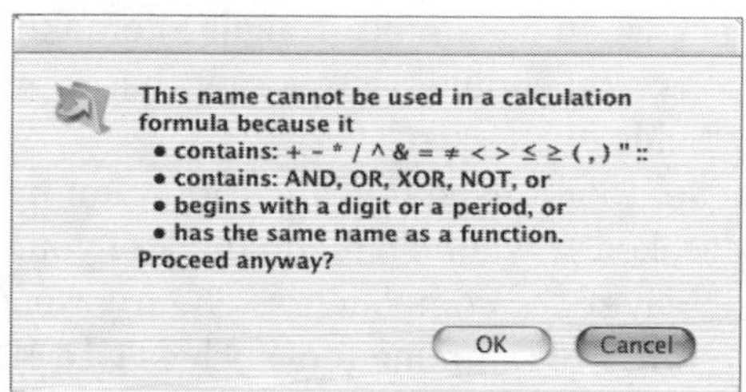

This name cannot be used in a calculation formula because it
• contains: + - * / ^ & = ≠ < > ≤ ≥ (,) " ::
• contains: AND, OR, XOR, NOT, or
• begins with a digit or a period, or
• has the same name as a function.
Proceed anyway?
OK
Cancel

Figure 2.1

No such dialog protects layout names, script names, or value list names, so these are areas where you want to be particularly watchful.

We've found that it's safe to use underscores, periods, and pipe characters. If you feel a need for symbols in your names, stick to those. High ASCII characters (such things as bullets, trademark symbols, accented characters) should definitely be avoided in object names.

Uniqueness

FileMaker will prevent you from having duplicate field, value list, and relationship names, but there's no such restriction on layout names or database names. Having multiple databases with the same name is obviously a bad idea, and you can easily imagine how a request to Orders.fp5 might go astray if there were two open files of that name at the designated IP address. Less obvious is why layout names should be unique. FileMaker doesn't require that layout names be unique because it uses an internal serial number to store and retrieve layout information. So, a script with a Go To Layout step in it doesn't care about ambiguous layout names.

A web request will usually specify which layout should be used to process the request (more on this later in the chapter). That request just specifies the layout name, so in the case of duplicate layout names, FileMaker uses the earliest one created to process the request. We wouldn't make such a big deal out of this if it hadn't been the source of a painful debugging episode a few years back.

Use of Global Fields, Calculations, and Summary Fields

When you think of your databases, try to make a mental distinction between fields that store data (text, number, date, time, and container fields), fields that act as variables (global fields), and fields that are derived from other fields (calculations and summary fields). All of these are useful and necessary when designing straight FileMaker solutions, but for web solutions, you should try to forget that your globals, calcs, and summary fields even exist.

This may be a hard mindset to get used to if your programming experience is limited to FileMaker. It will help if you think of your web applications as having distinct layers or components. The front end is the browser, the middleware is a programming tool such as CDML, PHP, Lasso, or XSL, and the back end is your FileMaker database system. The primary purpose of the back end is to act as a receptacle for data. It's a simple bucket-o'-data and shouldn't be bothered with requests for summarization or formatting. All of the middleware tools used for Custom Web Publishing have the ability to manipulate data, and they'll typically do it much faster than FileMaker. Your business logic and all of your data manipulation should, to the largest extent possible, reside in the middleware code. The middleware typically does much of the screen rendering as well, but the browser itself, via JavaScript or Cascading Style Sheets, can also play an important role in the "look and feel" of your application.

If you have a pre-existing solution that you intend to put on the web, you may be tempted to tap into the calcs and summary fields that you've painstakingly created. It will work, and that may unfortunately lead you to think that you're doing a good thing. The problem will be speed. Not only is FileMaker not particularly fast at summarizing large data sets, but the FileMaker Web Companion is single-threaded, which means that while it's processing one web request, all other requests must wait in a queue to be processed. Therefore, a time-consuming summary or calc not only impacts the requestor but also all of the other web users who won't have a clue why the site seems slow.

The mere presence of summary fields or calcs in your database tables isn't cause for alarm. If your system is used by FileMaker clients internally and web clients externally, you certainly can't just delete all of those fields. Don't request that they be displayed in the browser, and don't put them on the layouts that you access from the web. This may be the single best thing you can do to increase the performance of your web application.

Global fields are another story entirely. Global fields are variables. That is, they're temporary storage locations. They're local to each client on a FileMaker network, which essentially means that each user gets her own global fields that no other user can see. This fact means that global fields become a vital tool for implementing business logic in straight FileMaker solutions. For instance, maybe you set the user's access level into a global field upon logging into the system. It can then be referenced any time during that session when you need to validate access to something. Or you might choose to store search parameters in global fields so that upon searching again you can default the search to the last set of criteria.

The problem with accessing global fields from the web is that all of the web users share the same set of global fields. They're not unique for each web user—just for each FileMaker client. This means that if

Web User A stores something in a global field, then Web User B not only can potentially see what's stored there but can also change it. Business rules in web applications should never rely upon data stored in global fields.

Middleware applications typically have several types of variables that can be used in the roles where you had previously used global fields. PHP and Lasso, for instance, both have session variables that can act as temporary storage locations as the user navigates through your application.

As you're preparing existing databases for the web, you should be on the lookout for routines that rely on global fields. Don't worry about scripts that use globals as counters. Those are innocuous. Worry about any globals that need to persist as the user moves from place to place. More than likely you'll need to abandon them and come up with alternatives as you move to the web.

Use of Scripts

Our advice for the use of scripts depends on what tool you're using to web-enable your database. As we discuss in depth in Chapter 5, if you are using Instant Web Publishing, scripts are essential for customizing a site. But only a handful of script steps are IWP compliant, and they may have a very different meaning for IWP than they normally do.

If you're using one of the Custom Web Publishing methods, you have entirely different issues with scripts. Scripts are the lifeblood of many FileMaker solutions; they're typically how business logic is implemented and enforced. Remember our earlier discussion of application components? On the web, the middleware has the primary responsibility for business logic, and the back end is supposed to be a simple bucket-o'-data. This isn't an arbitrary distinction, but rather one that recognizes and exploits the strengths of each tool. Moreover, you'll find that having some business logic implemented in the middleware and some in the back-end database (and possibly some in the front end as JavaScript validation) complicates the maintenance of an application.

You should therefore be very choosy when it comes to running scripts from the web. The rule of thumb is to avoid running scripts unless there's a really good reason. There are a few reasons why this is so. The first is again one of performance. If FileMaker is running a script that takes a few seconds to execute, it won't be able to respond to other requests during that time. The other reason is that most scripts simply won't be useful. Scripts that navigate from one layout to another, for instance, have no impact whatsoever on what a web user sees on her screen. Other typical script functions, like searching, creating, and deleting records, should be done directly by calls to the Web Companion.

Be sure never to call a script from the web that brings up a dialog on the host computer, such as Show Message, or a delete confirmation. If this happens, you're in big trouble. The Web Companion can't process any requests until the dialog is cleared, and so your web site would be toast.

There are nonetheless a few situations where it is appropriate and desirable to invoke scripts directly from a web interface. Take, for instance, printing and exporting. Printing from a web browser is the Achilles' heel of the web, but with FileMaker scripting available to you, you can have a button on your web interface trigger a script that, say, prints to a PDF (you'd have the PDF driver selected as the default printer on your FileMaker Pro Unlimited machine) and moves the resulting file to a directory where it can be viewed or downloaded by the user. You will need the help of a plug-in for the file-moving part of the script, but you get the idea.

Typically, if you are creating a new solution and the only access is through a web interface, you will find that you do almost no FileMaker scripting. All of the business logic and navigation is done in the middleware instead. For existing solutions, don't worry at all about your existing scripts; just write new ones specific for the web as you need them.

Relationships, Portals, and Related Records

In complex FileMaker systems, many of the relationships between tables serve utilitarian, rather than structural, purposes. Examples of these include constant relationships that are used for setting and retrieving global values from other tables, relationships based on multivalued keys that are used for selection portals, and relationships that facilitate jumping to sets of related records. By and large, these utilitarian relationships have no place in a web solution.

Your structural relationships remain important not only because they enable you to access related fields, but also because they can be used to enforce referential integrity (i.e., cascading deletes). More important than the actual definition of a relationship, however, is that you have a coherent system of primary and foreign keys. You'll find that on the web, you use the keys themselves more than you use FileMaker relationships.

An example will help clarify what we mean by this. In FileMaker, if you wanted to navigate from a parent record to a set of children, you'd most likely use a Go to Related Record script step that requires a defined relationship between the two tables. In a web application, on the other hand, you'd end up accomplishing this by performing a search in the child table for records that have a certain parent key. It wouldn't matter whether or not there was a relationship defined in the underlying FileMaker database.

Portals—one of the most powerful tools in the FileMaker developer's toolbox—are used much less often on the web than in FileMaker. This isn't because of a dearth of tools for creating them. Indeed, there are CDML and Lasso tags for creating portals, and FileMaker's XML schema can represent sets of related records. The reason that they aren't used as much on the web is simply that there are other, perhaps even better, ways of rendering sets of related records. All of the middleware tools that we discuss have the ability to perform multiple database actions and return the results as a single HTML page. CDML and Lasso both refer to these actions as *inlines*, and we use that term as well to refer to any action whose result is available within the page itself (as opposed to actions that call other pages).

Let's look at an example of the functional resemblance of portals and inlines. Say you wanted to have a web page that displayed information about a company and you wanted a list of related contacts to appear on the page as well. In a straight FileMaker application, you'd create a relationship from company to contacts based on a company ID, and then you'd create a portal in the company record to show the related set of contacts. On the web, you could either use a portal, or you could do a search of the company table (based on the company ID) and an inline search of the contact table (also based on the company ID). The results of both searches could be displayed on the same web page, giving much of the same user experience as a portal. The inline approach is structurally similar to how other web database applications operate, so if you've done web development with other tools, you'll probably find inlines more intuitive than portals.

Portals have one major advantage over inlines—the ability to edit multiple records in one request. When you submit an update of a record that has a portal, both the parent record and all of the portal records are updated. It's very complicated to do multiple updates in one action if you've used inlines.

If you're using Instant Web Publishing, you'll find that portals on your layouts are rendered almost flawlessly, including alternate line coloring and a vertical scroll bar. You can even allow creation of related records like you would in FileMaker.

Even though you'll use fewer portals in your web applications, you'll still find it convenient to use related fields for displaying more information about a parent record. If you want to access related fields, you must explicitly request a layout that contains the related fields. The layout is an optional parameter that you send as part of a web request. Without it, the database uses what's known as Layout 0, a virtual layout that contains all the fields of the table (but no related fields).

As an example of when you'd use related fields, let's say that you wanted to display a list of all the records in the contact table, but you wanted to include the company name as one of the columns in your list. You certainly wouldn't want to do an inline search of the company database for each contact—that would be downright slow. Instead, you'd establish a FileMaker relationship from contacts to company, and then you'd put the company name field on your web layout in the contact table.

Our bottom-line advice is that if you're using any of the Custom Web Publishing tools to web-enable existing FileMaker databases, you should try to ignore utility relationships and portals. Plan on replacing them with inline actions. If you're building a new system, put in whatever structural relationships are useful for displaying related parent data and enforcing relational integrity. Outside of these pragmatic considerations, we don't architect a file structure any differently, whether we're planning a pure FileMaker interface or a web interface.

Layouts

We've already touched on the importance of layouts for web-enabling your databases. When you access a database through the FileMaker Web Companion, you generally want to tell it what layout to use to process your request. For certain requests, it's irrelevant, such as if you asked the Web Companion for a list of open databases or the number of records in a given table. Most requests, however, are layout specific, which is both a good thing and a bad thing.

Let's look at an example to clarify how important layouts are to web development. Say you have a CDML request to find all the records in the contact.fp5 database with a last name beginning with a B. Your request as a URL would look something like this:

```
http://<your IP address>/FMpro?-db=contact.fp5&-format=
  list.htm&last+name=B&-find
```

When the Web Companion receives this request, it looks at all of the information after the question mark and parses it into name-value pairs. So, in this case, it knows that we're interested in the contact.fp5 database, we want the results sent to the list.htm format file, we're interested in last names that begin with a B (begins with is the default search behavior), and we're doing a find action.

After performing a find action, the Web Companion creates a result set to pass back to the requestor. That result set contains data from all the fields on the specified layout for all of the records in the found set. In our example, since no layout was specified, FileMaker uses a virtual layout referred to as Layout 0 and includes *every* field as part of the result set. That's probably much more information than you need to display a search results screen. The bloated result is bad for two reasons. The first is simply that the set takes longer to move across the network. The other is that if you have summary fields in your database, FileMaker must evaluate those in order to prepare the result set in the first place.

Better by far would be to create a layout in the contact database that contains any possible search fields and all of the fields (including related fields) that you want to be returned as part of the results. Perhaps for our example we'd have a layout called WebFind with contact ID, First Name, and Last Name. Then, we'd restructure the request to look like the following.

```
http://<your IP address>/FMpro?-db=contact.fp5&-lay=
  WebFind&-format=list.htm&last+name=B&-find
```

The impact this has on performance is truly dramatic.

When preparing your databases, then, you'll want to create a slew of web-only layouts that have the minimal set of fields you need to accomplish the given task. Avoid putting summary fields or slow calculations on any of these. It's not uncommon to have a half dozen or more web-specific layouts in a table. These layouts take just seconds to create, as all you need is a simple form view with a handful of fields. Don't waste any more time than necessary with the formatting or maintenance of them.

While specifying layouts is a good thing and can greatly speed up your solution, there are, alas, a few things of which you need to be aware. The first is the situation where you've specified a layout but you don't have the right fields on it. If our WebFind layout above didn't have the First Name field on it and we tried to display it on the search results page, we'd simply have an empty column on our result page. The other situation to worry about is someone deleting or renaming one of your web layouts. Web layouts usually look disposable, and a well-meaning future developer may come along and ruin an entire solution "cleaning up" the database. To protect against this, we suggest that you put a big, bold message at the top of your web layouts that warns the viewer of the nasty consequences that await those who mess with that layout, as in Figure 2.2.

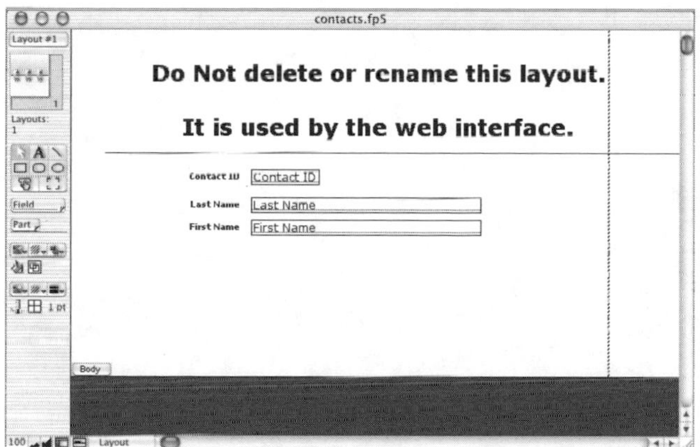

Figure 2.2

It's tempting to use just one or two layouts for all of your web needs, but pretty soon you end up with a giant utility layout with way more stuff on it than you need for any given task. Take the time to create request-specific layouts as you need them.

Our discussion of layouts pertains to all methods of Custom Web Publishing. For Instant Web Publishing, layouts are even more important. With IWP, your FileMaker layouts are instantly and entirely recreated in a web browser. For a complete discussion of Instant Web Publishing, please see Chapter 5.

Summary

In this chapter, we've tried to cover a broad range of things you should do and consider as you prepare your FileMaker database systems for the web. In our discussion of the four categories of web projects, we suggested that the choice of development tool could be partially determined by the project type. We presented some "best practices" naming conventions and discussed the problems you might encounter if your databases used names with certain special characters. We also discussed the performance and design implications of using global fields, calculations, summary fields, scripts, and portals. Finally, we explained why layouts are crucial to web requests and how you can use layouts specific to particular actions to optimize the performance of your solution.

Chapter 3

Configuring FileMaker for the Web

In the last chapter we discussed several strategies for preparing your databases for the web. The structure of your databases can have a big impact on how they'll perform over the web. The next subject we discuss is configuring the FileMaker application itself so that it can be securely accessed from the web. It's not terribly complicated, but there are several pieces involved, and it's good to know what they do. The topics covered in this chapter are:

- Choosing Instant vs. Custom Web Publishing
- Setting up the host machine
- Enabling the Web Companion
- Sharing the databases
- Securing your site
- Using the Web Server Connector

Choosing Instant vs. Custom Web Publishing

Broadly speaking, there are two methods for web-enabling FileMaker Pro databases. The first is referred to as Instant Web Publishing, or simply IWP. The beauty of IWP is that you don't need to write a single line of HTML code. When IWP is enabled, FileMaker generates and serves web pages automatically, basing the design on layouts that you've selected for various tasks. IWP was first introduced in FileMaker 4.0 and has been updated steadily in each major version since. The early IWP really wasn't suitable for building web apps of any complexity, but in FileMaker 6, IWP has some added features that give enough flexibility to finally be considered a viable web development tool. If you haven't seen IWP since its infancy, you should give it another look. We cover IWP in detail in Chapter 5 of this book.

The other method for publishing FileMaker databases to the web is referred to as Custom Web Publishing. Custom Web Publishing is really a catch-all term for using any of a number of tools to exchange data with FileMaker through the Web Companion. The majority of this book is in fact about Custom Web Publishing using CDML, Lasso, PHP, and XSML/XSTL.

Instant Web Publishing is utterly simple to set up and use, but it's not very programmable. You have some limited control over functionality, but for the most part, it gives you a set of features, and if they're not what you want, you're out of luck. You can't "look behind the curtain" to see what's going on or extend the functionality. IWP is suitable for relatively simple web applications. By "simple," we don't mean screen design or number of fields. In fact, since IWP renders your FileMaker layouts as HTML, it's very easy to produce beautiful looking pages. Rather, we mean "simple" in terms of the business logic that you're able to implement. If you recall from our discussion in Chapter 2 of the components of a web application, business logic is typically best implemented by the middleware layer. There is no middleware layer with IWP. So, for instance, you can't create conditional branches. If I click on a button, I can't have a rule where it takes me to one layout under conditions XYZ and a different layout under conditions ABC.

The decision to go to Custom Web Publishing comes with a bit of a learning curve. Even the simplest solution requires a bunch of coding. You'll need to be adept with both HTML and a tool for interacting with the Web Companion (PHP, Lasso, CDML, or XML/XST). Figure 3.1 illustrates the complexity vs. functionality trade-off of Custom Web Publishing.

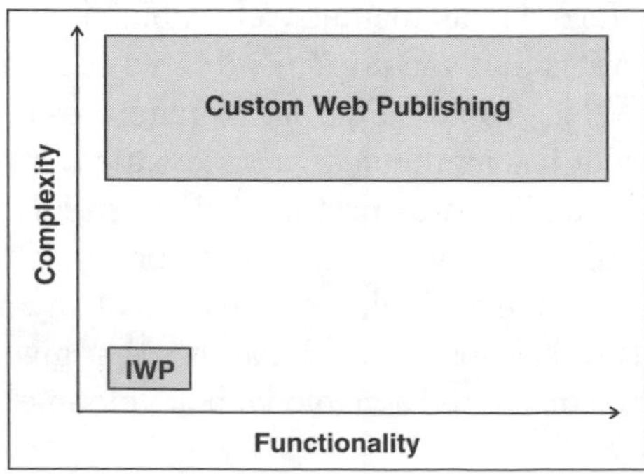

Figure 3.1

What we mean to show by this illustration is that there's no middle ground on the complexity side. Instead of a smooth transition from IWP to CWP, there's a big complexity gap. If you want more functionality than what IWP can provide, you're going to be in for more complexity.

Setting up the Host Machine

Regardless of which option you choose for publishing your database to the web—Instant Web Publishing or Custom Web Publishing—you should have a dedicated computer that will act as the web host. This machine can run any OS supported by FileMaker, including Windows NT/2000/XP/98 and Macintosh 9.x/10. We strongly recommend that the machine not be used for any tasks other than FileMaker web hosting.

Hardware Configuration

You don't need to run out and buy a server-class machine to act as the web host. But don't relegate your slowest and oldest workstation to this task either. We consider a mid- to high-end workstation sufficient. iMacs make great web hosts. The machine you choose doesn't need to have a large hard drive or gigabytes of RAM or any other bells and whistles. Its primary purpose is to serve data through the network, so the most important components are the network subsystem and the hard drive. The faster the machine can get the data to and from the disk and back to the network, the better. Splurge for a fast hard drive (Wide Ultra SCSI with high RPMs) rather than a large hard drive, and make sure you have a quality network card. Check also that your web host is connected as directly as possible to your high-speed Internet connection. That is, don't have the machine routed through a cheap hub on its way to your fast switch.

Your host machine needs to have a static IP address, and it should be connected to the Internet at all times. If your organization uses a firewall to protect its network, you might need to work with your IT department to place your machine outside the firewall.

Software

Your web host needs to have either FileMaker Pro or FileMaker Pro Unlimited installed and running. (We discuss the FileMaker 6 product line in this book, but just about everything applies equally as well to FileMaker 5.x.) You can't web-enable FileMaker Server. The difference between Pro and Unlimited is important to understand. FileMaker Pro is limited to receiving requests from ten different IP addresses every 12 hours. Further requests will be denied. This might be sufficient if you're using Instant Web Publishing so your outside sales reps can look up contact information, but it's clearly not for any kind of public site.

FileMaker Pro Unlimited has no such IP metering (hence the "unlimited" in the name), and it's the correct tool to use for most web applications. The IP metering is the only difference between the two products. You can develop and use databases with Unlimited exactly the same as you would with Pro. When you purchase FileMaker Pro Unlimited, you also receive the Web Server Connector, which is a Java servlet that allows you to integrate FileMaker's Web Companion with full-service web serving software (such as Microsoft's Internet Information Server (IIS), or Apache on OS X or Red Hat Linux). We discuss the Web Server Connector in detail at the end of this chapter. If you're using any sort of middleware to connect to the Web Companion, regardless of the number of IP addresses, you are bound under the FileMaker licensing terms to use FileMaker Pro Unlimited rather than Pro as your web host.

Both products come with a plug-in called the Web Companion; it's installed in your plug-in directory (FileMaker/System on Windows, FileMaker:FileMaker Extensions on Macintosh) as part of the typical installation. That's the tool that allows your database to respond to HTTP requests. In the next section we discuss how you enable and configure the Web Companion.

Whichever product or platform you're using, you'll have much better performance if FileMaker is the foreground application; it can't run as a service or daemon like FileMaker Server can. Disable any screen savers or other routines (like indexing) that may compete with FileMaker for resources.

Your Database Files

Any databases that you want accessible to the web need to be open on the host machine. The databases can either reside locally on the host machine, or they can be open as guests of FileMaker Server. Figure 3.2 illustrates the topology of these two configurations.

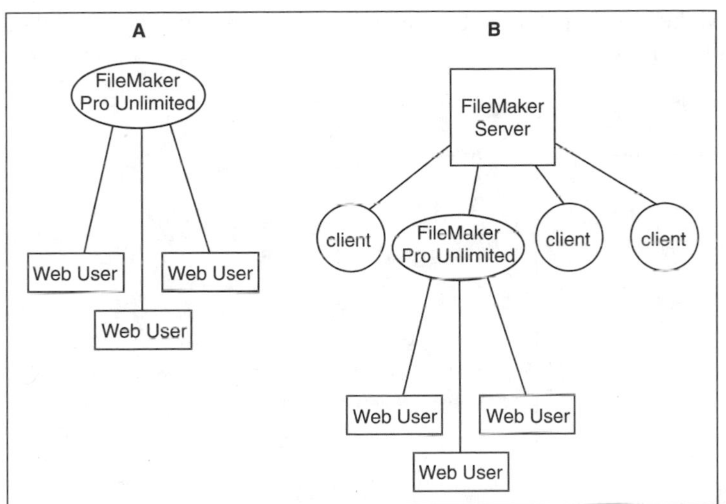

Figure 3.2

If the databases live on the host machine (as in Figure 3.2A), it really doesn't matter where you put them. The only restriction is that they should not be placed in the web folder within the FileMaker folder. That's the root folder for all web requests, and a web user can potentially download anything in that folder. Running with this topology, it doesn't matter what you set as your FileMaker network protocol. In fact, you'll probably want to disable peer-to-peer networking (access this under Edit>Preferences>Application). Similarly, it doesn't matter whether you set your files to be single-user or multi-user.

Under either topology, when you open the databases on the web host, the password you use must have the Export Records privilege. The Web Companion can't interact with a table that doesn't have this privilege. This is good because if there are certain databases that need to be open but shouldn't be web accessible, simply use a password without the Export privilege for those files.

If your web host is a guest of FileMaker Server (as in Figure 3.2B), be sure that the password you use to open the databases is not disconnected during idle time by the server. That was a feature added to FileMaker Server 5.0 that kicks off users who haven't had activity for some specified amount of time. The problem, of course, is that you might want to kick off regular users who have been inactive for two hours, but you certainly don't want your web server disconnecting during a lull in the middle of the night. You can prevent the disconnection at the password level simply by unchecking the Disconnect from

FileMaker Server when idle check box in the Define Passwords dialog (see Figure 3.3).

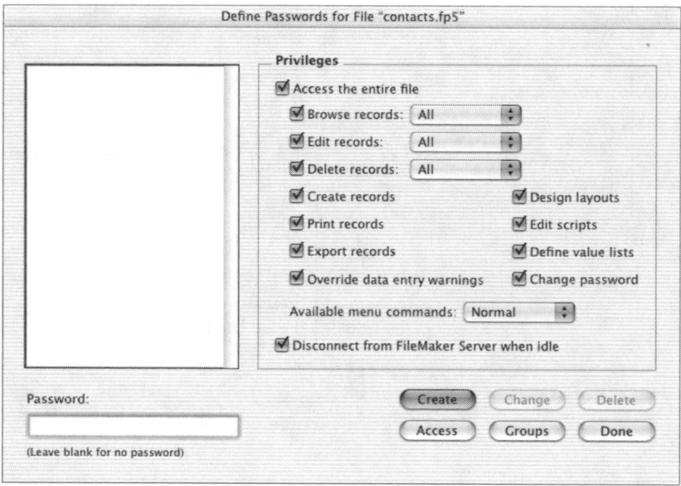

Figure 3.3

Enabling the Web Companion

Simply put, the Web Companion is a plug-in that responds to HTTP requests. It's installed as part of the typical installation of both FileMaker Pro and FileMaker Pro Unlimited. You don't need to buy or install anything special to use the Web Companion. It can act both as a Common Gateway Interface (CGI) to pass data to a web server and as a web server itself.

Keep in mind that since the Web Companion is a client-side tool, users on your FileMaker network might inadvertently (or even advertently...) permit access to your databases to web users through their machines. If you're the system administrator of a database with sensitive data, you might rest easier at night if you pull the Web Companion off your users' workstations.

Enabling and configuring the Web Companion is a breeze. On the host machine, launch FileMaker (it doesn't matter what database), go to Edit>Preferences>Application, and click the Plug-Ins tab. As shown in Figure 3.4, you'll see a list of plug-ins that are available for use on that machine.

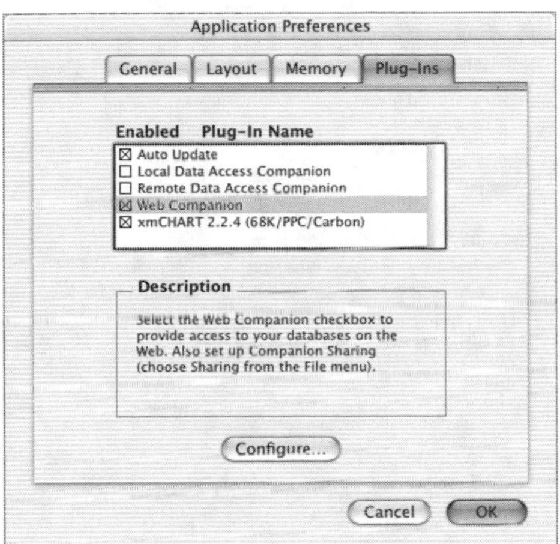

Figure 3.4

If you don't see the Web Companion listed among the choices, you'll have to manually find it and place it in the appropriate directory. Rather than reinstalling the application, it's probably easier to go to another machine and see if you can copy it over. On Windows machines, plug-ins are located in the System folder within the FileMaker application folder. On Macs, they're in the FileMaker Extensions folder within the FileMaker application folder. After moving files into the appropriate directory, you'll probably need to restart FileMaker to see the revised list of available plug-ins.

To enable the Web Companion, all you have to do is select the Enabled check box on the screen. See, we told you it was easy.

Configuring the Web Companion is only a hair more difficult. Click on the Web Companion plug-in to highlight it, and then click the Configure button. You're now at the configuration screen, which is shown in Figure 3.5. Keep in mind that you're configuring the FileMaker application itself, not an individual database. Any changes you make to the Web Companion configuration immediately affects all open databases.

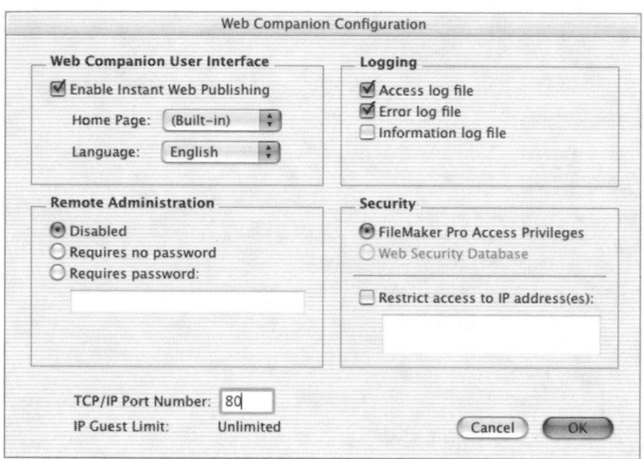

Figure 3.5

The following sections explain in detail what each of these configuration options offers.

Web Companion User Interface

By selecting or deselecting the check box in this section, Instant Web Publishing is turned on or off. If you're going to be using a tool like CDML, Lasso, PHP, or XML to web-enable your databases, you'll probably want to deselect this option. It's not that you can't do Custom Web Publishing with IWP enabled, but rather your databases will be accessible in a manner that you haven't planned for, so go ahead and disable IWP if you aren't planning on using it.

By the way, there's nothing that you need to do on the FileMaker side to allow for the use or restriction of a particular Custom Web Publishing tool. As long as the Web Companion is active, it will respond to any and all properly formatted inquiries.

If you have enabled Instant Web Publishing, you have the further option of having FileMaker generate a home page (that's the "built-in" option) or selecting one of your own design. Any document that's in the Web directory inside the FileMaker folder will be available to choose as the home page. We discuss the creation of custom home pages in Chapter 5.

The language selection again only applies if you've enabled Instant Web Publishing. It determines, as you might expect, the language in which the pregenerated IWP web pages are displayed.

Remote Administration

The Remote Administration area governs a handful of tasks that can be done remotely through a browser. The most important of these is administration of the Web Security Databases. Of course, if you haven't selected this as your security option, it's a moot point. Remote Administration also allows you to:

- Use the -dbopen tag to open a database
- Use the -dbclose tag to close a database
- Download .fp5 files from the web directory
- Upload files (of any type) to the web directory using HTTP PUT

You should only enable Remote Administration if you intend to modify user or database privileges remotely or if you need access to any of these other functions. If you do enable it, then of course you'll want to require a password. The other choice shouldn't even be presented as an option.

Logging

The Web Companion can create log files that allow you to monitor its activities. The logs, which are placed in the FileMaker application folder, can be opened by any text editor.

- The **Access Log** gives you a list of incoming requests, including the date, time, and requestor's IP address.
- The **Error Log** is a list of errors generated by the Web Companion.
- The **Information Log** records any text specified by the [FMP-Log] tag. You can use this to create your own custom logs as users move through your application. For instance, you might have the tag [FMP-Log: Order Submitted] in one of your format files.

If you enable these options, you probably want to periodically purge or archive their contents. The Access Log especially can become large rather quickly with a busy site. Some people wonder whether logging slows down their web application. We haven't found the difference to be noticeable, so if you think you'd benefit from having logs generated, go ahead and turn on these options.

Security

When you publish databases to the web, you can either use whatever passwords and privileges you've already set up to protect the database or you can use what are called the Web Security Databases to create web-only privileges. If you're using Instant Web Publishing, you really don't have a choice; only FileMaker's built-in security can be used.

When you first come to the Web Companion configuration screen, the option to select the Web Security Databases may be grayed out. This is because the Web Security Databases must be open before you can choose this as an option. The three files that comprise the Web Security Databases are found in the Web Security/Databases folder.

If you opt to use the Web Security Databases, these three files must remain open at all times on the host machine. You'll need to set up security for every file that you make accessible via the web.

There's no simple rule of thumb for when you should use FileMaker's access privileges and when you should use the Web Security Databases. Most people find that it's much simpler to use the built-in access privileges. One of the nice things about the Web Security Databases is that you can make changes to your security while your application is being used. Any new passwords or restrictions you set up take effect immediately.

In the Security section of the configuration window, you also have the option to restrict access to certain IP numbers. This is extremely good security for intranets or solutions where you know the identity of your users. You can enter up to 255 characters in the space provided. Lists of IP addresses should be separated by commas. You can specify an entire subnet by using a wildcard (i.e., 209.243.123.*) in place of the final number.

There's one final section of the configuration window. In the lower left-hand corner you'll see a place to enter the TCP/IP port number that the Web Companion uses. The default port for web applications is 80. If you know that this port isn't in use by another application, go ahead and use it. In the event that port 80 is in use, set the port number as 591. That is a registered number that shouldn't conflict with any other applications. Keep in mind that if you use anything other than port 80, all of your web requests will need to specify the port number. That is, a request might be 123.123.123.123:591/FMPro… instead of 123.123.123.123/FMPro…

Underneath the port number, you'll see the IP guest limit. This isn't something that you set. It lets you know whether you're running regular FileMaker Pro client (in which case, it says "10") or if you're using FileMaker Pro Unlimited (in which case, it says "Unlimited").

Sharing the Databases

Enabling and configuring the Web Companion allows the FileMaker application itself to respond to web requests. You then need to go into each of the databases that you want to be web accessible and explicitly set them up to share to the web. To do this, select File > Sharing—at which point you'll see the dialog shown in Figure 3.6.

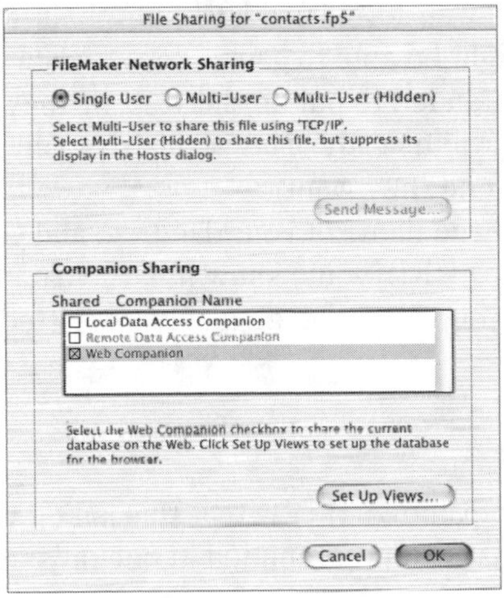

Figure 3.6

Under Companion Sharing, select the check box next to Web Companion. If you're going to be using Instant Web Publishing, you can proceed from here to set up your views. We discuss this in Chapter 5. For now, you're done—your database is accessible from the web.

Securing Your Site

There's one final and vital thing for you to consider when web-enabling a FileMaker database: security. We've already briefly discussed the two ways that security can be implemented for a web solution—using FileMaker's access privileges or using the Web Security Databases. In this section, we elaborate on each of these, focusing especially on the use of the Web Security Databases.

To begin, we're going to try to scare you a bit by telling you about some of the things that can happen to your databases if you don't secure them (or secure them improperly). Web users interact with the Web Companion by sending it HTTP requests. These requests are quite simple. They specify the IP address of your server and a string of commands that tell the Web Companion what to do and how to furnish a response. Typically, these requests are sent when a user clicks on a link or submits a form that you've created in your web solution. Would-be hackers can glean a lot of information about your databases by studying these valid requests. They can possibly find out the names of databases, layouts, and fields. They might even see record IDs pass by as they edit records. The hackers can then create their own malicious request simply by typing a well-formatted URL into their browser's address bar. They might be able to gain access to data in your database that you hadn't intended to put on the web, or they might change or delete records whimsically. They can also easily get a list of script names and run any one they want.

Even if a hacker knows only the name of your database and you haven't protected it, the following URL would show him the data from every field and every record of your database, all nicely formatted in an XML result set:

```
http://<your IP address>/FMpro?-db=myDatabase.fp5&-format=
  -dso_xml&-max=all&-findall
```

There's no way for the Web Companion to know that this isn't a valid request coming from a button that you programmed in one of your format files.

Hopefully, you're sufficiently scared now to read the rest of this section diligently. Setting up security properly takes time to plan, implement, and maintain, but that's better than the alternative.

Protecting Your Database with FileMaker's Access Privileges

If your database requires a password for entry, and you've configured the Web Companion to use FileMaker access privileges, any request to the web companion will trigger an HTTP authentication dialog, similar to that in Figure 3.7

Figure 3.7

It doesn't matter what, if anything, is entered as the user ID, but the password must match one of the passwords in the database. If it doesn't, the user won't be able to do anything. If it does, the privileges that user has within FileMaker extend to the web. There's no way to allow only certain passwords access from the web when you're using this security method. A user who knows any valid password can authenticate via the web.

A user is only prompted for authentication the first time a request is submitted to the Web Companion. The browser automatically sends this information with subsequent requests during the session. If the user attempts to perform an action he doesn't have the privilege to perform, he is prompted for the password again. Only by entering a valid password with that privilege is the request processed.

If you're designing a site that is used by the general public (say, a product catalog), you obviously can't require that a password be entered to access your data. Yet of course you still need to protect it. For these situations, you'll want to define a blank password in FileMaker and give it the bare minimum set of privileges needed to use your site. As long as they are performing actions permitted by a blank password, your visitors will not be asked for a password. But as soon as they attempt to do something they shouldn't, they will be.

Protecting Script Access

One of the hardest things to protect against is a web user running one of your scripts. You're probably thinking that they'd have to know the name of a script before they could run it. And you're correct. But it's trivial for a user with a limited password (or if you've set up a blank password) to get a list of all your scripts, simply by sending the following request:

```
http://<your IP address>/FMpro?-db=myDatabase.fp5&-format=
  -dso_xml&-scriptnames
```

Try this before setting up security on your databases and you'll be amazed at the result. Once someone knows the names of your scripts, they can run one with another simple request:

```
http://<your IP address>/FMpro?-db=myDatabase.fp5&-format=
  -dso_xml&-script=Super+Secret+Script&-findany
```

There's no way using FileMaker's built-in access privileges to grant a user some access to your data, yet protect the list of scripts or prevent any of them from being run. Running scripts might not cause much mischief in some systems, but there are an awful lot where it could.

One bad thing that can happen is the web hacker runs a script that causes a dialog box to appear on the host machine, perhaps a Show Message or a print dialog. Until that dialog is cleared on the host machine, the Web Companion is deaf to any other requests. Well, at least the hacker would be out of business for a while!

If you're concerned about this, you can add a few lines to the beginning of each of your scripts that detects whether or not it's being called by a web user. The Web Companion, being a plug-in, has external functions similar to those of other plug-ins. Using those, you can get information like the IP address that's currently using the Web Companion. At the top of your scripts, then, you might put the following code:

```
If [External("Web-ClientIP", "")]
     Halt Script
End If
```

The Web-ClientIP function doesn't take a parameter, so just put in "" as the second argument. Any script protected this way is harmless if called from the web, and you haven't sacrificed a bit of functionality. If you want to go beyond protection and try to hunt the hacker down, you can also write the IP address, date, time, and script name to a log file before halting the script.

While we're on the subject of the Web Companion's External functions, there's another place where you should consider using them. If you have a solution where users are adding records from a browser, create a field in your database that has the Web-ClientIP function auto-entered so you'll have it for future reference.

Protecting Fields

In addition to protecting your scripts, you should take the time to protect the contents of any fields that you wouldn't want displayed for a web hacker. You might, for instance, publish your company's phone directory database online, carefully making sure that you don't divulge sensitive data, such as salary or home phone numbers. A savvy user of your system, however, will potentially be able to see that information if you don't explicitly guard against it.

To see a list of all the fields in your database, a hacker with some access would simply submit the following request:

```
http://<your IP address>/FMpro?-db=myDatabase.fp5&-format=
   -fmp_xml&-view
```

They could also specify a particular layout name and see just the fields on that layout, as well as any formatting information, such as value lists. A list of your layouts is also quite accessible; it's available through the request:

```
http://<your IP address>/FMpro?-db=myDatabase.fp5&-format=
  -fmp_xml&-layoutnames
```

Knowing your field and layout names might not seem like a big deal, but for every field a hacker can see in your field list, he can also see data in that field. Assuming he had the privilege to browse records in the database, he'd just have to request:

```
http://<your IP address>/FMpro?-db=myDatabase.fp5&-format=
  -fmp_xml&-max=all&-findall
```

...and he'd see all of your data. Your best hope would then be that the size of the result set is so large that it causes the browser to time out while waiting for a response.

If you're using FileMaker's built-in access privileges to protect your system and there are fields that you don't want web users to see, you need to wander into the murky world of FileMaker's Access Privilege Overview screen to protect them.

First, set up a new group. Then go into the Access screen and click on the password that your web users will be using in the second column. While it's highlighted, click on the dot in front of your web group to add it to that group. Make sure that it's not part of any other groups. Then click on the name of your group to activate it. Now you'll be able to deselect those layouts and fields that you don't want that group to have access to. If you need more information about how to use the Overview screen, refer to the FileMaker Help system.

Once you've done this, web users won't even know these fields exist and won't have access to the data in them. Usually, in a pure FileMaker system, you can rely on hiding layouts to keep users from sensitive data. Be aware that if you have regular FileMaker users whose passwords allow access to those fields, they may have a backdoor into the data through the web companion. They can even set up their own workstation as the web server if they have the privilege to export records.

Protecting Records

It's relatively easy to protect certain records from being viewed, edited, or deleted from the web using FileMaker's built-in access privileges for security. This is done exactly the same way as if you were protecting records from regular FileMaker Pro users. When you set up your web password, you can leave the privileges for Browse, Edit, and Delete checked, but then in the pop-up menu next to the privilege, select Limited and put a condition on the use of that action.

Say that you had an event calendar online, and you only wanted web users to be able to view records with an event date within the next two weeks. In that case, you'd set up the following condition under Browse records:

```
EventDate >= Status(CurrentDate) and EventDate <=
  Status(CurrentDate) + 14
```

If a user tries to mine your entire database using the method that we described earlier, they'd get <No Access> for the fields of the events that didn't fit this criterion.

This concludes our discussion of how to protect web databases using FileMaker's built-in access privileges. If you take a few simple and reasonable precautions, you can rest easier knowing your data is safe.

Protecting Your Databases with the Web Security Databases

The other method for protecting your web site is through the Web Security Databases. Most people find that there's a slight learning curve associated with their use. The main advantages that the Web Security Databases have over FileMaker's built-in access privileges are that you can administer your security settings remotely, require both a user name and a password, and keep your web users and FileMaker users separate from each other.

Note: If you are using Instant Web Publishing, you cannot use the Web Security Databases. Access to your site will be controlled by FileMaker's built-in access privileges.

The three files that comprise the Web Security Databases are Web Security.fp5, Web Users_.fp5, and Web Fields_.fp5. You'll find them in the Databases folder within the Web Security directory. You can move the files if you like, but there's no need to. The Web Security Databases are ordinary FileMaker databases, and they're wide open. You can alter them if you want, but you probably shouldn't. Under no circumstances should you set these databases to share to the web—that would be a huge security risk. Similarly, you should never share the Web Security Databases with FileMaker Server or peer-to-peer. If you need the ability to edit the files remotely, use the Remote Administration capabilities built into the tool.

The Web Security Databases need to be open in order for you even to choose that option in the Web Companion Configuration. They must remain open at all times. If they aren't open for some reason, web users get an error and no requests are processed by the Web Companion.

When you first open the Web Security database, it will be empty and look something like Figure 3.8.

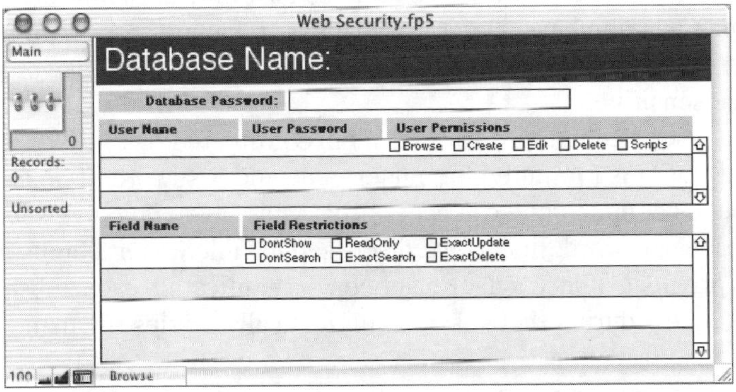

Figure 3.8

You'll need to create a record in this file for each database for which you want to provide security. On each record, you'll then enter the usernames, passwords, and access privileges in the top portal. You'll also be able to set field- and record-level restrictions in the bottom portal. The key that's used to relate the three files together is the database name itself, so if you ever have to modify the name of a table for some reason, all of the data in the portals will seem to disappear.

Any changes that you make to the Web Security Database take effect immediately. Even if a user has already authenticated, you can change his privileges anytime, even in the middle of his session.

You also have an opportunity on this screen to enter a database password. Its purpose is to allow you to tap into FileMaker's built-in access privileges and use them in conjunction with the Web Security Databases. If you enter here one of your FileMaker passwords, then no web user can have greater access than what is provided with that password. That is, the privileges you set up in the Web Security Databases can further restrict access, but they can't extend it. The privileges associated with the FileMaker password represent the maximum set of privileges that any web user could possibly have.

Setting Up Usernames

Usernames and passwords are entered in the top portal. If your solution contains multiple databases, you need to set up the same usernames and passwords for each of your tables. For each user, you can grant or restrict access for viewing, creating, editing, and deleting records. You can also prohibit that user from running any of your FileMaker scripts, which if you recall was something that you couldn't do using FileMaker's built-in access privileges.

Usernames and passwords should consist only of the letters A through Z and numbers. Don't use leading or trailing spaces, punctuation symbols, or any special characters. Usernames and passwords are *not* case sensitive.

Any user attempting to access a table protected by the Web Security Databases is prompted for a username and password. If no names have been set up, no one can access that table, even if you've specified a database password. Just as we discussed for FileMaker's built-in access privileges, once a user has been authenticated, each subsequent request during that session automatically carries the name and password information.

If you're creating a site that will be accessed by the public at large, you obviously can't set a password for each of your users. For these situations, there's a special username called All Users that you can use. You'd set that up as the username, leave the password blank, and then set any access restriction that you want to place on your guests. Figure 3.9 shows the setup that you'd use if you had a database that you wanted anyone on the web to be able to browse but not edit.

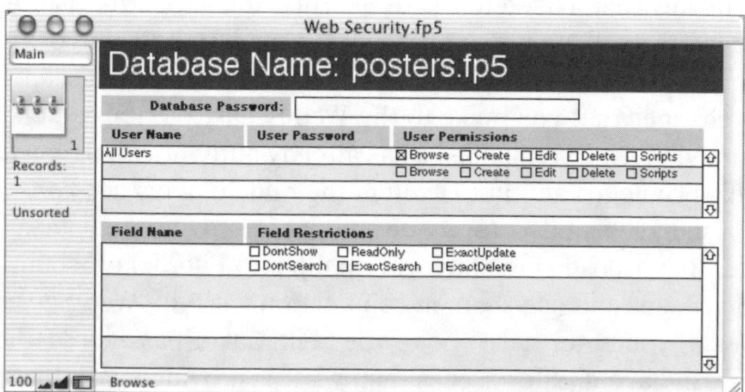

Figure 3.9

The All Users username functions similarly to how a blank password does if you're using the built-in access privileges. Depending on your solution, it may make sense to set up All Users with extremely limited privileges (say, browse only) and then set up other names/passwords for those who need additional access. As long as web users are doing things allowed by the All Users settings, they won't be prompted for a password, but as soon as they try to do something more, they are prompted to enter a password.

You can't define other names/passwords that are more restrictive than the settings for All Users. For instance, you can't grant All Users the privilege to delete records and then restrict it for other users. An explicitly defined user can always do what All Users can do, and they can also perform additional actions that they've been granted.

Setting Field and Record Restrictions

At the bottom of the Web Security.fp5 database, you have the opportunity to set up field and record restrictions. Any restrictions you set up apply to the table as a whole. That is, you can't allow some users access to a field but not others. The two portals are independent of one another.

There are six restrictions that you can define for a field, and although it's not very intuitive, three of them define field restrictions and three define record restrictions. Since this is probably the most nebulous part of the Web Security Databases, let's look at each of the restrictions and discuss how and why you might want to use it.

First, the field restrictions:

Don't Show

If you select the option to not show a field, you'll prohibit any web user from ever seeing data in that field. You'd probably want to set this up for every field that you're not displaying somewhere yourself in a format file. Earlier in this chapter we discussed how easy it could be for a web hacker to get information from any field in an unprotected database. Beware: Fields that are hidden using Don't Show can still be edited. In most cases, you'll want to select Read Only every time you select Don't Show.

Don't Search

This option restricts which fields can be used as search arguments from a web browser. Even if you've selected the Don't Show option for a field, that field could still be used as a search parameter. For instance, if you had a personnel database online and you set the Salary field to

Don't Show, a user who knew the name of the field could still search using that field and get back lists of employees that met the criteria they defined.

Read Only

As you'd probably expect, fields that have a read-only restriction can be viewed but not edited via a request to the Web Companion.

Now the record restrictions:

Exact Search

Exact Search is really a browse restriction. When you select Exact Search for a field, every search request that comes into the Web Companion needs to have that field as one of the search arguments. Then, only records where the incoming search argument matches exactly the data in that field will be returned. Clear as mud, right?

An example will hopefully shed some light on the matter. Say that you have a contact database online that's used by your outside sales folks, but you don't want them to be able to view each other's contacts. Create a field in the database called RecordKey or something similar and populate each salesperson's set of records with some kind of password that only he or she will know. In the Web Security.fp5 database, put an Exact Search restriction on the RecordKey field.

Then, when you build the web forms that the salespeople use to find contacts, stick an extra field on your search form so they can enter their secret record key. Say they search for all the "Smiths" and enter their record key as well. Only the Smith records with their record key would be returned. Any search that doesn't have a record key as one of its arguments fails. Similarly, a search with an empty record key also fails.

In your forms and URLs, you need to explicitly set the operator for the record key to "eq" when submitting these types of requests. The default operator is "begins with," and that doesn't work for any fields set with this Exact Search restriction. In a URL, just add &-op=eq before the Exact Search argument. In a form, you'll have a hidden input with a name of -op and a value of eq before the Exact Search argument. Operators always affect the following search parameter. Using CDML, your form might end up looking like the following:

```
<input type="hidden" name="-db" value="myContacts.fp5">
<input type="hidden" name="-lay" value="searchForm">
Last Name to Search for:<input type="text" name="Last Name"
  value=""><br>
```

```
<input type="hidden" name="-op" value="eq">
Record Key:<input type="password" name="RecordKey" value="">
```

As another example, say you have a large product database, but you only want information on a handful of products to be available on your web site. To achieve this, set up a field called ViewOnline and set it to some value (like 1) for those records that you want accessible. Then set up an Exact Search restriction for this field in the Web Security Database. As part of all of your search forms, you'd then have a hidden input field that sets ViewOnline to 1. All of the search requests would thereby be constrained to the set of records that you had flagged. Even if a hacker figured out what you were doing, he would still not be able to access unflagged records. Remember, in an unprotected database, the following URL would spit back every iota of data to a hacker:

```
http://<your IP address>/FMpro?-db=products.fp5&-format=
  -dso_xml&-max=all&-findall
```

With an Exact Search restriction, this command wouldn't do a thing. And even if the hacker knew the restriction and submitted this request:

```
http://<your IP address>/FMpro?-db=products.fp5&-format=
  -dso_xml&-max=all&-op=eq&ViewOnline=1&-find
```

...he would only see the records you allowed to be viewed on the web.

It is possible to set an Exact Search restriction for multiple fields, but that is seldom necessary. In that case, all of the restricted fields need to be included in the search. That is, it's an "and" restriction rather than an "or" restriction.

Another nice side effect of Exact Search is that it disables the -findall and -findany actions. Finally, you'll usually want to select the Don't Show restriction on fields where you've selected Exact Search.

Exact Update

The Exact Update restriction is very similar to the Exact Search restriction. The difference is that it governs the editing of records rather than the viewing of records. By placing this restriction on a field, any request to edit a record has to be accompanied by a record key.

This restriction usually causes some misunderstandings. It's not the case that in every record where the key exists, some value will be changed. It also has nothing to do with editing the restricted field.

To understand what it does do, it's helpful to review how to request edits via the Web Companion. With an edit request, you must always specify the internal ID of the record to edit. You also pass information about what fields you want to change. So, for instance, the following request might be used to change a contact's name from Fred to Joe:

```
http://<your IP address>/FMpro?-db=contacts.fp5&-format=
  -dso_xml&-recid=37&firstname=joe &-edit
```

The Exact Update restriction checks a passed parameter to make sure that value is in the record, and only if it is will the edit be allowed to proceed. So, if we wanted to protect Fred's contact record from being incorrectly updated, we might have an UpdateKey field in the database and set it to, say, "foo." Then the request to change this record would need to be changed to the following:

```
http://<your IP address>/FMpro?-db=contacts.fp5&-format=
  -dso_xml&-recid=37&firstname=joe&UpdateKey=foo&-edit
```

This request states that if the UpdateKey of record 37 is "foo," then the firstname field should be set to "joe." It doesn't set the UpdateKey, nor does it find records where the UpdateKey is equal to "foo."

A good example of when you might use this would be an internal employee directory where everyone can see everything, but where you need to confine users to only modify their own profile. You can't simply remove edit access; you need to restrict it. To do this, provide each employee with an update key of some sort and set an Exact Update restriction on that field. Then, when they go to the edit screen that you designed, you would require them to enter the key along with their changes. Again, you'll usually want to select the Don't Show restriction on fields where you've selected Exact Update.

Exact Delete

The Exact Delete restriction provides a mechanism for requiring record-specific authentication to delete records. It's very similar to the Exact Update restriction in its syntax. Record deletion also requires that an internal record ID be passed to the Web Companion. With Exact Delete set for a field, web requests require that an additional parameter be passed that matches a piece of existing data in that record. That is to say a user can only delete a record if he knows the key to that record.

As an example, consider a solution where you allow web users to post events to an online event calendar. When new events are submitted, you can have a random confirmation string generated by FileMaker and echoed back to the user (or e-mailed to them). Then, you can require that editing or deleting that event record requires the event key be entered by the user. This way, you're leaving users with the privilege of deleting records, but they can only delete records they've created.

Creating Global Security for "All Databases"

Just as you can define global security for All Users, you can also set up global security for "All Databases." Simply create a new record in the Web Security Database and name the database All Databases, and then set up your usernames and passwords as you would for any other database. Using the special All Databases name is helpful if you have many database tables with the same restrictions and many usernames to set up. You can still set up field-level restrictions as well, but think through whether it makes sense. For instance, you might elect to not show a Salary field no matter what database it appears in. It might not make as much sense, however, to set any of the Exact restrictions.

What happens, you might wonder, if you have a record for All Databases and another that's specific to a given table? It's quite similar to what happens when you have All Users set up as well as other users. Anything that can be done for All Databases can be done in any table. Other tables can grant additional privileges, but they can't be more restrictive.

Say, for instance, that you have "Fred" set up as a user in All Databases with the privilege to delete but not to run scripts. If you set security records for specific tables and define Fred as a user in those, you won't be able to take away his privilege to delete records, but you can grant him the privilege of running scripts if you want.

Use the All Databases and All Users settings with caution. If you've set up a record for All Databases, and you've given All Users access to Browse, Edit, Create, Delete, and Scripts, then you've essentially turned off security.

Remote Administration

One of the best things about the Web Security Databases is that you can administer them equally well through a browser interface as you can through the FileMaker interface. Recall from our discussion of the Web Companion configuration that you have an option there to enable remote administration. We strongly recommend that if you choose to enable remote administration that you select the option to use a password.

Beyond enabling remote administration, there's one other thing that you must do; in the Web Security folder, there's a folder called Security, and that's where all of the HTML pages for doing remote access can be found. You'll need to move or copy the entire Security directory into the Web directory. You probably shouldn't modify any of the actual web forms, as you may break things or introduce security holes.

Once you've enabled remote administration and moved the Security folder, you can view and edit your security settings from anywhere you have browser access to the server. To bring up the web interface, go to http://<your IP address>/Security. You'll be presented with the screen shown in Figure 3.10.

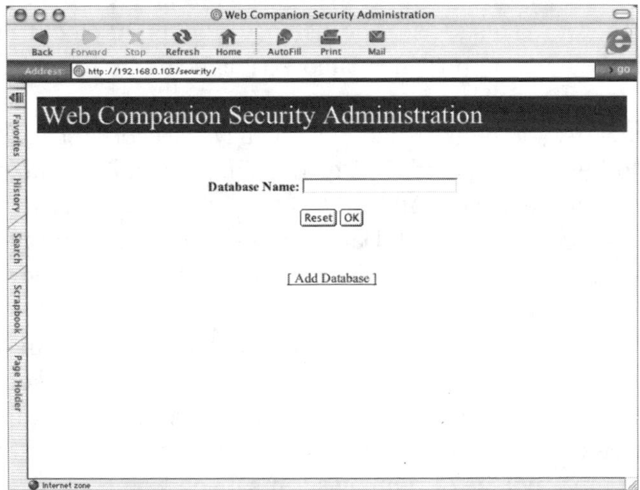

Figure 3.10

From here, you can either enter the name of the database that you want to administer or you can add a new database. If you've set up a password to access remote administration, you won't be prompted for it until you do one of these things (since that's the first time you're requesting any data from the Web Companion). You'll need to use "Admin" as the username in the authentication dialog and whatever password you set up on the configuration screen.

You'll find that the interface for remote administration is very similar to the FileMaker interface. Figure 3.11, for instance, shows what the database overview screen looks like through a browser.

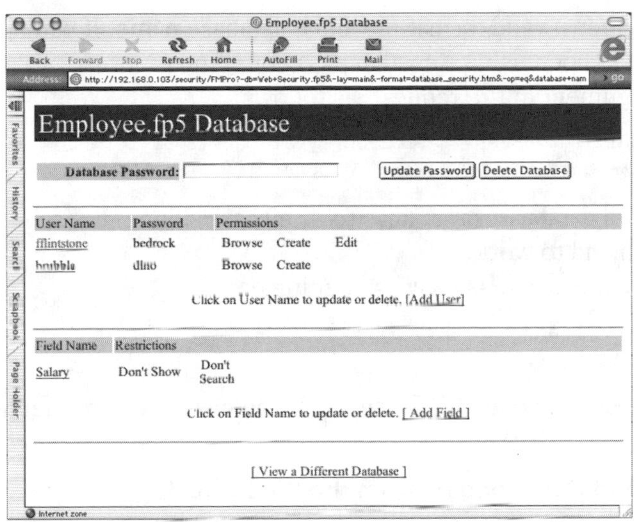

Figure 3.11

We think you'll have no problem navigating through the interface, so we're not going to bore you by going through every screen. All the functionality that we discussed in the previous section (both for setting up user accounts and field restrictions) is available to you. Any changes you make via Remote Administration are captured in the Web Security Databases, and they go into effect immediately.

Other Remote Administration Privileges

By turning on Remote Administration, you not only allow browser access to the Web Security Databases, but you also enable a few other important, but potentially dangerous, commands.

-dbOpen and -dbClose

The -dbOpen and -dbClose actions can only be used when Remote Administration is enabled, but they have nothing whatsoever to do with the Web Security Databases. Use of either command prompts the user for a password if one has been set. These commands are very useful if you ever need to close files for maintenance or restart them after a server crash.

The syntax to open a file is as follows:

```
http://<your IP address>/FMPro?-db=myDatabase.fp5&-format=
  -fmp_xml&-dbOpen
```

You must include a valid format file and a database name. If you'd like the database to open using a certain password, you enter that as an additional argument in the request, as follows:

```
http://<your IP address>/FMPro?-db=myDatabase.fp5&-format=
  -fmp_xml&-password=myPassword&-dbOpen
```

The requested database, or an alias to it, must reside in the web folder for this command to work.

Closing a file is just as easy as opening one:

```
http://<your IP address>/FMPro?-db=myDatabase.fp5&-format=
  -fmp_xml&-dbClose
```

Unlike -dbOpen, however, -dbClose works no matter where the file lives.

Uploading and Downloading from the Web Directory

With Remote Administration enabled, you can download any FileMaker file that lives in (or has an alias in) the web directory. You'll need a password, provided that you've set one up. To download a file, simply enter into your browser http://<your IP address>/myDatabase.fp5.

Files can be uploaded to the web directory as well using HTTP PUT. These can be very useful if you have a database hosted by an ISP that you need to periodically refresh.

You should always close a file before downloading it or you run the risk that your downloaded copy will be corrupted.

Protecting Your Format Files

In Chapter 6 we discuss how to create format files for rendering the responses to CDML requests. Format files contain your business logic and shouldn't be accessible by web users. To protect them, be sure to place them in the cdml_format_files directory, which is inside your FileMaker directory. FileMaker 6 is the first version of the product with this directory. In earlier versions, your format files needed to be placed in the web directory. Putting them there, however, potentially allows your source code to be viewed from a web browser. The cdml_format_files directory is not directly accessible from the web and is therefore secure from this type of attack.

Images and static files must still be placed in the web directory. You can put copies of them in the cdml_format_files directory, but they won't actually be served from there.

If you need additional information on securing your web applications, you can find a PDF document on web security in the Web Security folder. You'll also find security updates posted from time to time on FileMaker's web site (www.filemaker.com).

Using the Web Server Connector

In our discussion up to this point, we've assumed a configuration in which the Web Companion acts as both a CGI (Common Gateway Interface) and an HTTP server. It's also possible through the use of a tool called the FileMaker Web Server Connector (FMWSC) to have a full-service web server in the role of the HTTP server, freeing the Web Companion to focus on responding to database queries.

The Web Server Connector is a Java servlet that acts as an extension to a web server, passing requests for XML or CDML from FileMaker to one or more machines running FileMaker Pro Unlimited. By license agreement, the Web Server Connector can only be used with FileMaker Pro Unlimited (not FileMaker Pro), even if you don't exceed the ten IP addresses per 12 hours limitation. The FMWSC does not support Instant Web Publishing.

You should consider using the Web Server Connector in the following situations:

- You serve a lot of static HTML files and/or images.
- You need web server functionality that the Web Companion doesn't provide, such as secure socket layers (SSL) or server side includes.
- You want to set up a RAIC (Redundant Array of Inexpensive Computers) to increase performance and/or reliability.

The FMWSC can work with a variety of popular web servers, including Apache, Microsoft's Internet Information Server, Netscape Enterprise Server, and WebSTAR. When you purchase FileMaker Pro Unlimited, you receive a separate CD that contains the Web Server Connector, documentation, and example files. The documentation is quite good, and it contains detailed installation and configuration instructions, which we won't repeat here.

The Web Server Connector is always installed on the machine that contains your web server. It's this machine that users hit from their browser. For performance reasons, you don't want FileMaker Pro Unlimited on the same machine as your web server. Rather, you'll have one or more separate machines each running FileMaker Pro

Unlimited. You can place any static HTML files or images on your web server, but CDML and XSLT format files still live in the web directory on the FileMaker Pro Unlimited machine(s).

You can configure the Web Server Connector from a web browser at the following address:

```
http://<IP address of your web server>/FMPro?config
```

There are two options there for telling the Web Server Connector how to find your FileMaker Pro Unlimited machines. The first is by host. When you tell the FMWSC connector the IP address and port of the FMU machine, it gives you a list of the databases available at that address and you can check the ones to which you want requests sent. The other option is by database. Here, instead of starting with the address of your FMU machine, enter the name of a database. Then provide the WSC a list of IP addresses and ports where it can find that database.

The simplest deployment involving the Web Server Connector is to have all of your databases available on a single FileMaker Pro Unlimited machine. The FMWSC passes along all FileMaker requests from the web server to that machine. More advanced deployments involve using multiple machines in a RAIC, each having its own copy of FileMaker Pro Unlimited.

The typical reason that you want to involve multiple FileMaker Pro Unlimited machines is to provide load balancing and/or fault tolerance. Load balancing increases the performance of a web application by dividing requests among several machines. So, even while FMU machine 1 is bogged down processing a query, FMU machine 2 (3, 4, 5,…) is capable of processing the next query that comes into the web server. Fault tolerance means reducing the risk of downtime by not keeping all of your eggs in one basket. If each of several machines is equally able to process a request, a hardware or software problem that disrupts one machine doesn't disrupt the functionality of the system as a whole. The Web Server Connector is able to detect that a machine is unable to receive a request and simply passes it on to a different machine.

There are three typical configurations of a RAIC. Each has pluses and minuses that you need to weigh based on your requirements and resources. The first is having identical copies of your databases on several FileMaker Pro Unlimited machines. This represents the optimal fault tolerance, as well as the optimal load balancing, but requires that the databases are accessible for read only. Editing and adding data to independent copies of the databases doesn't simply present a synchronization problem either. Imagine that a web user submits a request that adds a record and then submits another request to view the record that they've just added. There's no guarantee that the second request is processed by the same machine, and so it appears that the data has disappeared. Typical examples of solutions that would be deployed using this configuration are things like catalogs or document retrieval systems.

The second configuration option is to have FileMaker Server host the databases and then have each of several FileMaker Pro Unlimited machines open all of the files as guests. This way, you are able to handle both reading and writing to the databases without worrying about which machine processes the request. However, any RAIC configuration that involves FileMaker Server is not optimally fault tolerant. The FileMaker Server becomes a weak link in the system. If a drive fails on that machine or some other disruption occurs, the system is down until it's fixed or replaced.

A third configuration to consider is routing requests for certain databases to one machine and requests for other databases to other machines. Perhaps you have an application where one database receives a majority of requests. To balance the load, you'd place that database on its very own FileMaker Pro Unlimited machine and put the other databases on another machine. It's irrelevant (for load balancing purposes) whether the files physically reside on the Unlimited machines or are simply open as guests of a FileMaker Server.

This last configuration gives you more control over exactly how the system is balanced. It's also a good first step beyond having everything hosted by a single machine. The downside, of course, is that it lacks fault tolerance—but then, so does having everything hosted on a single machine (and that's the most typical configuration there is). If performance is your primary concern, this configuration may be worth trying. If stability is your primary concern, then the first configuration we discussed offers the most hope.

Summary

We've covered a wide range of topics in this chapter. We began with instructions and advice for how to configure the Web Companion and allow your databases to be accessed from the web. We then had a lengthy discussion about securing your databases from hackers using either FileMaker's built-in access privileges or the Web Security

Databases. Finally, we examined situations where it makes sense to use the Web Server Connector.

This concludes the theory and setup portion of the book. From here, we begin looking closely at the tools themselves.

Chapter 4

Publishing Your FileMaker Data with XML

By now you've probably heard something about XML. It's been a heavily hyped technology for some years. But until FileMaker version 5, if you were a FileMaker developer, the buzz didn't matter, since FileMaker didn't do anything with XML. But now that's changed. As of FileMaker 5, the Web Companion can publish data in XML format. As of FileMaker 6, this capability has been augmented with the ability to import and export data directly in an XML format and apply *transformations* to XML-formatted FileMaker data. You can't avoid it any longer; you know you need to learn this technology. But what is it, and where do you start?

This book gives a very basic grounding in XML and its companion technology, XSL. We don't provide comprehensive coverage of either technology—each one could easily fill several books. But the basics are not hard to grasp. By the time we're done, you'll have a working knowledge of XML and be able to use the XSL transformation language to take FileMaker's raw XML output and transform it into a variety of text-based formats. We also leave you with a solid set of references to printed books and online resources that you can use to further your knowledge of XML.

In this chapter, we lay out a general introduction to XML and then delve into FileMaker specifics. If you already have a handle on what XML is and why it's (arguably) important, feel free to skim this first section or skip it completely and move on to the section "FileMaker and XML"), which introduces FileMaker's own XML capabilities. If you've worked with FileMaker's XML output already and are familiar with FileMaker's different XML "grammars," skip ahead to the section "Using XSL to Transform FileMaker's Output" in order to delve directly into stylesheet writing.

What Is XML?

XML is an acronym for Extensible Markup Language, but what is a "markup language"? In the simplest terms, a markup language is a set of rules for adding extra data to a document—data that can help tell us something about what the document contains and how it's organized. This is information that a human can often easily glean from inspecting a document, but it's very difficult for a computer to discern.

For example, we have a text file representing a poem, as follows:

O Rose Thou Art Sick
by William Blake

O Rose, thou art sick!
The invisible worm
That flies in the night,
In the howling storm,

Has found out thy bed
Of crimson joy:
And his dark secret love
Does thy life destroy.

As we read this poem, we are aware that the first line is a title and the second is an author. We're aware that subsequent lines are verse lines, and they're grouped into stanzas of four lines apiece. But how would a computer know that?

We could create a rule that a verse line is everything between two carriage returns. That wouldn't work well though, since the title and author would look like verse lines as well. We could create a rule that two carriage returns divide one stanza from the next, but that would make the title and author look like a stanza. We could hard-code everything and tell the computer the first line is a title, the second is an author, and all other lines are stanzas in groups of four. But what if there are two authors or the number of lines per stanza changes? Clearly, it's very hard to write rules for things that just depend on the plain format of the text. We need some way to add *semantics* to the text, to include information that says "this part is a title, this part is an author," and so forth.

This is exactly the problem that markup languages were designed to solve. Probably the best known modern markup language is SGML, which stands for Standard Generalized Markup Language. SGML was the crystallization of many ideas about electronic document representation that were percolating in the late '60s. These ideas resulted in the creation of something called GML around 1969 and SGML around 1974. By 1986, SGML was accepted as an international standard for document encoding.

Here's how the above poem might look marked up in some form of SGML:

```
<poem>
     <title>O Rose Thou Art Sick</title>
     <author>William Blake</author>
     <stanza>
          <line>O Rose, thou art sick!</line>
          <line>The invisible worm</line>
          <line>That flies in the night,</line>
          <line>In the howling storm,</line>
     </stanza>
     <stanza>
          <line>Has found out thy bed</line>
          <line>Of crimson joy:</line>
          <line>And his dark secret love</line>
          <line>Does thy life destroy.</line>
     </stanza>
<poem>
```

Notice that the interpretation of the document's structure is now made very plain. A computer could easily come in and find the author, the first stanza, the second stanza, and so forth. The text has been "marked up" according to a set of rules. SGML and its descendants are tools that help us define such rule sets.

SGML is a huge topic, so we include a range of resources and references at the end of the chapter. The basics are covered very briefly. One thing to note is that the ML in SGML is a bit misleading. It is not really a single markup language but a set of tools for defining such languages. SGML is a tool that lets us lay down the rule (expressed in the marked-up Blake poem) that a poem is something that contains a title, an author, and one or more stanzas grouped into lines. This set of rules is contained in something called a Document Type Definition (DTD). By comparing the marked-up document with a "poems" DTD, we can decide whether the document was indeed a valid instance of a poem. SGML is the language we use to write the DTD itself.

Why does this matter? Weren't we talking about XML? Well, XML is one of two relatives of SGML that are extremely important for the web. The first is HTML, the language of the web since its invention in 1989. The second is XML, which promises to remedy all the defects of HTML. Technically speaking, XML is, like SGML, a metalanguage (that is, a means for generating rule sets to describe documents). HTML, on the other hand, *is* such a rule set—a rule set that describes the permissible forms of markup for an HTML document. Think of XML as a simpler form of SGML—a way to generate sets of rules that describe document content. HTML, on the other hand, is a particular rule set, one that can be described in an SGML document definition.

So now we understand the concept of markup, but what problem does it solve? Here are a few:

- Proprietary data interchange formats
- Non-semantic data formats
- Non-hierarchical data formats

Ideally, a data format is a) open and b) tells you not only what the data is but what it *means*. Tab-delimited text, for example, is an open format, but it's non-semantic (that is, it doesn't tell you what any of the data inside itself actually means). There's no way to look at a file and know that the first column is personal name, the third is lung size, etc. It lacks metadata ("data about the data"). You can send along a list of column names or say that they live in the first row, and this works—but it's clumsy. With XML markup, as we saw with the Blake poem, we can include markup that tells us what the different pieces of the document are.

XML also leaps over the problem of proprietary data formats. Traditionally, there is a hard choice to make in sending documents. If you want a rich representation of the document, containing things like footnotes, bold text, and the like, you need to create it using a proprietary tool like a word processor so that the file could only easily be read by others with the same software. Many converters and intermediate formats exist to ease this process, of course, but the point remains. Or you can save the document in a purely textual format, which makes it simple for others to read but robs the document of most of its richness. Markup languages, in theory, give you the best of both worlds. XML (and SGML and HTML) documents are plain text and can be transmitted and read anywhere, while containing a great deal of rich data about the document.

On a more specialized note, XML also makes it easier to work with hierarchical data. This gets us closer to the database areas that are really the focus of this book. Let's say that I want to send someone some publishing data. I have data on magazines and data on magazine articles. Magazines can contain one or many articles. I can send this in tab-delimited text files, which will look like the dump from a relational database. I can include the field names as a first row. To do this I have to send two files, one for magazines and the other for articles. The data might look like this:

```
[magazines.txt]
mag id    mag name           mag year       mag month
001       Fine Soapmaking    1981           September
002       Styrofoam Artist   1990           August
003       Squirrel           1999           December
004       Meteor Monthly     1996           March

[articles.txt]
article id mag id author fname author lname  title
001         001    Jason        Saponard      Rose Essence and Paraffin?
002         001    Sarah        Lipidary      Five Kinds of Pumice
003         001    Agape        Sanders       99 44/100 Of What?
004         003    Harlan       Marquardt     Black Squirrels of the Andes
005         004    Janet        Choi          A New Take on the Leonids
```

Here's how this data might look in XML:

```
<magazines>
     <magazine>
          <mag_id>001</mag_id>
          <mag_name>Fine Soapmaking</mag_name>
          <mag_year>1981</mag_year>
          <mag_month>September</mag_month>
          <articles>
               <article>
                    <article_id>001</article_id>
                    <author_fname>Jason</author_fname>
                    <author_lname>Saponard</author_fname>
                    <title>Rose Essence and Paraffin?</title>
               </article>
               <article>
                    <article_id>002</article_id>
                    <author_fname>Sarah</author_fname>
                    <author_lname>Lipidary</author_fname>
                    <title>Five Kinds of Pumice</title>
               </article>
               <article>
                    <article_id>003</article_id>
                    <author_fname>Agape</author_fname>
                    <author_lname>Sanders</author_fname>
                    <title>99 44/100 of What?</title>
               </article>
          </articles>
     </magazine>
     <magazine>
          <mag_id>002</mag_id>
          <mag_name>Styrofoam Artist</mag_name>
```

```
        <mag_year>1990</mag_year>
        <mag_month>August</mag_month>
    </magazine>
    <magazine>
        <mag_id>003</mag_id>
        <mag_name>Squirrel</mag_name>
        <mag_year>1999</mag_year>
        <mag_month>December</mag_month>
        <articles>
            <article>
                <article_id>004</article_id>
                <author_fname>Harlan</author_fname>
                <author_lname>Marquardt</author_fname>
                <title>Black Squirrels of the Andes</title>
            </article>
        </articles>
    </magazine>
    <magazine>
        <mag_id>004</mag_id>
        <mag_name>Meteor Monthly</mag_name>
        <mag_year>1996</mag_year>
        <mag_month>March</mag_month>
        <articles>
            <article>
                <article_id>005</article_id>
                <author_fname>Janet</author_fname>
                <author_lname>Choi</author_fname>
                <title>A New Take on the Leonids</title>
            </article>
        </articles>
    </magazine>
</magazines>
```

At first glance this comparison doesn't look too promising for XML. It seems to be much more verbose and harder to read. Where exactly is the charm in this? The flat text files are much more concise and, to a trained database eye, express the structure and relationships of their data perfectly well.

XML is interesting to a certain degree for what it does and to an even greater degree for what can be done to it. One thing it does well is describe itself. The above document makes it clear that there is something called a magazine, which has an ID, a name, a month, and a year, and the magazine contains zero or more things called articles that in turn have some other information that describes them. This is a simple example, but almost any kind of document can be well represented by XML, even those that are typically not well representable by a database structure. Consider a book. It may have a foreword, or not, possibly one or more prefaces, a table of contents, a set of chapters that might be broken down into more sub-levels, possibly an index, possibly one or more appendices, and possibly an author biography. This kind of structure is quite painful to capture in a relational database structure, but it can easily be represented in XML. Best of all, the XML itself makes it clear what the structure of the document is supposed to be.

So XML is interesting because it can readily describe very complex documents and data structures, and it carries inside itself all the necessary information to understand how that data is organized. What can be done to it is equally interesting. Far more than being simply a big block of text, XML can be validated, parsed, and transformed. For purposes of using FileMaker's XML capabilities, the last of these is the most important. Let's look at each one.

- **XML can be validated.** If you send someone a flat text file or two, your recipient has no way to determine whether the contents of the files are really any good or not. They can tell whether you sent the right number of fields, but that's about it without importing the data into some application (like FileMaker, for instance) that can validate it further. XML, on the other hand, can be validated according to a set of rules that you send along with the document. These rules, known as a Document Type Definition (DTD), can be embedded directly in the XML document or stored and referenced as a separate document. (Side note: To a database designer, the kinds of validation possible within a DTD still appear rather weak. In particular, DTDs have very little support for data typing. This concern lies behind the movement to develop a more rigorously validated type of XML, called, appropriately enough, XML Schema.)
- **XML can be parsed.** You're probably thinking that it would be a large pain to pick through that whole XML document to find what you want. You envision writing complicated, text-parsing calculations in an environment like FileMaker and shudder. And you'd be right. Thankfully, you don't have to. There are many tools available that know how to read XML documents and pick out the pieces that you specify. Normally, these tools are invisible to you, the developer; they are incorporated into other tools (like FileMaker) that use them to do useful things with XML. There are many XML-parsing tools available—you won't need to write your own.
- **XML can be transformed.** This is the big one for us as FileMaker developers. By using an intermediate language called XSLT (Extensible Stylesheet Language Transformations), a single XML document can be transformed into a variety of useful output

formats, such as HTML, RTF, and PDF. XSL transformations provide a unified framework for publishing your data from FileMaker in a wide variety of formats, many of them suited for display or distribution over the web.

Why the Web?

Why does a discussion of XML belong in a book about FileMaker and the web? Well, XML documents are very well suited to web delivery. In a typical web scenario, a user types a URL into her browser and gets back an HTML document, which her browser then renders into a nice-looking document. But the remote web server could just as well return an XML document. In fact, the FileMaker Web Companion is able to do just that. Certain types of requests to the Web Companion result in an XML-formatted data set that can then be further manipulated or transformed.

To take matters one step further, the request for a web-based XML document need not come from a user clicking or typing in a browser. It can come from some remote machine that simply wants to fetch that XML data over the web for its own purposes. This kind of data provisioning is called a web service, and we discuss it in depth in Chapter 9. In addition to being able to publish its own data to the web via XML, FileMaker 6 can now also request XML data from remote web sources and import it directly into FileMaker. So XML can be a vehicle for publishing data from FileMaker to a variety of data formats for distribution via numerous media, including the web. XML can also be a means to allow FileMaker to request data from remote web servers, import it, and do something useful with it. XML is the interchange medium for a possibly two-way communication stream that moves data in and out of FileMaker via the web.

More about XML

Before learning more about FileMaker's XML capabilities, let's take another look at the structure of an XML document. XML documents are made up of *elements*. An element is simply a pair of tags with something between them. Take, for example, the following snippet:

```
<title>The Pardoner's Tale</title>
```

This code consists of an *element* called <title> and that element's *content*. The content is everything inside the element, delimited by the element's opening and closing tags. Notice that in XML, all tags come in pairs and must be closed properly. If the </title> tag were missing, the XML would not be valid, and XML parsers would inform you of this. This is in strong contrast to HTML, where many user agents (otherwise known as browsers) are very forgiving of lax syntax. XML is not forgiving. Think of it as HTML's mean uncle. Thankfully, you won't have to write much XML by hand yourself—XSL stylesheets are the notable exception.

Elements can contain other things. In the simplest case, they just contain some content. In the example above, the content of the title element is the text "The Pardoner's Tale." But elements may also contain other elements:

```
<magazine>
      <mag_id>004</mag_id>
      <mag_name>Meteor Monthly</mag_name>
      <mag_year>1996</mag_year>
      <mag_month>March</mag_month>
</magazine>
```

Here the magazine element contains four other elements and no content. Elements may also have *attributes*. Here's another way to write the code above:

```
<magazine mag_id="004" mag_name="Meteor Monthly" mag_year="1996"
  mag_month="March"/>
```

Well, hmm, this starts to look a bit more like some of the HTML we're used to seeing:

```
<form name="search_form" method="post" action="search.html">
```

This is valid HTML (well, it would need a closing </form> tag), and it's valid XML as well (with the same proviso). In XML slang, this is a form element with three attributes. Attributes are expressed in XML the same way they are in HTML—as name-value pairs. The attribute begins with the attribute name, followed by an equals sign and the attribute's value in quotation marks. In HTML the quotes are often optional. In XML, as you might guess, they are not.

There are a few more oddities to explore. What's with the odd characters (/>) at the end of the magazine element that has the attributes? The extra backslash indicates that this element has no content at all (just attributes), and so it can be considered closed with just the extra backslash without going to all the trouble of writing an ending </magazine> tag. So <magazine></magazine> is the long form, but if there's nothing between the two tags, <magazine/> is the legitimate short form in XML.

I mentioned that the two forms of the <magazine> element are identical. One stores information about the magazine as additional elements that are nested inside the <magazine> element. The other stores the magazine info as attributes of the magazine tag. The two are completely equivalent. So which is better? Neither. It's a matter of personal preference.

XML Documents Are Trees

We said earlier that XML documents are tree-like. We should state that a bit more strongly. XML documents *are* trees and often referred to as such in the literature. But what does that mean? Well, a tree is a hierarchy of associations, or links between things. Consider an organization chart or a family tree. In a family tree, the links are links of parentage—we are linked to the elements below us because they're our descendants, and we're linked to the elements above because they're our ancestors. We also have a relationship with elements at the same level; they're our siblings.

XML documents work just the same way, and we'll see that they even deliberately borrow the language of parent, child, ancestor, descendant, and sibling to describe relationships between different parts of a document. Here's how the "XML-ized" Blake poem might look, represented as a tree:

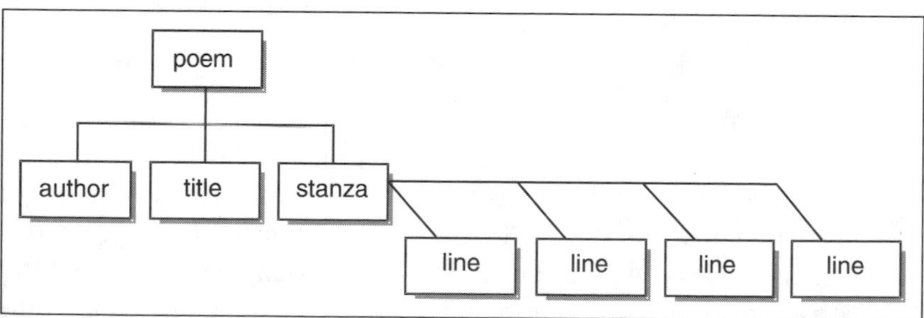

Figure 4.1

One thing to know about XML trees is that they can have just one element at the very top. In the Blake example, the topmost node is the <poem> element. Every valid XML document must have one and only one top-level element, often called the *root element*. Everything else is a descendant of the root element. Take a look at some of the relationships inside this document. The immediate children of <poem> are <author>, <title>, and a bunch of <stanza> elements.

The immediate children of a <stanza> are each a <line>. All the lines of a stanza are siblings, as are all the stanzas. A <line> is a descendant of the <poem>. The <poem> is an ancestor of every <line>. You get the idea.

Keep the idea of an XML document as a tree very firmly in mind. When we transform XML using stylesheets, we're actually changing one tree (the input XML document, often called the *source tree*) into another (the output document, often called the *result tree*). This completes our quick tour of some of the building blocks of XML—tags, elements, element content, and attributes.

FileMaker and XML

So what does this have to do with FileMaker? Let's walk through FileMaker's XML capabilities one small step at a time. At points along the way, you may feel slightly puzzled as to what these capabilities are good for. Just bear with us, and everything should become clear. We work with files from the book's downloadable content, so you may want to grab those first.

The simplest thing FileMaker can do with XML is export it. To see what this means, open the Animal.fp5 file (available in the downloadable files) and Show All Records. Select Export... from the File menu, and then select XML as the output format. Export the records to a file called animal.xml. Before you see the usual Export dialog, you see an XML Export dialog first. It prompts you to make two choices: First you need to choose an XML grammar and then, optionally, a stylesheet. Don't worry too much about what these choices mean for now. Choose FMPDSO as the grammar, and don't bother with a stylesheet. Once you've made those choices, you see the Export dialog. Do a Move All to make sure all fields get exported, and then export the data. The XML is now in a file, somewhere on your drive, called animal.xml. That's all there is to it.

That's all there is to what, though? What did I get, and what good is it? Good question. Let's look at animal.xml and see what it's got in it. There are two good ways to do this. One is to open it in the text editor of your choice. That way you can see exactly what information got exported. The problem is that it's not formatted very nicely. It's most likely all run together, without useful line breaks or indents. Another choice is to view it in a web browser. Currently only a few web browsers support an XML view. If you have one of these browsers (Internet Explorer 5 and above is a good choice), try opening the new file in the browser. You'll see the XML rendered as a nice tree that's expandable and collapsible at each level. Be warned, though, that IE is not showing you exactly what was exported. It is showing you a rendering of that XML data. As it happens, the rendering is very accurate, but some things do change. For example, if your XML contains elements with no content (like <herd></herd>), IE automatically converts those tags to the short form (<herd/>). If you don't expect little changes like this, they may surprise you. When in doubt, cross-check your expectations with the actual exported text as viewed in a text editor.

When we open animal.xml in a text editor, we see something like this:

```
<?xml version="1.0" encoding="UTF-8" ?>
<FMPDSORESULT xmlns="http://www.filemaker.com/fmpdsoresult">
     <ERRORCODE>0</ERRORCODE>
     <DATABASE>Animal.fp5</DATABASE>
     <LAYOUT></LAYOUT>
     <ROW MODID="0" RECORDID="1">
          <date_birth>4/23/1994</date_birth>
          <id_animal>A1</id_animal>
          <id_father></id_father>
          <id_mother></id_mother>
          <name>Great Geronimo</name>
          <weight_birth>107</weight_birth>
          <weight_current>812</weight_current>
     </ROW>
     [ numerous other rows here ...]
</FMPDSORESULT>
```

Let's look at the structure of this document. FMPDSO is one of two "grammars" of XML that FileMaker can work with. It's by far the most human-readable of the two. Again, every well-formed XML document has to have what's called a root element; there has to be one element that is the parent (or better, ancestor) of all the others. In our earlier document, the root element was called <magazines>. Here it's called <FMPDSORESULT>. According to our output, an <FMPDSO-RESULT> element can contain four other kinds of elements: an <ERRORCODE>, a <DATABASE>, a <LAYOUT>, and one or more <ROW> elements. Each of these is fairly straightforward. The <ERRORCODE> element contains the most recent error code, as if we'd written Status(CurrentError) in a calculation. <DATABASE> contains the name of the database that the data came from, and <LAYOUT> specifies the name of the layout that was in effect at the time, if any. Finally, the <ROW> elements have two attributes that give us the FileMaker record ID and some information about the last modification of the record. The <ROW> element then has other elements that appear to correspond to the database fields. In fact, the <ROW> element has one of each of these elements per exported field. We exported seven fields, so we get seven elements inside <ROW>, each with the name of the exported field.

All right—that was FileMaker's "readable" XML grammar. Let's look at the other one, called FMPXML. This is a more verbose format, full of metadata (again, "data about the data"). The FMPDSO grammar has a little metadata, like the database name and the layout, but it is missing potentially crucial information, like the data types of each of the fields. Let's re-export the data from Animal.fp5 again to an XML format, but this time let's choose the FMPXML grammar and save it to a file with a different name.

Here's what the result looks like, in part:

```
<?xml version="1.0" encoding="UTF-8" ?>
<FMPXMLRESULT xmlns="http://www.filemaker.com/fmpxmlresult">
    <ERRORCODE>0</ERRORCODE>
    <PRODUCT BUILD="06/13/2002" NAME="FileMaker Pro"
      VERSION="6.0v1"/>
    <DATABASE DATEFORMAT="M/d/yyyy" LAYOUT="" NAME="Animal.fp5"
      RECORDS="11" TIMEFORMAT="h:mm:ss a"/>
    <METADATA>
        <FIELD EMPTYOK="YES" MAXREPEAT="1" NAME="date_birth"
          TYPE="DATE"/>
        <FIELD EMPTYOK="NO" MAXREPEAT="1" NAME="id_animal"
          TYPE="TEXT"/>
        <FIELD EMPTYOK="YES" MAXREPEAT="1" NAME="id_father"
          TYPE="TEXT"/>
        <FIELD EMPTYOK="YES" MAXREPEAT="1" NAME="id_mother"
          TYPE="TEXT"/>
        <FIELD EMPTYOK="YES" MAXREPEAT="1" NAME="name"
          TYPE="TEXT"/>
        <FIELD EMPTYOK="YES" MAXREPEAT="1" NAME="weight_birth"
          TYPE="NUMBER"/>
        <FIELD EMPTYOK="YES" MAXREPEAT="1" NAME="weight_current"
          TYPE="NUMBER"/>
    </METADATA>
    <RESULTSET FOUND="11">
        <ROW MODID="0" RECORDID="1">
            <COL>
                <DATA>4/23/1994</DATA>
            </COL>
            <COL>
                <DATA>A1</DATA>
            </COL>
            <COL>
                <DATA></DATA>
            </COL>
            <COL>
                <DATA></DATA>
```

Chapter 4

```
                    </COL>
                    <COL>
                         <DATA>Great Geronimo</DATA>
                    </COL>
                    <COL>
                         <DATA>107</DATA>
                    </COL>
                    <COL>
                         <DATA>812</DATA>
                    </COL>
               </ROW>
               [ ... many other rows]
          </RESULTSET>
</FMPXMLRESULT>
```

This is similar to the other but contains more metadata and is less readable. The root element is now <FMPXMLRESULT> rather than <FMPDSORESULT>. It now also contains information about the product, as well as similar-looking information about the database and layout (though with more information about database settings). Then comes a section called <METADATA>, which is a bit different. <METADATA> contains one <FIELD> element per exported field, and each <FIELD> element has four useful attributes, mostly self-explanatory, which tell us whether the field may be empty (whether it "allows nulls," in database geek parlance), whether it's a repeating field (and if so, with how many repetititions), and what the field's name and data type are.

After the <METADATA>, we get a <RESULTSET>. This element contains numerous <ROW> elements—one per exported <ROW>, as always. Each row contains some number of <COL> elements (one per exported field), and each <COL> element contains a <DATA> element that contains that field's data for that record. Note that the <COL> elements do not explicitly name the field. To figure out with which field the data goes in, reference must be made to the <METADATA>, which fills you in on the details of the field that's in that particular spot in the numerical order. This data is really meant for further processing by XML parsers or XSL transformers, rather than being very legible to people.

So now we know that a set of FileMaker records can be exported in one of two XML formats ("grammars") called FMPDSO (think of it as "FMP Dead Simple Output") and FMPXML. So what can we do with these verbose outputs? Well, there are really two answers to that question.

First, we can do nothing with them. It may be that some other application out there needs data in XML format. Well, FileMaker can produce that output. It can be printed and sent (we're kind of joking about that one), sent in an electronic document, picked up via FTP for further processing—you get the idea. It can also, by the way, be broadcast over the web so that other systems can consume it. This is fundamental to the idea of a *web service*, a topic we discuss in a chapter of its own.

So our first choice is to do nothing with the XML and just send it along to some other service that knows how to read it and presumably has a use for it. This is appropriate if you are trying to engineer some kind of data exchange between systems with XML as the common exchange mechanism.

Aside from just shipping off the raw XML to another system, there is one other interesting thing we can do with it, and that is to *transform* it. With a certain amount of work, we can take any XML document and transform it into almost any other kind of document that can be represented by plain text. This means that, in theory, we can transform our XML documents into tab-delimited text, HTML, Rich Text Format, PDF, or almost anything else.

This is all accomplished through a technology called XSL (Extensible Stylesheet Language). XSL is really a group of languages developed and promoted by the World Wide Web Consortium (www.w3c.org). With these languages, we can write *stylesheets* that specify how XML can be transformed into other kinds of documents. Using different stylesheets, a single XML document can be transformed into comma-separated text, a PDF document, and an HTML presentation, to name just a few. (XSL technically consists of three technologies at the moment: XSLT, XPath, and XSL-FO. We're concerned with transformations, and we use the terms XSL and XSLT interchangeably to refer to XSL's transformation capabilities.)

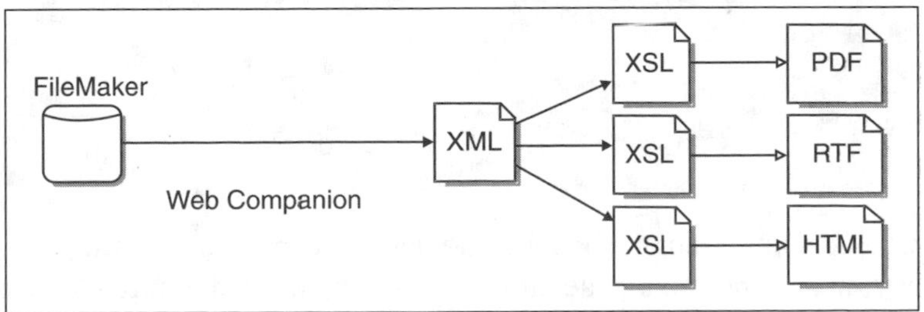

Figure 4.2

So what's inside these XSL "stylesheets"? Quite a lot, actually. XSLT is a language unto itself. You can certainly get started by modifying stylesheets that others have written (including the bunch that ship with FileMaker), but sooner or later you're going to want to roll your own. We take you through the basics and get you started writing simple stylesheets, but you also want to pick up one of the many good books that cover this topic in more depth.

Great, you say, another chapter, another language! Can I go home now? No, no, stick around. This is fairly interesting stuff, and the amount of flexibility and power it adds to FileMaker on the output side is nothing short of staggering. If you master XSLT, you can output from FileMaker to any text-based format imaginable.

XSLT is a full-fledged programming language. It is not terribly difficult to learn, but, like any new language, it requires patience and practice in order to become fluent. If it seems tricky or peculiar at first, be patient, and we'll try to introduce you to it one step at a time.

Using XSLT to Transform FileMaker's Output

Let's return to our Animal.fp5 database. Our state government has asked for herd information in a text-only reporting format. PDFs or other such output are not welcome. The government inspectors have told us they need a report that looks like this:

```
Herd Listing for Blue Horizon Bison Breeders
========================================
date_birth:   4/23/1994
id_animal:   A1
id_father:
id_mother:
name:   Great Geronimo
weight_birth:   107
weight_current:   812
========================================
date_birth:   6/1/1993
id_animal:   A2
id_father:
id_mother:
name:   Stellazura
weight_birth:   90
weight_current:   702
========================================
```

We need some kind of a header, the data on each animal with one field per row, and the records separated by rows of line delimiters. We can probably produce this output from FileMaker the old-fashioned way—create a big text calculation that chunks together all the record data into a single field and adds the record delimiters. This works but has irritating drawbacks (not least of which is the need to edit the field structure of the database). Good luck trying that during the business day in a production system! We can produce this output with an XSL stylesheet without altering the database fields in any way.

Let's start with a simple task and work our way up. Using your favorite text editor, create a new file with the following content, and save it as animal1.xsl:

```
<?xml version="1.0" encoding="UTF-8"?>
<xsl:stylesheet version="1.0"
  xmlns:xsl="http://www.w3.org/1999/XSL/Transform"
  xmlns:fmp="http://www.filemaker.com/fmpdsoresult">
    <xsl:output method="text" version="1.0" encoding="UTF-8"
      indent="no"/>
    <xsl:template match="fmp:FMPDSORESULT">
        <xsl:text>Herd Listing for Blue Horizon Bison
          Breeders</xsl:text>
    </xsl:template>
</xsl:stylesheet>
```

Now go into the Animal.fp5 file, Show All Records, and select Export Records. Choose XML as the output format, and, when prompted, choose FMPDSO as the XML grammar. Now let's turn our attention to the lower half of the XML options dialog where we're prompted to select a stylesheet. Click File and navigate to the animal1.xsl stylesheet that you just saved. Click OK, and then make sure all the fields are selected for export. Export the data to a file called animal1.txt. If FileMaker complains about your XML and throws up an XML error, make sure that your animal1.xsl looks just like the example above.

Assuming your export ran without any XML errors, you should have a file called animal1.xml somewhere on your hard drive. Navigate to it and open it in a text editor. It should only contain the single line "Herd Listing for Blue Horizon Bison Breeders."

Well, that was a lot of work for just one line. We could have typed that line quicker by hand, but let's look at animal1.xsl and see what's going on. The first thing to notice is that this XSL document is actually a valid XML document also. A quick glance should confirm this. So, what's inside it? It has a root element called <xsl:stylesheet>. All XSL stylesheets have this same root element. This node has a couple of attributes called "version" and "xmlns," which we'll skip over for now. Let's also skip the <xsl:output> tag for now—it provides a clue as to what kind of document is being produced (text, HTML, RTF, etc.).

The first really interesting tag is the <xsl:template> tag. Recall that the XML input that we are transforming is organized into a tree. XSL templates let us pick specific parts of that tree and take specific actions when we find them. The most usual action is to output some text. For example, we can use an <xsl:template> to output specific text every time we come to a new FileMaker <ROW> element; we get to that example shortly.

Back to our first example, the <xsl:template> tag has an attribute called "match". This attribute tells us what this particular template is looking for (whereas the content of the tag tells us what to do when we find it). Here the value of match is set to fmp:FMPDSORESULT. This indicates the root element of the document. So the moment we find the root element of the document, we perform the instructions in this template. Since there's only one root element, these instructions only get executed once. That makes this node's template a good place to put anything that needs to be output only once per entire document, such as a title.

Once we find the root element, we perform whatever instructions we find inside the <xsl:template> tag. In this case the only content is another tag (called <xsl:text>). This tag instructs the processor to copy the tag's text content to the output at this point. So in our case, when we find the root element, we copy the text string "Herd Listing for Blue Horizon Bison Breeders" to the output.

That's all this stylesheet does. There are no more templates, so no more pieces of the input are matched. This is a critical concept. We use templates to tell the XSL processor which parts of the input to look at. We use the content of the templates to tell the processor what to do. In this stylesheet, once we've looked at the root element, the processing is complete, and the output tree is actually output. The result is a document with a title and nothing else.

This is the basic mechanism of an XSL stylesheet. The processor is going to read through the input XML tree and check each piece of it to see if our stylesheet has any templates that match the current item. If so, the XSL processor looks at the template and decides what to do. Most interesting actions involve sending something to the output tree.

So now we have a stylesheet that can print a report header. This is not very interesting so far. Let's add some code to our stylesheet, as follows:

```
<?xml version="1.0" encoding="UTF-8"?>
<xsl:stylesheet version="1.0"
  xmlns:xsl="http://www.w3.org/1999/XSL/Transform"
  xmlns:fmp="http://www.filemaker.com/fmpdsoresult">
     <xsl:output method="text" version="1.0" encoding="UTF-8"
       indent="no"/>
     <xsl:template match="fmp:FMPDSORESULT">
          <xsl:text>Herd Listing for Blue Horizon Bison Breeders
```

```
</xsl:text>
        <xsl:apply-templates/>
    </xsl:template>


    <xsl:template match="fmp:ROW">
        <xsl:text>====================================
Row data goes here
</xsl:text>
    </xsl:template>
</xsl:stylesheet>
```

If you export the records from Animal.fp5 using this new stylesheet, you should get the following result:

```
Herd Listing for Blue Horizon Bison Breeders
0Animal.fp5====================================
Row data goes here
====================================
Row data goes here
====================================
Row data goes here
```

Let's take a look at what has changed. First of all, we have a new template element. This one matches on fmp:ROW. (The reasons for the "fmp" prefix are a bit arcane. "Fmp" here is an XML namespace, hence the "xmlns" attributes of the stylesheet tag in this document, and it refers to all the elements in the FMPDSORESULT grammar.) This template element instructs the XSL processor to stop every time it finds a ROW element and perform the instructions inside the template. In this case, the instructions consist of one xsl:text element that outputs the record separator, along with some boilerplate text announcing that we've found a record.

There's one other interesting difference in the new stylesheet, and that's the presence of the <xsl:apply-templates> tag inside the template that matches on the root element. If you're curious about what it does, try leaving it out. If you do, you'll discover that the processor stops after handling the root element. If we want it to continue, we need to issue the <xsl:apply-templates> tag to tell it to keep working its way down the tree. Without this tag, the processor never examines any of the child elements of the root and doesn't bother trying to apply the second template.

There's one problem with our output. Before the first record delimiter line, we've got what looks like some stray data—the string "0Animal.fp5." This data represents the content of the <ERROR-CODE> and <DATABASE> elements from the XML source. To make a long story short, our stylesheet doesn't say anything about what to do with these tags, so their contents get dumped into the output, whole and unadorned.

The real story is a bit longer than that. <ERRORCODE> and <DATABASE> are both children of the <FMPDSORESULT> node. The <FMPDSORESULT> node is matched by the / template that we provided. In our instructions for that match, we used the apply-templates command, instructing the processor to try to find templates that apply to all of <FMPDSORESULT>'s children. Again, there are no templates for <ERRORCODE> or <DATABASE>. Rather than skipping them, though, the XSL processor applies one of a set of default templates. As it happens, the default template for textual content, as well as for attributes, is to send the data straight to the output.

To fix this, we can supply templates for the <ERRORCODE> and <DATABASE> elements that specify that these elements should be ignored. All we need to do is add these two lines of code:

```
<xsl:template match="fmp:ERRORCODE"/>
<xsl:template match="fmp:DATABASE"/>
```

The two matches explicitly match the <ERRORCODE> and <DATABASE> elements. Since these templates don't actually output anything, the effect is to ignore these two elements, and we get the following result:

```
Herd Listing for Blue Horizon Bison Breeders
=======================================
Row data goes here
=======================================
Row data goes here
=======================================
Row data goes here
=======================================
```

(A better way to accomplish this is by adding some specificity to our <xsl:apply-templates> command. We can tell it to apply only the template for fmp:ROW and skip others, including the default template. We see shortly how to do this.)

This output is better, but we still need to do something with the row data. Each <ROW> element has a number of child elements—one for each database field. We'd like to somehow loop through these and output each on its own line—first the name of the element and then its content, which is the value of the database field.

Here's the stylesheet that does it:

```
<?xml version="1.0" encoding="UTF-8"?>
<xsl:stylesheet version="1.0"
  xmlns:xsl="http://www.w3.org/1999/XSL/Transform"
```

```
xmlns:fmp="http://www.filemaker.com/fmpdsoresult">
    <xsl:output method="text" version="1.0" encoding="UTF-8"
      indent="no"/>
    <xsl:template match="fmp:FMPDSORESULT">
         <xsl:text>Herd Listing for Blue Horizon Bison Breeders
</xsl:text>
         <xsl:apply-templates/>
    </xsl:template>

    <xsl:template match="fmp:ROW">
         <xsl:text>=====================================
</xsl:text>
    <xsl:apply-templates/>
    </xsl:template>

    <xsl:template match="fmp:ERRORCODE"/>
    <xsl:template match="fmp:DATABASE"/>
    <xsl:template match="fmp:ROW/*">
         <xsl:value-of select="name()"/>
         <xsl:text>: </xsl:text>
         <xsl:value-of select="."/>
         <xsl:text>
</xsl:text>
    </xsl:template>
</xsl:stylesheet>
```

(Note that, although we've had to break lines in our code to fit them onto a book page, in most cases those line breaks are optional. But this is not the case with our <xsl:text> elements. <xsl:text> outputs all of its content literally. In the above code, we've included carriage returns as part of the content of <xsl:text> in order to get these carriage returns into the final text output. So the carriage returns inside the <xsl:text elements> are significant and need to be preserved.)

We've added one more template element to match on all the children of any <ROW> element. We've also added the xsl:apply-templates element to the template for <ROW> to tell the XSL processor to keep applying other templates, rather than stopping once it is done with the <ROW> elements. The new template matches on fmp:ROW/*. This is XSL syntax for "match on any child of an fmp:ROW element." (Technically, this is not XSLT but rather an expression in the XPath language. XPath is the language that XSL uses to select portions of an XML document. We just refer to it as part of XSL for the sake of convenience.)

Inside this last template element is one more new XSL construct, the <xsl:value-of> tag. This tag is used to extract information from one or more nodes of an XML document tree and copy them to the output. <xsl:value-of> says "get me information about some piece of the source XML document," and the select attribute of the <xsl:value-of> tag says "get this particular piece of data."

In the first <xsl:value-of> tag, the select attribute is set to "name()". This is an example of an XSL function call. The name() function returns the name of the current element. In this case, for a child of a <ROW> element, the node name is actually the name of a database field. So this tag gets the name of the node. Then we have an <xsl:text> element, used only to output the colon-space combination that follows the field name. Then we get another <xsl:value-of> tag, and here the selector is set to ".". If you're familiar with command-line syntax for an operating system like Unix (or DOS, for that matter), you know that "." means "the current directory," or more generally "right where I already am." Its significance is similar in XSL; it refers to the current node being evaluated. This selector simply copies the content of the current node, whereas the previous selector deliberately extracted the tag's name.

We finish the template with a carriage return, courtesy of <xsl:text>. Our resulting output should look like this:

```
Herd Listing for Blue Horizon Bison
=======================================
date_birth: 4/23/1994
id_animal: A1
id_father:
id_mother:
name: Great Geronimo
weight_birth: 107
weight_current: 812
=======================================
date_birth: 6/1/1993
id_animal: A2
id_father:
id_mother:
name: Stellazura
weight_birth: 90
weight_current: 702
=======================================
```

Okay, very good; we're actually working our way up to something useful here. However, there are some changes that we'd like to make. Right now, the stylesheet picks up all fields (that is, all children of a <ROW>). It also doesn't give us any ability to specify which order they should come out in. Let's say that instead we wanted our database records to come out looking like this:

```
=======================================
Great Geronimo
```

```
Born 4/23/1994
Birth Weight: 107
Current Weight: 812
=======================================
```

So we want our fields formatted more nicely, and we want to limit ourselves to only four of them. As is often the case with XSL, there are a number of ways to do this. Later we look at one that showcases another feature of the <xsl:apply-templates> tag. So far, we've used <xsl:apply-templates> to keep working our way down the document tree. We haven't used it to limit what kinds of further matches we might be looking for. But it can be used in exactly this way by adding a "match" attribute to the tag to ensure that it only applies some templates, not all of them.

Clearly, we're going to have to do something with the part of the code that displays all the children of a <ROW> element. Right now, we have a template that matches any child of <ROW> (fmp:ROW/* is the match condition). We're going to need to replace that with templates that match the specific items we're looking for. Then we're going to have to make sure that those templates are applied in the exact order that we want the fields to come out in. Here's how it looks:

```
<xsl:stylesheet version="1.0"
  xmlns:xsl="http://www.w3.org/1999/XSL/Transform"
  xmlns:fmp="http://www.filemaker.com/fmpdsoresult">
     <xsl:output method="text" version="1.0" encoding="UTF-8"
       indent="no"/>
     <xsl:template match="fmp:FMPDSORESULT">
          <xsl:text>Herd Listing for Blue Horizon Bison Breeders
</xsl:text>
          <xsl:apply-templates/>
     </xsl:template>

     <xsl:template match="fmp:ROW">
          <xsl:text>=======================================
</xsl:text>
     <xsl:apply-templates select="fmp:name"/>
     <xsl:apply-templates select="fmp:date_birth"/>
     <xsl:apply-templates select="fmp:weight_birth"/>
     <xsl:apply-templates select="fmp:weight_current"/>
     </xsl:template>

     <xsl:template match="fmp:ERRORCODE"/>
     <xsl:template match="fmp:DATABASE"/>
     <xsl:template match="fmp:name">
          <xsl:value-of select="."/>
          <xsl:text>
</xsl:text>
     </xsl:template>
```

```
    <xsl:template match="fmp:date_birth">
        <xsl:text>Born </xsl:text>
        <xsl:value-of select="."/>
        <xsl:text>
</xsl:text>
    </xsl:template>

    <xsl:template match="fmp:weight_birth">
        <xsl:text>Birth Weight </xsl:text>
        <xsl:value-of select="."/>
        <xsl:text>
</xsl:text>
    </xsl:template>

    <xsl:template match="fmp:weight_current">
        <xsl:text>Current Weight </xsl:text>
        <xsl:value-of select="."/>
        <xsl:text>
</xsl:text>
    </xsl:template>
</xsl:stylesheet>
```

We've changed two things here. First, in the <ROW> element, rather than a single <xsl:apply-templates> that matches all children of <ROW>, we have four <xsl:apply-templates> commands. Each one has a "select" attribute that limits which templates are matched on and applied. They're ordered in the way we want our fields ordered in the output.

Correspondingly, instead of a single template that matches all children of <ROW>, we have four specific templates, one for each possible output field.

Remember that the <xsl:apply-templates> command acts within the context of the current position in the XML tree. Typically, it's only acting on children of the current node or element. So, from the vantage point of a <ROW> element, the logic is something like this: "go find me any of my children that are called name, and then apply the appropriate template. Then do the same for date_birth, weight_birth, and weight_current." The ordering of the <xsl:apply-templates> elements determines the order in which the fields are output. The content of the individual templates determines how the data is formatted for output.

Generating HTML

That was a lot of work just to generate a fairly dowdy-looking text report. We hope you can see how the stylesheet that we've written is already fairly flexible. Without needing to touch anything inside of

FileMaker, we can fairly easily alter which fields are displayed in the report, how they're displayed, and the order in which they appear. This was a useful way to learn the basic mechanics of XSL's template-based transformation process. But plain text is not a very attractive output format. In this section, we look at using XSL stylesheets to turn FileMaker data into HTML.

Let's say that we want to take the simple text output that we just finished creating and output something similar in HTML. (See Figure 4.3 for an image of the rendered HTML.)

Here's the stylesheet that produces that result:

```
<?xml version="1.0" encoding="UTF-8"?>
<xsl:stylesheet version="1.0"
  xmlns:xsl="http://www.w3.org/1999/XSL/Transform"
  xmlns:fmp="http://www.filemaker.com/fmpdsoresult">
     <xsl:output method="html" indent="yes"
       doctype-public="-//W3C//DTD HTML 3.2 Final//EN"/>
     <xsl:template match="fmp:FMPDSORESULT">
<html>
<head>
     <title>BHBB Herd Listing</title>
</head>
<body>
     <H2>Blue Horizon Bison Breeders</H2>
     <H3>Herd Listing</H3>
     <table border="">
          <xsl:apply-templates/>
     </table>
</body>
</html>
     </xsl:template>

     <xsl:template match="fmp:ROW">
     <xsl:apply-templates select="fmp:name"/>
     <tr>
     <xsl:apply-templates select="fmp:date_birth"/>
     <xsl:apply-templates select="fmp:weight_birth"/>
     <xsl:apply-templates select="fmp:weight_current"/>
     </tr>
     </xsl:template>

     <xsl:template match="fmp:ERRORCODE"/>
     <xsl:template match="fmp:DATABASE"/>
     <xsl:template match="fmp:name">
          <tr><td colspan="3"><b><xsl:value-of select="."/>
            </b></td></tr>
     </xsl:template>

     <xsl:template match="fmp:date_birth">
          <td>Born <xsl:value-of select="."/></td>
          </xsl:template>
```

Chapter 4

```
    <xsl:template match="fmp:weight_birth">
        <td>Birth Weight <xsl:value-of select="."/></td>
        </xsl:template>

    <xsl:template match="fmp:weight_current">
        <td>Current Weight <xsl:value-of select="."/></td>
        </xsl:template>
</xsl:stylesheet>
```

The mechanics of this stylesheet should be pretty clear to you by now. Our final HTML document has a lot of HTML code that only occurs once, like the <head> element and the initial large headers. Then it has a table with many items repeated inside it (these being the database records). In our stylesheet, then, the first thing we do is match on the root element and use that template to output all of our nonrecurring HTML: the <head> element, the <H2> and <H3> elements that make up the text header, and the <table>...</table> tags. Then, within the <table> element, we issue the <xsl:apply-templates> command, instructing the XSL processor to keep working downward from the root element to find other elements to process.

The only other element that we're interested in is the <ROW> element and its children. We match on the <ROW> element exactly as before and then hand off most of the processing to the templates that match the interesting children of <ROW>. There is a tiny amount of other work done by the <ROW> template. Notice that the last three <xsl:apply-templates> commands are wrapped in a pair of <tr>...</tr> tags. The reason for this is that the stylesheet is an XML document, and XML documents don't like to see unbalanced tags, even if they're HTML tags. All three fields that those templates match are intended to appear in a single HTML table row. We could have put the <tr> tags inside the template that matches on fmp:date_birth and the </tr> tag inside the template for fmp:weight_current, but in either case we'd have an unbalanced tag and the XSL processor would complain. The right thing to do is wrap all three templates up at the next higher level inside the <ROW> element with a pair of balanced <table>...</table> tags. We don't have this problem with the template for fmp:name because that table contains both the starting and ending tags inside itself, so nothing is unbalanced.

We can finish this example by adding a little polish to the output with some CSS styling for those browsers that support it (which nowadays is most of them). Change the fmp:ROW template to look like this:

```
    <xsl:template match="fmp:ROW">
    <xsl:apply-templates select="fmp:name"/>
```

```
<tr style="border-bottom: 1px solid silver">
<xsl:apply-templates select="fmp:date_birth"/>
<xsl:apply-templates select="fmp:weight_birth"/>
<xsl:apply-templates select="fmp:weight_current"/>
</tr>
</xsl:template>
```

...and the fmp:name template to look like this:

```
<xsl:template match="fmp:name">
      <tr><td colspan="3" style="color:red"><b><xsl:value-of
        select="."/></b></td></tr>
</xsl:template>
```

...to give a more polished appearance to the report. (You should also set the table to have border=0.)

Note: When you're outputting to different text formats, it's a good idea to pay attention to file suffixes. You should export all your HTML to files ending in .html, for example. Most operating systems will use the suffix to determine the file type, which will make life easier when you want to view the results.

Here's the full pipeline for this example, starting with the raw data and finishing with the rendered HTML:

1. Raw data:

```
Great Geronimo          4/23/94        107          812
Stellazura               6/1/93         90          702
Hohokam Glory            4/5/99        123          900
Chin-cha-pe              4/5/99         82          598
Shaw-Shaw wa Be-na-se    4/5/99        101         1032
Hector                  1/19/90        102          899
Harriet                 8/14/92         79          680
Sweetpea                 6/8/00         80          502
Sacajawea                6/8/00         94          856
Barleycorn               6/8/00         60          402
Scatters Them            6/8/00        100          789
Harlequin                7/1/01        112          500
Mandan                   8/1/01         90          412
Hedda                    3/1/02         85          200
```

2. FileMaker's DSO XML output:

```
<?xml version="1.0" encoding="UTF-8" ?>
<FMPDSORESULT xmlns="http://www.filemaker.com/fmpdsoresult">
      <ERRORCODE>0</ERRORCODE>
      <DATABASE>Animal.fp5</DATABASE>
      <LAYOUT></LAYOUT>
      <ROW MODID="7" RECORDID="1">
            <name>Great Geronimo</name>
            <date_birth>4/23/1994</date_birth>
            <weight_birth>107</weight_birth>
            <weight_current>812</weight_current>
```

Chapter 4

```
    </ROW>
    <ROW MODID="6" RECORDID="2">
        <name>Stellazura</name>
        <date_birth>6/1/1993</date_birth>
        <weight_birth>90</weight_birth>
        <weight_current>702</weight_current>
    </ROW>
    <ROW MODID="7" RECORDID="3">
        <name>Hohokam Glory</name>
        <date_birth>4/5/1999</date_birth>
        <weight_birth>123</weight_birth>
        <weight_current>900</weight_current>
    </ROW>
    <ROW MODID="7" RECORDID="4">
        <name>Chin-cha-pe</name>
        <date_birth>4/5/1999</date_birth>
        <weight_birth>82</weight_birth>
        <weight_current>598</weight_current>
    </ROW>
    <ROW MODID="9" RECORDID="5">
        <name>Shaw-Shaw-wa Be-na-se</name>
        <date_birth>4/5/1999</date_birth>
        <weight_birth>101</weight_birth>
        <weight_current>1032</weight_current>
    </ROW>
    <ROW MODID="5" RECORDID="6">
        <name>Hector</name>
        <date_birth>1/19/1990</date_birth>
        <weight_birth>102</weight_birth>
        <weight_current>899</weight_current>
    </ROW>
    <ROW MODID="4" RECORDID="7">
        <name>Harriet</name>
        <date_birth>8/14/1992</date_birth>
        <weight_birth>79</weight_birth>
        <weight_current>680</weight_current>
    </ROW>
    <ROW MODID="5" RECORDID="8">
        <name>Sweetpea</name>
        <date_birth>6/8/2000</date_birth>
        <weight_birth>80</weight_birth>
        <weight_current>502</weight_current>
    </ROW>
    <ROW MODID="6" RECORDID="9">
        <name>Sacajawea</name>
        <date_birth>6/8/2000</date_birth>
        <weight_birth>94</weight_birth>
        <weight_current>856</weight_current>
    </ROW>
    <ROW MODID="6" RECORDID="10">
        <name>Barleycorn</name>
        <date_birth>6/8/2000</date_birth>
        <weight_birth>60</weight_birth>
        <weight_current>402</weight_current>
```

```
    </ROW>
    <ROW MODID="5" RECORDID="11">
         <name>Scatters Them</name>
         <date_birth>6/8/2000</date_birth>
         <weight_birth>100</weight_birth>
         <weight_current>789</weight_current>
    </ROW>
    <ROW MODID="3" RECORDID="12">
         <name>Harlequin</name>
         <date_birth>7/1/2001</date_birth>
         <weight_birth>112</weight_birth>
         <weight_current>500</weight_current>
    </ROW>
    <ROW MODID="4" RECORDID="13">
         <name>Mandan</name>
         <date_birth>8/1/2001</date_birth>
         <weight_birth>90</weight_birth>
         <weight_current>412</weight_current>
    </ROW>
    <ROW MODID="4" RECORDID="14">
         <name>Hedda</name>
         <date_birth>3/1/2002</date_birth>
         <weight_birth>85</weight_birth>
         <weight_current>200</weight_current>
    </ROW>
</FMPDSORESULT>
```

3. The final version of our XSL stylesheet:

```
<?xml version="1.0" encoding="UTF-8"?>
<xsl:stylesheet version="1.0"
  xmlns:xsl="http://www.w3.org/1999/XSL/Transform"
  xmlns:fmp="http://www.filemaker.com/fmpdsoresult">
     <xsl:output method="html" indent="yes"
       doctype-public="-//W3C//DTD HTML 3.2 Final//EN"/>
     <xsl:template match="fmp:FMPDSORESULT">
<html>
<head>
     <title>BHBB Herd Listing</title>
</head>
<body>
     <H2>Blue Horizon Bison Breeders</H2>
     <H3>Herd Listing</H3>
     <table border="0">
          <xsl:apply-templates/>
     </table>
</body>
</html>
     </xsl:template>

     <xsl:template match="fmp:ROW">
     <xsl:apply-templates select="fmp:name"/>
     <tr style="border-bottom: 1px solid silver">
     <xsl:apply-templates select="fmp:date_birth"/>
     <xsl:apply-templates select="fmp:weight_birth"/>
```

```
    <xsl:apply-templates select="fmp:weight_current"/>
    </tr>
    </xsl:template>

    <xsl:template match="fmp:ERRORCODE"/>
    <xsl:template match="fmp:DATABASE"/>
    <xsl:template match="fmp:name">
        <tr><td colspan="3" style="color:red"><b><xsl:value-of
          select="."/></b></td></tr>
    </xsl:template>

    <xsl:template match="fmp:date_birth">
        <td>Born <xsl:value-of select="."/></td>
        </xsl:template>

    <xsl:template match="fmp:weight_birth">
        <td>Birth Weight <xsl:value-of select="."/></td>
        </xsl:template>

    <xsl:template match="fmp:weight_current">
        <td>Current Weight <xsl:value-of select="."/></td>
        </xsl:template>
</xsl:stylesheet>
```

4. HTML output from the stylesheet:

```
<!DOCTYPE HTML PUBLIC "-//W3C//DTD HTML 3.2 Final//EN">
<html xmlns:fmp="http://www.filemaker.com/fmpdsoresult">
<head>
    <meta http-equiv="Content-Type" content="text/html;
      charset=UTF-8">
    <title>BHBB Herd Listing</title>
</head>
<body>
<h2>Blue Horizon Bison Breeders</h2> <h3>Herd Listing</h3>
<table border="0">
    <tr>
        <td colspan="3" style="color:red">
            <b>Great Geronimo</b></td>
    </tr>
    <tr style="border-bottom: 1px solid silver">
        <td>Born 4/23/1994</td>
        <td>Birth Weight 107</td>
        <td>Current Weight 812</td>
    </tr>
    <tr>
        <td colspan="3" style="color:red">
            <b>Stellazura</b></td>
    </tr>
    <tr style="border-bottom: 1px solid silver">
        <td>Born 6/1/1993</td>
        <td>Birth Weight 90</td>
        <td>Current Weight 702</td>
    </tr>
    <tr>
```

```
        <td colspan="3" style="color:red">
            <b>Hohokam Glory</b></td>
    </tr>
    <tr style="border-bottom: 1px solid silver">
        <td>Born 4/5/1999</td>
        <td>Birth Weight 123</td>
        <td>Current Weight 900</td>
    </tr>
    <tr>
        <td colspan="3" style="color:red">
            <b>Chin-cha-pe</b></td>
    </tr>
    <tr style="border-bottom: 1px solid silver">
        <td>Born 4/5/1999</td>
        <td>Birth Weight 82</td>
        <td>Current Weight 598</td>
    </tr>
    <tr>
        <td colspan="3" style="color:red">
            <b>Shaw-Shaw-wa Be-na-se</b></td>
    </tr>
    <tr style="border-bottom: 1px solid silver">
        <td>Born 4/5/1999</td>
        <td>Birth Weight 101</td>
        <td>Current Weight 1032</td>
    </tr>
    <tr>
        <td colspan="3" style="color:red">
            <b>Hector</b></td>
    </tr>
    <tr style="border-bottom: 1px solid silver">
        <td>Born 1/19/1990</td>
        <td>Birth Weight 102</td>
        <td>Current Weight 899</td>
    </tr>
    <tr>
        <td colspan="3" style="color:red">
            <b>Harriet</b></td>
    </tr>
    <tr style="border-bottom: 1px solid silver">
        <td>Born 8/14/1992</td>
        <td>Birth Weight 79</td>
        <td>Current Weight 680</td>
    </tr>
    <tr>
        <td colspan="3" style="color:red">
            <b>Sweetpea</b></td>
    </tr>
    <tr style="border-bottom: 1px solid silver">
        <td>Born 6/8/2000</td>
        <td>Birth Weight 80</td>
        <td>Current Weight 502</td>
    </tr>
    <tr>
```

```
        <td colspan="3" style="color:red">
            <b>Sacajawea</b></td>
    </tr>
    <tr style="border-bottom: 1px solid silver">
        <td>Born 6/8/2000</td>
        <td>Birth Weight 94</td>
        <td>Current Weight 856</td>
    </tr>
    <tr>
        <td colspan="3" style="color:red">
            <b>Barleycorn</b></td>
    </tr>
    <tr style="border-bottom: 1px solid silver">
        <td>Born 6/8/2000</td>
        <td>Birth Weight 60</td>
        <td>Current Weight 402</td>
    </tr>
    <tr>
        <td colspan="3" style="color:red">
            <b>Scatters Them</b></td>
    </tr>
    <tr style="border-bottom: 1px solid silver">
        <td>Born 6/8/2000</td>
        <td>Birth Weight 100</td>
        <td>Current Weight 789</td>
    </tr>
    <tr>
        <td colspan="3" style="color:red">
            <b>Harlequin</b></td>
    </tr>
    <tr style="border-bottom: 1px solid silver">
        <td>Born 7/1/2001</td>
        <td>Birth Weight 112</td>
        <td>Current Weight 500</td>
    </tr>
    <tr>
        <td colspan="3" style="color:red">
            <b>Mandan</b></td>
    </tr>
    <tr style="border-bottom: 1px solid silver">
        <td>Born 8/1/2001</td>
        <td>Birth Weight 90</td>
        <td>Current Weight 412</td>
    </tr>
    <tr>
        <td colspan="3" style="color:red">
            <b>Hedda</b></td>
    </tr>
    <tr style="border-bottom: 1px solid silver">
        <td>Born 3/1/2002</td>
        <td>Birth Weight 85</td>
        <td>Current Weight 200</td>
    </tr>
</table>
```

```
</body>
</html>
```

5. Rendered HTML in the browser (IE 5.2 for Mac OS X):

Blue Horizon Bison Breeders

Herd Listing

Great Geronimo
Born 4/23/1994 Birth Weight 107 Current Weight 812
Stellazura
Born 6/1/1993 Birth Weight 90 Current Weight 702
Hohokam Glory
Born 4/5/1999 Birth Weight 123 Current Weight 900
Chin-cha-pe
Born 4/5/1999 Birth Weight 82 Current Weight 598
Shaw-Shaw-wa Be-na-se
Born 4/5/1999 Birth Weight 101 Current Weight 1032
Hector
Born 1/19/1990 Birth Weight 102 Current Weight 899
Harriet
Born 8/14/1992 Birth Weight 79 Current Weight 680
Sweetpea
Born 6/8/2000 Birth Weight 80 Current Weight 502
Sacajawea
Born 6/8/2000 Birth Weight 94 Current Weight 856
Barleycorn
Born 6/8/2000 Birth Weight 60 Current Weight 402
Scatters Them
Born 6/8/2000 Birth Weight 100 Current Weight 789
Harlequin
Born 7/1/2001 Birth Weight 112 Current Weight 500
Mandan
Born 8/1/2001 Birth Weight 90 Current Weight 412
Hedda
Born 3/1/2002 Birth Weight 85 Current Weight 200

Figure 4.3

XSL So Far

Here's a recap of the XSL commands and expressions that we've encountered so far and how they're used.

XSL Tags

- **xsl:template**

Syntax: <xsl:template match="*XPath expression*">

Description: xsl:template contains information to be output every time the match criterion is met. This could be as simple as some static text or as complicated as an expression that pulls in data from several other parts of the document (or even from another document altogether).

- **xsl:apply-templates**

Syntax: <xsl:apply-templates select="*XPath expression*">

Description: xsl:apply-templates is a command to specify which parts of the source XML document should be transformed next. Apply-templates is often used within a template definition. For example, you might have a template expression to output information about an invoice, and then within that template you would apply another template to output information about invoice line items.

- **xsl:text**

Syntax: <xsl:text>*Included text*</xsl:text>

Description: xsl:text is a simple way to include raw text in the output of your stylesheet.

- **xsl:value-of**

Syntax: <xsl:value-of select="*XPath expression*">

Description: xsl:value-of is used to extract content from an XML source file and include it in the output of the stylesheet. Anytime that you need to include some of the actual element content from your XML file, you need to use xsl:value-of to specify that content.

XPath Expressions

XPath is that part of XSL that is used to "point to" specific portions of the XML input. Very often, your XSL commands need to be told on which parts of the XML input to operate. XPath is the syntax that you use to do that. We talk more about complex XPath later in this chapter. So far we've seen syntax to match on all children of the current node that have a specified name.

The XPath expression is just what's inside the quotes following the match statement.

- <xsl:template match="fmp:ROW"> matches any child of the current element if that child is called fmp:ROW.

We've also seen XPath syntax to match on what could be called "grandchildren":

- <xsl:template match="fmp:ROW/*"> defines a template that matches any grandchild of the current element, as long as that grandchild's parent is called fmp:ROW.

We've also seen some miscellaneous XPath expressions that point to different pieces of the current data element:

- <xsl:value-of select="."/> fetches the data content of the current element.
- <xsl:value-of select="name()"/> fetches the name of the current element.

Calculation and Computation with XSL

So far we've treated XSL as a presentation tool. We've mostly been concerned with making our output look right. But XSL can do other kinds of work for us as well. Consider our well-worn Animal database. It's missing some information that we'd like to have. Specifically, it doesn't give us a way to see the average birth weight or average current weight for our animals.

Now, it's true that we can build those computations into the FileMaker file as calculations. But our focus here is on moving functions out of FileMaker. The less work (calculations, for example) we ask FileMaker to perform, the more quickly it can serve data to us. Ideally, we'd like it to return a bunch of raw data to us, and let us do the rest of the processing. In this case, we delegate the math to XSLT.

XSLT has a couple of functions that are similar to FileMaker's aggregate functions. They're called sum() and count(). Whereas FileMaker's functions of these names operate on groups of related records, their XSL equivalents operate on *node sets*. A node set is simply a group of nodes (we call them nodes because they could be elements, attributes, or other more specialized types of nodes we haven't encountered here) that's usually referred to by a match expression of some kind. So, to add up the birth weights of the entire herd, we can say <xsl:value-of select="sum(fmp:weight_birth)"/>. This will take the sum of all <fmp:weight_birth> elements that are children of the current node. If we want to limit the set of weights being added, we can change the selector. So <xsl:value-of select= "sum(fmp:ROW/weight_birth)"/> would add only the weights that were direct children of an <fmp:ROW> element, and that <fmp:ROW> element would have to be a child of the current node. In this document, that doesn't really change anything; all of the birth weight fields are children of a <ROW>. We see later, though, how this is useful in performing computations on subgroups, just as you would in a FileMaker sub-summary report.

XSLT, at least in the 1.0 version that's still prevalent, has no average() function. So we just have to make do with sum() and count(). Here's a stylesheet that computes the average birth and current weights for the entire herd. In order to do this, we need to take our last stylesheet and modify the template that matches on the root element. Once we're done applying templates to output all the rows, we want to output a final row that contains the averages for birth and current weights. The right place for this is in the template that matches the root element. The new template should look like this:

```
    <xsl:template match="fmp:FMPDSORESULT">
<html>
<head>
    <title>BHBB Herd Listing</title>
</head>
<body>
    <H2>Blue Horizon Bison Breeders</H2>
    <H3>Herd Listing</H3>
    <table border="0">
        <tr>
            <td>
                <xsl:apply-templates/></td>
            <td align="right">
                avg. = <xsl:value-of select='sum(fmp:ROW/
                  fmp:weight_birth) div count(fmp:ROW/
                  fmp:weight_birth)'/></td><td align="right">
                avg. = <xsl:value-of select="sum(//fmp:weight_
                  current) div count(//fmp:weight_
                  current)"/></td>
        </tr>
    </table>
</body>
</html>
    </xsl:template>
```

Here, we use the sum() function to add up all the birth weights (for example) and then divide by the count of all the birth weights to get an average. Sum() and count() are both functions that work on node sets, meaning that you need to hand them expressions that return one or more nodes from the source document. The expression fmp:ROW/fmp:weight_birth, for example, means "starting from the current node, find me all fmp:weight_birth elements that are children of fmp:ROW elements." This expression is evaluated relative to the current node, which in this case is the root element, called <fmp:FMPDSORESULT>. From there, it tries to find <fmp:ROW> elements that are children of <fmp:FMPDSORESULT>. Having found one or more ROWs, it looks into each one to see whether it contains a <weight_birth> element. Right now we're using these functions to sum up elements from the entire data set (a FileMaker Grand Summary, if that comparison helps). For sub-summary-style reports, though, the fact that functions like sum() and count() can operate on specific node sets turns out to be very useful.

More Complex Reporting with XML

So far, we've seen how to output a few different types of simple list reports in HTML format using FileMaker's XSL transformations. Let's look at some more complex reporting now—the kind we're used to doing with FileMaker sub-summary reports. The ride is a little bumpier here; it's not quite as easy as popping open FileMaker's report wizard, but with a little work, we can achieve some great-looking web reports.

Let's start with the most basic element of a sub-summary report: a header for each subgroup. Let's say that we want a report like the previous list but separated by herd, with a header for each herd. Before delving into XSL particulars, let's think about the necessary logic. We need an algorithm for outputting "herd breaks," and it goes something like this: If the herd for this animal is different from the herd for the previous animal, output a herd break; otherwise, don't. To this we need to add: If this is the very first animal in the list, output a herd break. (By the way, this is a good way to approach any programming problem; think about it in terms of general logic at first with as little reference as possible to the tool that you're planning to use.)

In order to work with herd information, we need to do a little more work. Right now the Animal.fp5 database has just the HerdID in it. We naturally want our report to show the herd names, so we need to bring these in somehow. Let's create a relationship from Animal.fp5 to Herd.fp5 called Herd_By_Herd_ID. We'll have to add the herd name (Herd_By_Herd_ID::HerdName) field to our export order as well. This will give us a chance to see how FileMaker exports related fields as XML. Here's what the new output will look like, in part:

```
<row modid="7" recordid="1">
     <name>Great Geronimo</name>
     <date_birth>4/23/1994</date_birth>
     <weight_birth>107</weight_birth>
     <weight_current>812</weight_current>
     <herd_by_herd_id.herdname>
          <data>North Branch</data>
     </herd_by_herd_id.herdname>
</row>
```

Notice how FileMaker handles the export of the related field. Instead of having one piece of content, it contains multiple <data> elements, each of which contains some data. We'll see how to handle this in a minute.

We're making one critical assumption here. Did you notice what it was? The assumption is that the records are going to come to us presorted by herd. We can write an XSL stylesheet that doesn't need to make that assumption, but it's a bit more complicated. So for now, we're going to have FileMaker sort these records by herd before exporting them (this is part of our export script).

So now we have our algorithm. How do we translate it into XSL? We need to make some kind of conditional test each time we hit a <ROW> element. Specifically, we need to drill into the <ROW>, extract the Herd_By_Herd_ID.HerdName element, and then dig into that element and extract its <DATA> element. (This nested data structure might seem odd, but it is how FileMaker represents related fields in its XML grammar. The reason for going a level deeper, rather than just having the herd name be the direct content of the <Herd_By_Herd_ID.HerdName> element, is that this structure allows for multiple related fields for a single record—in other words, a portal. In our example, each animal has only one herd, so this consideration doesn't apply here, but later we see an example of a more "portal-like" display.)

Once we have the current row's herd name, we need to compare it to the previous row's. If they're not equal, we output the herd break.

To perform a conditional test, we need a new XSL element called <xsl:if>. Its syntax looks like this:

```
<xsl-if test="a>b">
    a is greater than b!
</xsl:if>
```

<xsl:if> has a single attribute called test, which has a Boolean (that is, true-false) expression as its value. To use it for our purposes, let's start with the first test for herd breaks: We just want to know if the current <ROW> element is the first one in the document or not.

That's a bit trickier than it sounds. XSL has a function called position(), which sounds helpful. It returns the position of the current node, relative to what's called its *context*. The context of a node is determined not by the structure of the XML document but by how we write our stylesheet. In our stylesheet, in our template for <FMPDSORESULT>, we have an <xsl:apply-templates> call. It's in the context (that word again) of that <xsl:apply-templates> that we come upon the template for a <ROW> element. Recall what FileMaker's DSO XML output looks like:

```
<?xml version="1.0" encoding="UTF-8" ?>
<FMPDSORESULT xmlns="http://www.filemaker.com/fmpdsoresult">
      <ERRORCODE>0</ERRORCODE>
      <DATABASE>Animal.fp5</DATABASE>
      <LAYOUT></LAYOUT>
      <ROW MODID="0" RECORDID="1">
            <date_birth>4/23/1994</date_birth>
            <id_animal>A1</id_animal>
            <id_father></id_father>
            <id_mother></id_mother>
            <name>Great Geronimo</name>
            <weight_birth>107</weight_birth>
            <weight_current>812</weight_current>
      </ROW>
      [ numerous other rows here ...]
</FMPDSORESULT>
```

And here is our problem: The first <ROW> element is not the very first element in its context; it's the fourth—preceded by <ERRORCODE>, <DATABASE>, and <LAYOUT>. We can use position(), though, if we really want to. Here it is, by way of illustration. We would put this conditional in the template that matches on <ROW> elements:

```
      <xsl-if test="position()=4">
            This is the first row of the data set.
      </xsl:if>
```

This works for now, but what's wrong with it? Well, it's fragile. If the format of FileMaker's DSO output changes slightly, this could break. It can be pointed out that most stylesheets certainly break if the underlying XML structure that they're transforming changes. Though this is true, it still pays to make your code (XSL, FileMaker, COBOL, whatever) somewhat protected against such changes.

We'd rather have a test that asks whether a given element is the first one of its type in the document, no matter how the document is organized and no matter how we process it. That's a little more robust than depending on the first <ROW> being the fourth element in a given context. For each <ROW>, we'd like to look backward and ask, "Are there any other <ROW> elements before me in this document?"

This concept of "looking backward" brings us to the XSL concept of an "axis." More specifically, this construct is part of XPath. XPath, as you might recall, is the part of XSL that lets us point to things, usually to sections of a document tree. XPath lets us express concepts like "all elements named DATA, wherever they are in the document," or "all children of the current ROW node," or "all grandchildren of the current ROW node that are named DATA," or "all siblings of the current ROW node." Each of these has a corresponding XPath expression, and each of these expressions uses an axis, either explicitly or implicitly.

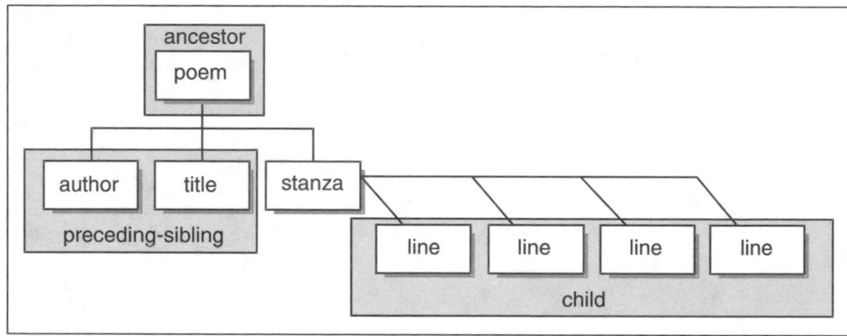

Figure 4.4

My, that sounds dense. We can feel your eyelids getting heavy. Let's go to some examples. Let's say that we want to write a template that matches a <ROW> node, and inside that template we want to find and output the herd name.

```
<xsl:template match="fmp:ROW">
     Herd: <xsl:value-of select='fmp:Herd_By_Herd_ID.HerdName/
       fmp:DATA'>
</xsl:template>
```

The interesting XPath expression is in the select attribute of the xsl:value-of element. This expression says "find me a child of the current <ROW> element called fmp:Herd_By_Herd_ID.HerdName. Then find me a child of that element called <DATA>." Notice the forward slash—this indicates that <fmp:DATA> is a child of <fmp:Herd_By_Herd_ID.HerdName>. If this slash makes you think of the way directory paths are written in some operating systems (notably Unix), so much the better—much of XPath uses a directory-like syntax. This is not surprising, since an XML document and a filesystem directory structure are both examples of a tree-like structure.

XPath syntax is fairly rich, and there are often a few ways to say the same thing. For example, this selector gets us the same result as the previous one:

```
<xsl:template match="fmp:ROW">
     Herd: <xsl:value-of select='.//fmp:DATA'>
</xsl:template>
```

Although this gives us the same result, it doesn't say exactly the same thing. This expression says "find me any descendant of the current node (a <ROW>) called <fmp:DATA>." It could be one level down; it could be ten levels down. If the single slash in the first expression meant "go down one level," the double slash here means "go down all the levels."

The other interesting point here is the dot (.) in the expression. Again, if you're familiar with some directory notations, the dot generally means "where I am now." So this expression means "starting where I am now (in this particular <ROW> node), go through all of this node's children, grandchildren, etc., all the way down, and find me any instance of <fmp:DATA>." Now we happen to know that there is only one of these per <ROW>, so this expression has the same result as the previous. It is, though, potentially much less efficient. The first selector gives an exact path (fmp:Herd_By_Herd_ID.HerdName/fmp:DATA). The second one just says "search the house." Depending on how many descendants a <ROW> element has, this search could take quite a bit longer. Of the two expressions, then, the first is much preferable for our purpose.

So what does this have to do with the ominous-sounding concept of *axes* (that would be "ax-eez," as opposed to hatchets)? Well, these two expressions use two different XPath axes. The first uses an axis called *child*, and the second uses an axis called *descendant-or-self*. (In fact, the second expression incorporates a third axis, called *self*, abbreviated by the dot.)

XPath 1.0 has a total of 13 axes (http://www.w3.org/TR/xpath#axes). A number of these can be represented by an abbreviated syntax, such as those we used above. For example, the child axis is effectively the default axis and can be omitted from any expression. The expression fmp:Herd_By_Herd_ID.HerdName/fmp:DATA is the same as the more verbose child::fmp:Herd_By_Herd_ID.HerdName/child::fmp:DATA. The expression .//fmp:DATA is equivalent to the more verbose self::node()/descendant-or-self::node()/child::fmp:DATA.

Not all of the 13 XPath axes have an abbreviated syntax. In particular, the one we need to solve our row-counting problem doesn't. It's called *preceding-sibling* and points backward from the current node through any previous siblings of the current node in document order. For a <ROW> node in our XML document from the Animal.fp5, the preceding-sibling axis contains all the previous nodes in the document that are children of the same parent, starting with the nearest one and going backward to the beginning of the document.

The following diagram shows some of the major axes in the document that we're working with. The numbers show the order in which elements are traversed as you go along each axis:

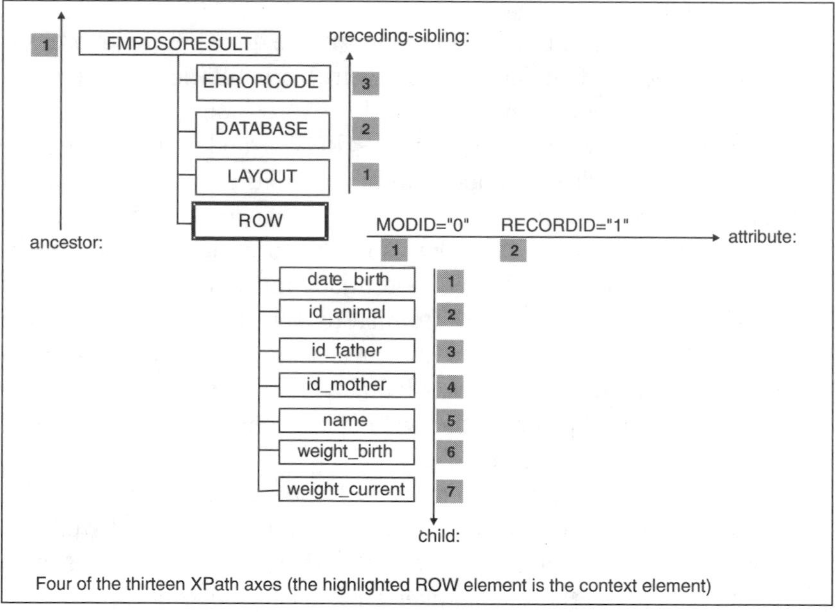

Figure 4.5

Our plan for using this axis is simple: We want to count all the nodes along it, starting from the current <ROW>. If the count is zero, we know this <ROW> is the first. But this is still not quite enough. The concept of "sibling" here doesn't necessarily mean that all siblings have the same name. In particular, among the children of the <FMPDSORESULT> element, <ROW> has many <ROW> siblings but also siblings called <LAYOUT>, <ERRORCODE>, and <DATABASE>. We can still count backward along the preceding-sibling axis, but we need to make sure that we're only counting ROWs. Here, without further ado, is how it looks:

```
<xsl:if test="count(preceding-sibling::fmp:ROW)=0">
     <xsl:apply-templates select="fmp:Herd_By_Herd_
       ID.HerdName"/>
</xsl:if>
```

Let's take this apart. The test expression is counting something using the count() function and checking to see if it equals zero. It's taking the count along the preceding-sibling axis, which is written in full since it has no abbreviated syntax. It looks back along that axis but only for <ROW> elements. It then counts those elements to see if there actually are any.

If you want true abstraction, there's one more step that you can take. The above expression works fine, but it only works for <ROW> elements. How can we generalize it so that it works for any element, regardless of its name? Our XPath expression needs to say something like "count all my preceding siblings that have the same name as me." Here's how that would look:

```
<xsl:if test="count(preceding-sibling::*[name() =
  name(current())])=0">
      <xsl:apply-templates select="fmp:Herd_By_Herd_
        ID.HerdName"/>
</xsl:if>
```

This is a pretty dense expression. It starts, again, by looking at everything along that same axis (preceding-sibling) and takes everything it finds there—this is expressed by the wildcard character *. It then applies a *predicate*, expressed by the square brackets. The brackets contain a logical test that's used to narrow down the node set. Here the test says "find me nodes where the name matches the name of the current node." This is a fairly complicated XPath expression. If you can get your head around that expression, you'll know most of the XPath that you'll probably ever need.

Notice that XPath lets us narrow down the node set in three different ways: by axis, by node name, and with a final predicate (inside the square brackets), which could be almost any kind of expression. This example is a bit complicated because the predicate test is actually a node name test as well. It could just as easily have said "find me all preceding siblings where the birth weight is greater than 200 pounds," as shown in the following:

```
preceding-sibling::*[birth_weight>200]
```

Or it could have been searching for a particular record ID attribute on the row:

```
preceding-sibling::*[@RECORDID=2]
```

(Here, by the way, the @ sign is abbreviated syntax for the attribute axis.) XPath is quite flexible and expressive, but there's no denying that it takes some getting used to. We can't cover every aspect of XPath (or XSL for that matter) exhaustively in this book. As you delve deeper into writing your own stylesheets, equip yourself with reference materials that cover these languages in greater depth. But don't worry—we leave you with more than enough XSL to modify other people's stylesheets and write some cool ones of your own.

After that dizzying dive, the expression for deciding if the current <ROW> is the first for its herd is not too bad by comparison:

```
<xsl:if test="preceding-sibling::fmp:ROW[1]/fmp:Herd_By_Herd_
  ID.HerdName/fmp:DATA != fmp:Herd_By_Herd_ID.HerdName/
  fmp:DATA">
      <xsl:apply-templates select="fmp:Herd_By_Herd_
        ID.HerdName"/>
</xsl:if>
```

Here, the expression again looks backward along the preceding-sibling axis. Recall that this axis starts with the immediately preceding sibling and works backward from there. Well, the immediately preceding sibling is just the one that we want. We refer to it this way:

```
preceding-sibling::fmp:ROW[1]
```

We want to know whether its herd is the same as that of the current node. Well, recall that the herd name is actually wrapped in the <DATA> element, which is wrapped in the <Herd_By_Herd_ID.HerdName element>, so it's a grandchild of <ROW>. Knowing that, the XPath syntax should be fairly clear.

Here's the whole stylesheet. We've added a little CSS styling that indicates the herd breaks in red on the browser:

```
<?xml version="1.0" encoding="UTF-8"?>
<xsl:stylesheet version="1.0"
  xmlns:xsl="http://www.w3.org/1999/XSL/Transform"
  xmlns:fmp="http://www.filemaker.com/fmpdsoresult">
      <xsl:output method="html" indent="yes"
        doctype-public="-//W3C//DTD HTML 3.2 Final//EN"/>
      <xsl:template match="fmp:FMPDSORESULT">
<html>
<head>
      <title>BHBB Herd Listing</title>
</head>
<body>
      <H2>Blue Horizon Bison Breeders</H2>
      <H3>Herd Listing</H3>
      <table border="0">
            <xsl:apply-templates/>
      </table>
</body>
</html>
      </xsl:template>

      <xsl:template match="fmp:ROW">
      <!--If this is the first ROW element, insert a herd break...-->
```

```
    <xsl:if test="count(preceding-sibling::*[name() =
      name(current())])=0">
          <xsl:apply-templates select="fmp:Herd_By_Herd_
            ID.HerdName"/>
    </xsl:if>
    <!--Or if this herd differs from the herd of the previous ROW,
      insert a herd break-->
    <xsl:if test="preceding-sibling::fmp:ROW[1]/
      fmp:Herd_By_Herd_ID.HerdName/fmp:DATA !=
      fmp:Herd_By_Herd_ID.HerdName/fmp:DATA">
          <xsl:apply-templates select="fmp:Herd_By_Herd_
            ID.HerdName"/>
    </xsl:if>
    <xsl:apply-templates select="fmp:name"/>
    <tr>
    <xsl:apply-templates select="fmp:date_birth"/>
    <xsl:apply-templates select="fmp:weight_birth"/>
    <xsl:apply-templates select="fmp:weight_current"/>
    </tr>
    </xsl:template>

    <xsl:template match="fmp:ERRORCODE"/>
    <xsl:template match="fmp:DATABASE"/>
    <xsl:template match="fmp:Herd_By_Herd_ID.HerdName">
          <tr style="color:red; border-bottom=2px solid;" >
            <td colspan="3"><b><xsl:value-of select="./fmp:DATA"/>
            Herd</b></td></tr>
    </xsl:template>

    <xsl:template match="fmp:name">
          <tr><td colspan="3"><b><xsl:value-of select="."/></b>
            </td></tr>
    </xsl:template>

    <xsl:template match="fmp:date_birth">
          <td>Born <xsl:value-of select="."/></td>
          </xsl:template>

    <xsl:template match="fmp:weight_birth">
          <td>Birth Weight <xsl:value-of select="."/></td>
          </xsl:template>

    <xsl:template match="fmp:weight_current">
          <td>Current Weight <xsl:value-of select="."/></td>
          </xsl:template>
</xsl:stylesheet>
```

That will do it. You might think that this was a lot of work just to output sub-summary group breaks. Yes, it was. We took you down that path because it's a useful tour of conditionals and complex XPath expressions, but it's not the most flexible way to transform XML data into grouped reports using XSL. For that, we need some more advanced tools.

Advanced Sub-summary Reporting in XSL

In this section we're going to look at a technique called the *Muenchian Method*, named for its progenitor, Steve Muench. The technique is well explained on the excellent XSLT pages of Jeni Tennison (http://www.jenitennison.com/xslt/grouping/muenchian.html) and demonstrated in the sub-summary stylesheet example that ships with FileMaker Pro 6. The stylesheet that we build here is quite similar to the FileMaker example, since, in addition to advanced summary reporting, it introduces a number of other useful XSL techniques.

There are a couple of problems with the technique that we illustrated in the previous section. First, it assumes the data is already sorted. Second, the "look-backward" technique that we use to decide if a row is the first in the entire dataset is inefficient. For every <ROW> the processor encounters, it has to count all the previous <ROW> elements. For a database of n rows, this means counting about $n^2/2$ elements—$(n^2 + n)/2$ to be exact. For those of you who have had some exposure to the analysis of algorithms, a computation that performs about n^2 operations for an input of size n is considered dangerously inefficient and should be avoided wherever possible. The situation is worse if the data is unsorted; in this case, we are unable to rely on the sorted relationship between each record and the one previous. Though we can actually replace the "very-first" test with a more efficient operation, we are still stuck doing the backward search for each and every <ROW>, which is devastating in a large data set. We need a different tool.

XSL is going to help us out with some constructs that are specifically designed to help in identifying subgroups within XML data sets. In particular, we use the <xsl:key> element and the corresponding key() function to solve our problems. Our plan is a "top-down" one. If we're grouping by herd, the first thing to do is to find all the different herds that are represented in the data set. Then we want to loop through that set (it will have two herds in it for our data set) and, for each distinct herd, output a list of all animals in that herd. That is enough for a one-level sub-summary.

<xsl:key> gives us an elegant way to pull out a group of nodes that correspond to certain criteria and, in effect, build an index into those nodes. The "look-back" XPath expressions that we used before were inefficient because they kept looking backward over almost the same set of nodes without taking advantage of any of that previous

processing. <xsl:key> lets you, in effect, index a group of nodes for faster lookup later. It looks like this:

```
<xsl:key name="animals_by_herd" match="fmp:ROW"
  use="fmp:Herd_By_Herd_ID.HerdName/fmp:DATA"/>
```

The <xsl:key> element has three attributes: name, match, and use (pronounced "yooz" and not "yoose," so it may help you remember the meaning better). The name is any name that you want to give the key. The match attribute specifies what *kind* of thing ends up in the result set. <xsl:key> creates a kind of dictionary—you use the match attribute to say what kind of thing each dictionary entry is. In our case, the dictionary contains instances of <fmp:ROW>. Lastly, the use attribute specifies which part of the entry is its actual key (that is, the part that we're going to look it up by). For each row, we're going to look it up by the herd ID, and the path to that data is fmp:Herd_By_Herd_ID.HerdName/fmp:DATA. (Remember, that's an XPath expression going along the default child axis down from a ROW element, so it means "the <fmp:DATA> element that's a child of the fmp:Herd_By_Herd_ID.HerdName that's a child of the current <fmp:ROW> node." The <fmp:ROW> node is the *context* for the XPath expression.)

We use <xsl:key> in what turns out to be a nested loop. We first want to find all unique herds in the data set. Then we want to loop through those herds and, for each herd, find all the animals for that herd and output them in sorted order. We use a couple more new elements to do this: <xsl:for-each> to perform the loops and <xsl:sort> to sort the records within groups.

We're glossing over an important step, though. Somehow we need to pull out a list that consists only of the unique herd names. What kind of test can give us that? Well, one way to rephrase the test is that we only want to keep a herd name if it's the first occurrence of that name in the data set. We know that a look-back expression along the preceding-sibling axis does this but at a serious cost to efficiency. This time, as we look at each <fmp:ROW> node, we're instead going to compare it to the set of nodes that our key expression extracts. For each <fmp:ROW>, we're going to look at the key-selected set of all the <fmp:ROW> nodes with the same herd name (remember, the herd name is the "match field" for the <xsl:key> element, shown by the use attribute). If the current <fmp:ROW> node is the same as the first one in the key-selected set, we keep it. Otherwise, we move on.

If this sounds obscure, think about how you do this in FileMaker Pro. Have you ever had to write a report that needed to behave like a sub-summary report but couldn't be displayed in Preview mode, possibly because it needed to perform scripts in response to user mouse clicks? Or possibly, your client doesn't like the fact that summary parts in FileMaker appear above or below groups, rather than inline. Imagine, for example, in our herd database, your user decides that he wants the herd name to appear next to the animal name but only for the first animal:

```
Herd                     Animal
-------------------------------
North Branch             Chin-cha-pe
                         Scatters Them
                         Hohokam Glory
Roaring Brook            Barleycorn
                         Sacajawea
```

In FileMaker, you'd want to create a calculated field to display the herd name. The calculation would say, in effect, "if this animal is the first for this herd, show the herd name; otherwise, don't." But what kind of calculation decides if a record is the first in its group? To solve this problem, you need a self-relationship based on whatever field you're trying to "de-dupe." Here you want to avoid duplicate display of the herd name, so you would create a self-relationship based on the herd name. Then, for any individual record, you want to ask whether it's the same as the first record found by that relationship. This means that you need to define both "same" and "first." For deciding about sameness, your records need a primary key. Two records are the same if and only if their primary key is the same. For our Animal.fp5 database, the key is the id_animal field. So if two records have the same id_animal, they're the same.

Then we get to the concept of "first." What's the "first" record in a related set? The concept really only has meaning if you've applied some ordering to that set (that is, if you've sorted it). So we want to sort our self-relationship. For right now, it is best to sort them by id_animal, since this has a unique value for each record; thus, the records are always fully sorted.

So we create a self-relationship on id_herd and sort it by id_animal. We then create a calculation called something like FirstForHerd, where the definition is:

```
id_animal = SelfByIDHerd::id_animal
```

We can then create a calculation called HerdDisplay to show the herd name for the first herd record in each group:

```
Case( FirstForHerd, HerdByHerdID::HerdName, "" )
```

Here is one last important note about this technique. There's a bit more to the choice of the sort order on the self-relationship than we said. What's important is that the self-related records have to be ordered in the same way that the animal records are ordered within each subgroup. If animals are going to be sorted by name within the herd group, the self-relationship should also be sorted by name. This is to ensure that the record that is first in the subgroup (which is where you want the herd name to display) is also "first" in the self-related records. If your ordering is different, the herd name shows up—not on the first line but on some seemingly random line farther down.

The only drawback to this technique in FileMaker is its speed. FirstForHerd is a calculation based on a related value, so it cannot be stored. In a big list view (which is of course where you want to do this), these self-related calcs can slow things down somewhat.

Back to XSL. The link is that the <xsl:key> construction that we saw above is almost exactly equivalent to the self-relationship in the FileMaker example: For a given node (record), the expression (relationship) pulls out all other records of the same set that somehow "match" it. In FileMaker, the match condition is set up in the self-relationship. In <xsl:key>, the match condition is actually established by the use attribute. If you think of use like a relational key, you are not far off.

Once our <xsl:key> is established, we invoke it using the key() function. (Keep the terms in mind: <xsl:key> is an element and key() is a function.) If we're on an <fmp:ROW> node (most likely in a template that somehow matches <fmp:ROW>), we can say:

```
key( "animals_by_herd", fmp:Herd_By_Herd_ID.HerdName/fmp:DATA )
```

That's an XPath expression that returns a node set consisting of all nodes with the same herd name as the current <fmp:ROW>. We can now apply a predicate to that node set to get the first one:

```
key( "animals_by_herd", fmp:Herd_By_Herd_ID.HerdName/fmp:DATA )[1]
```

We're almost there. We've picked out all the animals with the same herd name, using the more efficient key() function rather than the much-less-efficient lookback expressions. We've found the first one in that set. Now we just need to compare that node to the current one and decide whether they're the same. If they are, the current node is the first in its set, and we can act accordingly.

But here it gets sticky. XSL and XML don't really have any concept of sameness. If we're aware that each node of the type that we're working with has a unique value somewhere in it, we can just compare these values. So we could have a test like this:

```
fmp:id_animal = key( "animals_by_herd",
  fmp:Herd_By_Herd_ID.HerdName/fmp:DATA )[1]/fmp:id_animal
```

This means "look at the animal ID of the current node, and then go get the set of all nodes with the same herd name, get the first one, look at its animal ID, and compare the two." This works fine but only if the nodes that we're working on have some unique value like this. It won't work in a more general case where that unique value is either nonexistent or unknown. For that, we need to do more work.

We have a couple of choices here. One is to get XSL to generate the unique keys for us. XSL has a function called generate-id(), which generates a unique ID for any node. It is guaranteed to return the same unique ID for a given node within the context of a single XSL program. (We say "program" instead of "stylesheet" because it is possible to create XSL programs that are larger than a single stylesheet.) The ID is not guaranteed to be unique across multiple invocations of a program. So we can write the following test on an <fmp:ROW> node:

```
generate-id() = generate-id( key( 'animals_by_herd',
  fmp:Herd_By_Herd_ID.HerdName/fmp:DATA )[1]
```

This means generate IDs for the current <fmp:ROW> and for the first one in the key set, and compare them.

The other technique is more abstract. We can create a new node set by joining other nodes together using the union operator, which is written "|". We can try to create a set consisting of the current node and the first node in the key set, like this:

```
. | key( 'animals_by_herd', fmp:Herd_By_Herd_
  ID.HerdName/fmp:DATA )[1]
```

The dot, of course, is shorthand for the current node, while the key expression returns the first in the key set. Now, XSL forbids you from adding the same node twice to the same node set—a node can only appear once per set. So, if our set from above contains just one node, it means the two nodes were the same. We use the count() function to perform this test:

```
count( . | key( 'animals_by_herd', fmp:Herd_By_Herd_
  ID.HerdName/fmp:DATA )[1] ) = 1
```

This might seem a little odd, but it does work. Feel free to use whichever "find-first" technique makes more sense to you.

Are we there yet? Well, we're definitely out of the driveway. So far we've learned how to use XSL key constructs to: a) pull a list of all unique herds from our XML data set, and b) given a specific <fmp:ROW> element, pull a set of all the other <fmp:ROW> elements that share the same herd ID. From here, we need to write that nested loop that we mentioned, going through all the distinct herds one by one and, for each one, going through all the individual animal records and writing them out.

We haven't seen explicit looping in XSL so far. The closest we've come has been the <xsl:apply-templates> element. In fact, the two are very often interchangeable. It's up to you to choose the one that you think is easier to read or write. The "loop-ness" of our program is clearer with the <xsl:for-each> element, so let's go ahead and use that. Here's a full program to generate our grouped report using <xsl:for-each> and the key techniques that we just learned.

```
<?xml version="1.0" encoding="UTF-8"?>
<xsl:stylesheet version="1.0"
  xmlns:xsl="http://www.w3.org/1999/XSL/Transform"
  xmlns:fmp="http://www.filemaker.com/fmpdsoresult">
     <xsl:output method="html" indent="yes"
       doctype-public="-//W3C//DTD HTML 3.2 Final//EN"/>
     <xsl:key name="animals_by_herd" match="fmp:ROW"
       use="fmp:Herd_By_Herd_ID.HerdName/fmp:DATA"/>
     <xsl:template match="fmp:FMPDSORESULT">
<html>
<head>
     <title>BHBB Herd Listing</title>
</head>
<body>
     <H2>Blue Horizon Bison Breeders</H2>
     <H3>Herd Listing</H3>
     <table border="0">
          <xsl:for-each select="fmp:ROW[generate-id()=
            generate-id(key('animals_by_herd',
            fmp:Herd_By_Herd_ID.HerdName/fmp:DATA)[1])]">
               <tr style="color:red; border-bottom=2px solid;" >
                 <td colspan="3"><b>Herd: <xsl:value-of
                 select="fmp:Herd_By_Herd_ID.HerdName/fmp:DATA"/>
                 </b></td></tr>
               <xsl:for-each select="key('animals_by_herd',
                 fmp:Herd_By_Herd_ID.HerdName/fmp:DATA)">
                    <tr><td colspan="3"><b><xsl:value-of
                      select="./fmp:name"/></b></td></tr>
                    <tr>
                         <td>Born <xsl:value-of select="./fmp:date_
                           birth"/></td>
                         <td>Birth Weight <xsl:value-of
                           select="./fmp:weight_birth"/></td>
                         <td>Current Weight <xsl:value-of
```

Chapter 4

```
                                    select="./fmp:weight_current"/></td>
                              </tr>
                         </xsl:for-each>
                    </xsl:for-each>
               </table>
</body>
</html>
     </xsl:template>
</xsl:stylesheet>
```

The finished stylesheet turns out to be pleasingly compact. Much of the reason for this is the <xsl:for-each> structure. Where previous stylesheets that we worked with had as many as five templates, this has only one. In particular, all of the individual data fields are handled within the same template, rather than each having their own template. The result is perhaps more readable. In any event, it looks more like a traditional computer program, which depending on your point of view is either a good thing or not.

Sorting

We said that we'd add sorting to this report. To do this, we use the <xsl:sort> element. We use <xsl:sort> to force a specific ordering of data inside either an <xsl:apply-templates> or an <xsl:for-each> element. XSL lets us specify what data to sort on, what data type the data should be treated as (text or numeric), and whether to sort in ascending or descending order. It looks like this:

```
     <xsl:sort select="fmp:Herd_By_Herd_ID.HerdName/fmp:DATA"
       data-type="text" order="ascending"/>
```

We would place this immediately inside any <xsl:apply-templates> or <xsl:for-each> where we wanted to sort the matched elements. Both the data-type and order attributes are optional. The above statement tells the processor to sort by herd name—we'd place this right inside the first <xsl:for-each>. To further sort by animal name inside each herd, we'd add:

```
     <xsl:sort select="fmp:name" data-type="text" order="ascending"/>
```

We'd add that element just inside the second <xsl:for-each>. We won't reprint the whole stylesheet here with those additions; the next example incorporates several levels of sorting as well.

Multilevel Reporting

So far, all that pain doesn't seem to have bought us much. Our stylesheet still churns out pretty much the same report as before. It's true that it is more compact, and we swear it's more efficient for bigger data sets. But other than that, how does it help? Let's go ahead and extend it to a multilevel grouped report and see how that works.

Let's say that now, within each herd, we want to do subgrouping by animal gender. We can probably find a shortcut based on the fact that we know in advance that there are only two possible genders. But let's pretend that we don't know the range of possible choices there (just to cover the more general case).

Our situation is similar to the previous report, but now we need three nested loops instead of two. First we grab all the herds and loop through them. For each herd, we grab all the genders and loop through them. For each gender, we grab all the animals that match both that herd and that gender and output them somehow.

The main difference here is that since we have two grouping levels, we need to have two key elements. The first key, as in the previous example, gathers up all unique herd names. The second key gathers up all unique combinations of a herd name and a gender. The first key looks the same:

```
<xsl:key name="animals_by_herd" match="fmp:ROW"
  use="fmp:Herd_By_Herd_ID.HerdName/fmp:DATA"/>
```

For the second expression, we need a use attribute that somehow combines both the herd name and gender of the current record. We do this in XSL much the way that we might in FileMaker; we use string concatenation to create a value that includes both fields (herd name and animal gender). In FileMaker, we use the concatenation operator (&). In XSL, we can use the concat() function. Here's our second-level key expression:

```
<xsl:key name="herd_by_gender" match="fmp:ROW" use="concat
 ( fmp:Herd_By_Herd_ID.HerdName/fmp:DATA, ' ', fmp:gender)"/>
```

This doesn't get us all the way out of the woods. At the second level, the gender level, we need to make sure that we're only searching in the current herd. In the case of gender, this isn't such a strong restriction because the genders don't actually vary across herds. In other cases, we want to make sure that we did this. So the second-level key expression is going to be a bit more complicated. Let's look at the whole stylesheet and see what's going on.

```
<?xml version="1.0" encoding="UTF-8"?>
<xsl:stylesheet version="1.0"
  xmlns:xsl="http://www.w3.org/1999/XSL/Transform"
  xmlns:fmp="http://www.filemaker.com/fmpdsoresult">
  <xsl:output method="html" indent="yes" doctype-public="-//W3C//DTD
    HTML 3.2 Final//EN"/>

  <!--First-level key for herd grouping-->
  <xsl:key name="animals_by_herd" match="fmp:ROW"
    use="fmp:Herd_By_Herd_ID.HerdName/fmp:DATA"/>
  <!--Second-level key for subgrouping by gender within herd-->
  <xsl:key name="herd_by_gender" match="fmp:ROW" use="concat
    ( fmp:Herd_By_Herd_ID.HerdName/fmp:DATA, ' ', fmp:gender)"/>

  <xsl:template match="fmp:FMPDSORESULT">
    <html>
    <head>
      <title>BHBB Herd Listing</title>
    </head>
    <body>
      <H2>Blue Horizon Bison Breeders</H2>
      <H3>Herd Listing</H3>
      <table border="0">
        <!--Here we select our unique herd names-->
        <xsl:for-each select="fmp:ROW[generate-id()=generate-id
          (key('animals_by_herd', fmp:Herd_By_Herd_ID.HerdName/
          fmp:DATA)[1])]">
          <!--Here we sort the herds by name-->
          <xsl:sort select="fmp:Herd_By_Herd_ID.HerdName/fmp:DATA"
            data-type="text" order="ascending"/>
          <!--And output the herd break line-->
          <tr style="color:red; border-bottom=2px solid;" >
            <td colspan="3"><b><xsl:value-of select="fmp:Herd_By_
            Herd_ID.HerdName/fmp:DATA"/> Herd</b></td></tr>
          <!--Here we select the unique genders for this herd-->
          <xsl:variable name="animals" select="key('animals_by_herd',
            fmp:Herd_By_Herd_ID.HerdName/fmp:DATA)"/>
          <xsl:for-each select="$animals[generate-id()=generate-id
            (key('herd_by_gender', concat( fmp:Herd_By_Herd_
            ID.HerdName/fmp:DATA, ' ', fmp:gender))[1])]">
            <!--And output the gender break line-->
            <tr style="background-color: gray" ><td colspan="3">
              <b><xsl:value-of select="fmp:gender"/></b></td></tr>
            <xsl:for-each select="key('herd_by_gender', concat
              ( fmp:Herd_By_Herd_ID.HerdName/fmp:DATA, ' ',
                fmp:gender) )">
              <xsl:sort select="fmp:name" data-type="text"
                order="ascending"/>
              <tr><td colspan="3"><b><xsl:value-of select="./
                fmp:name"/></b></td></tr>
              <tr>
                <td>Born <xsl:value-of select="./fmp:date_birth"/>
                  </td>
                <td>Birth Weight <xsl:value-of select="./fmp:weight_
```

```
                birth"/></td>
              <td>Current Weight <xsl:value-of select="./
                fmp:weight_current"/></td>
            </tr>
          </xsl:for-each>
        </xsl:for-each>
      </xsl:for-each>
    </table>
  </body>
  </html>
</xsl:template>
</xsl:stylesheet>
```

We set up our two keys, as described above, with one based on herd name and the other on a combination of herd name and gender. We proceed as before, first pulling all unique herd names and looping through them. But the expression to pull all unique genders within a herd is more complicated. It's sufficiently snarly that we're going to use an <xsl:variable> element to minimize the confusion.

The <xsl:variable> lets us assign a name to a value. This is a convenient way to store complicated expressions, either for later reuse or just to make the code more readable. The name is actually misleading—typically we refer to a variable as a named value that can change (hence the term "variable"). Variables in XSLT can't change. Once they're set, there they stay. They're a bit more like what other languages would call a "constant."

Once a variable has been defined in XSLT, it can be referred to by prefixing it with a dollar sign. So this expression:

```
<xsl:variable name="animals" select="key('animals_by_herd',
  fmp:Herd_By_Herd_ID.HerdName/fmp:DATA)"/>
```

...creates a variable that we can refer to as $animals.

Here we use an <xsl:variable> to hold an XPath expression that points to the set of all the animals in the current herd. We want to pick the unique genders out of that specific group. We're using this to keep the next expression somewhat readable. Here it is:

```
<xsl:for-each select="$animals[generate-id()=generate-id
  (key('herd_by_gender', concat( fmp:Herd_By_Herd_ID.HerdName/
  fmp:DATA, ' ', fmp:gender))[1])]">
```

This is the for-each that is going to loop through all genders in a specific herd. We're using the familiar (if complicated) predicate that uses generate-id() to find the first gender records, but it's important that we limit our search to the current herd. Our $animals variable points to just those records, so it's in that group that we want to make our search.

Other than that, this stylesheet is very similar to the previous. Admittedly, this multilevel grouping is a bit of a chore. If that last expression made your head hurt, rest assured that the requirements for XSL 2.0, currently under development, include a call for a more straightforward multilevel grouping mechanism.

Displaying Hierarchical Data

Using XML and XSL, we can also work with data that is often difficult to manage in a traditional database. Take the example of hierarchical data. This is data, such as an organization chart or genealogy, that is structured like a tree. *Advanced FileMaker Pro 5.5 Techniques for Developers* from Wordware Publishing showed how to manipulate hierarchical data in FileMaker, which requires quite some effort to get a nice tree-like display in FileMaker. Here we're going to show you how to accomplish something similar using XSL.

That main difficulty with hierarchical data is that it's *recursive*. In a way, it looks somewhat like a traditional relational database structure. For example, there's a parent-child (or one-to-many) relationship between a given manager and her employees. But one of these employees might have others underneath him, and so on down the line. How deep do these relationships extend? We don't know. Thinking in terms of display, a portal shows us one "level" of children. So, for a given manager, a portal shows that manager's direct reports. But we want a display that goes all the way down. How far is that? There's no way to know. We have to keep following the tree until we reach the bottom.

The formula for doing this (the *algorithm*, in geek-speak) looks something like this: Find the top of the tree. Find all the immediate children. Display all the children. Then, for each of the children, repeat exactly the same process. If a node has no children, keep going. Draw yourself a tree structure on paper and work through this process by hand, and you'll see how it works. The process finishes when, and only when, you have touched each node in the tree, no matter how deep the tree is.

Let's look at an example of this, intended to output a family tree of Native American languages. Take a look at the NatAmLang.fp5 database included with the downloadable files, and you'll see a straightforward tree structure. All languages have a parent language ID, except for the language at the very top. We want a display that looks something like this:

```
Algonquian Language
     Central Algonquian Languages
          Cree Languages
               Attikamekw
               Cree
                    Michif
               Montagnais
               Naskapi
```

Our algorithm goes like this: First we want to find all the top-level languages. These are the ones with an empty id_parent field. For each of these, we want to indent one level, find all children of that language, and repeat the same process until we run out of children.

There are a few ways to do this. We're using one that illustrates an important new concept that helps in writing modular, reusable XSL code. This new construct is called a *named template*. A named template is very similar to a regular template, but it can be invoked directly. With <xsl:apply-templates>, you instruct the processor to find whatever template matches certain criteria. With a named template, you can point to one specific template and call it directly. Named templates are closely analogous to function calls in procedural languages. You can even pass parameters to a named template, just as you would to a function.

The easiest thing to do is examine the entire stylesheet:

```
<?xml version="1.0" encoding="UTF-8"?>
<xsl:stylesheet version="1.0"
  xmlns:xsl="http://www.w3.org/1999/XSL/Transform"
  xmlns:fmp="http://www.filemaker.com/fmpdsoresult">
     <xsl:output method="html" indent="yes"
       doctype-public="-//W3C//DTD HTML 3.2 Final//EN"/>

     <xsl:template match="fmp:FMPDSORESULT">
          <html>
     <head>
          <title>Languages</title>
     </head>
     <body>
     <h2>Partial Tree of Native American Languages</h2>
     <table border="0">
          <xsl:for-each select="fmp:ROW[fmp:id_parent='']">
                <tr><td><xsl:value-of select="fmp:name"/></td></tr>
                <xsl:call-template name="childLanguages">
                     <xsl:with-param name="langid" select="./
                       fmp:id_language"/>
                     <xsl:with-param name="indent" select="0"/>
                </xsl:call-template>
          </xsl:for-each>
          </table>
     </body></html>
```

```
    </xsl:template>

    <xsl:template name="childLanguages">
          <xsl:param name="langid"/>
          <xsl:param name="indent"/>
          <xsl:for-each select="/fmp:FMPDSORESULT/
            fmp:ROW[fmp:id_parent=$langid]">
                <tr><td>

                      <xsl:call-template name="Indenter">
                            <xsl:with-param name="iIndent"
                              select="$indent"/>
                      </xsl:call-template>

                      <xsl:value-of select="fmp:name"/>

                </td></tr>

                <xsl:call-template name="childLanguages">
                      <xsl:with-param name="langid"
                        select="fmp:id_language"/>
                      <xsl:with-param name="indent" select=
                        "$indent + 2"/>
                </xsl:call-template>
          </xsl:for-each>
    </xsl:template>

    <xsl:template name="Indenter">
          <xsl:param name="iIndent"/>
                <xsl:text>  </xsl:text>
                <xsl:if test="$iIndent>0">
                      <xsl:call-template name="Indenter">
                            <xsl:with-param name="iIndent"
                              select="$iIndent - 1"/>
                      </xsl:call-template>
                </xsl:if>
    </xsl:template>
</xsl:stylesheet>
```

Let's see what's going on here. Our first template, as usual, matches <fmp:FMPDSORESULT>, the root element. Here we output all the initial HTML for our page and then open a table. Then we use <xsl:for-each> to loop through all top-level languages, defined as those where id_parent is blank. Things begin to look different inside the <xsl:for-each>. Here we *call* a named template and pass it two parameters called langid and indent.

If you're at all familiar with functions from other languages, you'll understand the concept of parameters. These are named values that you pass off to another routine, usually as inputs to whatever processing it does. In FileMaker, most of the calculations take one or more parameters—the Length function takes one parameter (a field name) while the Left function takes two (field name and length). Here we're calling a template called childLanguages and passing it two parameters: langid, which is the ID of the language currently being processed, and indent, a value that tells us how much to indent the current element. From our top-level nodes, we pass down our own id_language and a current indent of zero.

Let's turn our attention to the childLanguages template proper. Unlike earlier templates, this one uses a name attribute. This is mandatory if we want to call the template by name. It also declares two parameters using an <xsl:param> element. These declarations are mandatory if we want to pass parameters to the template. Let's take a look at what the template actually does.

The template is going to do another <xsl:for-each> using the langid parameter to grab all languages that have langid as their parent. For each of those children, the template then calls another template called Indenter, passing along the indent value that was passed to the childLanguages template. This template simply adds space before the language name. Finally, the language name itself is output, and then, interestingly, the childLanguages template calls itself again. This time, though, it passes in the id_language from the current record and adds two to the indent parameter so that deeper levels of the tree are more deeply indented.

Finally, we can look at the Indenter template. This template really is just a looping construct. It outputs a pair of spaces for each value of $iIndent, meaning that if $iIndent is four, it indents the current name by eight spaces. You can see that it does this by repeatedly calling itself until it has counted from $iIndent backward to zero.

If you're new to recursive functions, you might be puzzled by the fact that childLanguages calls itself. Won't that create an infinite loop? That's a good question, and the answer is that it won't. Every recursion has a terminating condition (namely, a point at which the recursion does not go any deeper). In this case, the terminating condition comes from the fact that childLanguages is called from inside an <xsl:for-each> that operates on all the children of the current node. If the current node has no children, the <xsl:for-each> never gets off the ground, and the inner call to childLanguages doesn't get reached.

This is already pretty nice. Certainly, this kind of output seems a bit easier to achieve using XML than by operations inside FileMaker. Let's add a little refinement, all the same. In our chart, some of the elements, such as Micmac and Yurok, are actual languages. Others, though, are group names, like Arapaho Languages. Is there an easy way to distinguish between them visually?

We can choose any presentation styles for these elements. We just need some way for XSL to decide which records are languages and which are headers. The clear giveaway seems to be that the languages proper don't have children, while the headers do. (In comp-sci terminology, the language records are *leaf nodes* of the tree.) But there is one exception to our rule, the Cree language, which has the Cree-French hybrid Michif underneath it. So, though it's a little inelegant, we're going to say that any record with zero or one child is a leaf node, and we represent it differently. So now we want to write some XSL code that says "if this node has two or more children, represent it one way; otherwise, represent it some other way." Here's the code. It replaces the simple output of fmp:name with a more complex expression:

```
<xsl:choose>
     <xsl:when test="count(/fmp:FMPDSORESULT/fmp:ROW[fmp:id_
       parent=current()/fmp:id_language])&lt;2">
          <span style="color:red;"><xsl:value-of
            select="fmp:name"/></span>
     </xsl:when>
     <xsl:otherwise>
          <xsl:value-of select="fmp:name"/>
     </xsl:otherwise>
</xsl:choose>
```

Here we run into a few more of XSL's flow-of-control constructs. The outermost element is called <xsl:choose>. This element can be used to mimic what other languages call a switch statement, or an if-then-else construct. The <xsl:choose> element can contain any number of <xsl:when> elements and an <xsl:otherwise> element that applies if none of the <xsl:when> elements were used. In FileMaker, this is closest to the Case statement. Each instance of <xsl:when> has a test attribute that contains the logical test for the element. Here, our test is to count all records where the id_parent is equal to the id_language of the current row. We then check to see if that count is less than two. One irritating fact you should notice is that we've written the less-than symbol as <. This special encoding (called an entity reference) is necessary because the less-than symbol is reserved in XSL for opening a tag.

So, our logic here tells XSL to count the children and, if they're fewer than two, output the language name in red; otherwise, output it with no color applied. Now our languages come out in red and our headers in black.

So there you have it—an elegant hierarchical display of FileMaker data. If you feel like that technique made sense and you're game for a challenge, try writing a stylesheet that takes our Herd file and turns it into a family tree. Warning: Since each animal can have two parents instead of just one, it becomes more difficult. If we assume that bison are polygamous and can have more than one mate (which is the case), it becomes more difficult. A nice challenge.

Transforming FileMaker Data into Non-HTML Text Data

So far, all of our examples have demonstrated transformations of FileMaker data into HTML pages. That fits with the web focus of this book, and HTML is also both easy to read and fairly widely known. But, as we said earlier, XSL can produce data in any text format conceived by humanity. Let's look at a very popular format called RTF.

RTF, or Rich Text Format, is a Microsoft technology that was designed to make documents written in Microsoft's Word program more portable over networks. Text is inherently easier to send than the binary data that makes up most proprietary formats. Using RTF, a document can be sent over almost any kind of network connection and reinterpreted at the other end by an RTF-aware application with little risk of the contents being scrambled or misinterpreted. The fact that RTF is a text format is a huge boon to us. It means that we can use XSL to turn FileMaker data into documents that are readable by the widely popular Word program, among others.

This does introduce another speed bump. Just as we have to be able to read and write HTML to produce web pages as our XSL output, we also have to be familiar with the RTF format if we're going to write stylesheets that produce Word documents. But RTF is, frankly, an extremely dense and cryptic notation when compared to HTML. It's not that it can't be mastered, but it requires a bit of work. The RTF specification is available at http://msdn.microsoft.com/library/?url=/library/en-us/dnrtfspec/html/rtfspec.asp?frame=true. One good way to get a sense of what's involved in an RTF document is to take an application that can produce RTF and save a moderately complex document in RTF format. Open the resulting file in a non-RTF-aware text editor and feast your eyes. The odds are that you'll see something like the following repeated for perhaps several pages:

```
\rtf1\mac\ansicpg10000\uc1 \deff4\deflang1033\deflangfe1033{\
  upr{\fonttbl{\f0\fnil\fcharset256\fprq2{\*\panose
  00020206030504050203}Times New Roman;}{\f4\fnil\
  fcharset256\fprq2{\*\panose 00020005000000000000}Times;}
}{\*\ud{\fonttbl{\f0\fnil\fcharset256\fprq2{\*\panose
  00020206030504050203}Times New Roman;}{\f4\fnil\
  fcharset256\fprq2{\*\panose 00020005000000000000}Times;}}}}
```

These are RTF's internal formatting instructions. The good news is that many of them are optional.

It's hard to say more about the RTF code itself without going into a primer on the structure and syntax of RTF. To keep this book manageable, we can't delve into all the details, but here's a stylesheet that turns our list of languages into a lightly formatted RTF file that can be opened and read in Word and other RTF-aware programs (remember to save your output as a file ending with .rtf suffix):

```
<?xml version="1.0" encoding="UTF-8"?>
<xsl:stylesheet version="1.0"
  xmlns:xsl="http://www.w3.org/1999/XSL/Transform"
  xmlns:fmp="http://www.filemaker.com/fmpdsoresult">
     <xsl:output method="text" version="1.0" encoding="UTF-8"
       indent="no"/>
<xsl:template match="fmp:FMPDSORESULT"><xsl:text>{\rtf1\
  ansi\ansicpg10000\uc1 \deff4\deflang1033\deflangfe1033{\upr{\
  fonttbl{\f0\fnil\fcharset256\fprq2{\*\panose
  00020206030504050203}Times New Roman;}{\f4\fnil\
  fcharset256\fprq2{\*\panose 00020005000000000000}Times;}
  }{\*\ud{\fonttbl{\f0\fnil\fcharset256\fprq2{\*\panose
  00020206030504050203}Times New Roman;}{\f4\fnil\
  fcharset256\fprq2{\*\panose 00020005000000000000}Times;}}}}
\deftab288{Partial Tree of Native American Languages \par \par
  </xsl:text>

     <xsl:for-each select="fmp:ROW[fmp:id_parent='']">
               <xsl:value-of select="fmp:name"/>
               <xsl:call-template name="childLanguages">
                    <xsl:with-param name="langid" select="./
                      fmp:id_language"/>
                    <xsl:with-param name="indent" select="0"/>
               </xsl:call-template>
          </xsl:for-each>

          <xsl:text>}}</xsl:text>
     </xsl:template>
<xsl:template name="childLanguages">
          <xsl:param name="langid"/>
          <xsl:param name="indent"/>
          <xsl:for-each select="/fmp:FMPDSORESULT/
            fmp:ROW[fmp:id_parent=$langid]">
                 <xsl:text>\par </xsl:text>
                 <xsl:call-template name="Indenter">
```

```
                    <xsl:with-param name="iIndent"
                      select="$indent"/>
                </xsl:call-template>

                <xsl:choose>
                    <xsl:when test="count(/fmp:FMPDSORESULT/
                      fmp:ROW[fmp:id_parent=current()/
                      fmp:id_language])&lt;2">
                        <xsl:value-of select="fmp:name"/>
                    </xsl:when>
                    <xsl:otherwise>
                        <xsl:value-of select="fmp:name"/>
                    </xsl:otherwise>
                </xsl:choose>
            <xsl:call-template name="childLanguages">
                <xsl:with-param name="langid"
                  select="fmp:id_language"/>
                <xsl:with-param name="indent" select="$indent
                  + 2"/>
            </xsl:call-template>
        </xsl:for-each>
    </xsl:template>

    <xsl:template name="Indenter">
        <xsl:param name="iIndent"/>
            <xsl:text>\tab </xsl:text>
            <xsl:if test="$iIndent>0">
                <xsl:call-template name="Indenter">
                    <xsl:with-param name="iIndent"
                      select="$iIndent - 1"/>
                </xsl:call-template>
            </xsl:if>
    </xsl:template>

</xsl:stylesheet>
```


In fact, it's very similar to our HTML output template. From looking at what gets output, you can see that an RTF file consists of many dense codes wrapped up in nested braces. A typical RTF document is like an HTML document in that, in the simplest terms, it consists of a header and a body. As with HTML, most of what gets output in the template that matches on FMPDSO is header information. Our header is lightweight; the major items it specifies are the RTF version, the list of available fonts, and the character set. Near the end of that template, after the four closing braces, we finish the header and begin the body. The body is also lightweight; there's one command to specify how wide a tab stop is, and then the actual text begins. (For the curious, the tab unit is in "twips," meaning "twentieths of a point," with an inch containing 1440 twips. So these tab stops are .2 inches apart.) From there it's straightforward (except where HTML uses <br>, RTF uses

\par, and where HTML uses spaces to indent, we use \tab). Finally, at the end of the FMPDSO template, we output two closing braces to finish the body first and then the RTF document.

RTF is capable of many advanced formatting techniques. Explaining them all is beyond the scope of this book, but we hope this example has at least whetted your appetite to learn more about RTF and what it can do. In theory, you can publish an entire database as a formatted Word document with a table of contents, clickable cross-references, an index, and more. All that stands between you and glory is the RTF spec, and you know where to find that! With sufficient research into the RTF format, you should be able to turn out documents that take full advantage of indexes, tables of contents, embedded images, and other RTF features.

Resources and References

Books for Learning XML and XSL

- Kurt Cagle et al., *Professional XSL*. Wrox Press, 2001.
- Charles Goldfarb and Paul Prescod, *The XML Handbook*. Prentice Hall, 2000.
- Mark Birbeck, et al, *Professional XML*. Wrox Press, 2001.

Web-based Resources on XML and SGML

- http://www.oasis-open.org/cover/general.html—large compendium of links on XML and SGML
- http://etext.virginia.edu/bin/tei-tocs?div=DIV1&id=SG—introduction to SGML
- http://www.ucc.ie:8080/cocoon/xmlfaq—XML FAQ

"Official" W3C pages on XML and HTML

- http://www.w3.org/XML/
- http://www.w3.org/TR/html4/sgml/dtd.html

Chapter 5

Instant Web Publishing

Instant Web Publishing is a term used to describe FileMaker's ability to generate a web site based on the look and feel of a FileMaker database. It's not that FileMaker produces ready-to-host HTML pages or anything like that. Rather, when you enable Instant Web Publishing, FileMaker responds directly to a web query, and the web user sees the requested data in an interface that's virtually identical to a layout in the FileMaker database itself.

Most books and reference materials that we've seen don't cover Instant Web Publishing very well. They basically rehash the documentation, showing you how to configure the Web Companion and select themes and layouts. Those things are important (and easy), but they don't really give you a sense of what the tool is capable of. We'd like to plumb the depths of Instant Web Publishing. Our approach is to cover the fundamentals quickly and then walk leisurely through creation of a quasi-custom application. We hope to show you a few things along the way that you might not have thought possible with Instant Web Publishing.

If you'd like information about how Instant Web Publishing compares to Custom Web Publishing, please refer to our discussion of that topic in Chapter 3. There you can also find a thorough coverage of using FileMaker's built-in access privileges to protect the Web Companion (and hence, your IWP applications).

Getting Started

The concepts behind Instant Web Publishing are simple. Have FileMaker render layouts that you've developed in FileMaker as web pages. Have the security that you've already set up in FileMaker restrict what web users can do and see. Allow buttons on the web to run FileMaker scripts that affect the behavior of the web site. In short, bring the FileMaker experience to the web.

It's a great concept, and Instant Web Publishing gets stronger with each new release of FileMaker. Layout objects in FileMaker are stored internally as stylesheets that allow them to be rendered almost flawlessly in a browser. The web publishing themes provide an attractive and functional frame for your data. When you use Instant Web Publishing, the Web Companion not only acts as a web server, but it also generates 100 percent of the web interface for you, based on a handful of simple configuration options.

The first step down the IWP path is enabling the Web Companion. We covered this in detail in Chapter 3. It boils down to activating the Web Companion and then allowing each database to be shared to the web. By checking two check boxes, you've web-enabled your FileMaker Pro or FileMaker Pro Unlimited application.

If you've never done this before, we'd recommend trying that now so that you've got an idea of what the "vanilla" configuration gives you. Take an existing or new database (the simpler the better for now), set it to be shared to the web, and then fire up a browser and point to http://localhost/. If you have a static IP address (which you'll need for web serving), you can use that address in place of localhost. If you're not on a network, localhost should work, but in some cases you need to set your TCP/IP settings to a static address, like 10.10.10.10, and then use that in your browser.

If everything is configured properly, you should see a default home page with a list of accessible databases. If you've never used or seen IWP before, we'd urge you again to take ten minutes and do this now before you read any further.

There are a handful of configuration options that affect the look and feel of your IWP applications. Let's look at some of these now.

Home Page Options

When you enable Instant Web Publishing on the Web Companion configuration screen, you can choose to use what's called the "built-in" home page or you can create your own home page. Using the built-in home page, a user who types in the IP address of your server (or you, typing "localhost") sees something like what's shown in Figure 5.1.

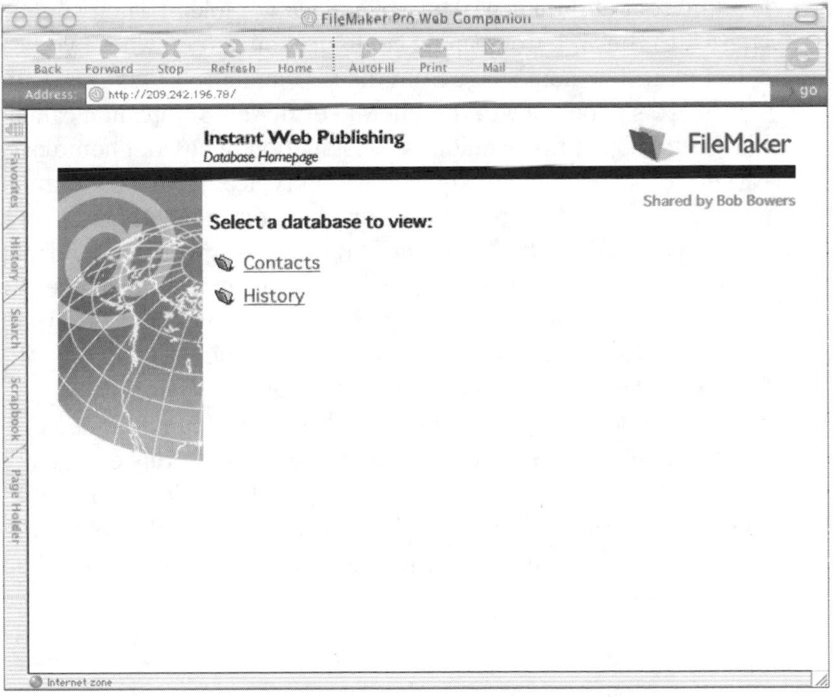

Figure 5.1

There are two ways to prevent open databases from appearing on this list. The first is to set those particular tables to not share to the web (this is part of the File>Sharing setup). The other way is to put an underscore at the end of the table name (i.e., contact_.fp5 instead of contact.fp5).

Creating Your Own Home Page

If you prefer that your web users see a different home page than the "built-in" screen shown in Figure 5.1, you can build a home page yourself and have IWP display that instead. If you have any experience at all creating web pages, it is fairly easy to build your own custom home page. Creating your own home page allows you to customize the look of the page with your own graphics, text, and links. You also have control over which databases are accessible and the ability to create links not only to the IWP form view (which is where the links on the built-in home page go) but also to any of the other IWP views (search, table, and new record).

Once you've built a new home page, put it in the Web folder, which is at the root of the FileMaker Pro application folder. Then you need to go back to the Web Companion configuration screen where you can select your new home page from the pop-up list.

There's a tool new to the FileMaker 6 Web Companion called the WebPortal object that facilitates construction of custom home pages. In earlier versions of FileMaker, you would typically build custom home pages by copying the complicated links generated by the built-in home page. The WebPortal is a JavaScript object that gives you information about the databases shared to the Web Companion. You can get the table names from it, the host user name, and most importantly, fully formed URLs to each of the views of each of your tables. It greatly facilitates the creation of custom home pages.

Let's look now at a simple example of how you might use the WebPortal object to create a custom home page. In this example, let's pretend that you have a database of rare books (called books.fp5) that you want visitors to your web site to be able to search. Let's start by creating a shell for the page with placeholders that we'll come back to later and replace with some fancy code.

```
<html>
<head>
     <title>Welcome!</title>
</head>
<body>
<br><br><br><br>
<table width=60% align=center>
<tr>
     <td align=center>
          <h1>Welcome to the Rare Book Emporium </h1><br><br>
          <h3>Please click on the link below to search our
            collection</h3>
<br><br>
     </td>
</tr>
<tr>
     <td align=center>
          <!--Here's where we want a link to the IWP search view-->
     </td>
</tr>
```

```
</table>
</body>
</html>
```

Save this page as home.htm, put it in the web directory, and configure the Web Companion to use that as its home page. It's a good idea to test at this point to make sure that you've got everything wired properly. That way, when you start adding code and something doesn't work, you know it's your code and not a configuration issue. Our fledgling page in its current state is shown in Figure 5.2.

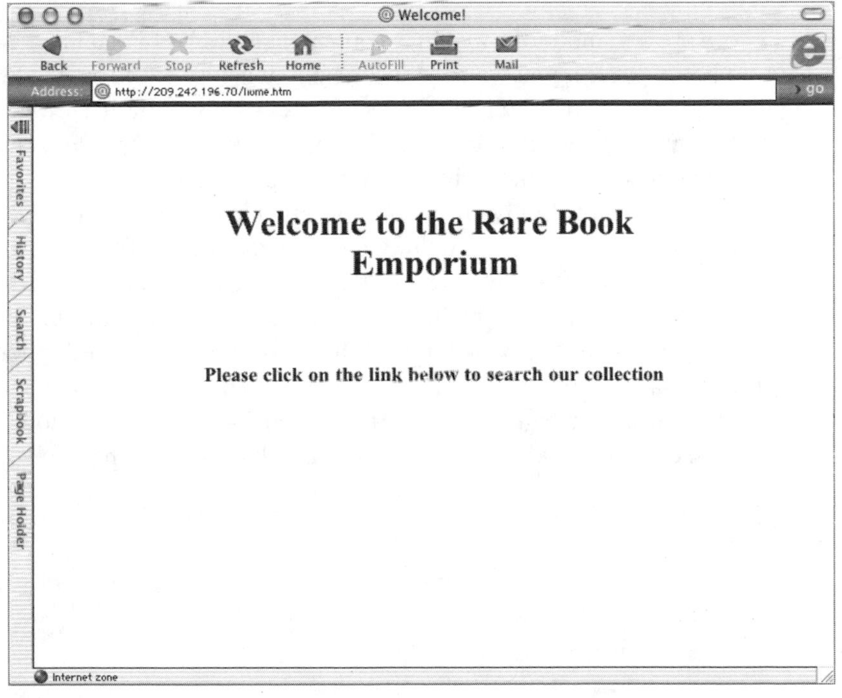

Figure 5.2

Now to the fun part. In order to generate the WebPortal object, insert the following line of code in the <head> portion of your page:

```
<script language="JavaScript" SRC="FMPro?-webportal"></script>
```

With that in place, every time this page loads, the Web Companion is queried for information about its shared databases; it returns a JavaScript object that you have access to for the remainder of the page. If you're curious to see exactly what it returns, just type http://<your IP address>/FMPro?-webportal into your browser.

The WebPortal object has the following properties:

- **window.webportal.databases**: An array containing the name of your databases and URLs to the various views. The elements of the array are name, defaultURL, formViewURL, tableViewURL, searchViewURL, and newViewURL.
- **window.webportal.username**: The identity of the FileMaker Pro host
- **window.webportal.language**: A code representing the language selected on the Web Companion configuration screen

There are a number of ways that you can use the WebPortal in a custom home page. If you want, you can simply list all of the available databases and allow the user to select links to any of their views. In our example, we want to confirm that our books.fp5 database is available, and if so, we'd like to build a link to its search page.

If you are absolutely sure that you only have one database available, you can simply use window.webportal.databases[0] to refer to that database. In the likelier event that there are several hosted databases, you won't know which position in the database array contains information about the books.fp5 database. We therefore need to look through each item in the array for our table. The following JavaScript function, which also goes in the <head> portion of the page, looks for the books database and builds a dynamic link to its search page.

```
function BooksSearchLink() {
     j= -1;
     for (i in window.webportal.databases) {
          if (window.webportal.databases[i].name == "books") {
               j = i;
          }
     }

     if (j == -1) {
          link = "<b>The collection is temporarily unavailable.
            Please try again later.</b>";
     } else {
          link = "<A HREF = /FMRes/" + window.webportal.data-
            bases[j].searchViewURL + ">Search</A>"
     }

     document.write (link);
}
```

If for any reason the books.fp5 database is unavailable, instead of a link to nowhere, the user is notified that the collection is unavailable. Another nice feature of building the page this way (as opposed to hard-coding a link yourself) is that if you ever decide to use a different layout in your database as the search view, the web site automatically and immediately reflects that change.

The only thing left to do to finish our custom home page is to call the BooksSearchLink function at the appropriate place in the body of the page. The full, final code is shown below.

```
<html>
<head>
     <title>Welcome!</title>
     <script language="JavaScript" SRC="FMPro?-webportal"></script>
     <script language="JavaScript">

     function BooksSearchLink() {
          j= -1;
          for (i in window.webportal.databases) {
               if (window.webportal.databases[i].name == "books") {
                    j = i;
               }
          }
          if (j == -1) {
               link = "<b>The collection is temporarily unavailable.
                 Please try again later</b>";
          } else {
               link = "<A HREF = /FMRes/" + window.webportal.data-
                 bases[j].searchViewURL + ">Search</A>"
          }
          document.write (link);
}
     </script>
</head>
<body>
<br><br><br><br>
<table width=60% align=center>
     <tr>
          <td align=center>
               <h1>Welcome to the Rare Book Emporium</h1>
               <br><br>
               <h3>Please click on the link below to search our
                 collection</h3>
               <br><br>
          </td>
     </tr>
     <tr>
          <td align=center>
               <script language="JavaScript">
                    BooksSearchLink();
               </script>
          </td>
     </tr>
</table>
```

```
</body>
</html>
```

Later in this chapter, we look at another method for creating your own home page. There, we actually use a FileMaker layout itself as the home page. For now, satisfied with the job that the WebPortal has done for us, we turn our attention to selecting styles and views.

Selecting a Style

For each database that you publish to the web using Instant Web Publishing, you can select a web style that determines the look of your site. To select a style, go to the File>Sharing screen (see Figure 5.3), highlight Web Companion under Companion Sharing, and select Set Up Views.

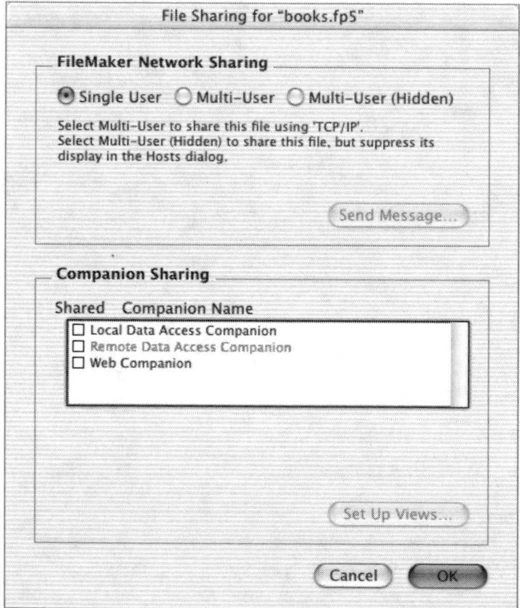

Figure 5.3

You then arrive at the Web Companion View Setup, the first screen of which is shown in Figure 5.4.

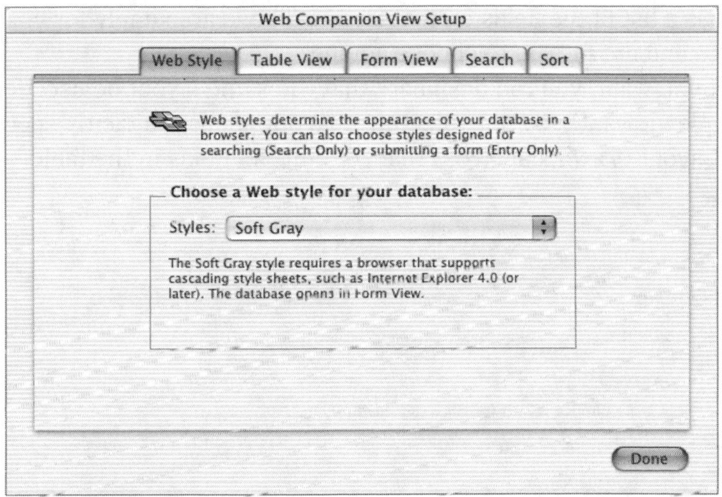

Figure 5.4

As you select a style from the drop-down list of choices, you see a brief description of the style and any browser restrictions that you need to be aware of. Most of the styles require a browser that supports Cascading Style Sheets, as those allow the Web Companion to accurately recreate your FileMaker layouts. In fact, only Fern Green and Blue and Gold 2 work with older browsers (before Internet Explorer 4/Netscape Navigator 3).

The Soft Gray, Lavender, and Wheat styles are very similar; they differ only in their color schemes. They are probably the most popular styles for Instant Web Publishing. The Search Only style restricts users to the Form View, Table View, and Search pages. Similarly, the Entry Only style confines users to the New Records page.

Selecting Your Views

Once you've selected a style, you're ready to move on to selecting your views. The middle three tabs in the Web Companion View Setup allow you to specify which layout FileMaker should render in response to IWP requests. The Table View layout (see Figure 5.5) is used anytime FileMaker needs to display sets of records, such as in response to a query. The Form View is used to display single records. You also select a layout as a Search page, but that layout is not rendered as-is on the web like Form View and Table View layouts. Instead, select a layout merely as a way of specifying which fields should be searchable. On each of the tabs, when you select a layout from the drop-down list, there is a list of the fields on that layout. Those are simply for your reference and not for you to choose among.

If you want, you can designate that the same layout be used for multiple views. Or, by not selecting a layout at all, you tacitly specify that Layout 0, a virtual layout that contains all fields in the table, is used.

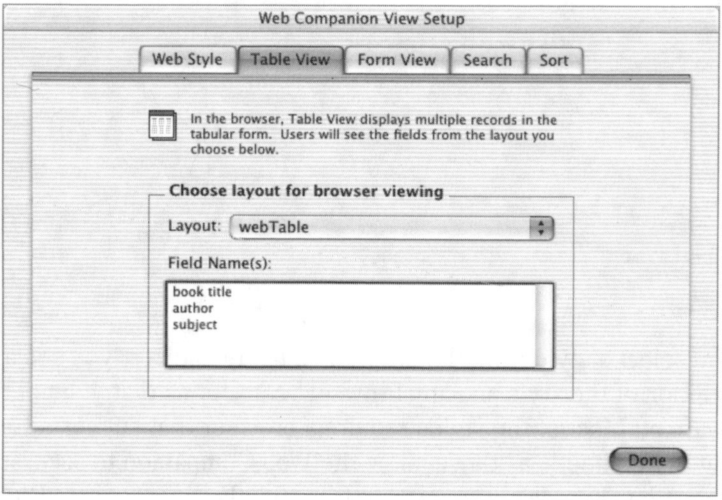

Figure 5.5

We recommend that you select layouts that you've specifically designed for the web. For the Table View, it doesn't matter what your layout looks like as a form or list in FileMaker. On the web, the fields on the selected layout are presented as a simple table. We find that it's best to choose as your Table View a layout that contains only the three to five most salient fields from a record. Including too many fields causes the data to extend off the edge of the browser window and look sloppy. Web users are unable to do any data editing or entry on the Table View itself. Clicking on a row in the Table View always takes the user to the Form View.

The Form View is where you can let loose your FileMaker layout design talents. We do have a few tips, however, on how to make layouts that look good in a browser:

- Use a white background for your parts. If you use a color and the user has a browser window larger than the part, they see white at the bottom. Making big parts to compensate only allows the user to scroll meaninglessly.
- Use colors and fonts that complement the style that you choose.

- Put a little more space between objects than you usually do. The browser doesn't always line up everything perfectly, so a little wiggle room helps.
- Don't put objects against the top or left edge of the layout. Because the style adds top and left elements, it looks best to have a bit of white space between them and your data.
- Put instructions on your layout that help users understand how to use the page.
- Don't use complicated layering of elements, as you run the risk that something won't quite line up right in the browser. Similarly, 3D effects don't render nicely on certain platforms and browsers.
- Be careful using field borders or placing boxes behind your fields. They may look great on the regular Form View, but clicking on any data entry field transforms the screen into an edit mode. In Edit mode, all data fields appear as either regular input fields or pop-up lists (if it has a value list attached to it on that layout). The edges of the input fields don't always line up with your field borders and background boxes on the web.
- When setting up a layout for your Table View, be sure to go into the Layout Options and set up the Table View in FileMaker to show the header and footer if you'd like to have those displayed on the web. The option to have the column headers act as sort buttons carries over to the web as well.

In the end, of course, nothing is better than trial and error. It's a good idea also to view your site from a few different machines and browsers.

The final bit of customization that you can do on the Web Companion View Setup screen is to select a sort option. As shown in Figure 5.6, there are three options you can choose from:

- You can choose not to allow sorting (in which case the link never appears).
- You can specify a set of fields that users can choose for sorting records displayed in the Form and Table Views.
- You can hard-code the sort order that you want the records to be sorted in. In this case, again, the Sort button disappears from the interface.

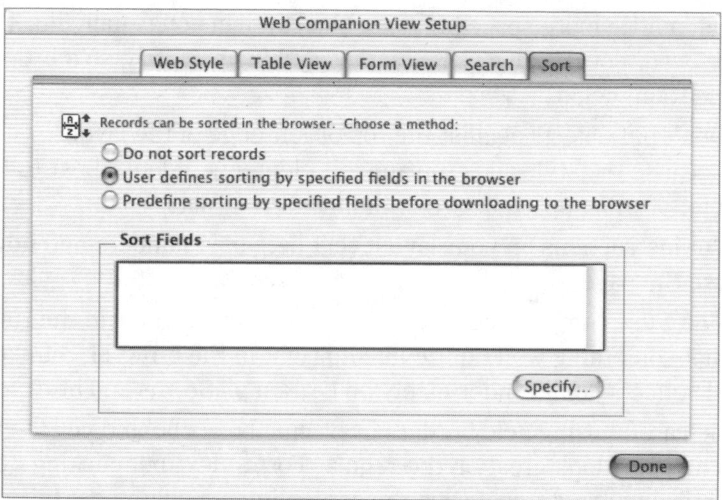

Figure 5.6

We caution you against the third option if you have large record sets. In such cases, forcing a sort before every download to the browser could slow your site substantially.

Layout Elements on the Web

The Web Companion does a great job of building web pages that look almost identical to your FileMaker layouts. Nonetheless, there are a few elements whose behavior on the web merits additional discussion.

Container Fields

There are no problems displaying images stored in container fields on your web page. FileMaker turns them into JPEGs on the fly. But web users are unable to put new images into container fields. In case you're curious, all of the graphic formatting options for alignment, cropping, and maintaining original proportions carry over perfectly to the web.

Value Lists

If you attach a value list to a field on any of your web layouts, those value lists display in the web browser as well. There are often a few minor formatting issues, however. For instance, pop-up lists and pop-up menus both render as pop-up menus. Lengthy check box and radio button lists display nicely as aligned columns in FileMaker. On the web, they lose their columnar shape and can appear very messy. Functionally, there are a few minor differences as well. The option to display Other as a choice with radio buttons and check boxes does not work on the web, nor does the Edit option. More importantly, if you've built a value list dynamically using the contents of a field and also selected the option to display another field (i.e., so your pick list has both part IDs and part names displayed), only the first value is displayed on the web. This can be a real nuisance. Building a calculation field that combines the two fields and using that field may seem like a good workaround, but keep in mind that the entire calculation is set into your field (not just the first value, as it is in FileMaker).

Field Formatting

Field formatting options that you set for number, date, and text fields should carry over to the web nicely. For instance, you can set a number to display using a currency symbol, right-align text in a field, and use custom date formats with no fear. Font, size, and color are also translated well.

Merge Fields

Text blocks that contain merge fields do not show up on your web layouts.

Portals

Portals display wonderfully using Instant Web Publishing. They can even have alternating row coloring and scroll bars. Best of all, when you drop into Edit mode, you can edit the content of multiple portal rows and even add a new related record through the portal.

Scripting

As if rendering FileMaker layouts on the web wasn't cool enough, the Web Companion also turns any buttons on your web layouts into clickable links. This allows you to use FileMaker's ScriptMaker to add functionality to your site. Only a small number of scripts steps are currently supported from the web, and most of them act a bit differently in IWP than they do normally in FileMaker.

Don't confuse IWP scripting and calling scripts from Custom Web Publishing applications.

When you call a script using CWP, you're in effect asking the host machine to run the script as if there were a user sitting at the machine. The script can be as long or as complex as you need it to be.

Scripting for Instant Web Publishing is very different. When a layout is requested via IWP, the scripts attached to your buttons are converted into JavaScript instructions for formulating a URL to which the Web Companion can respond. For instance, let's say that you have a button on your layout that calls the Sort script step. Clicking it from the web does not actually sort a darned thing. Instead, it takes you to the Sort page, as if you'd clicked the Sort button in the IWP frame. Nothing happens on the host workstation.

Besides having only a few commands at your disposal, there are some severe restrictions on the length of your scripts as well. In order to run from the web, your buttons can be connected to valid single script steps or to scripts of one to three lines long. Anything after the third line of a script is ignored. Also, the Web Companion stops reading as soon as it finds any unsupported script steps. So, since Beep isn't a supported script step, a script that went Sort, Beep would work, but not one that went Beep, Sort.

An important further restriction is that your script must include a change of mode, layout, or current record.

The following is a list of the IWP-supported script steps and a description of their behavior. Some script steps cannot be used in combination with other steps in multi-line scripts. Those that can are indicated with a "Yes" in the Multi column in the table below.

Script Step	Comments	Multi
Open	This allows you to navigate to another database. It's just like you've clicked on that table from the IWP home page. The specified database must be open and shared to the web on the host machine.	
Open URL	This creates a hyperlink to whatever address you've specified. You need to specify a full address, including the http://.	
Go to Layout	This takes you to a web version of whatever layout you've specified. Using Go to Layout extends your solution beyond the three layouts that you can specify in the View Setup screens.	Yes
Go to Related Record	This jumps you to the related set of records through the specified relationship. The other database must be open and shared to the web.	
Go to Record/Request/Page	The options to go to First, Last, Next, and Previous all function the way that you'd expect them to.	Yes
Go to Field	Changes to Edit mode	Yes
New Record Request	Changes to New Record mode	Yes
Enter Browse Mode	Navigates to the Form View defined for the database	Yes
Enter Find Mode	Navigates to the Search page defined for the database	Yes

Script Step	Comments	Multi
Show All Records	As you'd expect, this keeps the current view but with a found set of all records.	
Perform Find	Submits a search request. It doesn't care about any requests that you might have saved with the script.	
Exit Record	Submits a new record request, an edit request, or a search request, and automatically navigates back to the Form View	
Sort	Navigates to the Sort page	
Delete Record/Request	Deletes the current record. It can't be part of a script; it must be called directly by a button. It's performed with or without a dialog, as specified by the script step parameter.	
View as Table	View current layout as Table	Yes
View as Form	View current layout as Form	Yes
View as List	View current layout as Table	Yes
View as Cycle	Toggles between Form View and Table View	Yes
Open Help	Opens a new browser window with help for users on navigating using the Instant Web Companion tools	

In the next section we build an actual application using Instant Web Publishing, and we have occasion to write several scripts that further explain their use and behavior.

Building a Customized IWP Application

Most developers, when they think about Instant Web Publishing, think about a tool full of limitations. They appreciate its ease—select a style, select a few layouts—but lament the lack of control and extensibility. They are often surprised to discover that there's another facet to Instant Web Publishing, one that in fact provides a great deal of programmability.

To show you this other facet of IWP, we're going to use IWP tools to build a complete web application. It doesn't rival the complexity of the custom web apps we build later in the book, but it hopefully gives you some idea of the scope of applications that you can build with IWP.

For the inspiration for our application, we return to the fictional company that we invented in Chapter 1—Blue Horizon Bison Breeders. The breeders spend most of their time at the company's headquarters, but they also spend a lot of time on the road. For a contact management system, the company uses a simple FileMaker Pro database system that consists of two files, Contacts.fp5 and History.fp5. Contacts contains standard name, address, and phone info. History records notes from communications with a contact. They'd like to make the system available as part of their company intranet but don't want to spend a lot of time or money having a custom web solution developed. Let's see what they might accomplish in just a few hours using Instant Web Publishing.

Hiding the Frame

As we've discussed, one of the features of Instant Web Publishing is a built-in navigation frame. You can change the appearance of the frame some by selecting a different style, but that's the extent of your customization. You can't change the order of the links, add links, or insert your logo. Essentially, you're giving up flexibility in exchange for ease of use and development time.

If you'd like, however, you can get rid of the frame entirely. By doing so, you take responsibility for providing the user with all of the navigation that they need, and that's no trivial task. We think the increase in flexibility is well worth the effort. Once the frame is gone, what the web user sees in his browser is your exact FileMaker layout. You're in total control of the look, feel, and functionality. The constraints are those imposed by what you can and can't script, which we discussed in the previous section.

Turning the IWP frame off is trivial. Simply create a script with a single step—Toggle Status Area[Hide]—and set that script as a startup script. Do that by going under Edit>Preferences>Document, as shown in Figure 5.7. This signals to the Web Companion that it shouldn't include the navigation frame as it assembles web pages. The startup script is called with each and every IWP request to that database. If you have multiple tables in your solution, you want to set up this same startup script in each of them to ensure that navigating between databases doesn't inadvertently reactivate the frame.

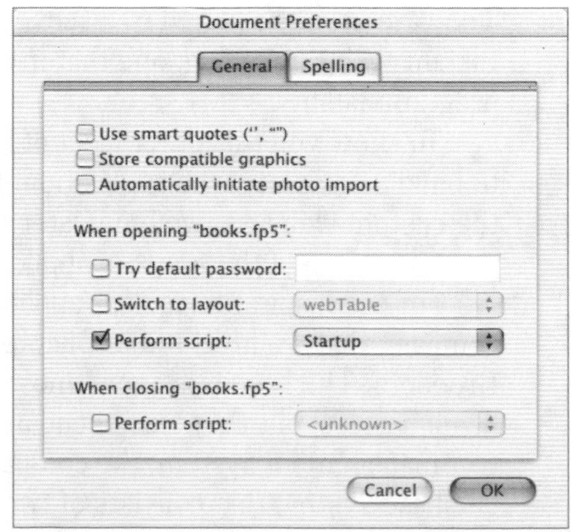

Figure 5.7

Using a Layout as Your Home Page

Earlier, we discussed how you can create your own home page and embed links to IWP-generated pages using JavaScript. There's also an easy way to use one of your FileMaker layouts as a home page, and that's what we do for the Bison Breeders WebContacts application. In a nutshell, our home page becomes a small HTML page that contains a redirect to a URL that renders one of our layouts.

First, let's look at the FileMaker layout that we want to use as our home page. It's shown in Figure 5.8. It's nothing fancy, but it's much easier to design a page using FileMaker's layout tools than any web-authoring tool we've ever used.

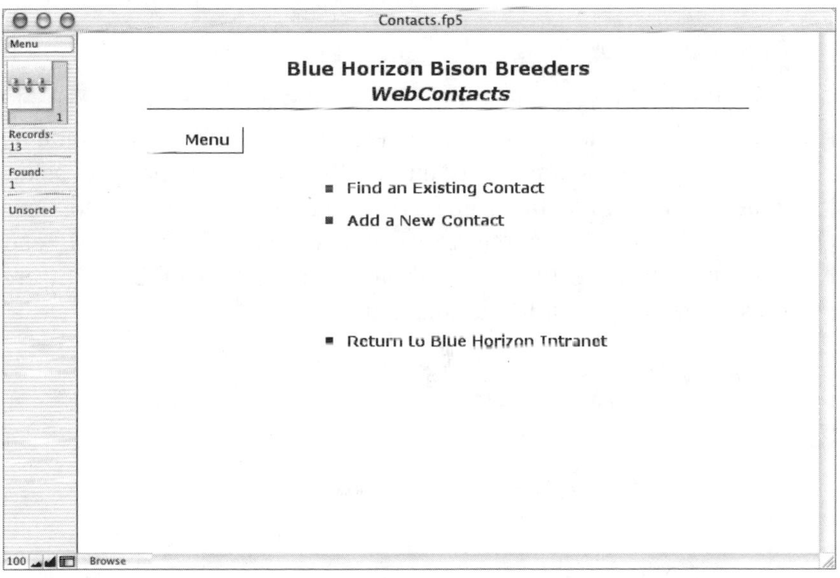

Figure 5.8

Next you need to determine the URL that displays this layout on the web. You might be able to deduce the logic of IWP URLs, but that's hardly necessary. If you temporarily configure the database to use this layout as its Form View and tell the Web Companion to use its built-in home page, you can simply copy the URL generated when you click the link from the home page. In our case, that URL is:

```
http://<your IP address>/FMRes/FMPJS?-db=Contacts.fp5&-layID=
  7&-token=25&-max=1&-format=formvwcss.htm&-mode=browse&-findall
```

Armed with this information, we're ready to create the redirect page. Let's call our new home page start.html. The entire page is as follows:

```
<html>
<head>
<title>Page Loading...</title>
<meta http-equiv="Refresh" Content="0; URL=/FMRes/FMPJS?-db=
  Contacts.fp5&-layID=7&-token=25&-max=1&-format=
  formvwcss.htm&-mode=browse&-findall">

</head>
<body>
<br><br><br>
<center>
<h3>One moment while the page loads...</h3>
</center>
</body>
</html>
```

After saving this document in the web directory of our host machine, we configure the Web Companion to use start.html as its home page. Now, anyone going to our IP address briefly sees a message asking them to wait while the page loads, and then they see our wonderful menu. These two screens are shown in Figures 5.9 and 5.10, respectively. Remember that we've already hidden the IWP frame by creating a startup script that hides the status area.

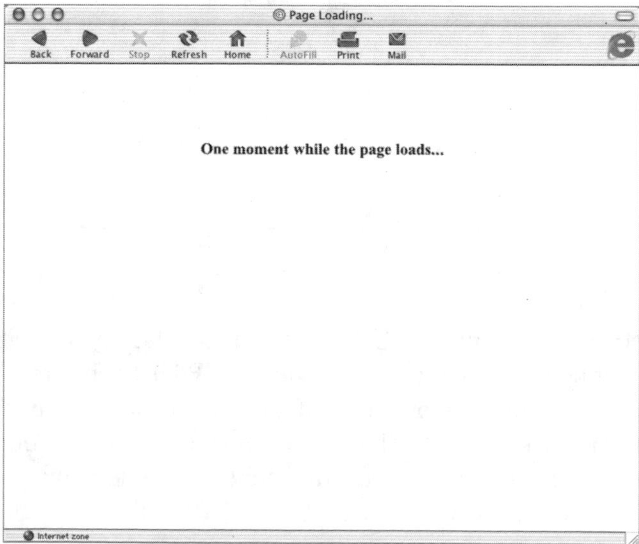

Figure 5.9

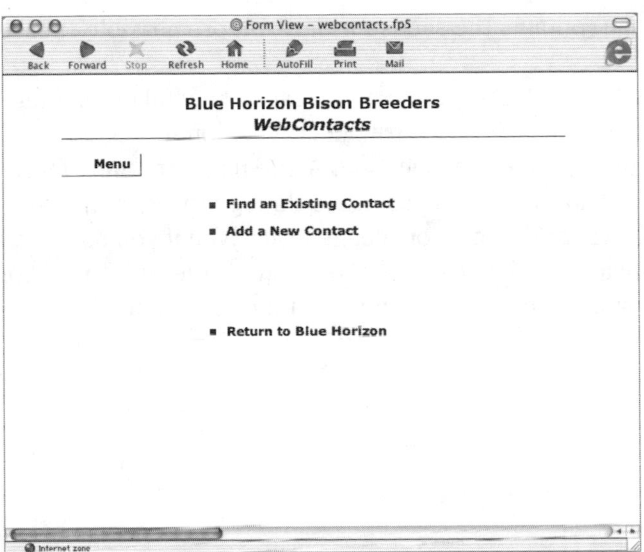

Figure 5.10

Planning the Site

With the home page in place, it's now time to think about functionality. We find it helpful to conceptualize our layouts as web pages and plan in advance the navigation from place to place. But know that designing web pages that flow well is very different from designing intuitive FileMaker solutions. In FileMaker, the same layout can easily be used for a variety of purposes, such as displaying, editing, or finding records, and there usually isn't a prescribed path through a system. In the majority of FileMaker solutions, users can switch layouts using the pop-up in the status area, they can move from table to table via the Window menu, and they can use menu commands or keyboard shortcuts to perform actions such as deleting or duplicating records. You can certainly create FileMaker systems with more user constraints, but the point is that you don't have to.

Web sites require more structure. If a user should have the ability to move from point A to point B or to perform some action, then you have to create a mechanism for him to do so. On the web, you must think in terms of requests and responses. A user submits a request for a set of records from a search page; the response is a list of records. A user requests a new record; the response is a blank form that the user needs to fill out. A user requests that his new record be submitted; the response contains the record data as a read-only form. Usually, each response page contains the seeds for one or more possible subsequent requests.

For the WebContacts system, we create a handful of FileMaker layouts, each of which serves a particular function. In Figure 5.11, you can see a site map for our application. A site map is nothing more than an overview of how a user can navigate through the system. It's a schematic of where the links on a page lead. Even if you don't create formal site maps suitable for display on your mother's refrigerator, a site map is an indispensable tool for creating web applications.

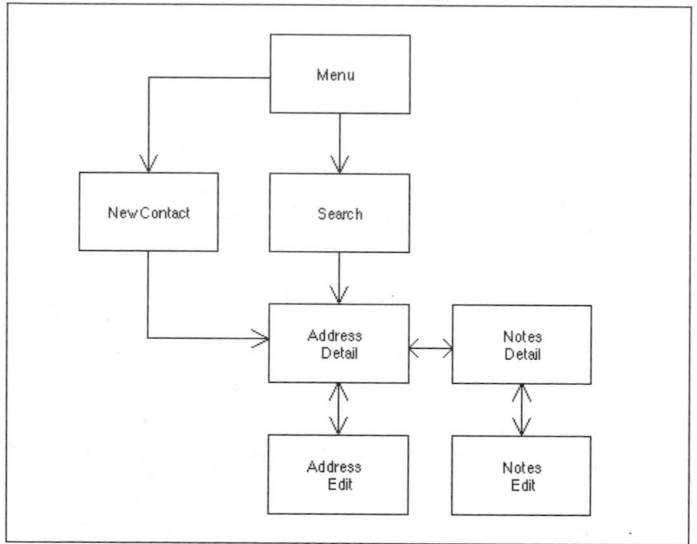

Figure 5.11

You can download the databases that we used for the WebContact system from www.wordware.com/files/fmweb and www.moyergroup.com/webbook. We suggest that you take the time to download them to your system and try them out. They're fully editable, so they also provide a place for you to play around and learn firsthand how FileMaker scripts work in IWP.

We don't describe in detail every button or layout of the solution. That would become tedious quickly. Rather, we look closely at a few of the key functional areas, and you can explore the rest of the screens at your leisure using the demo files.

The Search Routine

The first routine that we investigate is the search routine, which begins when the user clicks Find an Existing Contact from the main menu. Of course, before that link can be enabled, we must first build the destination layout/page so that we have some place to actually link to.

All you need for this is a FileMaker layout that contains the fields that you want to allow the user to search on. In our demo system, we've decided that searching on first or last name, city, or state is sufficient to find a set of contacts. Our search layout is shown in Figure 5.12. Even though we're just at the point of navigating *to* the search screen, you can see that we've stubbed in buttons that are eventually used to perform the find. Those buttons do absolutely nothing at this point, but they help us remember where we're headed.

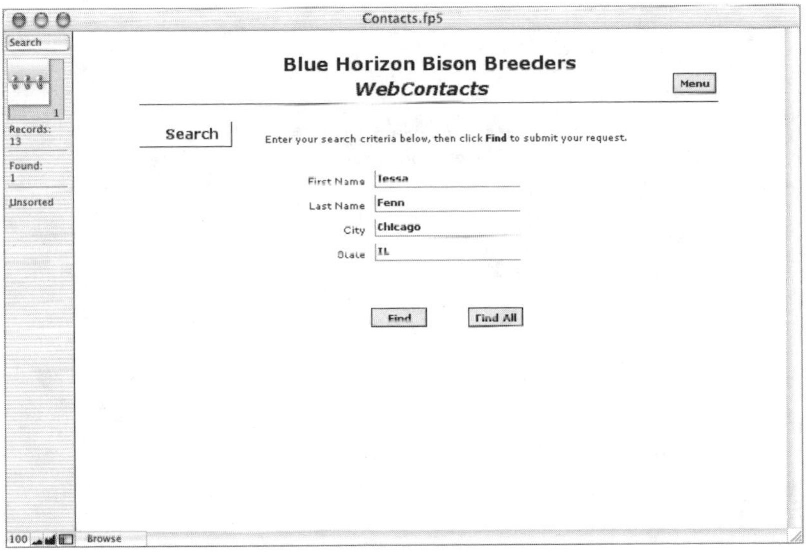

Figure 5.12

So how does the user manage to get from the menu to the search screen? If we were creating static HTML web pages, we'd create a hyperlink from one page to the other. But since we're using Instant Web Publishing, all we need to do is create a FileMaker script! All of the scripts that we are creating are quite simple, and none are more than three lines long. Keep in mind that some script steps behave differently for the Instant Web Publishing engine than they normally do.

You might find it helpful to refer back to our IWP scripting section from time to time.

We call our new script Go to Search Page, and we attach it to the top link on our menu layout. The script is simply the following two steps:

```
Go to Layout ["Search"]
Enter Find Mode
```

It doesn't make a bit of difference whether you choose the options to Restore Find Requests or Pause for the Enter Find Mode step. These are ignored for IWP purposes. There's of course no such thing as Find mode in a web browser. What FileMaker is doing is simply creating a form where the user can enter some text. That text is not turned into an actual find request until that form is submitted.

Figure 5.13 shows what the user will see in her browser when she clicks on the link.

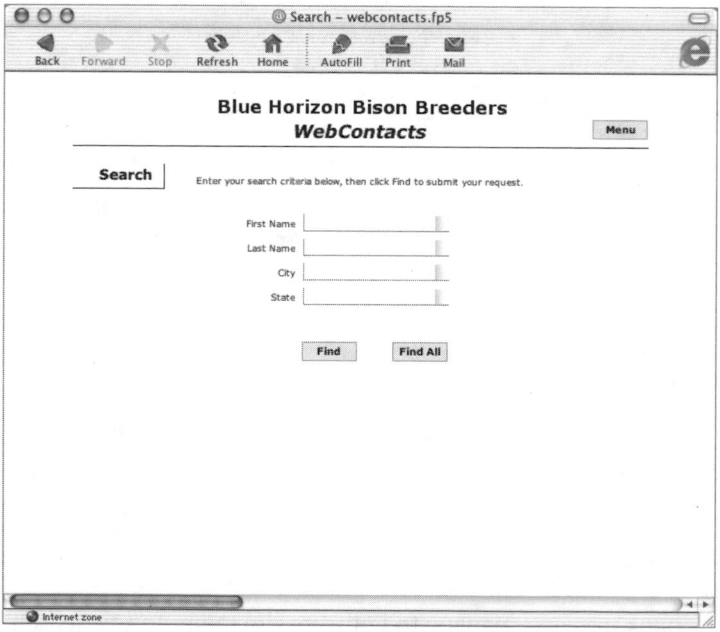

Figure 5.13

In case you're curious, the link from the menu to the search page was transmuted into the following link by the Web Companion:

```
http://localhost/FMRes/FMPJS?-db=Contacts.fp5&-layid=9&-format
  =searchcss.htm&-max=1&-token.0=25&-token.1=9&-mode=search&-lop=
  and&-findall
```

The "-layid" tells the Web Companion which layout to render, and the "-format" and "-mode" values tell it to render it as a search form.

Anytime you're in Find mode using IWP, clicking into one of the search fields brings up a palette of search options. All of the options available in FileMaker—from "..." for ranges to "!" for duplicates—are available to the user. It might seem trivial and hardly worth our mention, but if you had to create functionality like that from scratch in a typical web app, you'd know it was hardly trivial. There's no way to disable the search option palette, and that's something that you'll probably start to wish for. Although it adds fantastic functionality, it can get in the way sometimes.

Once our user is at the search page, we're going to give her three options for how to proceed: She can return to the menu (canceling the search), she can enter some search criteria and select Find, or she can select Find All. All of these actions can be accomplished through FileMaker scripting.

The script to return to the menu is very similar to the first script that we wrote:

```
Go to Layout ["Menu"]
Enter Browse Mode
```

The Find script needs to submit the user's request and go to the detail page (which we explore in a moment):

```
Perform Find
Go to Layout ["Address Detail"]
Enter Browse Mode
```

The Find All script is predictably similar:

```
Show All Records
Go to Layout ["Address Detail"]
Enter Browse Mode
```

The Perform Find step tells the Web Companion that it should take the form parameters of the submitted page and consider them to be a find request (as opposed to, say, considering them to be a new record). You must be in Search mode for a Perform Find to do anything. On a page where the mode is Browse or Table, a button with a Perform Find would not even be an active link.

You might wonder if the Enter Browse Mode at the end of each of these is redundant. It would be, of course, if this was a straight FileMaker script. On the web, however, after a Find is performed, the default mode is Table mode. We find that Table mode is unsuitable as a web tool, and so we go directly to a Form View instead.

There are three reasons that we avoid Table View. The first is an aesthetic reason; you can't customize a table view enough to make it look like it's part of your solution. You can put a header on a Table View layout, but you can't edit the column labels, you can't move the table away from the left edge of the browser, and you can't put fields in any arrangement other than side by side. So, it's really impossible to create a typical web-like hit list that users have come to expect from the web. Figure 5.14 shows what a table view might look like as a search results screen.

Figure 5.14

Lest you think we're just being petty to quibble over the interface, the second reason we avoid Table View is that you can't navigate off it well. Clicking a row in Table View automatically switches you to Browse mode on the same layout. You can't put a script over the row that, say, navigates to a different detail layout and goes to Browse mode.

The third reason is another functional issue. Without the IWP frame, there's no way to limit the result to a given number of records and have next and previous links to move through the found set (as you typically want on a hit list). Actually, instead of returning all of the records as one big set, the Table View automatically limits the set to

25 records. With no way to navigate, you'd never be able to see result records other than the first 25.

This concludes our discussion of the search routine. We turn next to the address detail screens and learn how to edit records.

Detail and Update Pages

In FileMaker, any time you're viewing a record, you're probably also going to be able to edit that record by clicking into a field. When you're done editing, you need to click out of the field or do something else to exit the record, and your changes are automatically saved.

That model doesn't translate well to the web. After making changes to a record, a user explicitly needs to submit that record through the browser to the Web Companion. The question then becomes whether you want the user to be in a perpetual edit mode or whether you'd rather differentiate between Browse and Edit modes. We think the latter is more web-like and makes for a better user experience. But it means a bit more development work to make this happen.

First, let's create some layouts to use for Browse mode. We can probably fit both the contact information and the note history on the same layout, but we thought it would be educational to show a tabbed interface implemented on the web. Figure 5.15 shows the layout that we came up with for browsing addresses, and Figure 5.16 shows the one we use for viewing notes.

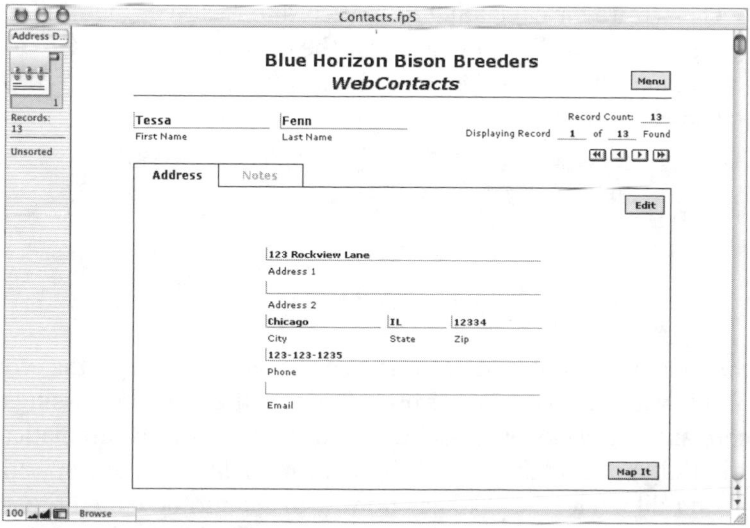

Figure 5.15

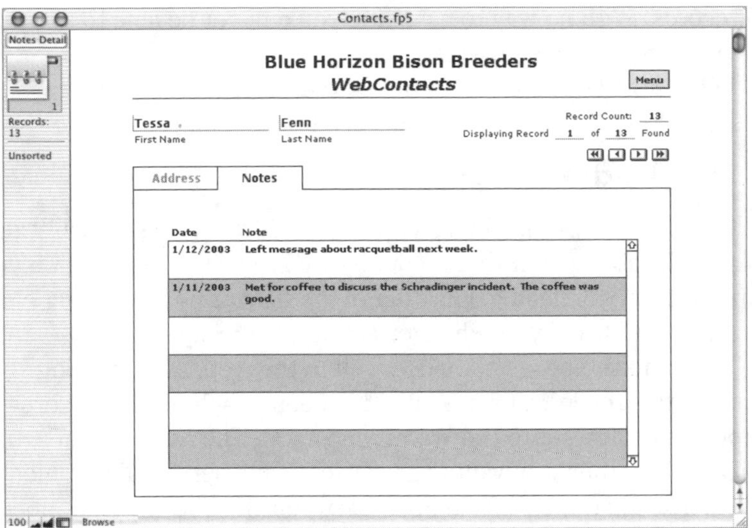

Figure 5.16

On both layouts, the Menu button runs the same script that we used earlier to get back from the Search page to the menu. The record counts in the top right were created as calculation fields that use basic Status functions: Status(CurrentRecordCount), Status(Current-FoundCount), and Status(CurrentRecordNumber). Remember that you should set calculations that reference status fields explicitly to be unstored so they keep updating.

The arrows for navigating from record to record call four different single step scripts. They're each just the obvious variant of Go to Record/Request/Page []. The tabs themselves are buttons set to call the following scripts:

```
Go to Notes Detail:
     Go to Layout ["Notes Detail"]
     Enter Browse Mode []

Go to Address Detail:
     Go to Layout ["Address Detail"]
     Enter Browse Mode []
```

Before looking at the Edit buttons, there's one other thing that you probably want to do on your browse layouts. If a user is browsing a record and she clicks on a field that allows entry, she is automatically put in Edit mode on the same layout. That might not sound so bad, but once in Edit mode, the user has no way to submit the edited record. We think the best way to avoid this is to set all of the fields on the browse layouts to not allow entry. (You do that by selecting the fields, going to Field Format, and unchecking the Allow Entry into field check box.)

By creating these two layouts and writing a few simple navigation scripts, a user should be able to perform a search (or find all records) at this point and easily comb through the search results. Figures 5.17 and 5.18 show how well the two browse layouts translated to the web. Without the status bar on the FileMaker screens and the button bar at the top of the web screens, it would be pretty darn tough to tell the two sets apart, wouldn't it?

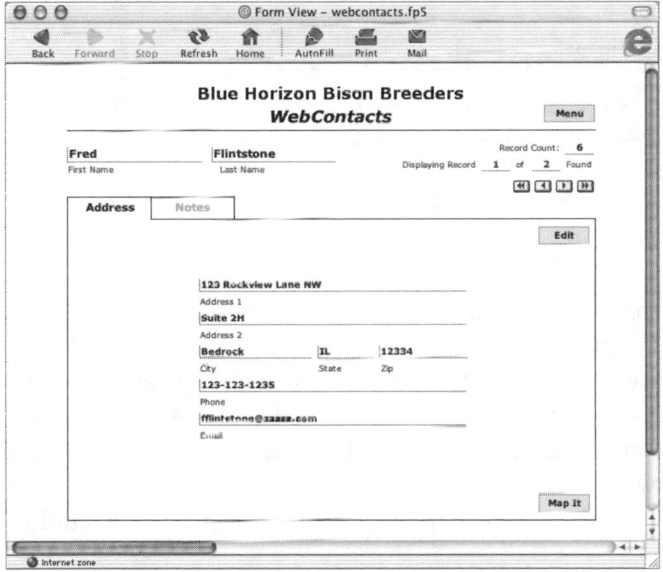

Figure 5.17

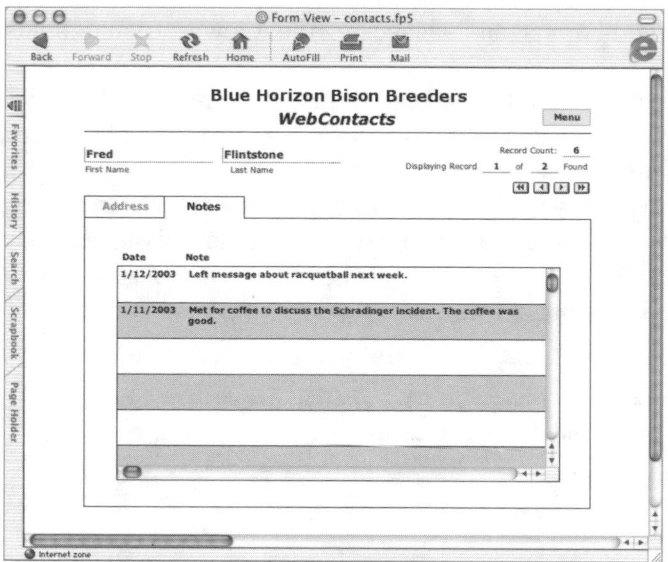

Figure 5.18

With the browse layouts already built, the edit screens are very easy to make. Just copy the layouts, turn on the ability to enter fields, and do a bit of scripting. Notice that we've also taken off the navigation tools. The idea is that a user drops into Edit mode, and the only way out is either to submit the record or cancel. There weren't any technical reasons why we did this; we just felt it made for a more intuitive and web-like user experience. The Address Edit page is shown in Figure 5.19.

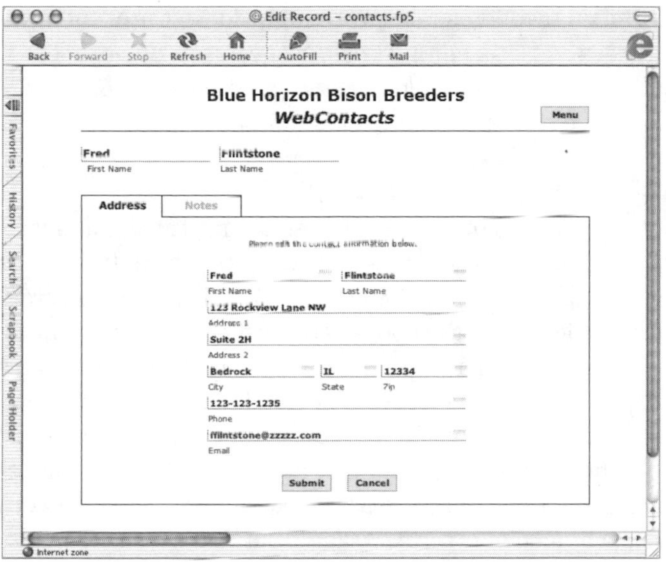

Figure 5.19

Once you've created the edit layouts, you can create navigation scripts from the browse pages. The script behind the Edit button on the Address tab is as follows:

```
Go to Address Edit;
     Go to Layout ["Address Edit"]
     Go to Field[]
```

The Go to Field step is what puts the user into Edit mode. It doesn't matter, by the way, if you have Go to Layout before or after Go to Field. For consistency, we've been putting Go to Layout as the first step in our navigation scripts.

The scripts to update the changed record and cancel are just as basic as the others that we've been working with:

```
Submit Add/Edit:
     Go to Layout ["Address Detail"]
     Exit Record/Request

Return to Detail:
     Go to Layout["Address Detail"]
     Enter Browse Mode[]
```

When you enter Edit mode, FileMaker generates a form and populates it with data from the database. It's the Exit Record/Request in the first script above that tells the Web Companion to update the database based on the values in the form.

The portal on the Notes tab surprisingly doesn't present any additional challenges as far as editing goes. You can edit one or more records in the portal or even add a new related item. All of these changes are saved once the user clicks Submit.

Validation

Hopefully, the examples of the search routine and the detail/update pages give you a better idea of how to use scripts to control the functionality and navigation of your IWP site. Instead of walking screen by screen through the rest of the app, we're turning now to two final topics: field-level validation and creating dynamic links to other web sites.

The reason we want to discuss field validation isn't because it's a particularly troublesome concept or hard to implement with IWP. Rather, we want to show an example of how IWP takes care of alert dialogs and errors. You don't have any programmatic control over the content or appearance of error messages, but that's a small price to pay when so much is done for you.

To see field validation at work, let's put an arbitrary restriction on one of the address fields. Say, perhaps, that you want two (and only two) characters in the State field. In the database, you'd set this up by adding a validation by calculation using the following formula:

```
Length (State) = 2
```

When that statement is true, the record passes our validation. If it's ever false, we'd like an error to stop the user from submitting the record.

Back on the web, if you were now to attempt to edit an address, putting in "Illinois" as the state, you'd see an error dialog similar to that in Figure 5.20.

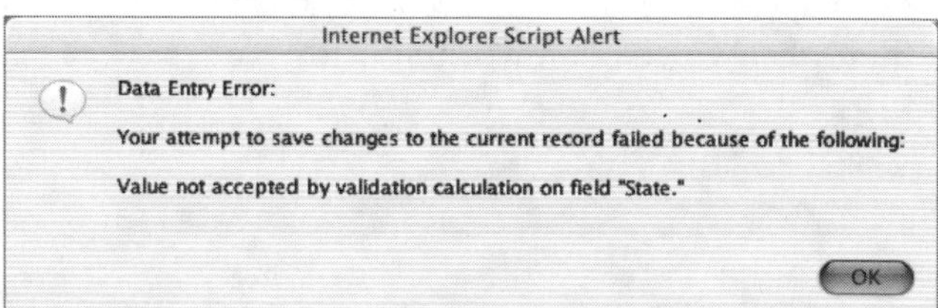

Figure 5.20

Note that it doesn't matter if you set the validation to be strict or not, nor will anything you set as a custom error message ever be seen on the web.

Building Dynamic Links to External Sites

The final experiment we conduct using the WebContacts system is to build a dynamic link to an external site. You may have noticed on the address detail screen a button that says Map It. It's finally time to see how that works. The concept is hopefully an intuitive one. Since we have address information on a contact, can't we just use an address service, such as mapquest.com, to get directions?

The first thing to do is figure out what a valid request to mapquest looks like. You can do this simply by running an address query manually and copying the URL that's generated. It should be easy to see which parts of the URL are from your query.

Once you know the general structure of a query, you can create a calculation field in your database that assembles a well-structured request. For our Map It button, we defined a new field called MapQuestLink with the following definition:

```
"http://www.mapquest.com/maps/map.adp?country=US" &
"&address=" & External ("Web-ToHTTP", Address1) &
"&city=" & External ("Web-ToHTTP", City) &
"&state=" & External ("Web-ToHTTP", State) &
"&zip=" & External ("Web-ToHTTP", Zip) &
"&homesubmit=Get+Map"
```

Remember that URLs should never have spaces in them. If we were simply to substitute an address like "123 Main Street" into the URL, our request would fail. To prevent this, we chose to use one of the External functions of the Web Companion. The Web-ToHTTP function takes a string and returns an HTTP safe version of that string. So for instance, "123 Main Street" would be encoded as "123%20Main-%20Street." You could easily do a substitution and replace spaces with %20s, but the Web-ToHTTP function takes care of other characters too, such as ampersands and angle brackets (< and >).

Finishing the task is easy. You simply define a new script with the single step OpenURL and tell it to open the URL given by your calculation field. Now hook that up to the button on the layout and test it out.

Summary

We hope that after reading this chapter you are inspired to try using Instant Web Publishing to build a simple web application. We began the chapter with an overview of how to configure a file for Instant Web Publishing. This included selecting a style and layouts for various views, as well as how to use the WebPortal object to create your own custom home pages. The next main topic was scripting. We discussed which script steps work with IWP and how their behavior differs in an IWP context.

In the context of building an actual web application, we then showed you how to hide the IWP frame and use a redirect to make it seem that one of your layouts is actually your home page. Once the frame is gone, IWP at last becomes somewhat of a development environment. If you've never tried doing this, you'll be amazed at how much quicker it is to develop pages and functionality using FileMaker rather than any other development tool.

Demo files containing the complete WebContacts application are available at www.wordware.com/files/fmweb and www.moyergroup.com/webbook.

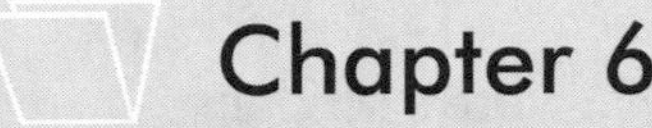

Chapter 6

Custom Web Publishing with CDML

By now your web skills are increasing. You may have used FileMaker's text calculations to publish static updates to your HTML-based web site. You've tinkered with XML and XSL to make the process more flexible and take the burden off of FileMaker itself. You've also web-enabled some databases using Instant Web Publishing. But you still want more. Well, who wouldn't? In the world of technology, more is usually available. The same is true with FileMaker web publishing. There are more tools and techniques ahead of you than behind you at this point, but they come with a steeper price. We're beginning to leave the point-and-click world of the native FileMaker interface and enter the wide world of text-based programming. From here on, a firm grounding in HTML is essential. Exposure to formal programming concepts are somewhat helpful as well, but if you don't have that exposure, there's nothing to worry about. We fully explain all the concepts as we go.

Introduction to CDML

CDML is a tag-based, server-side scripting language. Isn't that a mouthful? Let's examine that statement piece by piece.

CDML is a scripting language. A *scripting language* is an imprecise term that usually refers to a language that's used to automate or drive some other process or tie several disparate processes together as a kind of "glue." Examples of other scripting languages include AppleScript, WinBatch, Unix shell scripts, and languages like Perl, Python, and TCL.

CDML is a server-side language; when you write a script in FileMaker and that script is executed by someone running her own copy of the FileMaker software, the script is executed locally on the user's own desktop. The FileMaker client is responsible for finding the script, following its instructions, and giving the result back to the user. This is known as client-side execution. With most web technologies though (CDML included), the scripting instructions are processed by the web server itself, and only the result (which is generally a page of HTML) is actually returned to the user.

CDML is a tag-based language. Like the other web scripting languages we look at, CDML can be used inside pages containing regular HTML code. The CDML code stands out because it is usually contained inside CDML-specific tags that augment the regular HTML tag set. Whereas HTML might indicate bold text <b>this way</b>, CDML might use this syntax to refer to [FMP-Record]data that needs to be pulled from a record in a FileMaker database[/FMP-Record]. Everything inside the [FMP-Record]...[/FMP-Record] tags is pulled out and replaced with content from a database.

In order to develop using CDML, all you need is a regular, everyday copy of FileMaker. Assuming you're all set with FileMaker, let's go ahead and write a very simple CDML page that illustrates the idea of tag replacement.

Getting Started

The prerequisites for getting started with CDML are almost exactly the same as those for working with Instant Web Publishing. You need the following:

- A copy of FileMaker Pro with the Web Companion plug-in enabled
- At least one FileMaker database open on your development computer with the Web Companion enabled (this is done under File>Sharing, in case you've forgotten)
- A text editor of your choice (for Macintosh users we recommend BBEdit; Dreamweaver is a popular cross-platform choice with a graphical interface)

First, let's fire up your text editor and type in the following page:

```
<html>
     <head>
          <title>Server Date Test</title>
     </head>
     <body>
```

```
            <b>Date is: [FMP-CurrentDate] [FMP-CurrentTime]</b>
      </body>
</html>
```

Save the document to the Web folder inside your FileMaker folder. Name it date.html.

The first thing we want to remember is that the Web Companion is a web server in its own right. To see this, open a browser and type in the following URL (this assumes that you've configured your Web Companion to operate on port 591, which is what we recommend):

```
http://127.0.0.1:591/date.html
```

You should see a web page that shows the words "Date is [FMP-CurrentDate] [FMP-CurrentTime]." The Web Companion, acting as a web server, received our request for the document called date.html and sent it back to the browser.

We've seen that the Web Companion, all by itself, can serve up a web page, but the result isn't quite what we were looking for. There are some special instructions embedded in the date.html page, written in CDML. In particular, the [FMP-CurrentDate] is supposed to be a cue to the Web Companion to insert the current date at that point in the HTML document. Each time we refresh the page, we should see a different time inserted there, but all we got back was the raw CDML tag, exactly as we typed it in. Why is that, and how do we get the Web Companion to read that tag as CDML and do something with it, rather than reading it as plain text and shipping it unceremoniously back to the browser?

In order to tell the Web Companion to look for CDML tags inside the file that we wrote, we need to format our URL a little differently. Instead of calling the page directly, we need to call the Web Companion's CDML engine and tell it to do something with that page. Bear with us for a moment and follow these instructions, and we'll explain what's going on.

Open the BHBB_Product.fp5 file. Make sure it is shared via the Web Companion and that the Web Companion plug-in is enabled. Make sure that the database file is in Browse mode. Now go back to your browser and type the following URL:

```
http://127.0.0.1:591/FMPro?-db=bhbb_Product.fp5&-lay=Web&-format=
  date.html&-view.
```

There's our date.html page again, but this time the CDML tag has been replaced with the actual time of day. Hit your browser's Refresh button and watch the time update.

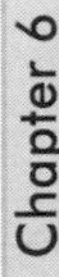

Okay, that works now, but what's with that hideous URL? It represents a string of commands to the Web Companion's CDML engine. This URL contains what's sometimes called a query string—everything before the question mark is the URL proper, and everything after the question mark is a set of specific commands that we're sending along. Notice that instead of calling the date.html page directly, we've accessed a URL simply called FMPro. A URL of the form http://<machine hosting Web Companion>[:optional port number]/FMPro represents a call to the Web Companion's CDML engine. The Web Companion, when it sees a URL of this form, knows that it's not trying to fetch an actual HTML page directly. It knows that the URL represents a call to the CDML engine, and that specific commands will follow.

All right then, what about that ugly query string? Its structure is very simple; it's a set of what is known as name-value pairs, four of them in this case. The string of name-value pairs begins at the question mark in the URL. Each name-value pair is separated from the next by an ampersand. (Query strings and name-value pairs, by the way, are not peculiar to the Web Companion at all. They're a standardized means of sending commands to pieces of middleware running on a web server. They're part of the HTTP standard.) Here we're using name-value pairs to send four specific pieces of information to the CDML engine: the name of a FileMaker database to use, a specific layout within that database file, a web page to process and display, and finally, the name of a database action to perform. So what this URL really says is this: "Hey, Web Companion, look at the web layout in the BHBB_Product.fp5 file, do a view action, take me to the page called date.html, and process all the tags you find inside it."

Well, this seems confusing. Why do we need to reference a database and a layout? We didn't do anything with any database data yet; we just asked to see the current time. Well, it's a foible of the Web Companion that it always requires you to give it at least three pieces of information: a database, a web page to display at the end, and the name of an action to perform. In many cases, you need to give the CDML engine the name of a layout as well. In this case, the action is "view," which for now we'll think of as meaning "perform no specific database action; just take me to the results page." Regardless of what was specified for the database, the layout, and the action, the Web Companion always processes the target page (the format file, as CDML calls it) and acts on any CDML commands that it finds in it.

Let's step back and review what we know so far about using CDML. In order to create a web page that contains CDML commands and have the Web Companion act on it, we do the following things: Write the page, with all necessary CDML instructions, and send a command to the Web Companion through a URL like the one we just saw, specifying a database, a layout, an action, and the CDML file that is the final page to display. When the Web Companion receives this string of commands, it performs the specified database action (so far it's a view, which doesn't do much), using the specified database file and the specified layout. Then it reads the specified results page (format file) and processes all the CDML commands in it, using, if necessary, the results of the just-completed database action. It then sends the resulting HTML page back to the user's browser.

This all becomes clearer if we move on to another example. Let's do something that requires an actual database action. We want to write a page that looks for all the animals in a database file and shows the user a formatted list of those records.

Let's open up the Animal.fp5 database we used in Chapter 4. Make sure the database is web-enabled (see Chapter 3 for a refresher on how to do this).

Now create the following web page, and save it in your Web folder as animals_all.html:

```
<html>
<head>
    <title>View All Animals</title>
</head>
<body>
<table>
    <tr>
         <th colspan="7">A listing of all animals in the Blue
           Horizons herd</td>
    </tr>
    <tr>
         <th>Name</th>
         <th>Born</th>
         <th>Father</th>
         <th>Mother</th>
         <th>Animal ID</th>
         <th>Birth Weight</th>
         <th>Current Weight</th>
    </tr>
[FMP-Record]
    <tr>
         <td>[FMP-Field: name]</td>
         <td>[FMP-Field: date_birth]</td>
         <td>[FMP-Field: id_father]</td>
```

```
            <td>[FMP-Field: id_mother]</td>
            <td>[FMP-Field: id_animal]</td>
            <td>[FMP-Field: weight_birth]</td>
            <td>[FMP-Field: weight_current]</td>
        </tr>
[/FMP-Record]
</table>
</body>
</html>
```

Now that the page is written, let's view it again in our browser: http://127.0.0.1:591/animals_all.html.

As usual, we get a plain text rendering of the page with all the CDML sitting in the page in unprocessed lumps. Now the fun begins. Enter the following URL into your browser:

```
http://127.0.0.1:591/FMPro?-db=Animal.fp5&-lay=Web&-format=animals_
  all.html&-findall.
```

This looks similar to the last one, but the database action is different; instead of -view, it's -findall. The meaning of the findall action command should be clear—it instructs the Web Companion to find all the records in the specified database. Then we go to the results page, animals_all.html, process whatever CDML we find there, and hand the result back to the user.

Let's look at the CDML for the page in more detail. There's not actually a whole lot of CDML there. There are a pair of tags called [FMP-Record]…[/FMP-Record] and a bunch of uses of the [FMP-Field] tag. What do these mean? Let's look at each one in turn.

The [FMP-Record] tags are an example of what CDML calls a replacement tag. Whenever CDML encounters a replacement tag, it removes it and replaces it with something else. In the case of a tag like [FMP-CurrentDate], CDML just replaces the entire tag with the current date. [FMP-Record], on the other hand, is an example of a looping replacement tag—everything between the start and the end of the tag is repeated some number of times. How many times depends on the exact tag being used. In the case of [FMP-Record], the replacement happens as many times as there are records in the current found set. If there are five records in the current found set, the code between the start and the end of the tags is executed five times.

Hold on, you say. What found set is that? Nothing in this page performs a search. How would I know how big the found set is? This is a great question, and it illustrates a point of fundamental importance, not only for CDML but for all forms of web programming, which we can state as follows: In order to figure out what's going on in a dynamic web page, you have to know not only where you are but where you came from. We can refine this still further for CDML. What you need to remember in CDML (and in Lasso as well) is this: In many cases, the database action is performed before the target page (format file) is processed. (This is generally true of what's sometimes called the "classic" CDML/Lasso programming style. We demonstrate a more powerful programming model that relies on *inline actions* later.)

Let's look again at the URL that we used to get to the animals_all.html page:

```
http://127.0.0.1:591/FMPro?-db=Animal.fp5&-lay=Web&-format=animals_
  all.html&-findall.
```

When the Web Companion sees this URL, the very first thing it does is perform the database action. That action then usually yields a found set; if the action was some sort of search, the found set contains everything in the specified database that met the search criteria. (Actions that edit or add a single record generally yield a result set of one record, namely the record being added or edited.) Once the action is completed, the file named in the -format tag is loaded and processed.

Let's look back at animals_all.html. Remember the earlier rule—we need to remember how we got here. In our case, we got here through a URL that included a -findall command. So we wrote the page with the assumption that it would be preceded by some kind of search that would give us a set of records to work with. What we want to do is build an HTML table with one table row per found record. So we want to loop through our found set and write an HTML table row for each record. That's exactly what the [FMP-Record]…[/FMP-Record] tag lets us do. The code inside the tag is repeated once for each record found.

If we inspect the code inside the [FMP-Record]…[/FMP-Record] tag, we see that it includes instances of another CDML tag called [FMP-Field]. This tag simply inserts the value of the specified field from the current database record. So when we say [FMP-Field:name], we're telling CDML, "replace this tag with the value of the name field from the current database record." Hold on again, you say. Current record? Which one is that? In a looping tag like [FMP-Record], the current record is going to change each time through the loop. The first time through the loop the [FMP-Field] tags pull values from the first record; the second time through they reference the second record and so on.

OK, let's review once more. When we call our animals_all.html page via the special Web Companion URL that we used before, here's

what happens: The Web Companion does a search for all database records. It holds the results in memory (assuming there were no errors on the search) and then loads the animals_all.html page and looks for CDML tags inside it. It finds the [FMP-Record] tag pair, which instructs it to loop through all the records in the found set and perform the actions inside the tags for each found record. This code, in turn, tells the Web Companion to extract certain fields from the current record, each time through the loop, and insert them into code that builds an HTML table row.

Variable Tags and Replacement Tags

If you've sufficiently recovered from that example, let's expand it a bit. In doing so, we learn about a distinction that may have been confusing to you up to this point. Let's look at the [FMP-Record entry in the CDML Reference in the appendix. Everything between the [FMP-Record] and [/FMPRecord] tags will be repeated for each record in the found set. The CDML Reference also directs our attention to the -Max and -Skip tags. If we look at those, we see that these commands give us a way to, for example, tell CDML the maximum number of records to show at one time. If -Max is set to 10, the [FMP-Record] tag pair in our page loops a maximum of ten times, regardless of how big the found set is.

That's all fine, but how do we specify a value for -Max? Do we put it somewhere inside the results page? If so, where? Looking at the CDML reference entry for -Max gives a clue. It shows a URL that includes the -Max parameter: `FMPro?-DB=Employee.fp5&-Lay=WebSearch&-Format=EmpList.html&-Max=15&-FindAll`. (There's also another flavor of the -Max command that uses an HTML form, but we're going to hold off on talking about that method for now.) So it seems that the value of -Max is something that gets set in a name-value pair, just like the values for -DB, -Lay, and -Format. Let's modify our "all animals" URL and see what happens: `http://127.0.0.1:591/FMPro?-db=Animal.fp5&-lay=Web&-format=animals_all.html&-Max=5&-findall`. Our page comes back as before but with only five records shown. That worked well. It limited us to five records, which is what we wanted. But it raises a puzzling question; it seems that we can issue CDML instructions in two different ways: either in name-value pairs that we put into URLs or in replacement tags that we put into results pages. Which is which, and what's the difference?

To start with, let's look at the CDML Reference Guide in the appendix. Look over the different tags and notice that we divide the available commands into three groups: request parameters, action parameters, and replacement tags. The request parameters and the action parameters all begin with a hyphen, whereas the replacement tags are enclosed in square brackets. Here's how to think about the difference: We said before that in order to figure out what happens when a results page (format file) gets processed, we need to know two things—not only what CDML code is in the current file but which commands we issued on the way to that page (database name, layout name, etc.). To understand the different types of CDML tags, we can rephrase that somewhat. CDML is divided into two types of commands—those that are processed on the way to a page (action and request parameters) and those that get processed when you get there. Commands of the first type always begin with a hyphen (in CDML syntax) and are passed along with the rest of the web request. So far, all of those requests have been in the shape of a URL, but we discuss another way later on. Commands of the second type (replacement tags) are placed into a text file and processed when that file is loaded as a results page (format file). Of those in the first group, some tags (the action parameters) specify a database action to be taken before the format file is loaded, while the rest (request parameters) specify additional information that CDML needs in order to perform the specified action.

To tie all this together, let's take one more look at how we issue commands to the Web Companion and get back a page with dynamic data in it:

1. We create a special URL that contains a number of named values. The minimum we need is to provide values for -db and -format (though we really should provide a specific layout as well) and provide an action command, such as -findall or -view.
2. When the user clicks or otherwise activates the URL, Web Companion performs the requested action against the specified database. If we've added any additional named values to the command, such as -Max, it takes those into account.
3. Web Companion loads the specified target page (CDML, again, calls this the format file, but we find the term "target page" more descriptive) and processes any CDML commands that it finds there. If any of those commands refer to database data, CDML uses the found set that resulted from the just-completed database action.

Building Applications Using CDML

Now that we understand the basic mechanisms that the Web Companion uses, it's time to write some software. Let's start with a few simple pages for our friends at BHBB and work up to a more complex application.

The Web Store Page

Recall that Karen wanted a way to pull weekly specials from her FileMaker database dynamically, rather than having to go in and edit the store's web page by hand each week. Her existing static page is a very simple document; it's really just a one-page brochure about the store with its hours and locations (BHBB actually maintains two stores, one on the reservation itself and one down in Lone Wolf, about 14 miles away). Instant Web Publishing is not really suitable for this, since Karen just wants to drop a little bit of dynamic data into a page of her own designing; she doesn't need anything like the full IWP interface, not even if she loads it down with password restrictions.

Karen keeps all her product information in a database file called, appropriately enough, Product.fp5. In the Product file is a field called Special, which can have a value of either "yes" or "no." To get the information on specials into a web page, Karen needs to do three things: create a Web Companion URL that searches for specials in the product file, create a CDML-ized version of the store page with code in it to display the dynamic data, and lastly, put the Web Companion URL in a place where someone can click on it to come to the store page.

Let's tackle the URL first. For a URL that performs a search, the action is -find. In addition, we need to specify some search criteria; we need the name of at least one field, along with the value that we want to search for in that field. Here's how it looks: `http://www.bhbb.com/FMPro?-DB=Product&-Lay=Web&-format=store.html&special=yes&-max=5&-find`. In this URL, the Web Companion knows that "special" is the name of a field and "yes" is the value it needs to look for in that field. Additionally, we use the -max tag to limit the search to five results at the most. Now Karen can drop that URL on the main BHBB page, and all she needs to do now is reformat the store.html page to contain some database-aware CDML code.

Right now Karen keeps the specials in an HTML table that looks like the following:

```
<table>
     <tr>
<td><b>Bison Rump Roast</b> - Our succulent roast should be
slow-cooked for six to eight hours and enjoyed with root vegetables
and an assertive red wine.</td><td>$8.49/lb</td>
     </tr>
     <tr>
<td><b>Lone Wolf Wild Rice</b> - Dark and nutty in flavor, our rice
pairs up extremely well with the Bison Rump Roast. Allow at least an
hour to cook before enjoying this native delicacy!.</td>
<td>$13.00/lb</td>
     </tr>
     <tr>
<td><b>Bison Skull</b> - Harvested from our own herd, from animals
that have died a natural death, our Bison Skull brings the grandeur
of this majestic Plains beast to your living room or
cubicle.</td><td>$500 (subject to availability)</td>
     </tr>
     <tr>
<td><b>Chicory Coffee</b> - What the cowhands drink at dawn. Wakes
You Up Right Quick (tm).</td><td>$6.49/lb</td>
     </tr>
     <tr>
<td><b>Plains Wall Poster</b> - Lovely depiction of the geographic
range of the major flora and fauna of the central Plains, based on
data gathered by the US Geographic Survey.</td><td>$30.00 (tube),
$50.00 (laminated), $175.00 (framed)</td>
     </tr>
</table>
```

Not only is it tedious to edit these table cells by hand, but it involves copying and pasting the descriptions from FileMaker into her web page editor. Tedious and, with CDML, unnecessary. In addition, CDML makes the code more compact. Here's how it looks:

```
<table>
[FMP-Record]
     <tr>
          <td><b>[FMP-Field:product_name]</b> - [FMP-Field:product_
            description]</td>
          <td>[FMP-Field:product_price]</td>
     </tr>
[/FMP-Record]
</table>
```

Short and sweet. How does it work? Remember that the first key to understanding a dynamic web page, whether you're using CDML, PHP, Lasso, or some other middleware tool, is to think about how you got to the page. CDML, as you recall, executes its database actions before loading the target page (with, again, the important exception of inline actions, which we cover later). This page, as it happens, is the target for a search action. What we want to do is build an HTML table, loop through the found set from the search, and write out a table row for each record. The [FMP-Record] tag loops through a found set and outputs whatever code is contained between the [FMP-Record] and [/FMP-Record] tags once for each found record.

So, before we issue the CDML command, we open the HTML table with a <table> tag and begin looping through records. For each one, we output all the code for an HTML table row. But all the data in the row is dynamic—it's inserted via three different [FMP-Field] tags, one each for name, description, and price. We format the HTML to assure that the product name is in bold and it is separated from the following description by a dash. CDML takes care of looping through the found records and inserting the field data from each one into the HTML.

That's it! If you're the hands-on type, build a quick search results page like this one and give these techniques a try.

Searchable Web Store

That exercise was fairly easy and took one irritating task off of Karen's plate. But like most successfully executed software tasks, it gets her thinking about what else she can do. Listing the specials is nice, but shouldn't she now provide a way for people to search the whole inventory of the store? Better yet, how about a way to see which of the two stores has a given item in stock? Like most of us, Karen needs more work like she needs a substantial cranial aperture, but that doesn't stop her from embarking on a task that seems new and exciting, as opposed to all the boring old tasks that are moldering in her in-box. She decides to lock the door for the weekend and build a searchable web store.

This job is going to be a bit more complex than the last one. For any software job that's going to take you more than a few hours to complete, the place to begin is always at the drawing board—pencil and paper, marker and whiteboard, whatever works for you. With web applications (like any other type of application design), a good storyboard goes a long way. (*Storyboard* is a term borrowed from the movie industry, referring to a hand-drawn depiction of the key frames of a movie sequence with notes. An application storyboard should have rough sketches of all the major interface screens, along with descriptions of what each button, hyperlink, or the like does and where it takes you.) Here's Karen's storyboard for the searchable web store:

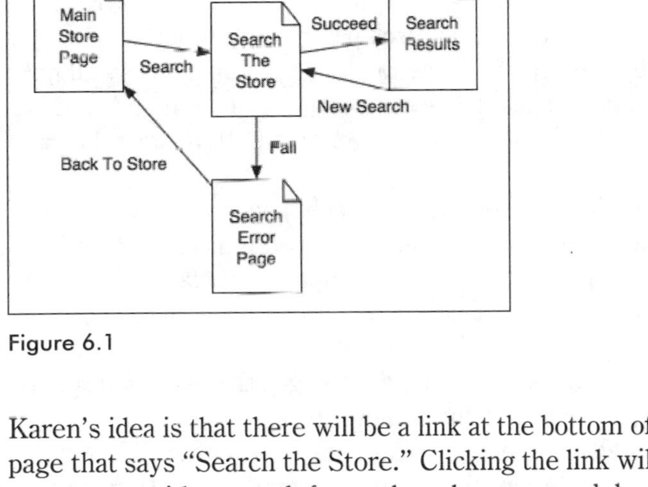

Figure 6.1

Karen's idea is that there will be a link at the bottom of the main store page that says "Search the Store." Clicking the link will bring the user to a screen with a search form where he can search by name, price, category, or description. The user will also be able to specify how many records he wants to view at once in the found set. If the search succeeds, the user will be taken to a page that shows a list view of the found set grouped according to the user's choice (five records at a time, ten records, all records). Each line will show the name, the category, the description, and the price. If the result set is broken up into groups of, say, ten records, there will be links at the bottom of each page to the previous ten records or the next ten, where applicable. Each results page (we often call such search results pages a *hit list*) will have links to return to the main store page or begin another search.

Besides the hit list pages, if the user's search fails for any reason, she will be taken to an error page that explains the error and gives her a place to click to begin another search. (A good storyboard, by the way, maps out not only what happens when the user's actions are successful but, perhaps even more importantly, what happens when they fail.)

So how many different pages does Karen need to write? It seems like three: one for the search form, one for the hit list, and one for a search error. Let's begin with the search form.

Search Forms in CDML

The last time we performed a database search, we did it by passing a hard-coded search criterion to the Web Companion in a URL. This time we can't hard-code the search parameters, since they're going to be defined by the user. So somehow, once the user enters all his search criteria, we need to take those criteria and embed them into a Web Companion URL and somehow trigger that URL to start the database action. Right?

Not quite. We've used the URL technique so far because it's easy (easier) to understand and because it provides a clear view of the commands that are passed to the Web Companion. In fact, a URL is one of two ways to send a command to the Web Companion. The other is in an HTML form. Submitting commands via a form is often more convenient and also has a few security advantages that we discuss later. But for now, let's just jump in and explore the form.

Karen needs two things to make this work: an HTML form capable of triggering Web Companion commands and an HTML table to format the search form nicely. Typically, we like to wrap the table around the form. Here's what Karen's search form is going to look like:

```
<table border="1">
<form action="FMPro" method="post">
<input type="hidden" name="-db" value="Product">
<input type="hidden" name="-lay" value="Web">
<input type="hidden" name="-format" value="product_hitlist.html">
<input type="hidden" name="-error" value="store_error.html">
<tr>
     <th>Name:</th>
     <td><input type="text" name="product_name"</td>
</tr>
<tr>
     <th>Price:</th>
     <td><input type="text" name="product_price"</td>
</tr>
<tr>
     <th>Category:</th>
     <td><input type="text" name="product_category"</td>
</tr>
<tr>
     <th>Description:</th>
     <td><input type="text" name="product_description"</td>
</tr>
<tr>
     <td colspan="2" align="center"><input type="submit" name=
       "-find" value="Search"></td>
</tr>
</form>
</table>
```

This looks superficially similar to some of the URLs that we've worked with. We have values for -db, -lay, and -format (as well as a new parameter called -error), and we also have the -find command at the end. But other than that, the syntax is alien. A programmer's first questions are probably "Why are there two different ways to send commands to the Web Companion? And how are they different?"

The answer to the first question is easy, but somewhat abstract; the two methods we've seen, namely sending commands in a URL and sending commands in a form, are not very different at all. For the technically curious, these two methods are the two standard methods that HTTP has for sending extra data to a web server. One of these methods, called GET, involves sending the extra data as a query string on the end of a URL (that's the question mark/ampersand syntax that we've used in our URLs so far, and it's standard HTTP). The other method, called POST, also sends a bunch of name-value pairs, but instead of appending them to the URL, it packages them up and sends them behind the scenes. Anything sent with a URL is automatically sent using the GET method. POST is generally done with an HTML form (as in the example above), but it is possible to force a form to use the GET method instead. Notice in the above example that the HTML <form> tag has an attribute called "method". In our example (and in all the examples we use), we set the method to post (capitalization doesn't matter—HTTP will send the method in all uppercase, as POST, but good HTML/XHTML/XML coding practice mandates that the value in any name-value pair be all lowercase). It is possible to set the method of a form to "get". We try that a bit later just to see what happens.

The important thing to understand about an HTML form is this: When the form is submitted, every named input in the form gets turned into a name-value pair. The name of the pair takes its name, of course, from the input name; in the above example, we have inputs named -db, -error, and product_price, to name a few. The value for the pair comes either from the input's "value" attribute (for non-editable inputs like the hidden inputs and the submit input) or whatever value the user has set the input to (for editable inputs like the text inputs in our example).

So the major difference between the URL syntax that we've been working with and the form-based method of sending commands to the Web Companion is this: Using the form allows the web user to specify values for some of the commands that we send to the Web Companion, as opposed to having those values hard-coded by the programmer. We most often need this for search forms, where we want the user to specify what to search for.

Note: There are other important differences between GET (sending commands in the URL) and POST (sending them via a form). One of the most obvious is that the parameters of the GET command are all visible in the address area of the user's browser. By manually editing the URL and resubmitting it, the user can send commands to the Web Companion other than those we intended. The POST method is somewhat more secure, though only marginally; the commands are not visible in the address, but they're visible the moment you select the View Source command (or its equivalent) in your web browser.

Another difference between these two methods is how much data can be submitted. According to the HTTP standard, a web server may not set any limit on the length of the URLs that it accepts, so in theory you can use a URL to transmit as long a command string as you want. However, the standard also says that a user agent (in other words, a web browser) may impose a limit on the length of the URLs it transmits. Some experimentation reveals that different browsers do indeed truncate the URL if it becomes "too long." Where they cut it varies by manufacturer, platform, and software version. It is not uncommon to truncate it at 1024 characters, but numbers as small (and as peculiar) as 219 characters can also be found. This means that the URL method is only suitable for short command strings. The POST method, by contrast, can send an unlimited amount of data, with no limits imposed by the browser.

This may seem like a long technical digression, but the mechanism of submitting commands to the web server via forms and URLs is at the heart of all web programming. All of these terms and concepts apply equally to all of the types of middleware that we're looking at in this book. They are by no means unique to CDML or to the Web Companion for that matter.

Finishing the Searchable Web Store v. 1.0

That takes care of the search form. What about our other two pages? As you recall, with most CDML commands, you tell the Web Companion where you want to end up if everything goes right. This is the -format parameter and, as we've seen, it means "take me to this page if everything works out all right." The search page that we just looked at adds another parameter, called -error. Its meaning, predictably enough, is "take me here if anything goes wrong." In each case, the value of the parameter is the name of a web page to load.

Let's look at these in order. In the first place we want to design the page that the user sees if her search returns some results. This page has been named product_hitlist.html, and it works in a fashion very similar to the simple store page with specials that we already examined. Like that page, product_hitlist.html is the target page for a search action. Unlike the specials page, the search data is being submitted from user input through a form, rather than hard-coded into a URL. That difference aside, the page looks and works about the same. Let's start with the core function of the page (displaying search results) and then go ahead and add some features to make it more usable. (In general, this is a good rule of thumb in software design—implement your features one at a time. That way, if something breaks, you have a much better idea of where the problem is.) Here's how the first draft looks:

```
<html>
<head>
     <title>Store Search Results</title>
</head>
<body>
     Your search found [FMP-CurrentFoundCount] records<br /><br />
<table>
     <tr>
          <th>Item Name</th>
          <th>Category</th>
          <th>Description</th>
          <th>Price</th>
     </tr>
[FMP-Record]
     <tr>
          <td>[FMP-Field:product_name]</td>
          <td>[FMP-Field:product_category]</td>
          <td>[FMP-Field:product_description]</td>
          <td>[FMP-Field:product_price]</td>
     </tr>
[/FMP-Record]
</table>
</body>
</html>
```

This is fairly bare-bones still, but it should look familiar. We're doing just what we did on the original specials page—using [FMP-Record] to loop through all the records in the found set and using [FMP-Field] to get data from each record as we come to it. The only thing that we've added is the [FMP-CurrentFoundCount] tag. Predictably enough, the Web Companion replaces this tag with the found count that resulted from the last operation; in the case of a search, like this one, this should tell us how many records the search found.

Lastly, we need the error page. If the search fails for any reason, we'll end up on a page called store_error.html. We could be here for a variety of reasons; it could mean that no records were found, but it could also mean that the search contained no valid criteria or that we tried to search for a field that either isn't in the database or, just as bad, isn't on the specific layout that we told the Web Companion to use. Here's what such a page might look like:

```
<html>
<head>
     <title>Whoops!</title>
</head>
<body>
Sorry, but the BHBB web store couldn't process your request. (Error
number was [FMP-CurrentError]). Please click your browser's Back
button to try again, or click <a href="store.html">here</a> to return
to our main Web Store page.
</body>
</html>
```

With that, our three-page web application is done. We've just implemented a stripped-down version of a design pattern called "search and hit list." In such a pattern, the user sees a search page, almost always implemented with an HTML form. That form targets a hit list page that's responsible for displaying the search results, if any. As with any web programming design pattern, there is also (at least) one error page, for handling any result that might be deemed an error.

Upgrading the Search Page

As we've said, the web store works, but it is fairly rudimentary. Karen's first complaint is with the hit list. Right now it dumps all the results into a single long list, whether the found count is one or a hundred. What she was hoping for is one of those nice displays at the top that says "viewing records 1-10 of 69 records found" and a pair of links at the bottom of the list that say "view next 10" and "view previous 10." Even better is if the user could choose how many records she wants to view in a single page. How is this possible?

You might recall from our discussion of variable and replacement tags that the Web Companion accepts a command called -Max. The -Max command tells FileMaker how many records to return at once. By default, with no specific value for -Max, the Web Companion returns records in groups of 25. Like all command parameters, it could be specified in a URL, like this:

```
http://127.0.0.1/FMPro?-db=Animals.fp5&-Lay=Web&name=Bigbull&
  -Max=20&-find
```

Or we could pass the command to the Web Companion through a form, like this:

```
<form action="FMPro" method="post>
<input type="hidden" name="-db" value="Product">
<input type="hidden" name="-lay" value="Web">
<input type="hidden" name="-format" value="product_hitlist.html">
<input type="hidden" name="-error" value="store_error.html">
<input type="hidden" name="-Max" value="20">
```

Whichever way we do it, the command gets passed to the Web Companion as a typical set of name-value pairs. It's worth stating (if we haven't already) that the order in which the Web Companion receives these values is unimportant. Both in the URL format and the form, we can put the items in any order that we please. By convention, we like to list the database first, then the layout, then any search parameters, then any other CDML command parameters like -Max and -Skip, and finally the action tag. But there's nothing magic about this order; it's just a convention that makes the code more consistent and readable.

Let's get back to Karen's problem and look first at her idea of returning the found records in pages. In our first cut, for purposes of illustration, we deliberately set the -Max value to "all," so all the records would be returned at once and displayed in a single page. In general, this is not a good idea. It is likely to be slow in any case and is completely impractical for databases of more than a few hundred records. We'd like the records to come back in sets of a fixed size and let the user flip through these sets like pages. This is a very common web programming design pattern that we'll call "paged result set."

For now, let's let the Web Companion break the result set up into groups of the default size of 25 records. So when we do a search, we actually only get the first 25 records in the database. We then need a link at the bottom of the page that says, in effect, "go run exactly the same search, and give me another 25 records, but start at record 26 this time instead of record 1." If the page was somewhere further down in the result set, we'd need links to take us to either the previous or the next 25. Finally, it's not uncommon for a paged result set to include links to take us to the very first or very last page of results.

There are two challenges here. The first is passing along all the search criteria involved in the current search. Remember, HTTP is a stateless protocol, and without some help from us programmers, the web server happily forgets all the details of our search once it has given us a result set back. The second challenge is getting the Web Companion to give us back a result set starting with something other than the first record.

Let's take the second challenge first. There's a CDML command parameter called -Skip, which tells the Web Companion how many records to skip before it begins returning results. So if we send the Web Companion a search command where we specify -Max as 30 and -Skip as 60, we get back records 61-90 of the result set, assuming that many records can be found.

Let's take a sample search in the Products database. Here's the URL version:

```
http://127.0.0.1/FMPro?-db=Products.fp5&-Lay=Web&-format=
  results.html&description=rice&-Max=20&-find
```

The Next link on our results hit list would need to look something like this:

```
http://127.0.0.1/FMPro?-db=Products.fp5&-Lay=Web&-format=
  results.html&description=rice&-Max=20&-Skip=20&-find
```

This is actually looking fairly complicated. The -Skip values of these URLs have to change from page to page, even though the actual CDML page that we're using is the same each time (it's the page called results.html). What's worse is we somehow have to capture all the search criteria (and sort criteria, which is a topic we haven't discussed yet) and get them into those URLs. Fortunately, CDML gives us a number of prepackaged replacement tags that automate this gruesome process and make it fairly easy. The tags that we're interested in are called [FMP-LinkFirst], [FMP-LinkNext], [FMP-LinkLast], and [FMP-LinkPrevious]. Unlike the -Max and -Skip command parameters, these are replacement tags. This means, again, that rather than be embedded in a form or a URL on the originating page, they are inserted into the HTML text of the destination page.

What these tags do is fairly straightforward. The contents of the tag are turned into a URL that performs the complex Web Companion command necessary to restore all previous search and sort criteria. These tags are also quite intelligent: If the user is on the first page of results, the [FMP-LinkFirst] and [FMP-LinkPrevious] tags do nothing, and the text in them is hidden. Likewise, on the last results page, the [FMP-LinkLast] and [FMP-LinkNext] tags do nothing either.

CDML thus gives us an easy way to build the paged result set. The other improvement we want to make to our search page is to let the user choose the number of records that are displayed in each result set page. All this means is letting the user specify a custom value for -Max, and this turns out to be just as easy as letting the user specify search criteria; we just add it into the form.

Here's what the beginning of the form looks like:

```
<table>
<form action="FMPro" method="post>
<input type="hidden" name="-db" value="Product">
<input type="hidden" name="-lay" value="Web">
<input type="hidden" name="-format" value="product_hitlist.html">
<input type="hidden" name="-error" value="store_error.html">
<tr>
	<th>Records per page:</th>
	<td>
		<select name="-Max">
			<option value="10">10</option>
			<option value="25">25</option>
			<option value="50">50</option>
			<option value="100">100</option>
			<option value="250">250</option>
			<option value="All">All</option>
		</select>
	</td>
</tr>
```

The way we've coded this page, the -Max parameter is going to take its value from the selection that the user makes using a drop-down menu. The menu here is coded as an HTML <select>, and we've given it the name of -Max so that the -Max command is sent to the destination page, along with the value that the user selected.

So far, so good. We've added the paged results set design pattern, and we've let the user select how many records he wants to view per page. Karen has one more modification to the search page in mind before she goes on to add some other features; she would like the user also to be able to specify how the result set is sorted (by name, by price, or by category). She also wants to offer the option to sort the results in either ascending or descending order so that, for example, a customer can see the most expensive items in the result set first.

How do we tell Web Companion how to sort a result set? You can probably guess. There are two command parameters that we can use for this purpose called -SortField and -SortOrder. Each occurrence of the -SortField tag tells the Web Companion to add a field to the sort order. (You would use multiple instances of -SortField if you want to sort by more than one criterion at once, such as sorting by customer and then by invoice date.) The -SortOrder parameter is optional, but if used, it goes directly after a -SortField tag and specifies whether the sort should be ascending, descending, or custom.

As we did with the -Max tag, we're going to add a place on the search layout where the user can specify both a sort field and a sort order. The database doesn't have many fields, so we're only going to allow the user to sort on a single field. Here's how the code looks:

```
<tr>
     <td>
          <select name="-SortField">
               <option value="name">Name</option>
               <option value="unit_price">Price</option>
          </select>
     </td>
     <td>
          <select name="-SortOrder">
               <option value="Ascending">Ascending</option>
               <option value="Descending">Descending</option>
          </select>
     </td>
</tr>
```

What we're doing should look familiar by now. We're creating HTML elements that have the same names as the command tags that we want to send. (This works because HTTP packages these up into name-value pairs, exactly the way the Web Companion wants to see them.) We're making sure that these user input areas only allow the right types of data to get into the field. For the -SortField command, the value must be the name of a FileMaker field. For -SortOrder, a value of Ascending, Descending, or Custom is permitted.

Here's what our heavily revised search page looks like:

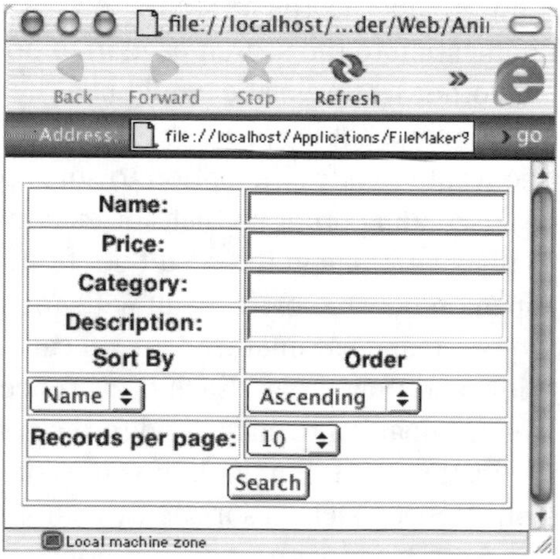

Figure 6.2

Here's the code that generates it:

```
<table border="1">
<form action="FMPro" method="post">
<input type="hidden" name="-db" value="Product">
<input type="hidden" name="-lay" value="Web">
<input type="hidden" name="-format" value="product_hitlist.html">
<input type="hidden" name="-error" value="store_error.html">
<tr>
    <th>Name:</th>
    <td><input type="text" name="product_name"</td>
</tr>
<tr>
    <th>Price:</th>
    <td><input type="text" name="product_price"</td>
</tr>
<tr>
    <th>Category:</th>
    <td><input type="text" name="product_category"</td>
</tr>
<tr>
    <th>Description:</th>
    <td><input type="text" name="product_description"</td>
</tr>
<tr>
    <th>Sort By</th><th>Order</th>
</tr>
<tr>
    <td>
        <select name="-SortField">
            <option value="name">Name</option>
            <option value="unit_price">Price</option>
        </select>
    </td>
    <td>
        <select name="-SortOrder">
            <option value="Ascending">Ascending</option>
            <option value="Descending">Descending</option>
        </select>
    </td>
</tr>
<tr>
    <th>Records per page:</th>
    <td>
        <select name="-Max">
            <option value="10">10</option>
            <option value="25">25</option>
            <option value="50">50</option>
            <option value="100">100</option>
            <option value="250">250</option>
            <option value="All">All</option>
        </select>
    </td>
</tr>
```

```
<tr>
     <td colspan="2" align="center"><input type="submit" name=
       "-find" value="Search"></td>
</tr>
</form>
</table>
```

Greater Control: Using CDML Tokens

So far we've just been working with the built-in parameters that CDML itself knows how to work with, such as the values -Skip and -Max. But if we want to do any sort of sophisticated programming, we need to be able to create our own kinds of parameters and pass them from page to page.

For example, Karen would now like to be able to include thumbnail images of BHBB products on the search results page. But she's concerned that since many of her customers and constituents live in rural, sometimes impoverished areas, they may not have access to a very fast web connection. So she'd like her web customers to be able to choose whether they want images displayed on their results page or they'd like a text-only page for faster download.

One of the significant limitations of CDML is that it gives us no direct, generalized way to inspect the values that are sent to a particular web page. This means that there's no way, in CDML, to write a program that says "if the -Script value sent to this page was Update-Record, do this; otherwise, do something else." CDML itself knows how to use the -Script parameter, but it doesn't give us, the programmers, a direct way to inspect that value. (CDML does include commands to inspect many of the commonly used page parameters, such as the -Max and -Skip values.) In order for us to be able to send our own customized values from one page to another in such a way that we can inspect them, we have to use a feature of CDML called *tokens*.

A token is nothing more than a specially written name-value pair. Here's an example, expressed as a hidden input:

```
<input type=hidden name="token" value="custom token">
```

If we put this into an HTML form that ends up sending us to a CDML page, that CDML page can inspect the value of "token" to see what value was sent. It used to be that CDML suppported only a single token. This meant that if you wanted to send multiple pieces of data, you had to somehow pack them into a single token and unpack them at the other end. CDML now supports up to nine tokens. They are referred to as token.1 through token.9 (or -token.1 through -token.9 when used in the URL syntax). If you're only using one token in a page you can omit the number, but we favor always using explicit token numbers—it cuts down on confusion, especially if you need to add other tokens to the same page later.

Tokens need not be expressed as hidden inputs. They can be used in a page in such a way as to capture a user's input and send it to another page where it can be checked and put to use. As an example, let's consider Karen's project to allow people to choose a text-only version of the product search results.

All that really needs to happen is for the following code to be added to the search page. We add it to the area for selecting sort orders:

```
<td>Display Results as:
     <select name="-token.1">
          <option value="1">Text Only (faster)</option>
          <option value="2">Text with Images (prettier)</option>
     </select>
</td>
```

Finally, we need to add some code to the results page to check this value and act accordingly. To do this, we need to conditionally add a column to the search results. If the token that we received is equal to 1 (for text-only display), we omit the image column. Otherwise, we include it. To pull this off, we need to use some of CDML's conditional logic. Here's how it looks:

```
[FMP-If: CurrentToken:1.eq.2]
     <td>[FMP-Image: thumbnail]</td>
[/FMP-If]
```

There are actually three new tags here. The first of these is [FMP-If]...[/FMP-If], which is used (not surprisingly) to write conditional statements in CDML. This tag has the same effect as If...EndIf in FileMaker. To use the FMP-If tag, we must include a logical test with the tag; here we want to test whether the first token is equal to 2 (2, as you recall, is the value that indicates the user wants to see text and images together).

To retrieve the value of that token, we need another new tag, called CurrentToken. CurrentToken can be used to indicate which of the nine possible tokens is the one we want. Here we specify that we want the first token, called CurrentToken:1. This lets us build the logical test that we need for the FMP-If tag. We want to test whether that token is equal to 2. To do that, we use CDML's equality operator, which is written .eq. (CDML does not use many of the usual symbols for its operators; instead of = it uses .eq, instead of > it uses .gt, and so on.)

So now that we've tested whether our custom token has the value that means "show me images in this page," all that remains is to show the image. We do that with the FMP-Image tag. FMP-Image is just like FMP-Field, except we use it when the field in question is a container field containing an image.

That does it. We've used CDML's token feature to extend the range of user choices in our small web application. With regular CDML, we can let the user choose how many records to show at once and how to sort them. Using tokens, we can add capabilities unknown in regular CDML, such as the ability to specify text-only and text-with-images views of a page. (Of course, we still had to do the programming that shows or hides the images depending on the value of the token.)

This is probably the most obvious use of tokens—to capture and store additional pieces of user input that you might need to pass from page to page.

Showing Portal Data in CDML

So far we've seen how to work with data from a single database table. CDML also gives us an easy way to pull data from a portal on a layout. Let's design some CDML pages that let us search for herd animals and see each one with a list of its offspring.

We'll also use the occasion here to broaden our skills in web application design. We're going to design using a pattern we call "integrated search page." Previously, we had one page that contained just a search form, and we then took the user to another page to display his results. Generally, for search forms that are small and uncomplicated, it's often nicer to display the results immediately underneath the search page. This makes it much easier for the user to input a fresh search, rather than have to click back to the previous screen and wait for it to load. In doing this, we effectively integrate our search and hit list pages.

Let's do a little design-think first. Doing it this way means that the display of the search results is conditional. We only want to display the results table if we reached this page as the result of a search. If we're coming to the page for the first time, we just want to show a message that says "no current search" or "please enter your search criteria above." So we need some way to know whether a search action is in effect or not. CDML gives us this ability.

As far as display goes, we're envisioning a results list with each row broken into two columns; the left column contains information about the current animal, and the right column is a mini-table of its offspring, pulled from a portal in FileMaker.

That's a fairly challenging page design, so let's get to work. As always, we want to design in pieces. The goal, in all software design, is always to break your task down into small, testable pieces. There are three tasks here—the search form, the results display, and some way of integrating the two. Obviously, the integration should come last. What should come first? Well, the search form by itself is not testable; until we write some kind of results page, we can't really know if the search form is working. So we start, oddly, with the results page because we can actually test the results page without a search form—we can just hit the page with a CDML -findall action passed via a URL. Once the results page looks good, we can make and test the search form and finally we bring them both together. So here it goes.

For the results page, we're envisioning a two-column table. The first column, again, contains basic data about the animal, while the second contains another table that lists the offspring. Here's how the page looks before any design improvements or graphical polish:

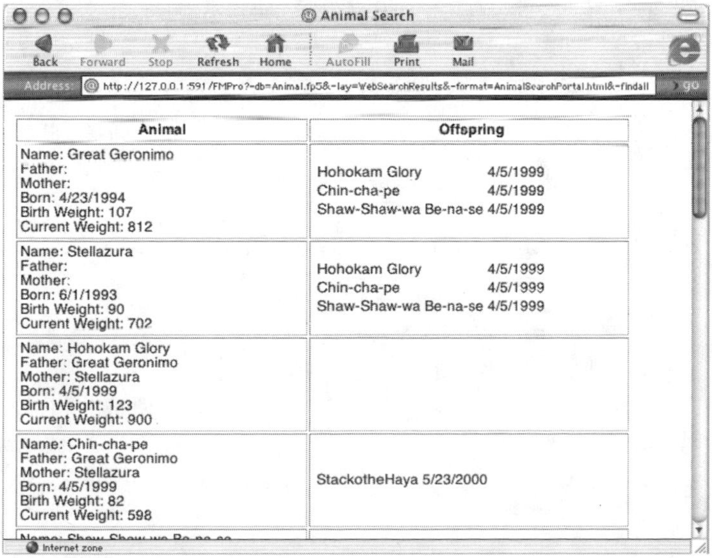
Animal Search
Back
Forward
Stop
Refresh
Home
AutoFill
Print
Mail
Address:
http://127.0.0.1:591/FMPro?-db=Animal.fp5&-lay=WebSearchResults&-format=AnimalSearchPortal.html&-findall
go
Animal
Offspring
Name: Great Geronimo
Father:
Mother:
Born: 4/23/1994
Birth Weight: 107
Current Weight: 812
Hohokam Glory 4/5/1999
Chin-cha-pe 4/5/1999
Shaw-Shaw-wa Be-na-se 4/5/1999
Name: Stellazura
Father:
Mother:
Born: 6/1/1993
Birth Weight: 90
Current Weight: 702
Hohokam Glory 4/5/1999
Chin-cha-pe 4/5/1999
Shaw-Shaw-wa Be-na-se 4/5/1999
Name: Hohokam Glory
Father: Great Geronimo
Mother: Stellazura
Born: 4/5/1999
Birth Weight: 123
Current Weight: 900
Name: Chin-cha-pe
Father: Great Geronimo
Mother: Stellazura
Born: 4/5/1999
Birth Weight: 82
Current Weight: 598
StackotheHaya 5/23/2000
Internet zone

Figure 6.3

We need a new layout and some other improvements to the Animal.fp5 database to support what we're trying to do here. We need several new relationships—one to view the animal's mother, another to view the father, and a third to view the offspring. For the first two, we just relate id_father and id_mother, respectively, to id_animal. To view the offspring, it's slightly trickier; we need a key in the Animal file that contains both the parent IDs. We create a new field called ParentIDs, defined as "id_father & "¶" & id_mother." Then we relate id_animal to that field to get the offspring.

We should also make a new layout for this search. Let's call it WebSearchResults. We need to make sure that the animal name from each of the related parent records is displayed, and we also need to make sure that there's a portal showing each animal's offspring. We want to display at least the name and date of birth. Once we have the layout and the new relationships built, we can start coding our results page. Let's call it AnimalSearchPortal.html.

The code looks like this for starters:

```
<!DOCTYPE HTML PUBLIC "-//W3C//DTD HTML 4.01//EN"
        "http://www.w3.org/TR/html4/strict.dtd">
<html>
<head>
     <title>Animal Search</title>
</head>
<body>
<table summary="Table of animal search results" border="1"
  width="600" cellspacing="2" cellpadding="3" frame="above"
  rules="all">
     <tr>
          <th>Animal</th>
          <th>Offspring</t>
     </tr>
     [FMP-Record]
     <tr>
          <td>
               Name: [FMP-Field:name]<br />
               Father: [FMP-Field:SelfByFather::name]<br />
               Mother: [FMP-Field:SelfByMother::name]<br />
               Born: [FMP-Field:date_birth]<br />
               Birth Weight: [FMP-Field:weight_birth]<br />
               Current Weight: [FMP-Field:weight_current]
          </td>
          <td align="top">
               <table>
                    [FMP-Portal: SelfByOffspring]
                         <tr>
                              <td>[FMP-Field: SelfByOffSpring::
                                name]</td><td align="right">[FMP-
                                Field: SelfByOffSpring::date_
                                birth]</td>
                         </tr>
                    [/FMP-Portal]
               </table>
```

```
            </td>
        </tr>
        [/FMP-Record]
</table>
</body>
</html>
```

If you create this document and then bring it up in your web browser with a URL like:

```
http://127.0.0.1:591/FMPro?-db=Animal.fp5&-lay=WebSearchResults&-
  format=AnimalSearchPortal.html&-findall
```

...you see a bare-bones version of the results page. Information on the individual is in the first column, and a list of offspring is in the second. Not much is new here except for the portal tags. To retrieve information from the portal on the layout, we use the [FMP-Portal] tag, specifying the name of the relationship that we want to use (again, a portal based on this relationship must be on the specified layout for this to work). [FMP-Portal] is a looping tag, like [FMP-Record]. This means that it outputs its contents multiple times. In the case of [FMP-Record], we get one loop per record in the current found set. With [FMP-Portal], we get one loop per record in the portal. Inside the portal tags, any reference to an [FMP-Field] tries to draw data from the current portal record.

Okay, we have a working and tested results page. Let's write a simple search page and wire it up. Here it is:

```
<!DOCTYPE HTML PUBLIC "-//W3C//DTD HTML 4.01//EN"
        "http://www.w3.org/TR/html4/strict.dtd">
<html>
<head>
     <title>AnimalSearchForm</title>
</head>
<body>
<form action="FMPro" method="post">
<input type="hidden" name="-db" value="Animal.fp5">
<input type="hidden" name="-lay" value="WebSearchResults">
<input type="hidden" name="-format" value="AnimalSearch.html">
<table>
     <tr>
          <td><b>Name</b></td><td><input type="text" name=
            "name"></td><td><input type="submit" name="-find"></td>
     </tr>
</table>
</form>
</body>
</html>
```

This is a very simple search form with just one search element—the animal name. Of course, we have the usual set of hidden inputs to establish the necessary Web Companion parameters, then the search element, and then a submit element with the name of -find, which executes our search. (Our dummy URL for testing the results page had an action of -findall, but that's not what we want here.)

Test your search-and-hit list page combination here and make sure everything is working. Now we're ready for the last stage, which is integrating them into a single page. Putting the search form at the top of the results page is easy. But if there are no search results, we don't want to display the results table. Even empty, it does not look pretty or professional. So we somehow need to test whether this page is being called with a -find action or not. CDML gives us the [FMP-Current-Action] tag to determine this. So let's test the value of that tag and only display the results if a search is in effect. Here's how that test looks:

```
    [FMP-If: CurrentAction .eq. find]
```

This test actually exposes some of the significant oddities of the CDML language. Though the CDML tag to determine the current action is called [FMP-CurrentAction] when it stands alone, inside the logical test it is instead written as CurrentAction. Despite the fact that the action value that we are looking for is the literal string "find," we don't enclose the value we're searching for in quotes since doing so causes the quotes to be part of the search string.

Here's the integrated version of the search page:

```
<!DOCTYPE HTML PUBLIC "-//W3C//DTD HTML 4.01//EN"
        "http://www.w3.org/TR/html4/strict.dtd">
<html>
<head>
     <title>Animal Search</title>
</head>
<body>
<form action="FMPro" method="post">
<input type="hidden" name="-db" value="Animal.fp5">
<input type="hidden" name="-lay" value="WebSearchResults">
<input type="hidden" name="-format" value="AnimalSearch.html">
<table>
     <tr>
          <td><b>Name</b></td>
          <td><input type="text" name="name"></td>
          <td><input type="submit" name="-find" value="Find"></td>
          <td><input type="submit" name="-findall" value="Find
            All"></td>
     </tr>
```

```
</table>
</form>
[FMP-If: (CurrentAction .eq. find) .or. (CurrentAction .eq.
  findall) ]
     <table summary="Table of animal search results" border="1"
       width="600" cellspacing="2" cellpadding="3">
          <tr>
               <th>Animal</th>
               <th>Offspring</t>
          </tr>
          [FMP-Record]
          <tr>
               <td>
                    Name: [FMP-Field:name]<br />
                    Father: [FMP-Field:SelfByFather::name]<br />
                    Mother: [FMP-Field:SelfByMother::name]<br />
                    Born: [FMP-Field:date_birth]<br />
                    Birth Weight: [FMP-Field:weight_birth]<br />
                    Current Weight: [FMP-Field:weight_current]
               </td>
               <td align="top">
                    <table>
                         [FMP-Portal: SelfByOffspring]
                              <tr>
                                   <td>[FMP-Field: SelfByOff-
                                     Spring::name]</td><td align=
                                     "right">[FMP-Field: SelfByOff-
                                     Spring::date_birth]</td>
                              </tr>
                         [/FMP-Portal]
                    </table>
               </td>
          </tr>
          [/FMP-Record]
     </table>
[/FMP-If]
</body>
</html>
```

As you can see, we've added the search form to the top of the page. That, more or less, works. The format file now points to this very same page, which means that this is the page on which the results are displayed as well. If that seems odd, look it over and give it some thought. A web page that targets itself is an extremely common and useful design pattern. Other than this, all we've added to the search form is a Find All button, which seems like a useful convenience.

The addition of the Find All button does complicate our test a little. Now, instead of just looking for an action of "find," we need to look for "findall" as well. You can see the appropriate syntax for that above.

That's it! We've not only learned how to pull related data into a web page, portal-style, but we've also seen how to apply some more sophisticated logic to control the display of an integrated search-and-hit list page. We still have a few more hills to climb before we're done with CDML, though.

Inline Actions: Performing Multiple Tasks in a Single Page

One of the odd things about CDML's execution environment is that we don't perform database actions once we get to the page, but rather, we somehow perform them "on the way" to that page. We launch a database action either by embedding CDML parameters in a URL's query string or by storing them in hidden inputs in an HTML form. Whichever technique we use, those parameters all get passed to the Web Companion, which follows this execution path:

1. Read all the incoming parameters (-db, -lay, -format, -Max, -find, and so forth).
2. Perform whatever database action is indicated.
3. Load up the HTML/CDML page specified by the -format parameter.
4. Using whatever found set was generated in step 2, process any CDML instructions in the format file.
5. Send the resulting HTML page back to the user.

The result of this way of doing things is that we can perform only one database action per page. We can search for something, *or* we can delete something, *or* we can update a user record, and so on. But most web applications frequently need to do more than one "database thing" per page. Let's say, for example, that we want to perform some kind of logging, creating a new database record every time a user views a page (we might be building a subscription-based information service that limits a user's page views per month based on a subscription level). Or we might want to perform some kind of conditional logic on a page; depending on a user's choice in a previous page, we might want to run one of two completely different searches in different databases. These kinds of accomplishments are difficult and, in many cases, impossible with "classic" CDML and its one-action-per-page execution model.

To get over this hurdle, CDML now offers us the inline action, or just "inline." Inlines are a technology inherited from Lasso, on which CDML is ultimately based. Lasso also offers a one-action-per-page execution model, but savvy Lasso developers avoid it for the most part. Instead, it's more common in Lasso to accomplish all database actions with inlines. We strongly advocate this technique for CDML development as well.

This sounds good, but what exactly is an inline? It's just another way of submitting a CDML request, which so far we've done through forms and URLs. Let's re-examine one of the URLs that we've already used:

```
http://127.0.0.1:591/FMPro?-db=Animal.fp5&-lay=WebSearchResults&-
  format=AnimalSearch.html&-findall
```

We're instructing the Web Companion to find all records in Animal.fp5 and display them using the AnimalSearch.html page. Here's how this might look as an inline:

```
[FMP-InlineAction: -db=Animal.fp5, -lay=WebSearchResults, -findall]
[/FMP-InlineAction]
```

We can see that we've taken most of the CDML parameters, namely the database, the layout, and the action, and included them in the inline tag. Two things are immediately interesting about this. First, this is a CDML replacement tag, meaning it expects to have some content inside of it. What goes between the opening and closing [FMP-Inline-Action] tags? Secondly, we've somehow lost our -format parameter along the way, so how do we display the results of our database action?

The answers to both of those questions are the same. Inline actions are, well, in-line. Rather than occurring on our way to some page that we specified with the -format parameter, they happen after we've arrived at the page. In that sense, the format file is really the current page. More accurately though, the format file consists of the contents of the inline tag (that is, whatever's inside it).

What we need to understand about this whole execution model is that every database action has a scope. Remember that, way back at the beginning of our CDML tour, we asked a question about which found set would be in effect when we got to our search results page. The answer was, "whatever found set we picked up on the way in via our database action." That found set is then in effect for the duration of the format page only. All references to records and record sets occur within the context or the scope of that found set or other database action.

Whenever you work with database data, you're always "inside" some database scope, usually a found set. Up to this point, that scope has always started at the top of the format page and ended at the bottom of it. With inlines, it's a little different. The scope of an inline is limited to its insides, so to speak. If your inline performs a search, you can only access the results of that search from inside the inline. Once you pass the [/FMP-InlineAction] tag, you're out of the inline context and back into whatever the original context was. Of course, the beauty of inlines is that you can launch another one right away and create an entirely different context to work with some other set of database data.

That's a lot of talk with few examples. Let's start small and see how to use an inline action to replace the portal tags that we used before. In reality, the portal tags suffice perfectly well for the task of displaying those related offspring, but showing the same example inline-style is instructive. All we need to change from the previous version is the part of the page that uses portal tags. We remove the portal tags and put in the following code instead:

```
[FMP-InlineAction: -db=Animal.fp5, -lay=web, ParentIDs={field:id
  animal}, -find]
     [FMP-Record]
     <tr>
          <td>[FMP-Field: name]</td><td align="right">[FMP-Field:
            date_birth]</td>
     </tr>
     [/FMP-Record]
[/FMP-InlineAction]
```

The first thing to notice is that this inline performs a search (-find). We're telling it which database and layout, and we're also telling it what to search for. This search replaces the relationship that drove the portal in the previous example, so it needs to do the same thing—search for all records that have the current record's id_animal somewhere in the ParentIDs field. The syntax for this is odd, to say the least. We're using what CDML calls its intratag syntax. This is a fancy way of saying that regular CDML tags change their syntax when they're used inside of other tags. Normally, to refer to the id_animal field of the current record, CDML has us write [FMP-Field:id_animal]. Since we're already inside another tag, though (the [FMP-InlineAction] tag), we need to change the syntax; we drop the FMP- prefix, put the tag inside curly braces, and make everything lowercase.

Confusing? You bet. Intratag syntax is one of those language quirks that we just have to live with when we're programming in CDML (and still to some extent in its parent Lasso, though Lasso 5 did introduce some more manageable syntax choices with its LassoScript feature).

Grumpy digressions aside, we've managed to reproduce, using inline syntax, the same effect that we were getting with the portal tags. Let's take a look at the idea of context in this example. There are actually two nested contexts here. One is made of the outermost page, and the other is made up of the insides of the inline. In the outermost, we have a set of master [FMP-Record]...[/FMP-Record] tags that loop us through a found set of animals. That master context is still in effect through the end of the first inline tag because in that first inline tag, we need to refer to a value from the current record in the outermost context—we need to grab the id_animal from the current animal and use it to run our search. Once we get inside the inline, though, the new search (for offspring) is the current context, and when we use another pair of [FMP-Record]...[/FMP-Record] tags inside the inline, we're looping through the results of our inner search. This loop has no effect on what's outside the inline, and once we're done with the contents of the inline, we go right on looping through records in the outer context. The key here is to understand that neither context can "see" the other; each is its own isolated environment.

Let's now take the next step with this search-and-hit list page. We're already driving the offspring search with an inline, so now let's see how to drive the master search with an inline as well. Due to some CDML limitations, this is not as easy here as it would be in Lasso. Here's a first cut at a new page intended to accomplish this:

```
<!DOCTYPE HTML PUBLIC "-//W3C//DTD HTML 4.01//EN"
       "http://www.w3.org/TR/html4/strict.dtd">
<html>
<head>
     <title>Animal Search</title>
</head>
<body>
<form action="FMPro" method="post">
<input type="hidden" name="-db" value="Animal.fp5">
<input type="hidden" name="-lay" value="WebSearchResults">
<input type="hidden" name="-format" value="AnimalSearchInline2.html">
<table>
     <tr>
          <td><b>Name</b></td>
          <td><input type="text" name="-token.1"></td>
          <td><input type="submit" name="-token.2" value=
            "Find"></td>
          <td><input type="submit" name="-token.2" value=
            "Find All"></td>
     </tr>
</table>
<input type="hidden" name="-view" value="view">
</form>
[FMP-If: (CurrentToken:2 .eq. Find) .or. (CurrentToken:2 .eq. Find
  All) ]
     [FMP-InlineAction: -db=Animal.fp5, -lay=web, name=
       "{CurrentToken:1}", -find]
```

```
    <table summary="Table of animal search results" border="1"
      width="600" cellspacing="2" cellpadding="3">
        <tr>
            <th>Animal</th>
            <th>Offspring</t>
        </tr>
        [FMP-Record]
        <tr>
            <td>
                Name: [FMP-Field:name]<br />
                Father: [FMP-Field:SelfByFather::name]<br />
                Mother: [FMP-Field:SelfByMother::name]<br />
                Born: [FMP-Field:date_birth]<br />
                Birth Weight: [FMP-Field:weight_birth]<br />
                Current Weight: [FMP-Field:weight_current]
            </td>
            <td align="top">
                <table>
                    [FMP-InlineAction: -db=Animal.fp5, -lay=
                      web, ParentIDs={field:id_animal}, -find]
                        [FMP-Record]
                        <tr>
                            <td>[FMP-Field: name]</td>
                              <td align="right">[FMP-Field:
                              date_birth]</td>
                        </tr>
                        [/FMP-Record]
                    [/FMP-InlineAction]
                </table>
            </td>
        </tr>
        [/FMP-Record]
    </table>
    [/FMP-InlineAction]
[/FMP-If]
</body>
</html>
```

Let's see what's changed. The first big change is in the names of our form inputs. Everything is now being passed as a token. The text input for the name field is passed as token 1, and the user's choice of find or find all is passed as token 2. We need to pass these as tokens because, again, CDML gives us no way to inspect all the parameters passed to a page, and we need to reuse these values. Lastly, we've added an additional hidden input to hold our action parameter. Remember, the action parameter, which is mandatory, tells CDML what database action to perform on the way to the target page. Well, our whole idea here is to perform no action on the way to the page but to perform all actions once we get there, via inlines. So we add this extra input specifying the database action is -view, effectively meaning "perform no action."

(In fact, it is relatively harmless to leave the two submit inputs the way they were, named as -find and -findall, and skip the additional -view action. The find or find all action gets performed on the way to the page and is then overridden by our inlines. But why waste the cycles on an unnecessary search action? Using -view guarantees that we don't waste time on a search that we're going to override right away.)

The next part is similar to the original code. Instead of checking the value of the current action, we check the value of token 2 instead. If token 2 is equal to find or find all, we know that one of the two buttons was pressed, and we can go ahead and perform the search. The search is now driven by a master inline that looks like this:

```
[FMP-InlineAction: -db=Animal.fp5, -lay=web, name=
  "{CurrentToken:1}", -find]
```

It's a search that is similar to the offspring search that we ran before. The only difference is that we're searching by name instead of id_animal, and we want to search for a value of the name equal to whatever the user entered in the search form, which we've arranged to be passed along as token 1. (Notice that CDML's token technology imposes a clear and fairly sharp limit on this way of doing things—with only nine tokens available, we're limited in the number of search choices we can pass to a page.)

There's one other difficulty with this page. It doesn't matter whether the user pressed Find or Find All; the master inline we wrote always performs a -find action. How can we perform different actions based on the different user choices? There are a few ways to do this, none as elegant as we'd like. One thing that we can do is change the Find and Find All buttons so their code looks like this:

```
<td><input type="submit" name="-token.2" value="-find"></td>
<td><input type="submit" name="-token.2" value="-findall"></td>
```

With this, token 2 now passes along the correct value of each of the possible actions. If we then write our inline like this:

```
[FMP-InlineAction: -db=Animal.fp5, -lay=web, name=
  "{CurrentToken:1}", {CurrentToken:2}]
```

...it works fine, pulling the name of the correct action from token 2. The problem with this is that HTML submit elements show their value to the user as a button label, which means the buttons are labeled -find and -findall in the user interface, which is not remotely elegant.

What about generating two different inline statements using some kind of condition logic? We'd like to write something that looks more or less like this:

```
[FMP-If: CurrentToken:2 .eq. Find]
     [FMP-InlineAction: -db=Animal.fp5, -lay=web, name=
       "{CurrentToken:1}", -find]
[FMP-ElseIf: CurrentToken:2 .eq. Find All]
     [FMP-InlineAction: -db=Animal.fp5, -lay=web, name=
       "{CurrentToken:1}", -findall]
[/FMP-If]
```

Then we'd like to have the rest of the page go on as before. Unfortunately, this is not kosher CDML. We would have the inline start tag inside the [FMP-If] tag and the inline closing tag somewhere else. CDML doesn't let us nest tags in this way. To do it like this, we'd have to include the entire inline inside the [FMP-If] clause for each of the two cases.

Hmm. We're definitely on the right track. This is the right kind of construct, but we have to avoid the code duplication.

Note: This style of programming, where we're building source code in a text editor, makes it very easy to duplicate code by cut-and-paste. It's tempting, but it's often a bad idea. If you duplicate the same logic all over your system and that logic later changes, you need to track down every place where you duplicated that code and make the change there. The possibilities for error multiply every time you duplicate code. Sometimes it's necessary, but do so with care.

In order to avoid this duplication, we're going to take all of that inner code and move it into its own file. We're then going to use a new CDML tag, called [FMP-Include], to reference that file. So let's make a new file, called AnimalSearchInner.html, with the following contents:

```
<table summary="Table of animal search results" border="1" width=
  "600" cellspacing="2" cellpadding="3">
     <tr>
          <th>Animal</th>
          <th>Offspring</t>
     </tr>
     [FMP-Record]
     <tr>
          <td>
               Name: [FMP-Field:name]<br />
               Father: [FMP-Field:SelfByFather::name]<br />
               Mother: [FMP-Field:SelfByMother::name]<br />
               Born: [FMP-Field:date_birth]<br />
               Birth Weight: [FMP-Field:weight_birth]<br />
               Current Weight: [FMP-Field:weight_current]
          </td>
          <td align="top">
```

```
				<table>
					[FMP-InlineAction: -db=Animal.fp5, -lay=web,
					  ParentIDs={field:id_animal}, -find]
						[FMP-Record]
						<tr>
							<td>[FMP-Field: name]</td><td align=
							  "right">[FMP-Field: date_birth]</td>
						</tr>
						[/FMP-Record]
					[/FMP-InlineAction]
				</table>
			</td>
		</tr>
	[/FMP-Record]
</table>
```

Let's rewrite the original file using our conditional logic in a way that references the new file:

```
<form action="FMPro" method="post">
<input type="hidden" name="-db" value="Animal.fp5">
<input type="hidden" name="-lay" value="WebSearchResults">
<input type="hidden" name="-format" value="AnimalSearchInline2.html">
<table>
	<tr>
		<td><b>Name</b></td>
		<td><input type="text" name="-token.1"></td>
		<td><input type="submit" name="-token.2" value=
		  "Find"></td>
		<td><input type="submit" name="-token.2" value=
		  "Find All"></td>
	</tr>
</table>
<input type="hidden" name="-view" value="view">
</form>
	[FMP-If: CurrentToken:2 .eq. Find]
		[FMP-InlineAction: -db=Animal.fp5, -lay=web, name=
		  "{CurrentToken:1}", -find]
			[FMP-Include: AnimalSearchInner.html]
		[/FMP-InlineAction]
	[FMP-ElseIf: CurrentToken:2 .eq. Find All]
		[FMP-InlineAction: -db=Animal.fp5, -lay=web, name=
		  "{CurrentToken:1}", -findall]
			[FMP-Include: AnimalSearchInner.html]
		[/FMP-InlineAction]
	[/FMP-If]
</body>
</html>
```

Here we have the necessary double statement of the inline to prevent nesting violations, but inside each inline, we simply reference the external file that contains the shared code. The inlines differ only in the kind of search they perform. Once the search is done, the page display is identical.

That was a lot of work. What exactly have we accomplished? Well, the main advantage of inlines is their increased readability. In pages built with "classic" CDML syntax, where all actions happen on the way to a page, it's a bit difficult to tell what the context is when you look at the target page. Have we come here via a search action, and if so, what are the possible search parameters? With the inline syntax, we can always tell what's going on. In the original version of this page, we didn't necessarily know that a user could choose either a find or a find all action. The inline syntax makes this very clear and also shows us that the search has only a single parameter—the name field.

Powerful as this technique is, we have to state again that CDML's limited token support also limits the usability of this technique. Lasso does lift the token limitation, so this technique can really come into its own with Lasso. In the PHP language, as we see later, the limitation against nested contexts is also lifted, allowing us to do things like interleave the results of two database searches, which is not really feasible in environments that limit us to one database context at a time.

Using CDML to Send E-mail

By now we've covered most of the major features of CDML, but there are still a few more to go. One important feature of CDML is its ability to send e-mails. This capability is also tailor-made for use with CDML's inline facilities, since e-mailing represents exactly the kind of "extra" in-page action that inlines are meant to support.

Before we get to inlines, though, let's start with something simpler. Karen wants to put a simple feedback form on the BHBB web site. It will be a place for customers, researchers, or the interested general public to submit questions. Of course, Karen could just use a simple mailto: link of the form <a href="mailto:karent@bhbb.com"> Contact Us</a>, but she doesn't favor this. This will kick off the user's local e-mail client, which may or may not be configured correctly. Further, ever mindful of her constituency, people using the BHBB web site (possibly at some public site like a library) may not even have a personal e-mail account. Karen would like to be able to gather the questions and post the responses on the web site itself in a kind of virtual bulletin board.

Let's illustrate here the simple form Karen needs to gather feedback:

```
<!DOCTYPE HTML PUBLIC "-//W3C//DTD HTML 4.01//EN"
        "http://www.w3.org/TR/html4/strict.dtd">
<html>
<head>
     <title>Contact Us</title>
</head>
<body>
     <form action="FMPro" method="post">
     <input type="hidden" name="-DB" value="Comment.fp5">
     <input type="hidden" name="-Format" value="CommentThanks.html">
     <input type="hidden" name="-MailTo" value="karent@bhbb.com">
     <input type="hidden" name="-MailFrom" value=
       "webserver@bhbb.com">
     <input type="hidden" name="-MailSub" value="Web Feedback">
     <input type="hidden" name="-MailHost" value="smtp.bhbb.com">
     <input type="hidden" name="-MailFormat" value="comment.txt">
     <table border="1">
          <tr>
               <th>Please enter your question or comment below,
                 then press the Submit button<br />
     (Please include your e-mail address if an e-mail reply is
       desired).</th>
          </tr>
     <tr><td><textarea name="comment" rows="50" cols=
       "60"></textarea></td></tr>
     <tr><td align="center"><input type="submit" name="-new"
       value="Submit"></td></tr>
     </table>
     </form>
</body>
</html>
```

That short piece of code deserves a good bit of dissecting. In the first place, let's talk about e-mailing in general. CDML needs a total of seven pieces of information to execute an e-mail action. Five of these are specific to e-mailing; the other two are just a database name and an action parameter, which are always mandatory in CDML requests. The e-mail-specific five are a subject, a From address, a To address, a mail server, and a *mail format file*. The first four of those are basic to any e-mail that you might send. The last is specific to CDML. The mail format file (which is indeed a separate physical file) contains the text that is sent as the body of the e-mail. It is important to know that file can contain CDML replacement tags, and these are evaluated in the current CDML context.

The context is a -new action, since this page is going to try to create a new record in a database for each comment submitted. The database is called Comment.fp5, and right now it just has a single field called "comment."

We've set up most of the e-mail parameters as hard-coded values using hidden form inputs. The e-mail always comes to Karen, it always comes from the BHBB web server, and it always has a subject line of "Web Feedback." The interesting piece that we need to look at is the mail format file. Let's look at comment.txt:

```
Date: [FMP-CurrentDate]
Time: [FMP-CurrentTime]
Comment: [FMP-Field:comment]
```

Note that this is a plain text file, not an HTML file (though it could be if you wanted to send HTML-enhanced e-mail, which some of us curmudgeons regard as a pernicious practice). It is executed "on the back end," so to speak, after and in the context of the specified database action, which is a -new action. In the context of a -new action, the fields from the just-added record are accessible to us using [FMP-Field]. So the comment in the above e-mail is the comment from the most recently added record.

There's one other format file of interest here, which is CommentThanks.html. We are not reproducing it here; this is just the page where the user lands after submitting a comment and that presumably contains a thank-you and a link back to the main page.

Let's consider a trickier example. Say that Karen has given her researchers a way to delete animal records from the hit list. In the rightmost column she's put a link that says Delete. But she suspects that records may occasionally be deleted in error, and she also wants to make sure the feature is being used as intended. So she wants to set things up such that before deleting any record, the system sends her an e-mail with the details of the outgoing record. Inspecting these e-mails lets her be sure that the feature is being used correctly, and the e-mails act as a "trash can" if any of the researchers come running to her needing to get their deleted records back.

To kick things off, let's add a third column to the hit list. To the right of each entry, we put a table cell that looks like this:

```
<td><a href="FMPro?-db=Animal.fp5&-lay=WebSearchResults&-RecID=
  [FMP-CurrentRecId]&-format=DeleteAnimal.fp5&-view">Delete</a></td>
```

The format of that URL should be familiar by now. It directs us to a page where the actual processing occurs. Since our action is -view, nothing special happens on the way. The only thing unfamiliar might be the RecID tag, which comes in two different flavors. RecID is a named value that we can pass along to our results page, and [FMP-CurrentRecID] gets the ID of the current record. We need the record ID on the results page to tell CDML which record we want deleted.

So what does DeleteAnimal.html look like? It needs to do two things—first, send an e-mail to Karen informing her of the deletion and send her the record data, and second, delete the record as instructed. (Actually, a competent implementation would first prompt the user for confirmation before deleting a record. We know you'd never leave this out of a production solution, but we're going to skip it here for clarity only.)

Well, a CDML page that needs to do two things probably has to involve inlines. In fact, we use one inline to send the e-mail and a second one to perform the deletion. Watch carefully because there are some extra wrinkles here:

```
<!DOCTYPE HTML PUBLIC "-//W3C//DTD HTML 4.01//EN"
       "http://www.w3.org/TR/html4/strict.dtd">
<html>
<head>
    <title>Delete Animal</title>
</head>
<body>
    <!--Send an e-mail message about the deletion-->
    [FMP-InlineAction: -db=Animal.fp5, -lay=WebSearchResults,
      -mailto=karen@bhbb.com, -mailfrom=webserver@bhbb.com,
      -mailsub=Animal Record Deleted, -mailhost=smtp.bhbb.com,
      -mailformat=deletemessage.txt, -RecID=[CurrentRecID], -find]
    [/FMP-InlineAction]

    <!--Delete the record-->
    [FMP-InlineAction: -db=Animal.fp5, -lay=WebSearchResults,
      -RecID=[CurrentRecID], -delete]
    [/FMP-InlineAction]
</body>
</html>
```

Here's the code for the mail format file:

```
<!--deletemessage.txt-->
Date: [FMP-CurrentDate]
Time: [FMP-CurrentTime]
id_animal: [FMP-Field:id_animal]
Name: [FMP-Field:name]
Mother: [FMP-Field:id_mother]
Father: [FMP-Field:id_father]
Birth Weight: [FMP-Field:weight_birth]
Current Weight: [FMP-Field:weight_current]
```

The first inline reprises the e-mail parameters from the previous example. But, while the previous example used a -new action, this e-mail inline uses a -find. We need to take the -RecID parameter that was shipped in by the URL and use it to find the record that's about to be deleted. This is important because we want our e-mail to send Karen specific information about the exact record being deleted, rather than just a generic notice that some record, somewhere, is now history. Remember, the mail format file (as well as the regular format file) operates in the current CDML context. To show information about a record, we need to find it first. (To be specific, CDML lets us work with information from a record that we have found, added, or updated.) Our e-mail message just sends Karen the date and time of the deletion and the critical fields from the record.

Once the e-mail is sent, we run a second inline to perform the actual deletion. We send along the same record ID (this time in the context of a delete action), and the record is presumably removed. I say presumably because our code is not really production quality. It doesn't account for the fact that the delete might fail or provide what to do if this happens. In a more powerful programming environment, we might set up the text of the e-mail beforehand and store it in some kind of variable and only send it if the delete succeeded. In CDML, we might instead check whether the delete inline succeeded and, if not, send another e-mail to Karen indicating the failure.

That's really all there is to know about CDML's e-mail capabilities. Virtually all web development environments worth their salt provide some kind of e-mailing facilities. More advanced tools like PHP and Lasso offer richer e-mail capabilities, such as the ability to add attachments to your e-mail.

Cookies

Though this is our last topic in the CMDL chapter, cookies are not specific to CDML at all. They're an almost universal feature of dynamic web programming.

A cookie is a programming device intended to overcome the stateless nature of the web. If I do some shopping on BHBB's web site, and they want to be able to greet me by name when I come back (disregarding the Big-Brotherish intrusiveness of this gesture), they have a problem. After all, when I, via my web browser (or mobile phone or doubtlessly soon my toaster), send a request to a web server, I don't identify myself by name. Among the few bits of useful information the remote web server can glean from my incoming HTTP request are my user agent (usually a browser but, again, possibly some other device entirely) and the IP address of my computer. But the user agent identifier is easily spoofed or altered and isn't good for much anyway. My IP address doesn't help to link my request uniquely to a person either; if I work in a DHCP environment, I might have different IP addresses on different days, and if I'm behind a NAT device or a proxy server, the IP address on the request may not even be traceable to my machine. But if I'm a remote web server, that's all I get.

A cookie is a piece of data that is stored on your computer, usually under the stewardship of your web browser. If I'm the BHBB web server, for example, whenever a user first comes to the site I can send the user a cookie with a specific name (say, BHBB_ID). Inside the cookie I can store a piece of information, such as the user's name (assuming he has given it to me). Think of the cookie as a database record that a web server stores on your local machine. The cookie's name is its primary key—when you visit the web server or web site again, it will ask for the cookie by name, and your local cookie manager (usually your browser or other user agent) will look up the cookie by that name and send it back to the remote server. Within the cookie there can be a single piece of data. The remote web server can read this data back out of the cookie. It can also update it, add new cookies, or remove its cookies from your machine altogether. The important thing to remember is that each cookie has one name and one associated value.

Cookies are a tricky and inelegant way to get past the fact that the web was never designed as a client-server platform. In typical client-server computing, remember that the server maintains a known connection with each client and is able to associate every action and request with a particular client. The web, by contrast, was intended to be lightweight, stateless, and request-oriented rather than connection-oriented. As the web moved from being a medium for the navigation of information to a medium for presentation as well (and now also for the operation of client-server applications), new technologies had to be grafted onto the original HTTP and HTML that were the basis for the web. To enable better presentation, HTML was "extended" (some would say polluted) with tags like <FONT>. To allow persistent computing, cookies were born.

Not everyone agrees that cookies are a good thing. Some see them as tools to invade privacy. The important thing to remember is that the user has (or should have) complete control over whether and how her user agent accepts cookies. Most modern browsers allow the setting of different levels of cookie security, including allowing all cookies with no prompting, allowing cookies but prompting you to accept each one, allowing only cookies from certain sites, and allowing no cookies at all.

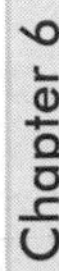

A good browser will have a cookie manager that lets you see what cookies are stored on your computer at any time, who sent them, and what their contents are. It should also let you delete cookies, either singly or en masse. This has an important ramification for you as a web programmer; if you design your site to depend on cookies and your user disables cookies in her browser, your application may not work. If you're building a private application (say, for use by paid subscribers or the members of a company intranet), you can probably communicate to all prospective users that cookies are mandatory to use the site. If you're building something for widespread public consumption, though, beware. Users may not like being told that they need to enable cookies. So just remember that cookies, like many other aspects of the web's user experience, are configurable by the user. At the very least, you may need to do some negotiation to make sure that your site works as expected. For more information on cookies (much more) visit www.cookiecentral.com, and be sure to check out their detailed FAQ.

Let's take a look at a simple file that exercises CDML's cookie capabilities:

```
<!DOCTYPE HTML PUBLIC "-//W3C//DTD HTML 4.01//EN"
        "http://www.w3.org/TR/html4/strict.dtd">
<html>
<head>
     <title>CDML Cookie Test</title>
</head>
     <body>

     <!--Check to see if the user has submitted her name to this page.
       If so, store it-->
     [FMP-If: CurrentToken .neq. ]
          Hello, [FMP-CurrentToken]. Welcome back!
          [FMP-SetCookie: name={CurrentToken}, expires = 1440]
     [FMP-Else]
          Hello, [FMP-Cookie:name]. Welcome back!
     [/FMP-If]

     <form action="FMPro" method="post">
          <input type="hidden" name="-db" value="Animal.fp5">
          <input type="hidden" name="-lay" value="WebSearchResults">
          <input type="hidden" name="-format" value=
            "CookieTest.html">
          Enter your name: <input type="text" name="-token"> <input
            type="submit" name="-view" value="Submit">
     </form>
     </body>
</html>-
```

This is a simple form with a place for a user to type in his name and submit it. It's stored in a CDML token and passed back to the same page, where, if the user has actually submitted a name, it's stored in a cookie. If you run this page repeatedly (changing the name if you like), the message always shows the most recently submitted name. By itself, this means nothing—this is happening simply because we're always passing the name back through using a token, so of course it's up to date. But the magic (such as it is) happens if you quit your browser, start it up again, and re-enter the same URL. Without submitting a name to the browser this time around, the last name you entered should appear in the message. That's because each name was being stored in the cookie by our code.

Inelegant as they are, cookies have many uses in web programming. The most important role for our purposes is their use in maintaining user sessions, a critical concept that we explore a bit further in the chapters ahead.

Summary

That finishes up our tour of CDML, the web publishing technology that's built into versions of the Web Companion from FileMaker 4 to FileMaker 6. It is a reasonably capable, tag-based web development language, and since it ships with FileMaker, it deserves our attention. Quite a number of simple tasks can be fairly easily accomplished using CDML, and if you stretch a bit more, you can use it to design a fairly sophisticated site. (There are capable commercial and public sites based entirely on CDML.)

All the same, we're going to argue that if you have the time, the energy, and the need to learn an actual web programming language, you might as well not stop with CDML. By all means, start there to test the waters and see how well you adapt to this style of programming. But we're going to argue that to really prosper as a web developer, you're going to want to learn a more powerful development language. CDML has been useful to us as a laboratory for learning some basic web programming concepts, but it's time to move on. In the chapters to come, we give you an overview of Lasso and then move on to PHP.

Chapter 7

Custom Web Publishing with Lasso

Lasso is one of the most long-lived available tools for web-enabling FileMaker Pro databases, having outlasted a number of the other early tools that became available when FileMaker added web capabilities to the product line. It is now a multi-platform web application tool that can work directly with data from FileMaker and from the popular open-source database MySQL. Lasso can also work with data from any JDBC-enabled data source, which includes most major relational database products. The current version, Lasso 6, runs on Mac OS X, Red Hat Linux, and Windows 2000 and XP.

Lasso runs in the classic middleware fashion; it's installed alongside a dedicated web server (Apache or WebSTAR in the case of Mac OS X, Apache for Linux, and Microsoft's IIS in the case of Windows) and does special extra processing to certain files. In a typical scenario, the web server will be instructed to hand all files with a .lasso suffix to Lasso for processing. As with CDML, these pages contain special markup code that represents instructions to Lasso. The difference between CDML and the other, more powerful Custom Web Publishing languages is simply in the range of available features, but the underlying mechanism is just the same.

The newest version of Lasso has some considerable strengths. Most outstanding is Lasso's ease of installation and powerful graphical tools for administering databases, database hosts, and other web application settings. Also very nice is the inclusion of Lasso MySQL, a licensed version of the popular open-source database MySQL. Lasso uses MySQL internally for keeping its database of administrative information, but you can use this powerful relational database engine for your own purposes in any Lasso application that you build, accessing it as easily as your FileMaker data. MySQL is able to handle extremely large data sets and complex queries that might be beyond the capabilities of FileMaker; if one of your database tables is hugely and disproportionately large or complex, you could store that data in MySQL instead of FileMaker, for example. (Our personal favorite among open source databases is PostgreSQL, but hey, you can't have everything!) Also noteworthy is the ability to compile your Lasso programs into LassoApps that can be deployed without releasing the application source code. (We've never needed such a feature, but we can see how, if you wanted to market a "shrink-wrap" style of application, you might.)

In this chapter, we show you some of the basic and advanced features of Lasso. For additional information, you can consult Duncan Cameron's *Lasso Professional 5 Developer's Guide* from Wordware Publishing for a full range of code examples.

Lasso is a commercial product, which means you must purchase it in addition to FileMaker Pro Unlimited. If you're interested in testing the product or just following along with our examples, you can download a 30-day evaluation copy at http://www.blueworld.com.

Configuring Lasso for FileMaker

We're going to assume that you've installed Lasso successfully. All Lasso configuration is done, appropriately enough, through a web interface, which is accessed at <your.server.address>/lasso. If you're working from the install machine, opening a browser and going to http://127.0.0.1/lasso should get you started. Here's how the opening screen should look.

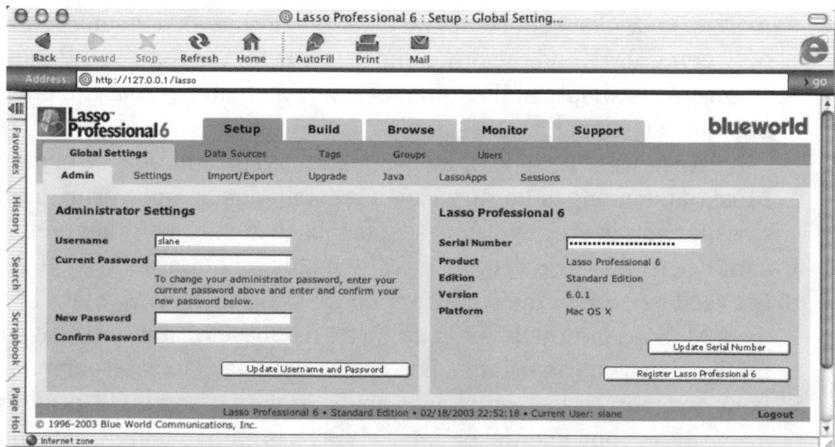

Figure 7.1

Once you've established your administrative username and password and added your serial number, you're ready to tell Lasso where to find some FileMaker Pro files. To do this, go to the **Setup>Data Sources>Hosts** tabs. Here's what you should see once you click the name of a host in the left-hand panel:

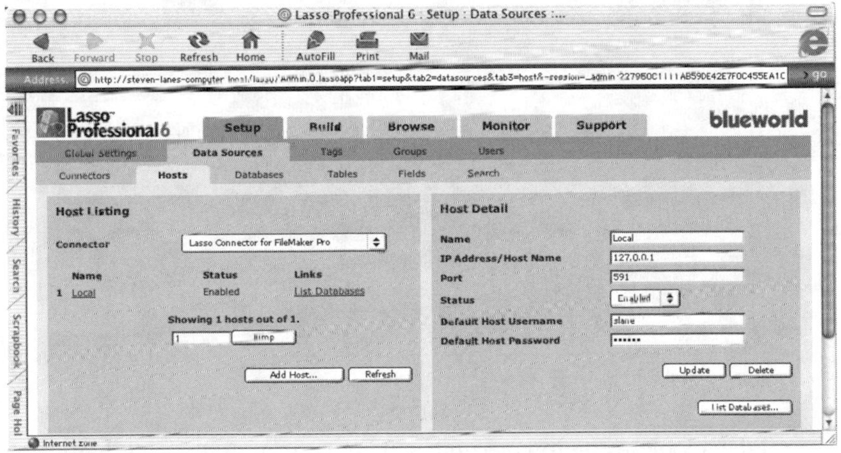

Figure 7.2

After selecting **Lasso Connector for FileMaker Pro** from the Connector pull-down menu and clicking the **FileMaker Local** link in the left panel (this is a host that we already configured—you need to set up your own), the details of the selected FileMaker host appear in the panel to the right. Here we've specified a FileMaker installation running on the same machine as Lasso (127.0.0.1, by the way, is an IP address that always points to the current machine) on port 591 (the Apple-registered port for Web Companion). We can work with as many hosts as we want, FileMaker or otherwise. We just need to use the Add Host button to make sure they get correctly configured and included in the list.

Finally, if we click the List Databases link for a given host, we see the available databases on that host in the left panel, and if we click on a database, we see a number of specific settings for that one database in the right panel.

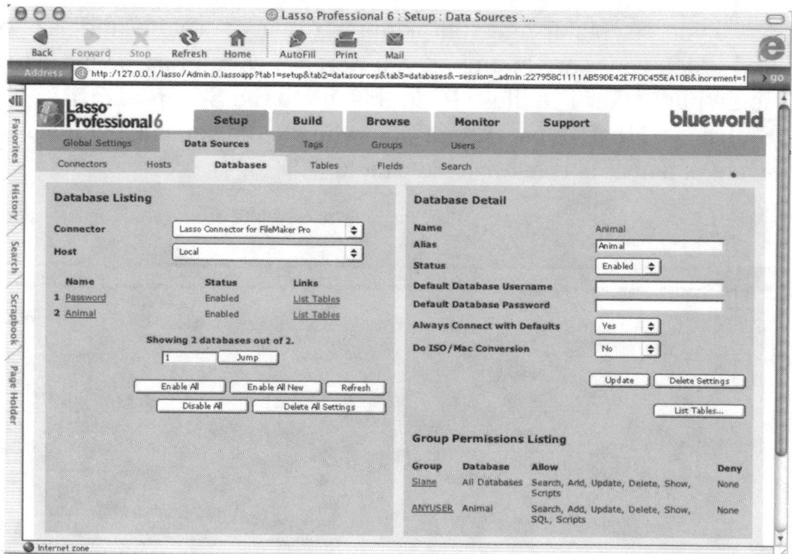

Figure 7.3

Take a look at the lower right-hand corner of Figure 7.3. Notice that, for the selected database, there's a listing of what are called Group Permissions. This is just the tip of the great iceberg that is Lasso's security system. Lasso has an extremely full-fledged security system built into it. It's so full-fledged that it can seem somewhat intrusive until you get used to it. For any database, you can control access based on layouts, fields, database actions, or even individual Lasso tags. A full exposition of Lasso's security system would take up a bit too much space here, but the important thing to realize is that Lasso takes a fairly restrictive stance by default; unless you specifically permit an action on a particular database, it is generally assumed to be forbidden. So if you configure a FileMaker connector, set up some databases for web sharing, and start writing Lasso pages to hit those databases, you may find yourself faced with a host of permissions errors.

When you're developing in Lasso, we recommend that you open up the permissions as wide as possible. If you want to make Lasso's security a part of whatever security scheme you devise for your Lasso-driven sites, you can add restrictions later in your production configuration. For now, we recommend effectively disabling Lasso's built-in security so that you can get on with your development.

To do this, you need to open the permissions on each database that you want to work with. There are two steps involved here. In the first place, referring again to Figure 7.3, you want to make sure that each database you want to work with is marked as Enabled on the database detail screen.

Once a given database is enabled, open up the group permissions on that database. Lasso's security model has some similarities to FileMaker's: In Lasso, permissions are granted to *groups* rather than to individual users. Users get privileges (or are denied them) by virtue of being in one or more groups. You, as the system administrator, can create as many users as you like and divide them up into groups any way you like. But there are also special built-in entities called Any User and Any Group. Any User is by definition a member of the group Any Group. By manipulating the permissions for these entities, you can open up whole classes of privileges quickly and easily.

To allow all users to perform all actions on a specified database, click on Setup>Groups>Databases in the Lasso administrative interface. If the pull-down menu at the upper right is not already set to AnyUser, change it to AnyUser. Make sure that you have the right host and connector selected in the left-hand panel (we're choosing the FileMaker connector and our own local host machine). Once you see the list of databases at the left, select one to edit its group permissions. Your screen should look something like this:

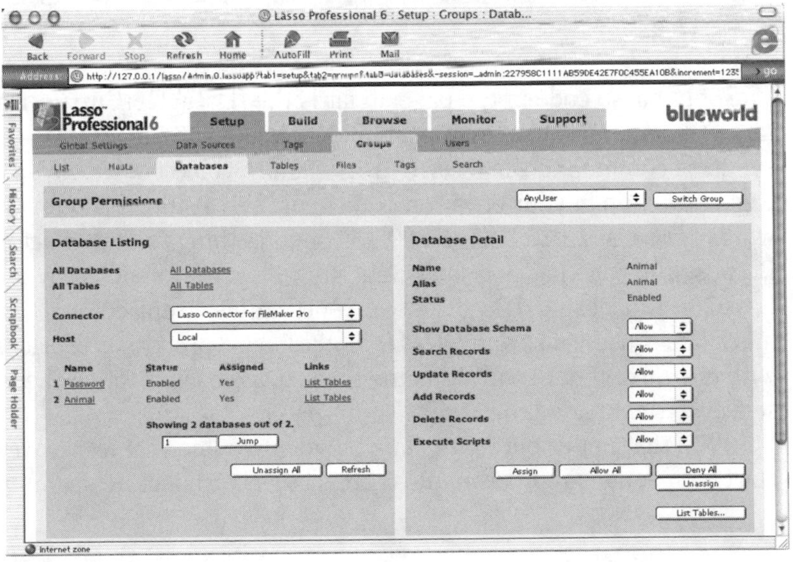

Figure 7.4

In order to allow unfettered access to the selected database during development, you need to make sure that the detail listed at the right shows that the database is enabled and that all six specific privileges are set to Allow. There's an Allow All button that will set these all at once. Once the database is enabled and all actions are allowed to the Any User group, you should be able to develop freely without any permissions errors.

Building an Application with Lasso

At first, Lasso may seem to you to be a more powerful CDML. The syntax and approach are similar, but the differences become more and more apparent the more you work with it. We're going to come back to the Blue Horizon databases and start developing some more powerful pages for them.

Before we get started, though, let's write a very minimal Lasso page just to make sure everything works. Create the following document and save it somewhere in your web server's directory structure as datetest.lasso:

```
<html>
    <head>
        <title>Lasso Date Test</title>
    </head>
    <body>
        Date is: [Date_GetCurrentDate]<br />
    </body>
</html>
```

The only Lasso code in the page so far is the [Date_GetCurrentDate] tag. The square-bracket syntax should look familiar from CDML; this syntax is common to the CDML-Lasso family. Once you've saved this page, load it up in your browser. You should see a simple page with the words "Date is: 12/26/2002 18:02:15" or something to that effect. Because the page has a .lasso suffix, the web server sends it over to Lasso for processing. [Date_GetCurrentDate] is a replacement tag, much like those we saw in CDML, so the Lasso processor replaces it with the current date and ships the whole page back through the web server to the user's browser.

With that under our belts, let's move into some real work. We start with some simple examples. Let's begin with a basic search page.

A Simple Search in Lasso

Let's start with a simple page for searching the BHBB herds by animal. We want users to be able to look for animals by a variety of criteria. Here's what our page looks like:

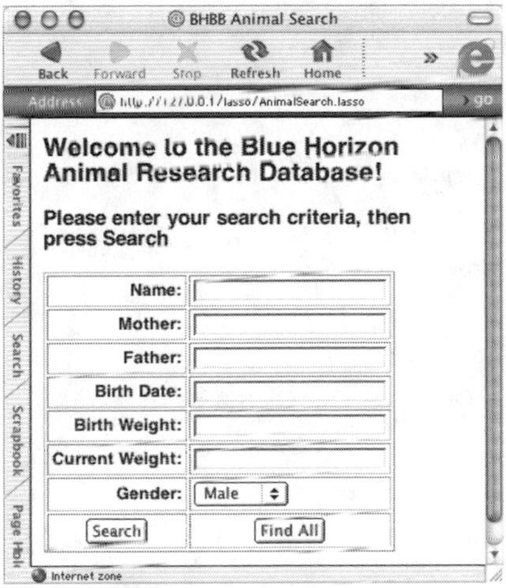

Figure 7.5

Here's the code:

```
<!DOCTYPE HTML PUBLIC "-//W3C//DTD HTML 4.01//EN"
        "http://www.w3.org/TR/html4/strict.dtd">
<html>
<head>
     <title>BHBB Animal Search</title>
</head>
<body>
     <H2>Welcome to the Blue Horizon<br />Animal Research
       Database!</H2>
     <H3>Please enter your search criteria, then press Search</H3>
     <form action="AnimalSearchResults.lasso" method="post">
     <input type="hidden" name="-Database" value="Animal">
     <input type="hidden" name="-Layout" value="WebSearchResults">
     <table border cellspacing="2" cellpadding="3">
     <tr>
          <th align="right">Name:</th>
          <td><input type="text" name="name"></td>
     </tr>
     <tr>
          <th align="right">Mother:</th>
          <td><input type="text" name="SelfByMother::name"></td>
     </tr>
     <tr>
          <th align="right">Father:</th>
```

```
            <td><input type="text" name="SelfByFather::name"></td>
        </tr>
        <tr>
            <th align="right">Birth Date:</th>
            <td><input type="text" name="date_birth"></td>
        </tr>
        <tr>
            <th align="right">Birth Weight:</th>
            <td><input type="text" name="weight_birth"></td>
        </tr>
        <tr>
            <th align="right">Current Weight:</th>
            <td><input type="text" name="weight_current"></td>
        </tr>
        <tr>
            <th align="right">Gender:</th>
            <td>
                <select name="gender">
        <option label="Male" value="Male">Male</option>
        <option label="Female" value="Female">Female</option>
                </select>
            </td>
        </tr>
        <tr>
            <td align="center">
                <input type="submit" name="-Search" value="Search">
            </td>
            <td align="center">
                <input type="submit" name="-FindAll" value="Find
                  All">
            </td>
        </tr>
</table>
        </form>
</body>
```

As usual, we've wrapped our search form in a table for nicer formatting. It's a straightforward search form, and in fact so far it's very similar to the form that we would write if we were working in CDML. At the top, we have two hidden inputs called -Database and -Layout to specify the database and layout. At the bottom we have two buttons, one of which triggers a Find action and the other of which triggers a Find All.

The following figure shows the search results page after pressing Find All:

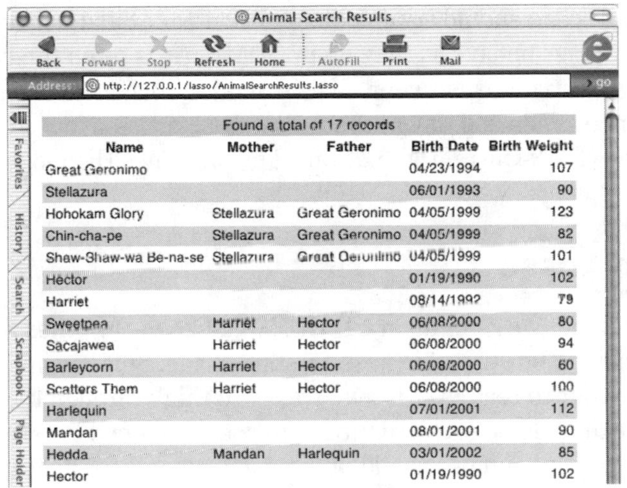

Figure 7.6

Here's the code for AnimalSearchResults.lasso:

```
<!DOCTYPE HTML PUBLIC "-//W3C//DTD HTML 4.01//EN"
        "http://www.w3.org/TR/html4/strict.dtd">
<html>
<head>
     <title>Animal Search Results</title>
</head>
     <body>
          <table border="0" cellspacing="2" cellpadding="3">
     <tr bgcolor="CCCCCC">
          <td colspan="5" align="center">Found a total of
            [Found_Count] records</td>
     </tr>
     <tr>
          <th>Name</th>
          <th>Mother</th>
          <th>Father</th>
          <th>Birth Date</th>
          <th>Birth Weight</th>
     </tr>
     [Records]
     <tr>
          <td>[Field:'name']</td>
          <td>[Field:'SelfByMother::name']</td>
          <td>[Field:'SelfByFather::name']</td>
          <td align="right">[Field:'date_birth']</td>
          <td align="right">[Field:'weight_birth']</td>
     </tr>
     [/Records]
</table>
     </body>
</html>
```

The result page code should again look familiar—the [Field] tag and [Found_Count] tags behave as they do in CDML. As is often the case, there are slight variations between CDML and Lasso syntax; the CDML parameters -db and -lay become -Database and -Layout in Lasso, and the [FMP-CurrentFoundCount] tag becomes [Found_Count].

Variables in Lasso

Let's do something we *can't* do in CDML. We'd like every other row of our results table to be striped in a contrasting shade. Some people think this is easier to read. As always, we try to think through the logic of what we need to do before committing to code. We need to decide whether a given row number is odd or even and color it (or not) depending on that result. Conceptually, we need some way to count the rows and then some way to examine the current row count and decide if it's odd or even.

If we were doing this in FileMaker, we might use a global field for our row counter. We'd set it to zero initially and then add 1 to it every time through a loop. This FileMaker global would be an example of the general programming concept of a *variable*. A variable could be defined as "a named value that can vary." If you can remember your basic algebra, with x and y in equations, the concept of a variable will be very familiar.

In Lasso, you declare a variable by saying [Variable: 'LoopCounter']. This creates a variable called LoopCounter and allows you to assign values to it. If you want to assign an initial value to it (called, appropriately enough, *initializing* the variable), you could write [Variable: 'LoopCounter' = 0]. If you think that's a lot to type just to set one variable, you can use the shorter syntax [Var: 'LoopCounter' = 0]. Most economical is to use Lasso's new short variable keyword, written $. This lets us say [$LoopCounter=0]. (This, as we see, is how PHP and other languages refer to their variables; it's both more standard and economical, and we encourage you to use it where possible. The one place this compact syntax can't be used in Lasso is when you're declaring a variable for the first time. So in our current example, we have to at least say [Var:'LoopCounter'=0], to get the variable to be created.)

So we can initialize a variable called LoopCounter to 0. We can increment it each time through the [Records] loop by using Lasso's *increment* operator, written ++. So by saying [++$LoopCounter], we add 1 to LoopCounter. Finally, for a given value of LoopCounter, we need to decide whether it's odd or even. To do this, we can use a *modulus* function, often just called *mod*. A mod operator performs division and looks at the remainder. We want to divide our row number by 2 and look at the remainder (the modulus). If it's 1, the number is odd. If it's 0, the number is even.

We can write the mod check in a couple of ways. There's a more verbose way, like this: [Math_Mod: $LoopCount, 2]. And there's a more economical way, like this: [$LoopCount %2]. Lasso tries to group its functions into families with consistent prefixes, so all the math functions are accessible under names that begin with Math_: Math_Mod, Math_Add, Math_Div, etc. At the same time, sensitive to programmers who may feel that [Math_Add: 2, 2] is a bit harder to write and more obscure than, say, [2+2], the language has a number of "shortcuts" for more commonly used language elements like math operators.

With that in mind, we can go ahead and rewrite the page using Lasso's variable capability and the mod operator to do our work. Here's how it looks:

```
<!DOCTYPE HTML PUBLIC "-//W3C//DTD HTML 4.01//EN"
        "http://www.w3.org/TR/html4/strict.dtd">
<html>
<head>
     <title>Animal Search Results</title>
</head>
     <body>
          <table border="0" cellspacing="2" cellpadding="3">
     <tr bgcolor="CCCCCC">
          <td colspan="5" align="center">Found a total of
            [Found_Count] records</td>
     </tr>
     <tr>
          <th>Name</th>
          <th>Mother</th>
          <th>Father</th>
          <th>Birth Date</th>
          <th>Birth Weight</th>
     </tr>
     [Var:'LoopCount' = 0]
     [Var: 'OddEven']
     [Records]
     [$OddEven = $LoopCount % 2]
     [If: $OddEven == 1]
          [Var:'BackColor'='FFFFFF']
     [Else]
          [Var:'BackColor'='DDDDDD']
     [/If]
```

```
        <tr bgcolor="[Output: $BackColor]">
              <td>[Field:'name']</td>
              <td>[Field:'SelfByMother::name']</td>
              <td>[Field:'SelfByFather::name']</td>
              <td align="right">[Field:'date_birth']</td>
              <td align="right">[Field:'weight_birth']</td>
        </tr>
        [/Records]
</table>
        </body>
</html>
```

In the code, we initialize our LoopCount variable to 0 and create a variable called OddEven, without initializing it. Each time through the [Records] loop, we set OddEven equal to LoopCount %2, which will be either 1 or 0 depending on whether the row number is odd or even. We then write a conditional statement using [If]...[Else] syntax very similar to CDML's to set a new variable called BackColor. If the row is even, it will be white; otherwise, it will be a light gray.

That's a very simple introduction to Lasso variables. Suffice it to say that you need to use variables for almost any significant work that you do in Lasso. We recommend that you use the short form for variable references ($) wherever possible to save keystrokes. The only place you can't use $ to refer to a variable is during the process of creating it. So the minimum work to create and use a variable looks like this:

```
[Var:'LoopCount'=0]
[Output:++$LoopCount]
```

Error Handling in Lasso

As we program, we expose our code to all kinds of possible errors. Some are simple and direct, such as mistyped program syntax. Others, especially in a middleware application, are more complex; the network might be down, or the remote copy of FileMaker might be unavailable for some other reason. Lasso has a well-developed system for providing error feedback to the programmer. Let's say, for example, that we introduce an error into our search results page above. We're going to mistype the closing square bracket on one of the Lasso tags, like this:

```
[Var:'LoopCount' = 0}
```

Then we're going to run a search and load the page again. We get an error message from Lasso that looks like the following:

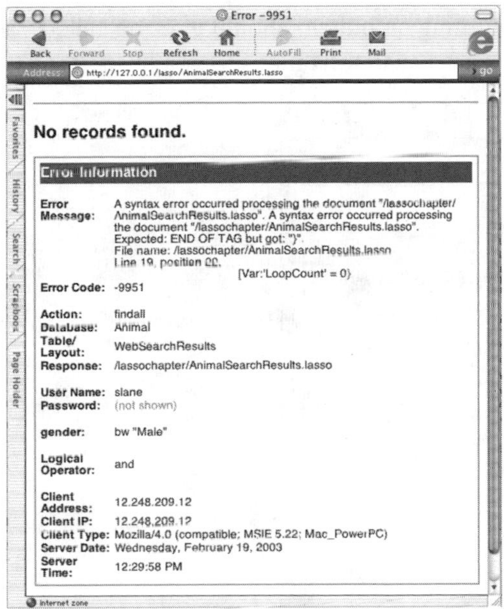

Figure 7.7

The main error message at the top of the page is a bit misleading. It says "No records found," but in fact, the problem is the syntax error. In the meat of the error output, Lasso identifies the exact line and character position of the suspected error and highlights what it believes to be the offending code. Now, Lasso does not always point you to the correct spot, nor does any code processor—there are many syntax errors you can make that will bamboozle a code parser into pointing to some other section of the code. This is true of languages like C and Java, and Lasso is no different. Overall, it gives you extremely rich and generally accurate feedback on all error conditions. In addition to the core error message, you can also see what action was being performed, against what database, with what search parameters, from what IP address, and a number of other important details. In general, if your program encounters an error, Lasso gets you a long way toward debugging the problem.

Error handling doesn't just result in messages to the screen. Error handling is also built into Lasso's system of action handling. When you set up an action, such as a search, Lasso (like CDML) lets you specify not only a format file (a page to go to if the action is successful) but also a number of error files as well, which represent pages to go to if certain types of errors are encountered. To learn more about this, let's run an unsuccessful search on the Animal file. We're searching for a buffalo called Cody (something no buffalo should ever be called), and the search fails. Here's what Lasso tells me:

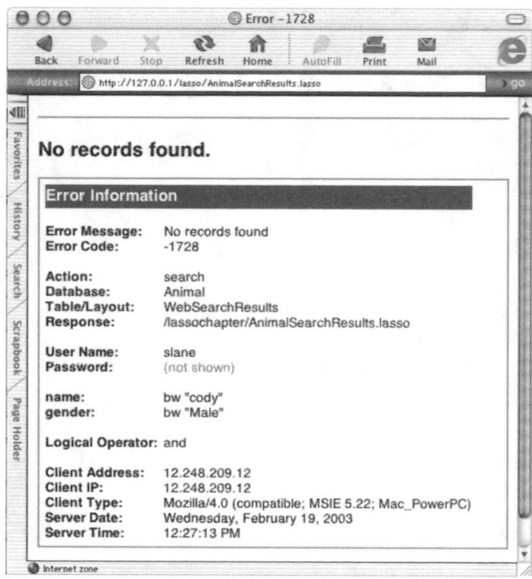

Figure 7.8

It says "No records found" again, but this time it really means it. In the absence of any other handling, Lasso considers this an error and takes us to a default Lasso error page. We can change this behavior by giving Lasso a value for a parameter called ResponseNoResultsError. If no records are found, we'd like to go back to our search page and show a message that says so. We need to modify AnimalSearch.lasso in two ways. First we need to make sure that any search error comes back to this page. Secondly, we need to add code to check for whether a search error has occurred and if so to display a message.

To point any errors back to this page, we can add this to the HTML <form> in AnimalSearch.lasso:

```
<input type="hidden" name="-ResponseNoResultsError" value=
  "AnimalSearch.lasso
```

If we simply add this to the search page and repeat our failing search, we are brought straight back to the search page. This isn't very good form, since it doesn't tell the user what happened and will most likely convince him that the page doesn't work at all. We need to check to see whether a search is in effect. If so, and we return to this page, the search must have failed, and we can output an error message of some kind. We need to add the following code:

```
[If: Lasso_CurrentAction == 'Search' || Lasso_CurrentAction ==
  'FindAll']
    <tr>
         <td colspan="2">Sorry, your search did not find any
           records.</td>
    </tr>
[/If]
```

The [Lasso_CurrentAction] tag, appropriately enough, returns the value of the current Lasso action. In this case, if the action is either Search or FindAll (|| is the operator for "or," by the way), we know we came here as a result of a failed search. If so, we output a table row with the error message at the top of everything.

Lasso's -ResponseNoResultsError is an example of a response parameter. In addition to this one, Lasso has response parameters for quite a number of possible outcomes of database actions—both failures and successes. Check the Lasso Reference (a web-based help system available from the Lasso Administration interface) under the Response category for a full listing of these. You can use these parameters to specify custom response pages for a variety of successful or unsuccessful actions.

One important note is that the response page mechanism really only has meaning in what's called "classic" Lasso, meaning the programming style in which you trigger database actions by including action parameters (such as Search, FindAll, Add, and Duplicate) in HTTP requests, either URLs or HTML forms. In general, as we mention in the previous chapter, we recommend that you stop using the "classic" style as soon as you feel comfortably able to and begin using inlines. We feel the same way about an application architecture based around response pages; it works perfectly well for relatively small applications, but for larger programs we like to centralize things a bit more, rather than spreading logic across dozens of small response pages. As long as you're programming in "classic" style, though, it's very worthwhile to know how to use response pages.

Folding Up the Search Pages

In general, we advocate a programming style that uses fewer individual code files rather than more. Often, this means rolling a couple of different functions together into a single page. First we'll show you how to fold the search page and the results page into a single combined page using "classic" Lasso style. Then we'll redo it in the preferred inline style and try to work as much as possible with inlines from there on. This design won't work very well if there's a huge number of fields that we need to search on; in that case, a separate search form is better. For a lightweight search form, it should work fine. We take a few of our fields out to make it a bit lighter.

Here's how the new page looks prior to a search:

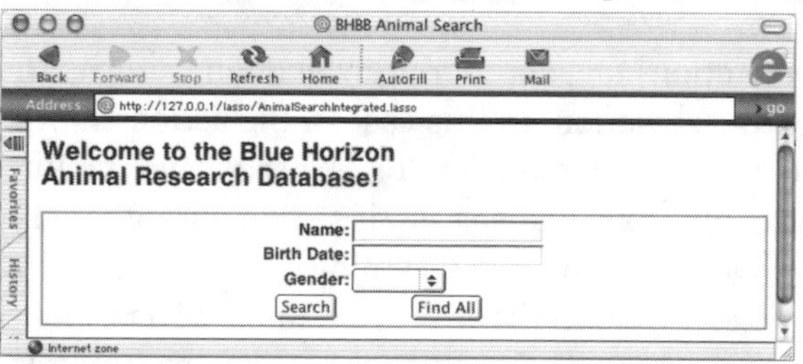

Figure 7.9

Here's how it looks after a failed search:

BHBB Animal Search

http://127.0.0.1/lasso/AnimalSearchIntegrated.lasso

Welcome to the Blue Horizon
Animal Research Database!

Name:
Birth Date:
Gender:
Search Find All

Sorry, your search did not return any records

Figure 7.10

Here's the result of a successful search:

BHBB Animal Search

http://127.0.0.1/lasso/AnimalSearchIntegrated.lasso

Welcome to the Blue Horizon
Animal Research Database!

Name:
Birth Date:
Gender:
Search Find All

Found a total of 17 records

Name	Mother	Father	Birth Date	Birth Weight
Great Geronimo			04/23/1994	107
Stellazura			06/01/1993	90
Hohokam Glory	Stellazura	Great Geronimo	04/05/1999	123
Chin-cha-pe	Stellazura	Great Geronimo	04/05/1999	82
Shaw-Shaw-wa Be-na-se	Stellazura	Great Geronimo	04/05/1999	101
Hector			01/19/1990	102
Harriet			08/14/1992	79
Sweetpea	Harriet	Hector	06/08/2000	80
Sacajawea	Harriet	Hector	06/08/2000	94
Barleycorn	Harriet	Hector	06/08/2000	60
Scatters Them	Harriet	Hector	06/08/2000	100
Harlequin			07/01/2001	112

Figure 7.11

Let's look at the code that accomplishes this:

```
<!DOCTYPE HTML PUBLIC "-//W3C//DTD HTML 4.01//EN"
        "http://www.w3.org/TR/html4/strict.dtd">
<html>
<head>
     <title>BHBB Animal Search</title>
</head>
<body>
     <H2>Welcome to the Blue Horizon<br />Animal Research
       Database!</H2>
     <form action="AnimalSearchIntegrated.lasso" method="post">
     <input type="hidden" name="-Database" value="Animal">
     <input type="hidden" name="-Layout" value="WebSearchResults">
     <input type="hidden" name="-ResponseNoResultsError"
       value="AnimalSearchIntegrated.lasso">
     <table border cellspacing="0" cellpadding="3" width="600">
     <tr align="center">
          <td colspan="6">
               <table border="0"cellspacing="0">
                    <tr>
                         <th align="right">Name:</th>
                         <td><input type="text" name="name"></td>
                    </tr>
                    <tr>
                         <th align="right">Birth Date:</th>
                         <td><input type="text" name=
                           "date_birth"></td>
                    </tr>
                    <tr>
                         <th align="right">Gender:</th>
                         <td>
                              <select name="gender">
                    <option label="" value=""></option>
                    <option label="Male" value="Male">Male</option>
                    <option label="Female" value="Female">Female
                      </option>
                              </select>
                         </td>
                    </tr>
                    <tr>
                         <td align="center">
                              <input type="submit" name="-Search"
                                value="Search">
                         </td>
                         <td align="center">
                              <input type="submit" name="-FindAll"
                                value="Find All">
                         </td>
                    </tr>
               </table>
          </td>
     </tr>
     </form>
```

```
    [If: Lasso_CurrentAction == 'Search' || Lasso_CurrentAction ==
      'FindAll']
                <tr>
        [If: Found_Count == 0]
                    <td colspan="6" align="center" bgcolor=
                      "#CCCCCC"><b>Sorry, your search did not
                      return any records</b></td>
                </tr>
                </table>
        [Else]
                    <td colspan="6" align="center" bgcolor=
                      "#CCCCCC"><b>Found a total of [Found_Count]
                      records</b></td>
                </tr>
                <tr>
                    <th>Name</th>
                    <th>Mother</th>
                    <th>Father</th>
                    <th>Birth Date</th>
                    <th>Birth Weight</th>
                </tr>
                [Var:'LoopCount' = 0]
                [Var: 'OddEven']
                [Records]
                [$OddEven = LoopCount % 2]
                [If: $OddEven == 0]
                    [Var:'BackColor'='#FFFFFF']
                [Else]
                    [Var:'BackColor'='#DDDDDD']
                [/If]
                <tr>
                    <td bgcolor="[Output: $BackColor]">[Field:
                      'name'] </td>
                    <td bgcolor="[Output: $BackColor]">[Field:
                      'SelfByMother::name'] </td>
                    <td bgcolor="[Output: $BackColor]">[Field:
                      'SelfByFather::name'] </td>
                    <td bgcolor="[Output: $BackColor]"
                      align="right">[Field:'date_birth'] </td>
                    <td bgcolor="[Output: $BackColor]" align=
                      "right">[Field:'weight_birth'] </td>
                </tr>
                [/Records]
        </table>
        [/If]
    [Else]
        </table>
    [/If]
</body>
</html>
```

Design-wise we've created one big table. The first row has another table nested inside it, which contains the slimmed-down search form. The next row displays a status message (if a search has been run), and the rest of the table consists of the search results. The search form always gets displayed, so we begin with that code. Then we come to a conditional where, as before, we check the current action. If it's a Search or a Find All, we begin to do some other processing. If there are no found records, then as before, we write a message to that effect. Otherwise, we begin to output the same results list that we have previously stowed in a different page file. The result is a single integrated page.

There are two schools of thought on this. One school says "one action, one page." That way, it's easier to understand what each page is supposed to do. Another school says "one user screen, one page." The thought there is that if a user can perform five actions from a single screen, that one page file should handle them all. This is the idea that we tend to lean toward. It does make the page more complex, and it requires more discipline to manage that complexity.

If we lean in that direction, we run into a problem with "classic" Lasso. The classic style only allows one database action per page request, since the action command is sent along with the HTTP request (whether POST or GET), and Lasso only recognizes one database action per request. The only way to leap that limitation is to use inlines, so that's where we head next.

Writing the Folded Page with Inlines

Inlines in Lasso are conceptually very similar to inlines in CDML. They allow a programmer to perform multiple database actions in a single page file, and they each represent their own special context where different things can occur. (Lasso's *named inlines* are an important exception to this rule.) Let's redo the "folded search page" with an inline.

Right now, the only actions that the page performs are a search and a Find All. These searches are performed by Lasso "on the way to the page," as we've been saying it. When we rewrite it as an inline, it happens *in* the page, but to get this to work, a few other things have to happen. First, we need to *not* send a real Lasso action parameter to the page. If we send a -Search or -FindAll parameter, that action gets performed. Instead, we send what's called a "nothing action," as follows:

```
<input type="hidden" name="-nothing" value="">
```

This tells Lasso not to perform any database actions prior to loading the page. This is important because the database actions are going to be performed by our inline once we're actually inside the page. We also need to change the names of our two buttons. We can't call them -Search and -FindAll anymore because when Lasso sees those names, it performs them as database actions. Instead, we call them both "action".

We still have some more work to do. When we call the inline, we need to tell it what database action to perform. To do this, we create a variable called DBAction. If we reached this page because the user pressed one of the search buttons, the name of that search button has been sent to this page as part of a name-value pair. We somehow need to ask whether either name has been sent to the page, and if it has, we act accordingly.

CDML gave us no way to inspect all of the name-value pairs that are passed to a page. Different commands, such as [FMP-Current-Format], let us inspect particular parameters that were passed to a page, but there was no mechanism to inspect any one we chose. Lasso uses the [Action_Param] tag to do this. What we want to do is create a new variable called DBAction and set it to the correct action parameter for either of the search buttons, if a search button was indeed pressed. We do it like this:

```
[If: (Action_Param: action) == 'Search' ]
         [Var: 'DBAction' = '-Search' ]
[ Else: (Action_Param: action) == 'Find All' ]
         [Var: 'DBAction' = '-FindAll' ]
[/If]
```

If the user presses the Search button, the page receives the name-value pair action=Search. If she presses Find All, the page receives the name-value pair action=Find All. If either of these is true, we set the DBAction variable to the appropriate database action. Finally, we perform our inline:

```
[Inline: (Action_Params), $DBAction, -Database='Animal', -Layout=
  'WebSearchResults' ]
```

For the inline to work, we need to pass it the same parameters that we normally pass through a form or URL. This includes a value for -Database, one for -Layout, a specific database action, *and* all of the name-value pairs that make up the search request. In the case of this search, a number of parameters are sent back to this page via the search form. These parameters include values for name, birth date, gender, and a database action. All four of these values are sent when the user presses Search or Find All. In Lasso, you can use the [Action_Params] tag to grab all of these named values and hand them off to an inline. [Action_Params] is in fact a Lasso *array*, a data type that we haven't looked at yet. In any case, adding (Action_Params) to the inline causes all of these values to be handed off to the inline for it to use. Since the form is no longer passing a database or a layout name (the previous example did but we've omitted those lines this time around), we need to supply those explicitly to the inline—though if we added them back to the search form as hidden inputs (as they were before), we wouldn't even need to do that. Note the *intratag* syntax of (Action_Params), by the way; we're inside a tag already, the Inline tag, so we have to use rounded parentheses instead of square brackets to enclose this inner tag. So this inline tells Lasso to run the specified request (either a Search or a Find All) and then execute the code inside the inline in the context of the specified database action (which, again, is some kind of search).

Here's the complete code for the folded page:

```
<!DOCTYPE HTML PUBLIC "-//W3C//DTD HTML 4.01//EN"
        "http://www.w3.org/TR/html4/strict.dtd">
<html>
<head>
     <title>BHBB Animal Search</title>
</head>
<body>
     <H2>Welcome to the Blue Horizon<br />Animal Research
       Database!</H2>
     <form action="AnimalSearchIntegratedInline.lasso" method="post">
     <input type="hidden" name="-nothing" value="">
     <table border cellspacing="0" cellpadding="3" width="600">
     <tr align="center">
          <td colspan="6">
               <table border="0"cellspacing="0">
                    <tr>
                         <th align="right">Name:</th>
                         <td><input type="text" name="name"></td>
                    </tr>
                    <tr>
                         <th align="right">Birth Date:</th>
                         <td><input type="text" name=
                           "date_birth"></td>
                    </tr>
                    <tr>
                         <th align="right">Gender:</th>
                         <td>
                              <select name="gender">
                    <option label="" value=""></option>
                    <option label="Male" value="Male">Male</option>
                    <option label="Female" value=
                      "Female">Female</option>
                              </select>
                         </td>
                    </tr>
```

```
                    <tr>
                         <td align="center">
                              <input type="submit" name="action"
                                value="Search">
                         </td>
                         <td align="center">
                              <input type="submit" name="action"
                                value="Find All">
                         </td>
                    </tr>
               </table>
          </td>
     </tr>
     </form>
     [Var: 'DBAction']
     [If: (Action_Param: action) == 'Search' ]
          [Var: 'DBAction' = '-Search' ]
     [ Else: (Action_Param: action) == 'Find All' ]
          [Var: 'DBAction' = '-FindAll' ]
     [/If]

 [If: $DBAction == '-Search' || $DBAction == '-FindAll' ]
               <tr>
     [Inline: (Action_Params), $DBAction, -Database='Animal',
       -Layout='WebSearchResults' ]
          [If: Found_Count == 0]
                    <td colspan="6" align="center" bgcolor=
                      "#CCCCCC"><b>Sorry, your search did not
                      return any records</b></td>
               </tr>
               </table>
          [Else]
                    <td colspan="6" align="center" bgcolor=
                      "#CCCCCC"><b>Found a total of [Found_Count]
                      records</b></td>
               </tr>
               <tr>
                    <th>Name</th>
                    <th>Mother</th>
                    <th>Father</th>
                    <th>Birth Date</th>
                    <th>Birth Weight</th>
               </tr>
               [Var:'LoopCount' = 0]
               [Var: 'OddEven']
               [Records]
               [$OddEven = LoopCount % 2]
               [If: $OddEven == 0]
                    [Var:'BackColor'='#FFFFFF']
               [Else]
                    [Var:'BackColor'='#DDDDDD']
               [/If]
               <tr>
                    <td bgcolor="[Output: $BackColor]">[Field:
```

```
                              'name'] </td>
                           <td bgcolor="[Output: $BackColor]">[Field:
                              'SelfByMother::name'] </td>
                           <td bgcolor="[Output: $BackColor]">[Field:
                              'SelfByFather::name'] </td>
                           <td bgcolor="[Output: $BackColor]" align=
                              "right">[Field:'date_birth'] </td>
                           <td bgcolor="[Output: $BackColor]" align=
                              "right">[Field:'weight_birth'] </td>
                      </tr>
                      [/Records]
                 </table>
                 [/If]
                 [/Inline]
          [Else]
                 </table>
          [/If]
</body>
</html>
```

Adding More Actions to the Page

This is all well and good, but we'd talked about adding other functions to this page as well. Suppose we'd like a column at the right with a link that privileged users could click on to delete a record. Naturally, once the record is deleted, we want to show this same page again, minus the deleted record. So it's natural enough to want this page to do the processing. The challenge here is that once the delete happens, we need to rerun the original search so that they see exactly the same found set, minus one.

So we need two things to do this: a way to trigger a delete command from this page that comes back to this page to perform the action and some code that deletes a specific record and then reruns a previous search that is somehow being saved. It seems like this is all much easier in FileMaker! So it is. This is one way to appreciate how much work FileMaker actually does on your behalf.

The Lasso -Delete action, when used with FileMaker records, needs to be told which record to delete. To do this, we give Lasso the internal FileMaker *record ID*, which is a number generated by FileMaker that uniquely identifies a database record. Here's a little HTML form that instructs Lasso to delete a specific record by its ID:

```
<form action=action.lasso method="post">
      <input type="hidden" name="-Database" value="Animal.fp5">
      <input type="hidden" name="-Layout" value="Web.fp5">
      <input type="hidden" name="-KeyValue" value="12312">
      <input type="submit" name="-Delete" value="Delete">
</form>
```

The -KeyValue parameter specifies the exact record ID that we're going to delete. Right now it's hard-coded, but that needs to change. What we want to do, remember, is put a Delete button at the end of each row of our search results that will send Lasso the command to delete that specific record. There are two wrinkles to this. Firstly, we can't hard-code the -KeyValue parameter since it changes from line to line. Secondly, once we come back to the page and perform the delete operation, we need to somehow rerun the previous search so that we can show the old results list minus the deleted record.

Let's look first at how to make the key value dynamic. We can write a little form to wrap around each Delete button:

```
<form action="AnimalSearchIntegratedInlineDelete.lasso"
  method="post">
 <input type="hidden" name="-Database" value="Animal.fp5">
 <input type="hidden" name="-Layout" value="Web.fp5">
 <input type="hidden" name="-KeyValue" value="[Keyfield_Value]">
 <input type="submit" name="-Delete" value="Delete">
</form>
```

Lasso replaces the [Keyfield_Value] tag with the record ID of the current FileMaker record. (The [Keyfield_Value] tag's behavior is different for SQL database sources with which Lasso can also work.) Now it happens that we don't actually want to send a real -Delete parameter back to our page. That's "classic" Lasso style, and we're doing this with inlines. If Lasso sees a -Delete coming back, it tries to execute that action. Instead, as before, we pass the name of the desired action in a named value called "action," and we pass "-nothing" back as our Lasso action.

So our Delete button looks like this:

```
<form action="AnimalSearchIntegratedInlineDelete.lasso" method=
  "post">
     <input type="hidden" name="RecordId" value=
       "[Keyfield_Value]">
     <input type="hidden" name="-nothing" value="">
     <input type="submit" name="action" value="Delete">
</form>
```

As with the search actions, our page can now check for this "action" parameter and do the appropriate thing when it finds it:

```
[If: (Action_Param: 'action') == 'Delete' ]
     [Inline: -Database='Animal', -KeyValue= (Action_Param:
       'RecordId'), -Delete]
     [/Inline]
     [$DBAction = (Action_Param:'prevaction')]
[/If]
```

(Don't worry about the "prevaction" value for now; it's explained further later in this chapter.) We have one more detail to attend to: Once the deletion has happened, we want to rerun the previous search. Here's our strategy: When we issue the delete command (by submitting the form that we just saw), we pass back the user's search choices, as well as the specific type of search (Search or Find All). Once we're done with our deletion, we reuse the page's search logic to rerun the search.

So our Delete form/button is actually going to look like this:

```
<form action="AnimalSearchIntegratedInlineDelete.lasso" method=
  "post">
     <input type="hidden" name="RecordId" value="[Keyfield_Value]">
     <input type="hidden" name="name" value="[Action_Param:'name']">
     <input type="hidden" name="gender" value="[Action_Param:
       'gender']">
     <input type="hidden" name="date_birth" value="[Action_Param:
       'date_birth']">
     <input type="hidden" name="-nothing" value="">
     <input type="hidden" name="prevaction" value="[$DBAction]">
     <input type="submit" name="action" value="Delete">
</form>
```

The different [Action_Param] values are the user's search criteria, if any, while the $DBAction variable is either Search or FindAll, depending on which the user chose. We can pass all these values back to the page in the course of the delete, and then our page logic looks like this:

```
<!DOCTYPE HTML PUBLIC "-//W3C//DTD HTML 4.01//EN"
       "http://www.w3.org/TR/html4/strict.dtd">
<html>
<head>
     <title>BHBB Animal Search</title>
</head>
<body>
     <H2>Welcome to the Blue Horizon<br />Animal Research
       Database!</H2>
     <form action="AnimalSearchIntegratedInlineDelete.lasso"
       method="post">
     <input type="hidden" name="-nothing" value="">
     <table border cellspacing="0" cellpadding="3" width="600">
     <tr align="center">
          <td colspan="6">
               <table border="0"cellspacing="0">
                    <tr>
                         <th align="right">Name:</th>
                         <td><input type="text" name="name"></td>
                    </tr>
                    <tr>
                         <th align="right">Birth Date:</th>
```

```
                <td><input type="text" name="date_
                  birth"></td>
            </tr>
            <tr>
                <th align="right">Gender:</th>
                <td>
                    <select name="gender">
            <option label="" value=""></option>
            <option label="Male" value="Male">Male</option>
            <option label="Female" value="Female">Female
              </option>
                    </select>
                </td>
            </tr>
            <tr>
                <td align="center">
                    <input type="submit" name="action"
                      value="Search">
                </td>
                <td align="center">
                    <input type="submit" name="action"
                      value="Find All">
                </td>
            </tr>
        </table>
    </td>
</tr>
</form>
[Var: 'DBAction']

[If: (Action_Param: 'action') == 'Delete' ]
    [Inline: -Database='Animal', -KeyValue= (Action_Param:
      'RecordId'), -Delete]
    [/Inline]
    [$DBAction = (Action_Param:'prevaction')]
[/If]

[If: (Action_Param: 'action') == 'Search' ]
    [Var: 'DBAction' = '-Search' ]
[ Else: (Action_Param: 'action') == 'Find All' ]
    [Var: 'DBAction' = '-FindAll' ]
[/If]

[If: $DBAction == '-Search' || $DBAction == '-FindAll' ]
        <tr>
[Inline: (Action_Params), $DBAction, -Database='Animal',
  -Layout='WebSearchResults' ]
    Error = [Error_CurrentError], [Error_CurrentError:
      -ErrorCode]
    [If: (Found_Count) == 0]
            <td colspan="6" align="center" bgcolor=
              "#CCCCCC"><b>Sorry, your search did not
              return any records</b></td>
        </tr>
```

```
            </table>
        [Else]
                <td colspan="6" align="center" bgcolor=
                  "#CCCCCC"><b>Found a total of [Found_Count]
                  records</b></td>
            </tr>
            <tr>
                <th>Name</th>
                <th>Mother</th>
                <th>Father</th>
                <th>Birth Date</th>
                <th>Birth Weight</th>
                <th> </th>
            </tr>
            [Var:'LoopCount' = 0]
            [Var: 'OddEven']
            [Records]
            [$OddEven = LoopCount % 2]
            [If: $OddEven == 0]
                [Var:'BackColor'='#FFFFFF']
            [Else]
                [Var:'BackColor'='#DDDDDD']
            [/If]
            <tr>
                <td bgcolor="[Output: $BackColor]">[Field:
                  'name'] </td>
                <td bgcolor="[Output: $BackColor]">[Field:
                  'SelfByMother::name'] </td>
                <td bgcolor="[Output: $BackColor]">[Field:
                  'SelfByFather::name'] </td>
                <td bgcolor="[Output: $BackColor]" align=
                  "right">[Field:'date_birth'] </td>
                <td bgcolor="[Output: $BackColor]" align=
                  "right">[Field:'weight_birth'] </td>
                <td bgcolor="[Output: $BackColor]" align=
                  "right">
                    <form action="AnimalSearchIntegratedIn-
                      lineDelete.lasso" method="post">
                        <input type="hidden" name="RecordId"
                          value="[Keyfield_Value]">
                        <input type="hidden" name="name"
                          value="[Action_Param:'name']">
                        <input type="hidden" name="gender"
                          value="[Action_Param:'gender']">
                        <input type="hidden" name="date_
                          birth" value="[Action_Param:
                          'date_birth']">
                        <input type="hidden" name="-nothing"
                          value="">
                        <input type="hidden" name=
                          "prevaction" value="[$DBAction]">
                        <input type="submit" name="action"
                          value="Delete">
                    </form>
```

```
                    </td>
                </tr>
                [/Records]
            </table>
            [/If]
            [/Inline]
        [Else]
            </table>
        [/If]
</body>
</html>
```

Now, in the course of performing the Delete action, we also set the variable DBAction equal to the value for "prevaction" that got passed back to the page. This is a setup for the logic that performs the search; when it sees a correctly set value for DBAction, it re-performs the specified search. The user's old search criteria are automatically reused in the search by virtue of the (Action_Params) value that is passed in to the search inline.

All right, our users can now delete records to their hearts' content. What else might they want to do on this page? Well, how about adding records? After all, it's easy to build a single layout in FileMaker that lets users create, delete, and edit records all in the same place. Can it be that much harder on the web? Not really—it's just a matter of adding more actions to the page.

Let's say that we want to add a new row just under the column headers with editable areas where the user can enter data. At the end of the row, instead of a Delete button like we used on the search results rows, we'll put an Add button instead. From here the user can fill in these fields, hit Add, and the new record will be added. As always, we rerun the previous search to make sure the displayed set of records stays the same.

Here's how the page looks:

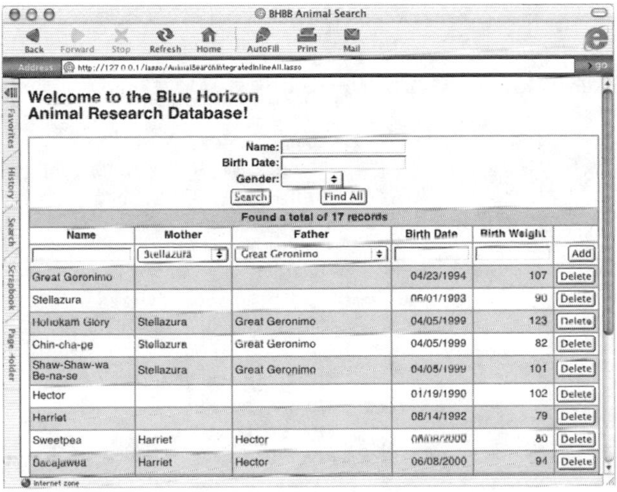

Figure 7.12

To fit this new row in, we need to change the structure of the page quite a lot. Things are getting crowded in there, so we're also going to resort to a fairly new and quite useful Lasso feature called *named inlines*. Lasso lets us give a specific inline a name and refer to the results of that inline later. In the new add row we're building, the Mother and Father columns each have a drop-down menu in them. In the Mother column, the names are those of all the female animals, while the Father column is a list of all the males. Each of those is built with a named inline:

```
[Inline: -InlineName='FemaleAnimals', -Database='Animal', -Layout=
  'WebSearchResults', 'gender'='Female', -Search][/Inline]
```

Once the inline has a name, we can refer to its results elsewhere without needing to do so inside the context of the inline. So later on we can say:

```
[Records: -InlineName='FemaleAnimals']...[/Records]
```

...anywhere we want to use the records from that inline (assuming it found any, which is an issue we have to deal with in our page). We also use a named inline for the main user search, since it makes some things more convenient. Here's the code for the new page:

```
<!DOCTYPE HTML PUBLIC "-//W3C//DTD HTML 4.01//EN"
        "http://www.w3.org/TR/html4/strict.dtd">
<html>
<head>
```

```
    <title>BHBB Animal Search</title>
</head>
<body>
    <H2>Welcome to the Blue Horizon<br />Animal Research
      Database!</H2>
    <form action="AnimalSearchIntegratedInlineAll.lasso"
      method="post">
    <input type="hidden" name="-nothing" value="">
    <table border cellspacing="0" cellpadding="3" width="600">
    <tr align="center">
        <td colspan="6">
            <table border="0"cellspacing="0">
                <tr>
                    <th align="right">Name:</th>
                    <td><input type="text" name="name"></td>
                </tr>
                <tr>
                    <th align="right">Birth Date:</th>
                    <td><input type="text" name=
                      "date_birth"></td>
                </tr>
                <tr>
                    <th align="right">Gender:</th>
                    <td>
                        <select name="gender">
                <option label="" value=""></option>
                <option label="Male" value="Male">Male</option>
                <option label="Female" value=
                  "Female">Female</option>
                        </select>
                    </td>
                </tr>
                <tr>
                    <td align="center">
                        <input type="submit" name="action"
                          value="Search">
                    </td>
                    <td align="center">
                        <input type="submit" name="action"
                          value="Find All">
                    </td>
                </tr>
            </table>
        </td>
    </tr>
    </form>
    [Var: 'DBAction']

    [Inline: -InlineName='FemaleAnimals', -Database='Animal',
      -Layout='WebSearchResults', 'gender'='Female',
      -Search][/Inline]
    [Inline: -InlineName='MaleAnimals', -Database='Animal',
      -Layout='WebSearchResults', 'gender'='Male', -Search][/Inline]
```

```
[If: (Action_Param: 'action') == 'Add' ]
      [Inline: -Database='Animal', -Layout='WebSearchResults',
        'name'=(Action_Param:'a_name'),
      'id_mother'=(Action_Param:'a_id_mother'),
        'id_father'=(Action_Param:'a_id_father'),
      'date_birth'=(Action_Param:'a_date_birth'),
        'weight_birth'=(Action_Param:'a_weight_birth'), -Add]
      [/Inline]
      [$DBAction = (Action_Param:'prevaction')]
[/If]

[If: (Action_Param: 'action') == 'Delete' ]
      [Inline: -Database='Animal', -KeyValue= (Action_Param:
        'RecordId'), -Delete]
      [/Inline]
      [$DBAction = (Action_Param:'prevaction')]
[/If]

[If: (Action_Param: 'action') == 'Search' ]
      [Var: 'DBAction' = '-Search' ]
[ Else: (Action_Param: 'action') == 'Find All' ]
      [Var: 'DBAction' = '-FindAll' ]
[/If]
<!--Error = [Error_CurrentError], [Error_CurrentError:
  -ErrorCode]-->

[If: $DBAction == '-Search' || $DBAction == '-FindAll' ]
            <tr>
      [Inline: -InlineName='UserSearch', (Action_Params),
        $DBAction, -Database='Animal', -Layout=
        'WebSearchResults' ]
            <!--Error = [Error_CurrentError], [Error_CurrentError:
              -ErrorCode]-->
            [Var: 'UserFoundCount' = (Found_Count) ]
            [If: $UserFoundCount == 0]
                        <td colspan="6" align="center" bgcolor=
                          "#CCCCCC"><b>Sorry, your search did not
                          return any records</b></td>
                  </tr>
            [Else]
                        <td colspan="6" align="center" bgcolor=
                          "#CCCCCC"><b>Found a total of
                          [Found_Count] records</b></td>
                  </tr>

            [/If]
      [/Inline]
[/If]

<tr>
      <th>Name</th>
      <th>Mother</th>
      <th>Father</th>
      <th>Birth Date</th>
```

```
        <th>Birth Weight</th>
        <th> </th>
    </tr>
    <tr>
        <form action="AnimalSearchIntegratedInlineAll.lasso"
          method="post">
            <td><input type="text" name="a_name" size="20"></td>
            <td>
                <select name="a_id_mother">
                    [Records: -InlineName='FemaleAnimals']
                    <option value="[Field:
                      'id_animal']">[Field:'name']</option>
                    [/Records]
                </select>
            </td>
            <td>
                <select name="a_id_father">
                    [Records: -InlineName='MaleAnimals']
                    <option value="[Field:
                      'id_animal']">[Field:'name']</option>
                    [/Records]
                </select>
            </td>
            <td align="right"><input type="text" name=
              "a_date_birth" size="15"></td>
            <td align="right"><input type="text"
              name="a_weight_birth" size="15"></td>
            <td align="right"><input type="submit"
              name="-nothing" value="Add"></td>
            <input type="hidden" name="prevaction"
              value="[$DBAction]">
            <input type="hidden" name="action" value="add">
        </form>
    </tr>

    [If: $UserFoundCount > 0 ]
            [Var:'LoopCount' = 0]
            [Var: 'OddEven']
            [Records: -InlineName = 'UserSearch']
            [$OddEven = LoopCount % 2]
            [If: $OddEven == 0]
                [Var:'BackColor'='#FFFFFF']
            [Else]
                [Var:'BackColor'='#DDDDDD']
            [/If]
            <tr>
                <td bgcolor="[Output: $BackColor]">[Field:
                  'name'] </td>
                <td bgcolor="[Output: $BackColor]">[Field:
                  'SelfByMother::name'] </td>
                <td bgcolor="[Output: $BackColor]">[Field:
                  'SelfByFather::name'] </td>
                <td bgcolor="[Output: $BackColor]" align=
                  "right">[Field:'date_birth'] </td>
```

```
                    <td bgcolor="[Output: $BackColor]" align=
                      "right">[Field:'weight_birth'] </td>
                    <td bgcolor="[Output: $BackColor]" align=
                      "right">
                         <form action="AnimalSearchIntegratedIn-
                           lineAll.lasso" method="post">
                              <input type="hidden" name="RecordId"
                                value="[Keyfield_Value]">
                              <input type="hidden" name="name"
                                value="[Action_Param:'name']">
                              <input type="hidden" name="gender"
                                value="[Action_Param:'gender']">
                              <input type="hidden" name="date_
                                birth" value="[Action_Param:'date_
                                birth']">
                              <input type="hidden" name="-nothing"
                                value="">
                              <input type="hidden" name=
                                "prevaction" value="[$DBAction]">
                              <input type="submit" name="action"
                                value="Delete">
                         </form>
                    </td>
               </tr>
               [/Records]
          </table>
     [Else]
          </table>
     [/If]
</body>
</html>
```

The bold sections represent changes to the original code. Let's begin our analysis of the code with the last bold section, which represents the new "add" row. There are two things of note. Firstly, notice that we've prefixed all the HTML element names with "a_." It's important to do something like this because the search form already contains elements whose names match those of some of the database fields. If we put elements in the add row with any of these same names, a number of different kinds of confusion are possible. Unless we have a special purpose in mind, we try not to have several different HTML elements share the same name. So we adopt the a_ prefix here to distinguish the elements in the add row. The other item of note is the way in which the mother and father drop-down menus are built using the results of two named inlines.

Turning to the first bold section, here we see the two named inlines for the mother and father menus. There's no particular reason to have them up here, other than to keep them out of the way. They could just as well be closer to the code for the add row. Also in this section is the conditional code dealing with the "add" action. Here we have an inline with an -Add action, in which all the fields are specified by name and value. We can't simply send the inline the [Action_Params] array as we've done elsewhere because our element names for the -Add action don't match up with the database names. So we have to map from these names to the database field names explicitly.

Adding Error Handling

Error handling is the bugaboo of every complicated program. If you're writing high-quality code, you need to check for errors at every point where they can possibly occur. In our case, that generally means database actions. Any of our database actions could fail. If they do, we need to diagnose the failure and report this gracefully to the user. Lasso gives us two mechanisms for catching and handling errors. The simplest technique uses the [Error_CurrentError] tag. More sophisticated error handling is possible using combinations of the [Protect] and [Handle] tags.

The [Error_CurrentError] tag simply reports the most recent Lasso error as a text message. It can also return the numeric code associated with that error when written like this: [Error_CurrentError: -ErrorCode]. Any error code other than zero indicates some type of error. Lasso also provides replacement tags that correspond to particularly common errors, including the "no error" state; these tags have names like [Error_NoError], [Error_FileNotFound], and the like. These can be used for the sake of convenience when checking for errors. So it's common to write:

```
[If: (Error_CurrentError) == (Error_NoError)]
```

...when checking for the absence of errors. We can use this to add simple error handling to each of our inlines. For example, the inline that performs the search could be rewritten like this:

```
[Var: 'UserFoundCount' = 0]
     [If: $DBAction == '-Search' || $DBAction == '-FindAll' ]
               <tr>
          [Inline: -InlineName='UserSearch', (Action_Params),
            $DBAction, -Database='Animal', -Layout=
            'WebSearchResults' ]
               [If: (Error_CurrentError) == (Error_NoError)]
                    [$UserFoundCount = (Found_Count) ]
                    [If: $UserFoundCount == 0]
                             <td colspan="6" align="center"
                               bgcolor="#CCCCCC"><b>Sorry, your
                               search did not return any
```

```
                                    records</b></td>
                              </tr>
                        [Else]
                                    <td colspan="6" align="center"
                                      bgcolor="#CCCCCC"><b>Found a total
                                      of [Found_Count] records</b></td>
                              </tr>
                        [/If]
                  [Else]
                              <td colspan="6" align="center" bgcolor=
                                "#CCCCCC"><b>An error occurred during
                                your search: [Error_CurrentError]
                                ([Error_CurrentError: -ErrorCode])
                                </b></td>
                        </tr>
                  [/If]
            [/Inline]
      [/If]
```

This simply wraps the inner logic in an error check and, if any error is present, substitutes an error message for the found set message. But this kind of error handling gets cumbersome quickly. You need to check for errors after each database action, and only continue executing the page if no error is found. You rapidly get deep into nested conditional statements ("do this, and if there's no error do this, and if there's no error do this" and so on). A more elegant style of error handling lets you specify what in some languages are called *try* and *catch* blocks and in Lasso are called [Protect] and [Handle] blocks.

These two tags, [Protect] and [Handle], work together. [Protect]...[/Protect] creates a code block that traps all errors inside itself. Any error that occurs inside this block is never presented directly to the user. It can, however, be handled inside a [Handle] block at the end of the [Protect] block. Further, Lasso provides a way to skip directly to the [Handle] sections inside any [Protect] block by using a tag called [Fail]. [Fail] is a way of saying "stop whatever you're doing and skip directly to the [Handle] sections."

A [Handle] block without any qualifiers traps all errors that occur in an enclosing [Protect] block. We can also add conditional expressions to [Handle] to tell it to handle only certain types of errors. For example:

```
[Protect]
      [Var: 'Error']
      [Inline: -Database='Animal.fp5', -Layout='Web', -FindAll]
            [$Error = (Error_CurrentError)]
            [If: $Error != 0]
                  [Fail]
            [/If]
```

```
    [/Inline]

    [Handle: $Error == (Error_InvalidDatabase)]
         Sorry, the specified database could not be found.
    [/Handle]

    [Handle: $Error == (Error_NoPermission)]
         Sorry, you don't have permission to search the Animals
           database.
    [/Handle]
[/Protect]
```

Here, we run an inline that does a search in the Animals database. If we find any error, we capture its value and issue a [Fail] command. The enclosing [Protect] block has two [Handle] clauses, each with a conditional statement that triggers the use of that particular block. If the error we failed on was a problem with the database's validity, we execute the first block. If it's a permissions error, the second block gets executed instead.

This way of doing things creates an implicit branching structure that makes it fairly easy to handle a number of different possible errors neatly. We can have multiple [Fail] or [FailIf] statements inside a [Protect] block, each one triggering a different type of error handler. This allows us to put all of our error-handling code in one place—inside one or more [Handle] blocks that are grouped together at the end of the [Protect] structure.

Here's how the core of our integrated animal search page looks, rewritten with [Protect] and [Handle]:

```
    [Var: 'DBAction']
    [Protect]
         [Inline: -InlineName='FemaleAnimals', -Database='Animal',
           -Layout='WebSearchResults', 'gender'='Female',
           -Search][/Inline]
         [Inline: -InlineName='MaleAnimals', -Database='Animal',
           -Layout='WebSearchResults', 'gender'='Male',
           -Search][/Inline]

         [If: (Action_Param: 'action') == 'Add' ]
              [Inline: -Database='Animal', -Layout=
                'WebSearchResults', 'name'=(Action_Param:'a_name'),
              'id_mother'=(Action_Param:'a_id_mother'),
                'id_father'=(Action_Param:'a_id_father'),
              'date_birth'=(Action_Param:'a_date_birth'),
                'weight_birth'=(Action_Param:'a_weight_birth'),
                -Add]
                   [If: (Error_CurrentError) != (Error_NoError)]
                        [Fail]
                   [/If]
              [/Inline]
```

```
        [$DBAction = (Action_Param:'prevaction')]
    [/If]

    [If: (Action_Param: 'action') == 'Delete' ]
        [Inline: -Database='Animal', KeyValue= (Action_
          Param:'RecordId'), -Delete]
            [If: (Error_CurrentError) != (Error_NoError)]
                [Fail]
            [/If]
        [/Inline]
        [$DBAction = (Action_Param:'prevaction')]
    [/If]

    [If: (Action_Param: 'action') == 'Search' ]
        [Var: 'DBAction' = '-Search' ]
    [ Else: (Action_Param: 'action') == 'Find All' ]
        [Var: 'DBAction' = '-FindAll' ]
    [/If]
    <!--Error = [Error_CurrentError], [Error_CurrentError:
      -ErrorCode]-->

    [Var: 'UserFoundCount' = 0]
    [If: $DBAction == '-Search' || $DBAction == '-FindAll' ]
            <tr>
        [Inline: -InlineName='UserSearch', (Action_Params),
          $DBAction, -Database='Animal', -Layout=
          'WebSearchResults' ]
            <!--Error = [Error_CurrentError], [Error_
              CurrentError: -ErrorCode]-->
            [If: ((Error_CurrentError) != (Error_NoError))
              && ((Error_CurrentError: -ErrorCode) !=
              -1728 )]
                [Fail]
            [/If]
            [$UserFoundCount = (Found_Count) ]
            [If: $UserFoundCount == 0]
                <td colspan="6" align="center" bgcolor=
                  "#CCCCCC"><b>Sorry, your search did not
                  return any records</b></td>
            </tr>
            [Else]
                <td colspan="6" align="center" bgcolor=
                  "#CCCCCC"><b>Found a total of
                  [Found_Count] records</b></td>
            </tr>

            [/If]
        [/Inline]
    [/If]

    [Handle: (Error_CurrentError) != (Error_No_Error)]
        <td colspan="6" align="center" bgcolor=
          "#CCCCCC"><b>An error occurred: [Error_
          CurrentError] ([Error_CurrentError:
```

```
                    -ErrorCode])</b></td>
            </tr>
            [/Handle]
        [/Protect]
```

We've now wrapped all of our database actions in a [Protect] block. After each action, we check the current error status, and if necessary, we [Fail]. In general we fail if the error code is other than zero (in other words, if [Error_CurrentError] is something other than [Error_NoError]). The only exception is in our search routine, where, if we find no records, Lasso returns an error of –1728. We'd rather handle that error a little differently, so we make an exception for that case and output a specific error message. Otherwise, all errors are handled by the [Handle] block. Notice that the code in the [Handle] block will *always* execute once all the other code in the [Protect] block is done, *unless* we add a conditional statement to the [Handle] block. Here we just add a conditional that checks to make sure there really is an error in effect. If not, we skip the [Handle] block.

This is a fairly simple application of [Protect] and [Handle], but these constructs can be used for complex error handling in a way that reduces the overall number of conditional branches needed to handle errors and brings all the error-handling code together in one place. Once your pages become as complex as the ones we've been working with, you'll benefit from learning to use these more advanced error-handling constructs.

Using Arrays and Maps to Create a Value List Library

Lasso, like PHP and other more advanced programming languages, has a number of built-in data types that offer the programmer elegant solutions to a variety of programming problems. For the handling of more complicated data structures, Lasso offers us the array and the map. (PHP refers to both of these structures simply as arrays, by way of comparison.) An *array* is an ordered list of elements where each item is distinguished by its position, while a *map* is a list of element pairs where each pair consists of a key and a value.

For example, we can use an array to create a list of possible salutations, like this:

```
[Var:'Salutations' = (Array: 'Ms.', 'Mrs.', 'Mr.', 'Dr.', 'Fr.',
  'Rev.')]
```

Once the array is created, we can access its elements using the Get function. So to get the third element of the array, we would write:

```
[Var;'Sal3' = $Salutations->(Get:3)]
```

...which would cause the variable Sal3 to be set to the value "Mr." There are quite a number of other functions that operate on arrays as well (about a dozen in all). There are functions to add items to an array, remove items at any position, merge two arrays, flatten an array into a string, sort an array, and get the size of an array (the number of elements).

A map is a similar concept, except each value in the map has a *key* instead of a numeric index. Let's say that you're taking a population survey and you have a set of codes that correspond to various ethnic backgrounds. Each possible background has a short two-letter code and a longer description. A map can store both of these together and use the shorter code to look up the longer description. For example:

```
[Var:'Backgrounds' = (Map: 'CR'='Cree', 'AB'='Athabasca',
  'MC'='Micmac', 'SX'='Sioux', 'KW'='Kiowa', 'KS'='Kansa',
  'SK'='Sauk', 'FX'='Fox', 'DW'='Delaware', 'MN'='Mandan') ]
```

We can then extract elements from the array by saying:

```
[Var:'CurrentTribe'=$Backgrounds->(Find:'CR')]
```

...which retrieves the mapped value corresponding to the key of CR and places it into the variable CurrentTribe.

Let's take a look at how we can use these structures to store value lists in our application. Of course, FileMaker itself can store value lists, and there are specific Lasso tags that let us work with FileMaker value lists. But we've decided that we'd rather not do a database query into FileMaker every time we want to use a value list of some kind. In any case, FileMaker value lists are not able to hold key-value pairs of the type that we often want to use in web applications.

Instead we construct a special file with all of our value list data in it. When we need a value list, we can include that file using Lasso's [Include] tag. So here's a sample ValueList.lasso file:

```
[Var:'BackgroundsVL' = (Map: 'CR'='Cree', 'AB'='Athabasca',
  'MC'='Micmac', 'SX'='Sioux', 'KW'='Kiowa', 'KS'='Kansa',
  'SK'='Sauk', 'FX'='Fox', 'DW'='Delaware', 'MN'='Mandan') ]

[Var:'PlainsStatesVL' = (Map: 'KS'='Kansas', 'MO'='Missouri',
  'NE'='Nebraska', 'OK'='Oklahoma', 'SD'='South Dakota', 'ND'='North
  Dakota') ]
```

```
[Var:'IncomeLevelsVL' = (Map: 'LT10'='Less Than $10,000',
  '10-15'='$10,000-$15,000', '15-25'='$15,000-$25,000', '25+'='Over
  $25,000')]
```

We could have quite a number of other value lists in that same file as well. Once we've built the value list file, all of our value lists are there waiting to be used. We can write some simple Lasso code to take any of our value lists, which are stored as Lasso maps, and turn them into HTML. For example, to turn a value list into an HTML SELECT structure, we could write something like this:

```
[Var:'StateCount' ]
[Var:'CurrentPair']
[$StateCount =$PlainsStatesVL->Size]
<select name="PlainsStates">
[Loop: -LoopFrom=1, -LoopTo=$StateCount]
     [$CurrentPair=$PlainsStatesVL->(Get:(Loop_Count))]
     <option value=[$CurrentPair->First]>[$CurrentPair->
       Second]</option>
[/Loop]
</select>
```

This code pulls items off the selected map in "pairs." In Lasso, a *pair* is simply that—a two-element structure that can have its elements accessed with the First and Second functions, as we see here. First we count the number of elements in the chosen value list. Then we loop from one up to that number, and each time through the loop we grab the current pair from the map. We then use its first and second elements to create the value and the actual display text for the menu item, respectively.

Well, that was straightforward enough. But we're likely to have to do that kind of thing over and over again, every time we want to make an HTML menu out of one of our arrays. Isn't there some way to package up that code in one place so we don't have to type it again and again? Yes there is, and that's what we're going to show you next.

Coding for Reuse: Lasso Custom Tags

Any programming language worth its salt will have some way to define custom chunks of reusable code. In traditional procedural programming languages, these reusable units are often called *functions*. In Lasso, they're known as *custom tags*. If you're used to languages like C, PHP, and Java, Lasso's custom tags are definitely a bit more cumbersome than traditional functions, but they accomplish the same goals.

The first chunk of code that we want to write is one that spits out map structures that correspond to our different value lists. We could just define each one as a separate variable, as we did above, but they'll be slightly easier to use if we write a custom tag that accepts the name of the value list as an input and returns the desired data map as its output. Here's how that looks:

```
[Define_Tag:'getValueListData', -Required='valueListName']
     [Var:'returnMap']
     [Select: (Local: 'valueListName')]
          [Case: 'BackgroundsVL']
               [$returnMap=(Map: 'CR'='Cree', 'AB'='Athabasca',
                'MC'='Micmac', 'SX'='Sioux', 'KW'='Kiowa',
                'KS'='Kansa', 'SK'='Sauk', 'FX'='Fox',
                'DW'='Delaware', 'MN'='Mandan')]
          [Case: 'PlainsStatesVL']
               [$returnMap=(Map: 'KS'='Kansas', 'MO'='Missouri',
                'NE'='Nebraska', 'OK'='Oklahoma', 'SD'='South
                Dakota', 'ND'='North Dakota')]
          [Case: 'IncomeLevelsVL']
               [$returnMap=(Map: 'LT10'='Less Than $10,000',
                '10-15'='$10,000-$15,000', '15-25'=
               '$15,000-$25,000', '25+'='Over $25,000')]
     [/Select]
     [Return: $returnMap]
[/Define_Tag]
```

There are several important new tags here. [Define_Tag] is the first of these. This is the master construct that encloses all of our custom code. Within the [Define_Tag] tag, we also need to specify what parameters the custom tag is going to take and whether they're required. In our case, we only need one parameter, which is the name of the value list whose data we're going to retrieve. This is a required parameter, so we use the -Required keyword and follow it with the name of our parameter, which is called valueListName. This is enough to finish defining the tag.

Now that the tag is defined (that is, it has a name and a list of parameters), we need to fill in its innards so that it can do some work. The logic is fairly simple; we're going to change the value that was passed in for valueListName, and if it's a name that we recognize, we're going to generate a map that contains the data for that value list. Lastly, we need to *return* the appropriate map to the user of our custom tag.

Inside our tag, we use a [Select] command to distinguish between different incoming values of valueListName. [Select] is a tag that lets us choose among many different values for a single variable and take a potentially different action for each one. Lasso's [Select] is similar to the *switch* construct in languages such as C, Java, and PHP. There's a wrinkle here, though; in order to access the incoming value for valueListName, we need to use the Lasso [Local] tag. To understand this, we need to understand a little bit about a topic called *variable scoping*. This is a point where novice programmers often get confused, so pay close attention if this concept is unfamiliar to you.

Our custom tag has a single *parameter* called valueListName. When a user calls our tag, she does so like this:

```
[getValueListData: 'BackgroundsVL']
```

In this case, the string BackgroundsVL is our inbound parameter. This means that inside the body of our function, the *value* BackgroundsVL is known by the *name* of valueListName. Now, if there's already some variable named valueListName in use somewhere outside our custom tag, these two variables are *not* the same, despite sharing the same name. The one defined outside our tag is the *global* version of the variable, and the one defined inside our tag is called the *local* version (because it's "local" to our tag code).

In many programming languages, the distinction between a global variable and a local variable of the same name is handled transparently; references to variables inside a function, in a language such as C or Java, are implicitly understood to refer to local variables. If no local variable by a given name can be found, an error results. Lasso does things the other way around; even inside a custom tag, all variable references are global by default, unless the [Local] keyword is used. If, instead of using the [Local] keyword, we just treated valueListName like a plain old variable and said this:

```
[Select: $valueListName]
```

...you'd get a Lasso error that states "the global variable 'valueListName' has not been declared." In other words, there's no variable by that name outside the tag, which is where Lasso looks by default. In order for Lasso to look at the inbound valueListName parameter, we have to force it to do this by saying [Local: 'valueListName']. For purposes of comparison, as you go on to learn other programming languages, realize that it is far more typical for a modular unit of code to see its own *local* variables by default and require special prompting to see variables in the global namespace. In Lasso, it's just the other way around.

So, we have a [Select] statement based on whatever value the user passed in for the valueListName parameter. Based on its value, we assign one of a number of different maps to a variable called return-

Map. Once we're done with our [Select] statement, we return whatever value is in returnMap. Note that returnMap is also a local variable; we declared it as such by saying [Local:'returnMap'], and later, when we refer to it, we use the special # character. In just the same way that $variable is shorthand for referring to a global variable named "variable," #variable is shorthand for referring to a local variable of the same name.

To use our new custom tag, we can just write:

```
[getValueListData: 'BackgroundsVL']
```

We should see the following in our Lasso page:

```
map: (AB)=(Athabasca), (CR)=(Cree), (DW)=(Delaware), (FX)=(Fox),
  (KS)=(Kansa), (KW)=(Kiowa), (MC)=(Micmac), (MN)=(Mandan),
  (SK)=(Sauk), (SX)=(Sioux)
```

Okay, so far so good. We've written one custom tag to spit back maps that contain value list data based on some value list name that we pass in. But what we really want is some reusable custom code to turn a given value list's data into, say, an HTML SELECT or a set of HTML radio buttons. Somehow, we want to package up that code that we wrote before into a custom tag. It should let us specify the name of the value list to use, just like the tag we just wrote. It should also allow us to specify a currently selected value so that if the user has made a menu choice, the output reflects that. Here's how the tag looks, along with an example of its use:

```
<!--Here's the definition of the tag-->
[Define_Tag: 'HTMLSelect', Required='selectName',
  -Required='valueListName', -Required='currentValue']
     [Local: 'dataMap' = (getValueListData: #valueListName )]
     [Local: 'vlCount'=#dataMap->Size]
     [Local: 'currentPair']
     [Local: 'selectText']
     [Local: 'htmlResult']
     [#htmlResult = '<select name="' + #selectName + '">' ]
     [Loop: -LoopFrom=1, -LoopTo=#vlCount]
          [#currentPair=#dataMap->(Get:(Loop_Count))]
          [If: #currentPair->First == #currentValue]
               [#selectText=' selected']
          [Else]
               [#selectText='']
          [/If]
          [#htmlResult = #htmlResult + '<option value=' +
            (#currentPair->First) + #selectText + '>' +
            (#currentPair->Second) + '</option>']
     [/Loop]
     [#htmlResult = #htmlResult + '</select>']
     [Return: #htmlResult]
```

```
[/Define_Tag]

<!--Here's how we use it-->
[HTMLSelect: 'background', 'BackgroundsVL', 'KW']
```

Our new tag has three required parameters: selectName, which is the name that the actual HTML element will have; valueListName, which is the name of our value list data, as before; and currentValue, which indicates the currently selected value in the value list (though required, this value may blank, indicating no selection). Our new tag does quite a bit with local variables, but it's really just a rewrite of the code that we used before made more generic. The only substantive differences are that we call on our other piece of custom code, getValueListData, to get back the data map corresponding to the inbound value list name, and we check each value as we loop to see whether it's the same as what was named as the currently selected value. If so, we output the HTML "selected" keyword; otherwise we don't. Lastly, we concatenate all of our HTML code together into a single local variable called htmlResult, which is what we ultimately return.

Custom Types: Writing Object-Oriented Code in Lasso

In the last couple of sections, you've probably noticed some syntax that appears a bit confusing at first glance. You've seen notations such as $PlainsStatesVL->Size and $CurrentPair->Second. What is that right-pointing arrow all about? It indicates that the thing to its left is an *object* and the thing to its right is one of that object's *member functions* (or *member tags*, as Lasso calls them). In the first example above, $PlainsStatesVL is a map, and all maps have a member tag called Size that returns the number of elements in the map. Maps have a number of other member tags, which would be called in a similar way—$PlainsStatesVL->Find or $PlainsStatesVL->Insert, for example. In all of these cases, $PlainsStatesVL is an *object*, an instance of the Map class, and it's capable of calling a variety of different member tags that operate on its own data.

Lasso has fairly strong support for creating new types of objects. As with custom tag definition, if you're used to the way this works in a language like Java, you may find that the Lasso method requires a tiny bit more typing, but the overall functionality is the same. If you're not very familiar with object-oriented programming concepts, follow along anyway and see how much you can pick up. (For reference and to become more familiar with object-oriented concepts, we recommend giving the early chapters of Bruce Eckel's *Thinking in Java* a glance. It's available online at www.bruceeckel.com.)

By way of demonstration, we're going to write a custom type (which most other languages would call a *class*, so we use that terminology from now on) that wraps up some of the functionality of an HTML table. Our particular table class is designed to display a set of database records. It allows us to color rows or columns with a specified color shade. Since we frequently display database result sets in HTML tables, we should get a lot of use out of our table class.

A proper HTML table class that provides an interface to all of the possible attributes of an HTML table would be a pretty complicated entity, so we're going to keep it simple for the sake of illustration. We allow the user to select a border width, whether they want to stripe some of the rows and in what color, and whether to write the field names into a header row. We also allow them to use column headers that are different from the underlying field names. So here then is the code for our table class. We've included both the class definition and some sample code that exercises the class.

```
<!--This custom type defines a class for handling HTML tables that
  display database data-->

[Define_Type: 'HTMLTable']
     [Local: 'inlineName']
     [Local: 'fieldNameArray']
     [Local: 'fieldLabelArray']
     [Local: 'rowStripeInterval' = 1] <!--default, means no row
       striping-->
     [Local: 'rowStripeColor' = '#CCCCCC']
     [Local: 'useHeaderRow' = 1] <!--if 1, output a header row with
       field names-->
     [Local: 'border' = 'null']
     [Local: 'recordCount' = 0]

     [Define_Tag: 'generateHTML']

          [Local: 'htmlOutput'='']
          [Local: 'fieldCount' = (Self->'fieldNameArray'->Size)]

          <!--begin table-->
          [If: (Self->'border'=='null')]
               [#htmlOutput += '<table border>']
          [Else]
               [#htmlOutput += '<table border="' + (Self->'border')
                 + '">']
          [/If]
```

```
        <!--generate header row if required-->
        [If: (Self->'useHeaderRow') == 1 ]
            [#htmlOutput += '<tr>']
            [Loop: #fieldCount]
                [#htmlOutput += '<th>']
                [#htmlOutput += (Self->'fieldLabelArray'->(Get:
                  (Loop_Count)))]
                [#htmlOutput += '</th>']
            [/Loop]
            [#htmlOutput += '</tr>']
        [/If]

        <!--generate data rows-->
        [Records: -InlineName=(Self->'inlineName')]
            [#htmlOutput += '<tr>']
            <!--loop through array of field names-->
            [Loop: #fieldCount]
                [#htmlOutput += '<td']
                <!--stripe the row if necessary-->
                [If: (Self->'rowStripeInterval' > 1 ) &&
                  ((Self->'recordCount') % (Self->
                  'rowStripeInterval') == 0) ]
                    [#htmlOutput += ' bgcolor="' + (Self->
                      'rowStripeColor') + '"']
                [/If]
                [#htmlOutput += '>']
                [#htmlOutput += (Field: (Self->
                  'fieldNameArray'->(Get: (Loop_Count))))]
                [#htmlOutput += '</td>']
            [/Loop]
            [#htmlOutput += '</tr>']
            [++(Self->'recordCount')]
        [/Records]

        [#htmlOutput += '<table>']
        [Return: #htmlOutput]
    [/Define_Tag]

[/Define_Type]

<!--code to test the class-->

<!--named inline to generate data-->
[Inline: -InlineName='FemaleAnimals', -Database='Animal',
  -Layout='WebSearchResults', 'gender'='Female', -Search][/Inline]

<!--declare an instance of the class-->
[Var:'myTable' = (htmlTable)]

<!--set up all attributes of the object-->
[$myTable->'border' = 0]
[$myTable->'rowStripeInterval' = 3]
```

```
[$myTable->'fieldLabelArray' = (Array: 'Name', 'Birth Date', 'Birth
  Weight' )]
[$myTable->'fieldNameArray' = (Array: 'name', 'date_birth',
  'weight_birth' )]
[$myTable->'inlineName' = 'FemaleAnimals']

<!--generate HTML-->
[$myTable->generateHTML]
```

The entire class (or custom type, again, in Lasso terminology) is wrapped in the [Define_Type]...[/Define_Type] tags. Inside those tags we find two things: definitions of *member variables* and definitions of *member tags*. Member variables represent the class's data, while member tags represent the internal functions that can operate on that data. In the case of our table class, our member variables, for the most part, represent user-settable attributes of the table, such as its border width, the names of column headers and data fields, the name of a named inline from which to draw the data, and so forth. The only exception is the recordCount variable that we use to keep track of which rows need to be striped. This class of ours has only one member tag, called generateHTML, which is responsible for generating all the HTML for our table and returning it as a string.

The member variables are fairly straightforward. Many of them are initialized to reasonable default values so that the user still gets a decent-looking table even if he doesn't specify values for all of them. Our default table has no row striping, has a default stripe color (if we do choose striping) of a medium gray, displays a header row, and has no border. All of these can be overridden by the user.

Let's turn our attention to the sole member tag, generateHTML. Its mechanics are fairly simple. It has a few local variables of its own, one to hold the HTML code as it's built up and the other to hold a count of the fields being displayed. It begins by outputting an opening table tag. We allow a value of null for the border width because some browsers display <table border> differently from <table border="0">.

Next we check to see if the user has opted to display a header row. If so, we loop through the array called fieldLabelArray and output each of its items in a <th>...</th> tag pair. This separate label array allows us to have column headings that differ from the underlying field names.

Next we generate the data rows. Our particular table class assumes that it will be displaying dynamic data from a named inline, and it requires an inline name to be set up for the object. It uses the

[Records: -InlineName] tag to loop through the inline's records. For each record in the result set, it loops across through the fieldName-Array and outputs the value of each specified field for the current record. Inside this loop, it checks to see whether striping has been turned on and, if so, whether the current row should be striped. It writes this into the table cell (<td>) tag. Once it's done looping through all the data records, it closes up the table and returns the HTML as a string.

That's all there is to the innards of our table class. Much of the beauty, though, is in how easy it is to use. In the test usage code that follows the class definition, we first set up a named inline (stealing one from our earlier examples). We then create a new instance of our table class by creating a variable of that type:

```
[Var:'myTable' = (htmlTable)]
```

Then we set the table's border and stripe interval, set up one array of field labels and another of actual field names, and finally set the table's inline name. Then, to generate and output the HTML for the table, we simply say:

```
[$myTable->generateHTML]
```

Our "in-page" code has become much, much simpler with our table class. Most likely we will put the class definition in a library file somewhere and make it available with an [Include] statement or the like. So the class definition will not clutter the pages in which we use it. All we see is the [Include] statement, probably near the top of the page, and then some code very similar to what we just reviewed that creates the new object, sets up its parameters, names its inline, and outputs the HTML.

This kind of abstraction can be very powerful. We still need to do quite a lot of work with our fledgling table class to make it production quality. For example, we need a way to put things other than database data into table cells—like delete buttons or hyperlinks. We also need a much fuller interface to manipulate all of the other possible HTML and CSS (Cascading Style Sheet) attributes, but we have a solid foundation for adding all of those features.

If programming features like functions ("custom tags") and classes ("custom types") are new to you, we strongly urge you to become very familiar with their uses. Functions and classes are the foundation of almost all advanced, modular programming, web or otherwise. We have more to say about these concepts in Chapter 8, "Custom Web Publishing with PHP."

Preserving State: Sessions in Lasso

No tutorial on advanced web programming would be complete without some mention of sessions. It's an important enough topic that we go into it twice, once here in the context of Lasso and again in the next chapter in the context of PHP. All heavy-duty middleware has some kind of support for sessions. We begin here with an overview of the important concepts and then look at how they're applied in Lasso.

As we've said in a few places, the web is very different from FileMaker's client-server model. The FileMaker Server tries its best to keep a dedicated connection open to each of its FileMaker clients. It knows which one is which and can distinguish between them. A web server, on the other hand, is an amnesiac; once it's sent you something, it forgets who you are and has no easy way to identify multiple different HTTP requests as originating from the same source. It can look at things like IP addresses, but for reasons we explain elsewhere, this data is possibly misleading or inaccurate.

Sessions are a way to overcome this limitation. The term *session* is a generic term for any technique that allows us to associate some persistent chunk of data with a particular user in the context of a web application. We really want something roughly equivalent to FileMaker's globals—persistent data that's unique to each user of the system. To do this on the web, our middleware needs to provide us with two things: a *persistence* mechanism and an *identification* mechanism. In other words, we need a place to store user data, and we need a way to associate a particular web request with a particular set of user data.

Middleware products generally offer a variety of persistence mechanisms. Lasso, by default, stores its session data in its built-in MySQL database in a way that's more or less transparent to us. PHP, which we discuss in the next chapter, stores its user data in disk-based text files by default, but it can be configured to store its session data in a database of the programmer's choosing as well. It's really the identity mechanism that requires the most work. Each user session needs a unique identifier of some kind. The middleware needs to generate that ID, associate it with the user's data, *and* somehow make sure that each web request from that user comes in bearing the key that allows us to find that user's data.

In order to make a Lasso page "session-aware," we need to use the Lasso [Session_Start] tag. The tag name, like PHP's session_start() function, is named in a slightly misleading fashion, since the appearance of this tag starts a brand new session if none exists yet for that user, or it continues the use of an existing session if one has already begun. Regardless, we need to put this tag at the beginning of any page that uses a session. It does not need to come at the very beginning of the page, but it's an extremely good idea to always put this tag early enough that it precedes any actual output from the page.

When Lasso encounters the [Session_Start] tag, it first tries to decide if this user already has a session going. If the user does have a session going, he'll be carrying around a session identifier with him, and it will be found in one of two places: Either the session ID will have come to the page as a GET or POST variable with the name -Session, or the ID will be available in a cookie that Lasso has set. (See Chapter 6 for a longer discussion on cookies.)

If Lasso finds that session data has been passed to this page, either over HTTP (GET/POST) or in a cookie, it assumes that a pre-existing session is being continued and fetches the user data associated with the given session key. Otherwise, it generates a brand new session key, which is a long, randomly generated character string whose only purpose is to uniquely identify a session.

When we start or continue a session in Lasso, we can specify what method we want Lasso to use to propagate the session ID. If we want the key to be passed in URLs and forms, we can write this:

```
[SessionStart: -Name='BHBBSession', -Expires=180, -UseLink]
```

The -UseLink parameter will force Lasso to automatically add the session ID to any internal URL links that it finds, as distinguished by the <A HREF=...> tag. Although Lasso handles propagating the session ID through any URLs that it finds, it's still up to the programmer to make sure that any and all forms also pass the session ID. Here's how such a form might look:

```
<form action="AnimalSearchIntegratedInlineAll.lasso" method="post">
  <input type="hidden" name="RecordId" value="[Keyfield_Value]">
  <input type="hidden" name="name" value="[Action_Param:'name']">
  <input type="hidden" name="gender" value="[Action_Param:'gender']">
  <input type="hidden" name="date_birth" value=
    "[Action_Param:'date_birth']">
  <input type="hidden" name="-nothing" value="">
  <input type="hidden" name="prevaction" value="[$DBAction]">
  <input type="hidden" name="-Session" value=
    "BHBBSession:[Session_ID: -Name='BHBBSession']">
  <input type="submit" name="action" value="Delete">
<form>
```

We've added the bold line to a form based on a previous example. Here we create a hidden input called -Session and assign it a value composed of two things: the name of the current session and the uniquely generated ID. The [Session_ID] tag, coupled with the name of the session, gives this to us.

So this is how propagation of the session ID via URLs and forms would work. But there are a number of serious drawbacks to this way of doing things. Firstly, Lasso can only automatically add the session ID to hyperlinks that are of the typical <A HREF=...> form. If you dynamically generate any of your hyperlinks or dynamically change them using technologies like JavaScript, Lasso may not be able to detect all of your URLs and modify them accordingly. Needing to remember to pass the session ID manually through each and every form is cumbersome and fragile. Instead, we're going to argue (and we know there are those who disagree) that the best way to handle session IDs is to pass them around using cookies. To do that, we write the [Session_Start] tag in the same way, but instead of -UseLink, we write -UseCookie.

Now, there are drawbacks to cookies as well. Some people are convinced that they are evil and only useful for invading privacy. For this reason, some users disable them. In our view, if that opposition exists, it's a hurdle that you need to overcome. It may be trickier for public-oriented sites, but certainly for internal intranet applications you ought to be able to mandate certain browser settings to anyone who wants to use your application. For example, for most of our custom applications, we mandate that users enable cookies and JavaScript. If you're working in a consulting mode for an organization whose IT practices you're not completely familiar with yet, it's very important to inquire up front whether these restrictions are acceptable. We know of at least one quite large firm that does not permit JavaScript to be run on any browser internally for security reasons. So be sure to do some due diligence before mandating any browser settings. With that said, in environments where it can be done, we recommend propagating all your session data using cookies.

Let's look at a small example to illustrate the use of sessions. We're going to return to our custom table class, but we're going to add a place on the display page where the user can set her preference for a striping interval. By itself, this is not too spectacular, but the point of our page is that the user can leave the page and come back again or even close her browser completely and come back to the page at a later time and her preference will still be retained. Let's look at the modified code:

```
<!--Code to handle session-->
[Session_Start: -Name='Table', -UseCookie]
[If: (Action_Param:'stripeCount') > 0]
     [Var: 'stripeCount' = (Action_Param:'stripeCount')]
[/If]
[Session_AddVar: -Name='Table', 'stripeCount']

<!--This custom type defines a class for handling HTML tables that
  display database data-->

[Define_Type: 'HTMLTable']
     [Local: 'inlineName']
     [Local: 'fieldNameArray']
     [Local: 'fieldLabelArray']
     [Local: 'rowStripeInterval' = 1] <!--default, means no row
       striping-->
     [Local: 'rowStripeColor' = '#CCCCCC']
     [Local: 'useHeaderRow' = 1] <!--if 1, output a header row with
       field names-->
     [Local: 'border' = 'null']
     [Local: 'recordCount' = 0]

     [Define_Tag: 'generateHTML']

          [Local: 'htmlOutput'='']
          [Local: 'fieldCount' = (Self->'fieldNameArray'->Size)]

          <!--begin table-->
          [If: (Self->'border'=='null')]
               [#htmlOutput += '<table border>']
          [Else]
               [#htmlOutput += '<table border="' + (Self->'border')
                 + '">']
          [/If]

          <!--generate header row if required-->
          [If: (Self->'useHeaderRow') == 1 ]
               [#htmlOutput += '<tr>']
               [Loop: #fieldCount]
                    [#htmlOutput += '<th>']
                    [#htmlOutput += (Self->'fieldLabelArray'->
                      (Get: (Loop_Count)))]
                    [#htmlOutput += '</th>']
               [/Loop]
               [#htmlOutput += '</tr>']
          [/If]

          <!--generate data rows-->
          [Records: -InlineName=(Self->'inlineName')]
               [#htmlOutput += '<tr>']
               <!--loop through array of field names-->
```

```
                [Loop: #fieldCount]
                        [#htmlOutput += '<td']
                        <!--stripe the row if necessary-->
                        [If: (Self->'rowStripeInterval' > 1 ) &&
                          ((Self->'recordCount') % (Self->
                          'rowStripeInterval') == 0) ]
                                [#htmlOutput += ' bgcolor="' + (Self->
                                  'rowStripeColor') + '"']
                        [/If]
                        [#htmlOutput += '>']
                        [#htmlOutput += (Field: (Self->
                          'fieldNameArray'->(Get: (Loop_Count))))]
                        [#htmlOutput += '</td>']
                [/Loop]
                [#htmlOutput += '</tr>']
                [++(Self->'recordCount')]
        [/Records]

        [#htmlOutput += '<table>']
        [Return: #htmlOutput]
    [/Define_Tag]

[/Define_Type]

<!--code to test the class-->

<!--named inline to generate data-->
[Inline: -InlineName='FemaleAnimals', -Database='Animal',
  -Layout='WebSearchResults', 'gender'='Female', -Search][/Inline]

<!--declare an instance of the class-->
[Var:'myTable' = (htmlTable)]

<!--setup all attributes of the object-->
[$myTable->'border' = 0]
[If: $stripeCount > 0]
     [$myTable->'rowStripeInterval' = $stripeCount]
[Else]
     [$myTable->'rowStripeInterval' = 3]
[/If]
[$myTable->'fieldLabelArray' = (Array: 'Name', 'Birth Date', 'Birth
  Weight' )]
[$myTable->'fieldNameArray' = (Array: 'name', 'date_birth',
  'weight_birth' )]
[$myTable->'inlineName' = 'FemaleAnimals']

<!--generate HTML-->
[$myTable->generateHTML]

<form action="TableClass.lasso" method="post">
     Choose a stripe interval: <input type="text" name="stripeCount"
       size="5">
     <input type="submit" name="-nothing" value="Submit">
</form>
```

Again, the bold areas show the code that's changed from the previous version of the page. At the very top of the page, we use the [Session_Start] tag so that this page will be session-aware. We refer to our session by the name Table, and we tell Lasso to use cookies to propagate the session ID. This requires the user to have cookies enabled. Next we check to see if an action parameter called stripeCount has been passed to the page. If so, we put that value into a variable called stripeCount. Lastly, we add the stripeCount variable to the session. This is a critical step; only variables that are added to a session in this way are stored with the session and passed from page to page. This step assures us that Lasso stores the stripeCount value with this user's session.

Any time that we return to this page, the [Session_Start] command finds all the variables added to the user's session and their values and restores them into the page. The first thing that happens is that Lasso finds the stripeCount variable in its session storage and creates a variable in the page called stripeCount with the stored value. Next, if the user has submitted a new value for stripeCount by filling in the box and pressing Submit, that value is put into stripeCount and overrides the value stored by the session. Finally, the [Session_AddVar] tag makes sure that the session is aware of the variable and stores the current value when the page is done.

Later on, our code checks the value of the stripeCount variable, and if it's been set to something greater than zero, it uses that value. Otherwise, it uses a default value of 3. Finally, we've added a little form at the bottom of the page where the user can submit new values of stripeCount back to the page.

This is a very small illustration of the power of sessions. One very good way to use sessions in a dynamic web site is to store data that needs to come from a database, but that is not likely to change over the course of a user's visit. If you need to carry around a number of different pieces of data about a user that are fetched from a database, sessions are the way to go. Say you're building a web site for sales reps to log into and record contact information. Each sales rep might have a region and a state. They might be able to view information for all other sales reps in their region and edit information for all contacts in their state. This information is stored in a database, but you're likely to need to refer to it on every page of your web site. You could query the database for this information on each page, but since sales reps don't change region and state very often, this needlessly slows things down. It is better to query for the information once when the user logs in, then store the region and state in session variables and carry them from page to page that way. (It's true, by the way, that Lasso is in turn storing the session data in a database and doing a database query on every page where you invoke the session using [Session_Start]. But we gain two things from this: Lasso stores the session data in its built-in MySQL database, which is likely to be faster than FileMaker, and in any case, having Lasso handle this behind the scenes simplifies our code.)

Summary

Lasso is one of a number of powerful tools available for advanced web publishing of FileMaker databases. Its strengths are its ease of installation, its unified feature set (no need to install or enable third-party software to add functionality), and its graphical administrative interface. The embedded MySQL database is also an attractive addition. It has become quite easy to set up "out of the box" and includes everything that you need to get started. Programmers used to more traditional languages may still find its syntax somewhat verbose and particular, but the new LassoScript syntax helps this somewhat, and it's an obstacle that can be overcome. If you don't want to wrestle around much with installation and configuration, Lasso is a fine choice. In the chapter that follows, we delve into a powerful, non-commercial middleware solution—the open-source tool PHP.

Chapter 8

Custom Web Publishing with PHP

So far, we've discussed how to create web applications using Instant Web Publishing, CDML, and Lasso, and we've even used XML to move data from FileMaker to the web. The last, but certainly not least, tool that we focus on is PHP. We think (indeed, hope) that you'll find many similarities between PHP, CDML, XML, and Lasso. Knowing any one of them makes learning the others easier, and knowing several of them gives you a wide range of tools to choose from for your Custom Web Publishing needs.

In the first section of this chapter, we give you a bit of background about what PHP is and how it fits into the web publishing landscape. Figuring that many of you have never seen PHP before, we then provide a brief overview and tutorial that covers general PHP programming skills. Next, we focus on how PHP can send XML queries to the Web Companion. It's here that we introduce you to a fabulous tool called FX. Finally, we bring everything together as we create an entire web application using PHP and FileMaker. But first things first....

What Is PHP?

PHP is a powerful, open-source middleware tool for building web applications, especially data-driven applications. With native connections to over 20 relational database systems, PHP is the tool of choice for thousands of web developers worldwide. From modest beginnings in the late '90s, it has risen to an installed base of over one million servers serving over ten million domains in the most recent Netcraft survey (www.php.net/usage.php). Its combination of power, versatility, and open-source licensing have contributed greatly to its popularity.

PHP is a procedural language with full support for user-defined functions and relatively weak enforcement of data types (in this way, it's similar to other scripting languages like JavaScript). PHP has all of the syntax elements and flow-of-control structures that one would expect of a modern programming language (rich set of built-in operators, for loops, while loops, switch statements, and the like). In addition, PHP can also be used in an object-oriented (OO) fashion to define traditional OO classes and methods for those who are used to working in an OO programming style.

PHP is freely downloadable from the project site at www.php.net. It is usually distributed in the form of source code but can be downloaded in precompiled ("binary") form for a variety of platforms, including Windows and Mac OS X. PHP can be built with support for dozens of different modules and additional libraries, and for this reason many developers prefer to compile it themselves from source code. For those lacking the technical expertise or the inclination to build PHP for themselves, the available binaries are usually configured with support for many of the most popular add-ins. A basic configuration of PHP also comes preinstalled with Mac OS X, as does an appropriately configured copy of the Apache web server. As a result, OS X is a great open-source web development platform right out of the box.

There is no printed documentation available for PHP, but the distributions come with copious electronic documentation that provides detailed installation instructions. Additionally, there are numerous excellent third-party books on PHP. The project site (www.php.net) also contains extensive documentation for installing and programming with PHP.

PHP is configured as an extension to an existing web server. The most popular web server choices for this purpose are Apache (on Unix/Linux platforms, including Mac OS X) and Internet Information Server (on platforms based on Microsoft technology), though other web servers such as WebSTAR and the Zeus server are supported. Regardless of platform, PHP is installed in such a way that the host web server will hand off requests for certain types of pages to the PHP processor. These pages contain PHP code, which the PHP processor will execute before returning an HTML page to the web server to be sent to the client. In this way PHP is no different from other widely popular middleware tools like JSP, ColdFusion, and ASP.

The only tool that you need to write PHP code is a text editor. Our favorite editor for Macintosh is Barebone's BBEdit, and on Windows it's Macromedia's HomeSite (now a part of the Dreamweaver MX product line). In addition to HTML editing tools, both offer syntax coloring to make your PHP code more readable.

Put simply, the job of a PHP programmer is to insert programming logic into HTML pages. Let's look at a simple example to illustrate this point.

```
<html>
<head>
     <title>PHP Test1</title>
</head>

<body>

<?php

$myDate = getdate();
echo "<center>Today is ". $myDate['weekday'] . "</center>";

?>

</body>
</html>
```

Type this into a text editor and save it as test1.php on a web server on which PHP is configured. Figure 8.1 shows the result of requesting this page via a browser.

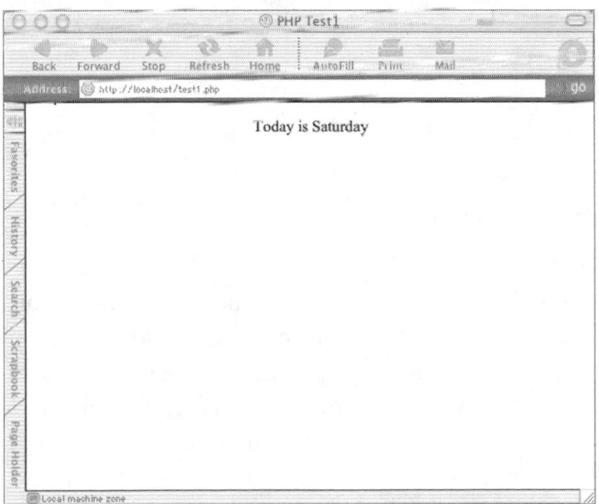

Figure 8.1

So how does this work? As part of the installation of PHP, you configure your web browser to pass on requests with certain extensions to

PHP. Typically, the extension is .php, but you could send .foo requests there if you wanted. In our example, then, the request for test1.php comes into the web server, and the .php extension tells the web server that this page should be processed by PHP. PHP looks for code blocks that are demarcated by <?php and ?>. Anything between these tags is processed by PHP; it ignores anything (HTML, JavaScript) outside of these tags.

The first line of PHP code in our example calls the built-in PHP function getdate(). This function returns an associative array containing information about the current local time (of the web server). The second line of code uses the echo function, which is used to print stuff (text, HTML) to the browser screen. In this case, we're sending some HTML formatting instructions, some literal text, and the "weekday" element of the $myDate array.

Once PHP is done processing all of its commands, it hands a document back to the web server containing all of the text that it didn't process (everything outside the <?php and ?> tags) and all of the output results of the PHP commands that it did process (such as the stuff in our echo function). The web server then sends that resultant document back to the browser that requested it. If you were to view the browser source of Figure 8.1, you'd see the following:

```
<html>
<head>
     <title>PHP Test1</title>
</head>

<body>

<center>Today is Saturday</center>
</body>
</html>
```

Thus, a person requesting this document has no idea what the original PHP commands were, which is a good thing. It means that your programming logic is completely hidden from the end user.

We hope this short example is enough to give you an idea of how a PHP page is processed. We cover the nuts and bolts of PHP programming in the next section and then move on to see how PHP can communicate with FileMaker.

Coding in PHP—General Principles

PHP is a relatively easy programming language to learn and use. If you have any procedural programming experience (such as C++, Perl, and Visual Basic), you'll pick up PHP in no time. Even if you don't, you'll find learning PHP quicker than just about any other language out there.

In this section, we cover the basics of PHP programming. We don't intend this to be a complete or exhaustive PHP reference—that would require a book of its own—but rather a sort of primer or tutorial to give you the tools that you'll need to get started (and understand the examples through the rest of the chapter).

Let's start with some coding conventions. First, we've seen that PHP code blocks are set apart from other code by the use of <?php and ?> tags. The opening tag can actually be written either as <?php or simply as <?, which is how we usually write it for brevity's sake. You can put any number of PHP code blocks in a document; they can even appear in the middle of HTML commands, like this:

```
<a href="<? echo $myURL;?>"> Click here</a>
```

All single-line PHP commands must end with a semicolon. Multiple-line constructs, such as conditionals and loops, must be surrounded by curly braces, such as { and }. By convention, usually only one command is placed on a line, but this isn't a requirement. PHP doesn't care about any white space between or within commands. Thus, the following two code blocks do exactly the same thing:

```
    <? $x = 1; $y = 2; $z = $x + $y; echo $z;?>
```

and

```
<?
    $x    =    1;
    $y    =    2;
    $z    =    $x + $y;

    echo $z;
?>
```

You'll find that liberal amounts of spacing help keep your code legible. If you have multiple programmers coding on a project, you'll probably want to come up with some orthography conventions. Coding typically isn't a good outlet for individualism.

There are two ways to add comments to your PHP code. The first is to use a //, which indicates that everything on the remainder of the line is a comment and should be ignored. To comment multiple lines, you can use /* at the beginning and */ at the end of a block. For example:

```
<?

// this is a comment line; anything I write here is ignored by PHP

$x = "hello";    // here we've added a comment to the end of a line

/*
Everything in here
Is a comment
*/

?>
```

Try to get in the habit of thoroughly commenting your code. Most FileMaker programmers don't have good commenting habits since it's a bit cumbersome to comment with FileMaker. It's so easy in PHP that you don't have any excuses not to. (Being lazy isn't a good excuse.)

Working with Variables

It's very easy to define and work with variables using PHP. All variables begin with a $, must consist of letters, numbers, and underscores, and must begin with a letter or underscore. So, $foo, $foo2, and $foo_2 are all valid variable names, but $2foo is not. There's no restriction on the length of a variable name, but they are case sensitive. Thus, $foo and $FOO refer to two distinct variables. We typically use all lowercase (myvarname) or camel case (myVarName) to name variables.

You can define a variable simply by a statement like:

```
var $myVar;
```

Unlike other languages, however, you don't need to define variables before using them. The first time you set them, they are declared automatically. Thus:

```
$myVar = "blah";
```

...creates a variable called myVar and sets it to the string "blah." (We're going to stop putting <? and ?> around all of our code snippets, but don't let that confuse you. You still need them.)

Unlike C++ and Java, PHP is a loosely typed language, which means that a variable can hold any of several different types of data, including strings, integers, floating-point numbers, pointers, objects, and arrays. Consider the following examples:

```
$var1 = 23;                                    // var1 is an integer
$var2 = 4.34;                     // var2 is a floating-point number
$var3 = "My name is Fred";                     // var3 is a string
$var4 = array ('banana', 'dirty socks', 'toothbrush') // var4 is an
                                               // array with 3 elements
$var5 = new Customer();                        // var5 is an object
```

When defining a variable to hold a string, you can use either single or double quotes. The only difference is that if you use double quotes, PHP will evaluate any variables referred to in the string. That is, if:

```
$var = "My name is $name";
$var2 = 'My name is $name';
```

...then if $name is "Fred," $var would be the string "My name is Fred" but $var2 would be the string "My name is $name."

If you want to put a single or double quote within a text string, you need to "escape" them using a backslash. Consider the following code snippets:

```
$myVar = "And then he said, "Wow!"";        // this won't work, you'll
                                            // get a syntax error
$myVar = "And then he said, \"Wow!\"";      // this will work, because
                                            // the internal quotes are
                                            // properly escaped
```

There are a few other characters that need to be escaped in text strings. These include $, \, tabs (\t), carriage returns (\r), and new lines (\n).

Once you've declared a variable, there are a zillion ways that you can manipulate it. Let's look at just a few math and string manipulations.

Addition, subtraction, multiplication, and division are performed using the +, –, *, and / operators. The ^ symbol is used to raise a number to some power, and the % symbol is used for modulo division. You can use parentheses to specify order of operation. Consider the following:

```
$a = 20;
$b = 5;

$c = $a + $b;          // $c is 25
$d = $a - $b;          // $d is 15
```

```
$e = $a * $b;           // $e is 100
$f = $a / $b;           // $f is 4

$g = $b ^ 3;            // $g is 625
$h = $a % 3;            // $h is 2, since 20 / 3 = 6 remainder 2

$i = 3 + 4 * 5          // $i is 23; order of operations is
                        // multiplication/division before
                        // addition/subtraction
$j = (3 + 4) * 5        // $j is 35
```

There are also special shorthand operators for incrementing or decrementing numbers. These get frequent use in looping constructs, so be sure you understand what they do.

```
$x = 5;
$x++;               // increases the variable by one. Shorthand for
                    // $x = $x + 1 (x = 6)
$x--;               // decreases a variable by one. Shorthand for $x = $x
                    // - 1 (x = 5)

$x += 5;            // adds 5 to x.  Shorthand for $x = $x + 5; (x = 10)
$x -= 5;            // subtracts 5 from x.  Shorthand for $x = $x - 5
                    // (x = 5)
```

There are dozens of functions built in to PHP for manipulating text strings, but there are really only a few that you need to know about to get started. The most basic string manipulation is concatenating two strings together. The concatenation operator is a period. So:

```
$a = "foo";
$b = "bar";
$c = $a . $b;    // $c = "foobar";
```

Similar to the shorthand math operators, there's a shorthand operator (.=) for appending to a string.

```
$a = "foo";
$a .= "bar";     // $a = "foobar".  Shorthand for $a = $a . "bar"
```

Arrays

If you've never used arrays before in your programming, they can be a bit difficult to sink your teeth into. But it's going to be crucial for you to have a good understanding of arrays when we start talking about PHP and FileMaker, so take your time going through this section.

An array is really just a set of "things." Those things can be numbers, strings, other arrays, or even objects. Perhaps it will help to think of an array as a bag that you toss stuff into. For instance, consider the following:

```
$myArray = array ("banana", "toothpaste", "race car");
```

We've just declared that $myArray is an array that contains three text strings. When you simply throw things into a set like this, each thing is assigned a number (starting at zero unless we specify otherwise) that can be used to retrieve the values. We call those numbers "keys." You use a key to retrieve a value from an array. If you want to refer to a specific element of an array, place the key after the name of the array name surrounded by square brackets. So, for example:

```
$a = $myArray[0];              // $a would be the string "banana"
$b = $myArray[2];              // $b would be the string "race car"
```

You can toss additional items into an array by using empty braces and asserting equality to some value. For example:

```
$myArray[] = "chocolate chip cookie"; // this added a new element to
                                      // the end of $myArray.
```

We can also add a new element, which itself is an array:

```
$myArray[] = array ("Beethoven", "Bach", "Mozart", "Brahms");
// we've added an element to $myArray (the 5th element...), which is
// itself an array with 4 items
```

Nesting arrays like this is quite powerful and, as we see soon, very common. If you wanted to refer to an element in a nested array, you'd just "drill down" into it:

```
$z = $myArray[4][2];           // $z would be "Mozart," since it's the
                               // 3rd element of the 5th element of
                               // $myArray (remember that we're 0 based)
```

The arrays that we've been using are often referred to as indexed arrays. The other type of array is what's known as an associative array. Essentially, this let's you define a key for each "thing" in the array, which can make retrieving it later much simpler (since you won't need to know its position in the array). There are a few ways to create associative arrays.

```
$myNewArray = array ('color' => 'green', 'size' => 'small',
  'smell'=>'not unpleasant');
```

The => symbol is used to assign a value to a key. There are three things in this new array, but we can retrieve them by the name of the key now:

```
$color = $myNewArray['color'];  // $color would be the string "green"
```

The single quotes around color are not required but are conventionally used. You can add elements to an associative array just by asserting them:

```
$myNewArray['capacity'] = 200;  // we've just added a new element to
                                // the array
```

Just as you can manipulate strings and numbers, there are many things that you can do to arrays. For instance, you can count the number of items in them, you can sort them, and you can search through them. We see some of these functions in our examples later, but you certainly don't need to know all of them at this point. For now, it is sufficient if you can conceptualize arrays well and recognize them if you see them.

In an earlier example, we saw the echo function, which is used to output information to a user's browser screen. Echo works fine for rendering strings and numbers, but it can't show an entire array. As you're writing and debugging PHP code, it's frequently desirable to see everything that's in an array. To do this, you can use the print_r function to dump out the entire array to the screen.

```
print_r ($myNewArray);
```

In your browser window, the array dump can be difficult to read since it sprawls across the screen. If you ask your browser to display the source code for the page, however, the array will be nicely formatted for you.

The Include Function

One of the first and most important functions we use in our web application at the end of this chapter is the include function. The include function lets you modularize your code for easy reuse and maintenance. Essentially, it pulls the entire contents of a document into another document. An example will clarify this. Say you have a whole bunch of HTML pages with different body content but they need the same header information on each page. If you put the HTML code for the header in each page and decide later that you want to change something, you might have to go through dozens or hundreds of documents to make the change. Or, you can place the common code in its own file and simply include that file at the top of the other files. What's nice is that any variables that you've declared can be referenced inside of the included file. It's really as if PHP is cutting and pasting the contents of the included file into the main file.

Let's look at an example of this. Say you have a file called "header.php" with the following code:

```
<html>
<head>
```

```
<title>
<? echo $title; ?>
</title>
</head>
<body bgcolor="red">
<img src="mylogo.jpg">
```

Now, this obviously isn't a well-formed HTML page and isn't intended to be requested directly from a web browser. But consider having the page info.php as follows:

```
<?
$title = "Information about our company";
include ("header.php");

?>
<!--lots of HTML here...!-->
</body>
</html>
```

Hopefully you can see right away what will happen. When a user requests info.php, PHP will assemble a response page from the snippets of the header file and the info page itself. Hundreds of other pages could also include the same header page. Yet since the title is a variable set in the calling document, it has the appearance of being customized for each page. If you ever wanted to change the header, simply changing the one document would cause anything that included it to change as well.

The include happens on demand as a browser requests a page. It's not compiled or stored in any way. You can put includes anywhere you want in your document. Your includes can themselves include other files.

Conditional Statements

If you're comfortable with If/Else/End If conditional scripting in FileMaker, then you'll have no problem with it in PHP. The concept is essentially the same; if some condition holds, do these things, or else do these other things. The syntax may look strange until you get used to it, but this will likely be one of the easier aspects of PHP to master. Let's look at a few examples:

```
if ($someVar == 10) {
    echo "Hello";          // these lines will only be executed
    $foo = 123;            // if $someVar is equal to 10
} else {
    echo "someVar is equal to $someVar";
}
```

There are several things that we'd like to point out in this example. First, notice that we use a double equal sign to test for equality. A single equal sign is only used when you're setting variables. Be careful that you use the double equal sign; you won't get a syntax error if you don't, but your code won't work. Notice next that the conditional test is within parentheses. Outside of the parentheses, you indicate with a left brace ({) the opening of a set of instructions to perform if the conditional statement evaluates as true. The else statement is optional; if it's used, you enclose the statements to perform with curly brackets. The spacing and indentation shown in our example is simply our convention to make if statements easily readable.

There are other types of conditional statements in PHP that we won't go into now (such as ternary operators and the switch function), but we would like to discuss a few useful constructions of the conditional statement itself. First, if you want to test multiple conditions, use && (two ampersands) or || (two pipes) to indicate AND or OR logic, respectively. For example:

```
if ( $a == 10 && $b == 5)          // means "if $a is 10 and $b is 5"

if ( $a == 10 || $b == 5)          // means "if $a is 10 or $b is 5"
```

You can use parentheses to create more complex conditions, such as:

```
if ( $a ==10 && ($b == 5 || $b == 1))       // means "if $a is 10 and
                                             // $b is either 5 or 1"
```

Finally, you can test for things other than equality. You can test for existence, nonexistence, and inequality, as the following examples show:

```
if ( $myVar )                  // returns true if $myVar is set to
                               // anything
if ( $myVar != null )          // alternate syntax for above

if ( !$myVar )                 // returns true if $myVar doesn't exist
if ( $myVar == null )          // alternate syntax for above

if ( $myVar >= $myOtherVar)        // returns true if $myVar is greater
                                   // than or equal to $myOtherVar
if ( count ($myArray) > 0 )        // returns true if the array $myArray
                                   // contans at least one item
```

The ! symbol is a negation symbol. So, != means "does not equal."

Looping Constructs

As with conditional statements, a familiarity with the FileMaker Loop/End Loop script steps makes it easier to conceptualize PHP looping constructs. A looping construct is a mechanism for performing a series of commands repetitively until some condition "breaks" the loop. PHP actually has several types of looping constructs that you'll want to be familiar with. Here, we discuss the for and foreach statements.

For Loops

For loops are a core element of most every programming language. They are most often used if you know in advance the number of times you want your loop to iterate. Consider the following example:

```
for ($i = 1 ; $i <= 10 ; $i++) {
    echo "Line $i <hr />";
}
```

This would render the following in a browser:

```
Line 1
Line 2
Line 3
Line 4
Line 5
Line 6
Line 7
Line 8
Line 9
Line 10
```

The for statement always takes three arguments separated by semicolons. The first argument contains one or more commands to execute before the loop begins. Here, we're simply setting a variable $i to 1. The second argument defines the conditions that must be true for the loop to go through another cycle. Here, as long as $i is less than or equal to 10, it will keep chugging along. The final argument defines one or more commands to execute in between loops. Typically, this third argument will increment a variable, as in our example. The incrementing happens *before* the exit condition is evaluated. That is, after completing an iteration of the loop, the variable increments; then if the condition still holds, all of the commands between the curly braces will be executed again.

Foreach Loops

The foreach loop is used to walk through the elements of a variable-length array. As a simple example:

```
$myArray = array ("blue", "yellow", "white", "orange", "peanut
  butter');

echo "Which of the following things is not like the others?<br />";

foreach ($myArray as $thing) {
     echo "<li>". $thing . "</li><br />";
}
```

This would render in a browser as:

```
Which of the following things is not like the others?
 - blue
 - yellow
 - white
 - orange
 - peanut butter
```

When you use a foreach loop, you walk through the array elements as an ordered set. With each iteration, the next item from the array is set into the variable that you've named (here, $thing). The loop ends automatically after the statements inside the loop have executed for each item in the array.

If you have an associative array, you can grab both the key and value of the items as you iterate through them. Consider the following:

```
$myArray['name'] = "Fred Flintstone";
$myArray['hobby'] = "Bowling";
$myArray['pet name'] = "Dino";

foreach ($myArray as $key_name => $value ) {
     echo $key_name . " - " . $value . "<br />";
}
```

This would render in a browser as:

```
name - Fred Flintstone
hobby - Bowling
pet name - Dino
```

You can see that each time we grab an element, we assign its key to the first variable that we've specified ($key_name) and its value to the second variable ($value).

We see a lot of the foreach loop later on for displaying sets of records returned from FileMaker.

Functions

Functions are among the most useful and important programming tools. A function is essentially a subroutine that you can call whenever you like. The code within a function only executes, in fact, if the function is called. Functions can be placed anywhere in a page, but they are typically placed near the top or in separate documents. The latter is particularly useful if the functions need to be called from multiple documents. Functions can be passed inputs (also called arguments), and they can return a value as well. Functions are all about modularity, code reuse, and stability.

To create a function, simply declare it and specify the commands that it performs. For example, the following function, displayError, could be used to display error messages to the user:

```
function displayError ($errorMsg) {
     echo "An error has been generated.<br /><br />";
     echo "The error message is: <b>$errorMsg</b>";
}
```

Once you've written this function, instead of having to explicitly echo out an error message every time there is an error, you can just call this function:

```
if (!$someValue) {
     displayError ("someValue was empty");
}

if (!$db_connect) {
     displayError ("Could not connect to the database");
}
```

Do you see how it's more efficient to have the code that actually renders the error only written once? Not only does it mean writing fewer lines of code, but if you ever need to change the error display, you can do it in a single place.

Let's look at a slightly more complex example of a function—this time one that returns a value:

```
function computeTaxAmount ($state, $amount) {
     $state_rates = array ('IL'=>8.25, 'MI'=>6.25, 'CA'=>9.75)
     $tax_rate = $state_rates[$state];

     $tax = $amount * $tax_rate / 100 ;
     return $tax;
}
```

This function expects to be passed two arguments. It puts the values that are passed in into the $state and $amount variables. Then, the function grabs a tax rate from an array based on the $state it was passed and uses this to calculate the amount of sales tax that should be charged. That tax amount is then returned as the result of the function. This function might be used as follows:

```
$myAmount = 84.54;
$myState = 'MI';
$theTax = computeTaxAmount ($myState, $myAmount)

$total = $myAmount + $theTax;
```

There are several benefits of encapsulating the tax computation in a function. The first is, again, reuse. Any time you need to find the sales tax amount, just call the function and you'll have your answer. Using a function also gives your code stability because you don't have to worry about the potential for inconsistency in your application. Did you compute the tax one way here and a different way over there? Did you forget to update the new rates in all six places where you compute the tax? If you're using a function, you won't have those sorts of worries.

Putting code into functions also makes your applications easier to debug. If you've written your function correctly and tested it thoroughly, you can rest assured that if you pass it good arguments, it gives you a good result. If there's a bug in your code, you won't waste time and effort looking through that code. In essence, you are modularizing your application logic so you can test each bit independently and have greater overall stability.

There's much more that you can learn about functions in PHP, but hopefully you understand the purpose and syntax of functions at this point. We have many opportunities to look at examples of functions in the web application at the end of this chapter.

Objects

The final topic that we cover in our brief PHP tutorial is an overview of object-oriented (OO) programming. We only scratch the surface of OO, but having at least some understanding of how to use objects is important when we start discussing FX, an object designed to let PHP talk to FileMaker Pro. Hopefully, the topic intrigues you and you'll do some further investigation into OO programming on your own.

First off, let's define, or rather describe, what we mean when we say "object." An object has attributes, which are called properties, and it can perform actions, which are called methods. Methods are nothing more than functions that act on the properties of the object. Think of an object as a generic template or idealized representation of something. In your programming, you then "instantiate" the object, breathing life into it by setting its properties and having it do things by invoking its methods. An example will help clarify this. Imagine an object called "dog." Try to think of a dog as a concept rather than thinking of a particular dog. Conceptually, you might identify properties that exist for dogs in general, such as "name," "age," "breed," "owner," and "gender." Then think about the things that dogs, in general, can do. Your list of methods might include such things as "roll_over," "beg_for_food," and "go_for_walk." It doesn't matter at this point if all dogs do these things; we're trying to define a lexicon that describes the things that a dog will potentially do. When we instantiate an actual dog, we can choose the actions that we want it to perform from the items in that lexicon. From this, the important things to remember are that properties are attributes of the object and methods are what it can do. If it helps you, try thinking of the properties as similar to field definitions of a FileMaker database and methods as similar to its scripts.

We look at the syntax for defining your own objects in a moment, but let's first discuss using objects that other programmers have created. This is akin to adding plug-ins to your FileMaker solutions. Say someone has created an object for drawing circles—they've determined a list of properties that belong to circles and have come up with a canonic set of functions that can be applied to them. The circle object might have properties like radius and color and methods like draw and move. To draw a circle, all you'd need to do is instantiate a new instance of circle, set its properties, and draw it. Instead of having to know lots about rendering graphics, all you need to know is how to use the object. Large amounts of programming complexity are entirely hidden from you. It's like driving a car without having to build it yourself or, indeed, even knowing how it works.

So, an object is a tool. You can create your own tools or you can use tools that others have developed, in which case you need to learn how to use the tool (not necessarily how the tool works). Implicit is a trust that if used properly, the tool will produce the desired and expected results.

To define an object in PHP, you use a class statement. Below is what the code might look like for defining our dog object:

```
class dog {
     var $name;
     var $age;
     var $breed;
```

```
    var $owner;
    var $gender;

    function roll_over() {
        // some code here
    }

    function beg_for_food($from_whom) {
        // some code here
        if ($from_whom == "Rebecca" ) {
            return true;
        } else {
            return false;
        }
    }

    function go_for_walk() {
        // some code here
    }
}
```

As with functions, the code within a class declaration will only execute if it's called explicitly. Typically, class declarations will be placed in their own files, which will be included in pages where they'll be called. To use our object, then, we might have the following code:

```
include ("class_dog.php"); // class_dog would have the code above...

$myDog = new dog();

$myDog->name = "Jasper";    // the -> symbol denotes a property of an
                            // object
$treat = $myDog->beg_for_food("Rebecca");
```

Above, we've used the keyword "new" to create a new instance of the dog class; the variable $myDog now refers to that instance. It doesn't matter what variable name you use to instantiate the object. Then, we've set the name property of the instance using the $myDog-> name syntax. Finally, we've invoked the beg_for_food method, passing "Rebecca" as an argument and putting the value returned by the function into the $treat variable. We don't need to know the complex logic involved in determining whether or not a dog will be given a treat. All we need to know is that the function needs to be told from whom food is being begged and that it returns a Boolean true or false.

We have ample opportunity in the coming sections to learn more about objects. For now, our whirlwind overview of PHP programming is complete. It's finally time to turn to integrating PHP with FileMaker.

Using PHP with FileMaker

Now that you know a little about PHP, you might be wondering how it works with FileMaker and what advantages or drawbacks it has compared to the other Custom Web Publishing methods that we discuss in this book. Let's focus first on how PHP works with FileMaker. Put simply, PHP sends requests to the Web Companion and receives XML back in response to those requests. The requests and responses look exactly the same as they would have, had they been requested directly by a web browser. In just a bit, we tell you about an object called FX that makes all of the XML interaction between FileMaker and PHP transparent to you, but before we do, we think it will be helpful for you to have an idea of what the communication between PHP and FileMaker looks like.

First, let's assume that we have set up a machine running FileMaker Pro Unlimited to act as our web host, and the IP address of that machine is 127.0.0.2. We further assume that we have a separate web server with Apache and PHP properly configured, and the IP address of that machine is 127.0.0.1. There are three databases open on the FileMaker Pro Unlimited machine, all of which have been set to share to the Web Companion. The Web Companion itself has been configured to use port 591 and not to do Instant Web Publishing.

Now, if you were sitting at a third machine, a plain old workstation with a browser (say, for now, Internet Explorer), and you typed the following URL into your browser:

```
http://127.0.0.2:591/FMPro?-format=-fmp_xml&-dbnames
```

...you'd see the following result in your browser window (Figure 8.2).

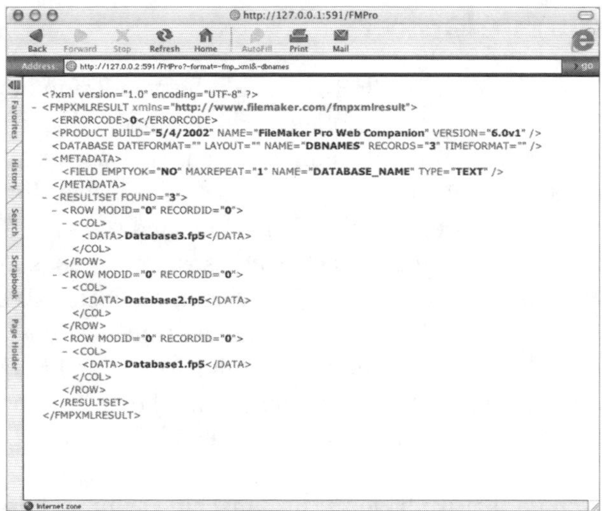

Figure 8.2

All we've done is issue a request directly to the Web Companion to give us a list of the open, shared databases and return the results using the fmp_xml grammar (we could have asked for the dso_xml grammar just as easily). Now, let's see how we can write a PHP page that performs this same request. The page, which we call getFileNames.php, is saved in the root web directory of the web server.

```
<html>
<head>
     <title>Get File Names</title>
</head>
<body>
<?

$request = "http://127.0.0.2:591/FMPro?-format=-fmp_xml&-dbnames";

$fp = fopen($request, "r");      // opens the file for reading
$myXML = fread($fp, 4096);       // reads the first 4096 characters
                                 // of the file
echo htmlentities($myXML);       // prints the raw code to screen

?>
</body>
</html>
```

Now, were we to request this page from our web server, we'd see the following result (Figure 8.3):

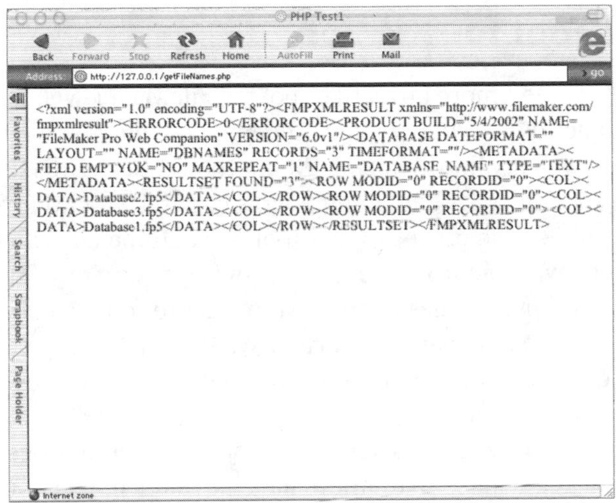

Figure 8.3

This is pretty similar to what we obtained submitting the request directly to the Web Companion, isn't it? Our four lines of PHP code in getFileNames.php are fairly straightforward. First, we set a variable called $request to a string containing our request. We then used the fopen command (file open) to submit the request, we read (using fread) the first 4,096 characters of the file into a variable called $myXML, and then we echoed that response string to the browser. The htmlentities function simply allows the XML to be displayed properly in the browser.

In real life, what we'd do next is parse through the incoming XML using PHP string functions and then display HTML back to the user. Summing up, we're using PHP to submit requests for XML to the Web Companion, and rather than spitting that raw XML back to the user or writing XSL stylesheets to turn that XML into HTML, we can use PHP to do our XML parsing and display appropriate HTML.

One of the big advantages of having PHP talk to the Web Companion, rather than having the Web Companion respond to individual browser requests (CDML or XML), is that you can completely hide the structure of your solution. A user never needs to see the names of your databases, layouts, or fields. They might not even know you're using FileMaker at all. This greatly reduces the chances of someone attempting to "hack" your databases. Moreover, since all of the requests to the Web Companion are coming from your web server, you can configure the Web Companion to only respond to requests from that IP address. The fact that it's free, fast, and secure certainly makes PHP an attractive choice for your FileMaker web publishing needs.

FX: The Right Tool for the Job

FX makes PHP an even more attractive tool for FileMaker web publishing. It would get quite cumbersome indeed if you needed to create an entire custom web application using the methods that we discussed in the previous section. Thankfully, someone's created a tool that simplifies and streamlines the process. That tool is a PHP object called FX, and it's freely available from the web site www.iviking.org. The author of FX, Chris Hansen, has even written easy-to-follow instructions and demo files to help get you started. We think FX is a great tool, and Chris deserves much thanks for his contribution to the FileMaker and PHP communities.

Recall from our earlier discussion about object-oriented programming that when using objects that others have developed, you don't need to know how the object works; you just need to know how to use the object. In this section, we're going to teach you how to use FX. All the code is open and available for you to peruse if you're curious about how it's put together, but we're essentially going to ignore all of the XML parsing and query assembling that Chris built in the FX class.

When you download FX from the www.iviking.org site, among the files that you receive is something called FX.php. That's the actual object code. You need to copy that file to your web server and then include it in any pages that you create. Just for comparison, if we wanted to use the FX class to get a list of open databases, we could create the following page:

```
<html>
<head>
     <title>Get File Names</title>
</head>

<body>
<?
include ("FX.php");

$FMAddress = "127.0.0.2";
$FMPort = "591";

$request = new FX ($FMAddress, $FMPort);
$result = $request->FMDBNames();

print_r ($result);
?>
</body>
</html>
```

If you were to run this script, PHP would execute the same fopen that we saw earlier, and then FX would parse the resulting XML into a multidimensional associative array. The $result array would appear as follows:

```
Array
(
    [linkNext] => /getFileNames2.php?skip=0&
    [linkPrevious] => /getFileNames2.php?skip=0&
    [foundCount] => 3
    [fields] => Array
        (
            [0] => Array
                (
                    [emptyok] => NO
                    [maxrepeat] => 1
                    [name] => DATABASE_NAME
                    [type] => TEXT
                )
        )
    [data] => Array
        (
            [0.0] => Array
                (
                    [DATABASE_NAME] => Array
                        (
                            [0] => Database2.fp5
                        )
                )
            [0.1] => Array
                (
                    [DATABASE_NAME] => Array
                        (
                            [0] => Database3.fp5
                        )
                )
            [0.2] => Array
                (
                    [DATABASE_NAME] => Array
                        (
                            [0] => Database1.fp5
                        )
                )
        )
    [URL] => http://127.0.0.2:591/FMPro?-db=&-format=-fmp_xml&-max=
      &-dbnames
    [errorCode] => 0
    [valueLists] => Array
        (
        )
)
```

The object represented by the FX class is a FileMaker XML request. It might not be as intuitive to conceptualize an XML request object as it was to imagine a dog object. In essence, every time you create an instance of an FX object, it represents a query that you can have PHP submit to FileMaker. It's sort of like being handed a blank order form to fill out. You check off the things that you want and submit the order form. Your order is processed and the results are handed back to you. Think of FX as an endless stack of blank order requests.

In order to submit an FX request, you need to do three things. First, create an instance of the object. Second, specify request parameters. Finally, specify the action to perform. Let's look at each of these in detail.

Creating an Instance of FX

The syntax to create a new instance of FX is as follows:

```
$newInstance = new FX ($dataServer, $dataPort);
```

This syntax is slightly different than what we learned earlier in our dog class example. Here, we're asked to pass arguments to the class as part of its creation. If you were to look at the FX class definition, you'd see a function there known as a constructor, which is called automatically every time an instance of the class is created. The constructor function is named FX, just like the class, and is shown below:

```
function FX ($dataServer, $dataPort=591) {
      $this->dataServer = $dataServer;
      $this->dataPort = ":" . $dataPort;

      $this->ClearAllParams();
}
```

This function takes the attributes passed to it and sets them into the dataServer and dataPort properties. Then, it calls the ClearAllParams method, presumably just as insurance that there are no vestigial bits of previous requests still floating about.

The $dataServer should be the IP address of the machine with the Web Companion. The $dataPort is an optional argument that you can pass to specify the port that the Web Companion is configured to use. If you don't specify a $dataPort, it assumes you're using port 591. That's what the "=591" part of the function definition indicates.

It's generally a good practice to set variables equal to the IP address and port and then use those as you instantiate the object. That way, if you ever change the IP address or port or move the site, you'll just need to change one or two variables rather than dozens of direct function calls. Those variables should be placed in their own file and included on every page you write. So, you'll have a file called prefs.php that contains the following code:

```
<?

$FMAddress = "127.0.0.2";
$FMPort = 591;

// put any other "constants" in this file

?>
```


Then, in all of your other pages, you'll have something like the following:

```
<?
include ("FX.php");
include ("prefs.php");

$request = new FX ($FMAddress, $FMPort);

// the rest of your code...

?>
```

The names of the variables don't matter. If you want to use $IPAddress or $IP instead of $FMAddress, go for it.

Specifying Request Parameters

Once an instance of FX has been created, you can then specify request parameters. We've listed all of the request parameters below. Certain actions require that you've specified certain parameters. Later in this section we have a matrix that specifies which parameters are required and optional for each of the actions. In general, it doesn't matter in which order you specify the parameters; there are a few exceptions that we point out when we come to them.

SetDBData

Syntax: SetDBData ($database, $layout="", $groupSize=50)

Example:

```
$myQuery = new FX ('127.0.0.2', '80');
$myQuery->SetDBData('contacts.fp5', 'webFind', 'All');
```

The SetDBData method specifies to which database and layout a request should be sent. You must call this method for every action with the exception of DBNames. The first parameter tells FX what database to specify in the action. It will become the -db parameter of the XML request. The second parameter, the layout, is optional in all cases, but it's highly recommended that you use it. Refer back to the discussion in Chapter 2 to refresh your memory about the importance of specifying a layout when sending requests to the Web Companion. In a nutshell, it's a performance issue. The only time you wouldn't want to set a layout parameter is if you'll be calling the LayoutNames method.

The final parameter, groupSize, is only relevant when performing a find. By default, the Web Companion will send back a maximum of 25 records at a time. If you plan on displaying a result set in chunks of, say, 10 or 20 records at a time, you'll want to set this parameter accordingly. If you want the Web Companion to send back the entire result set, set the groupSize to "All."

SetDBPassword

Syntax: SetDBPassword ($password)

Example:

```
$myQuery = new FX ('127.0.0.2', '80');
$myQuery->SetDBData('contacts.fp5', 'webFind', 'All');
$myQuery->SetDBPassword ('blah');
```

If you've protected your database with a password, you'll need to send that password as part of every request to that file. See our discussion in Chapter 3 for more information on securing databases while web publishing.

AddDBParam

Syntax: AddDBParam ($name, $value, $operator="")

Example:

```
$myQuery = new FX ('127.0.0.2', '80');
$myQuery->SetDBData('contacts.fp5', 'webFind', 'All');
$myQuery->SetDBPassword ('blah');
$myQuery->AddDBParam('FirstName', 'Fred', 'eq');
$myQuery->AddDBParam('LastName, 'Fintstone', 'eq');
```

The AddDBParam method is used differently for different actions. When performing a find, it's how you'll specify the search criteria. When adding or editing records, it's how you'll send the data to add or edit. For editing and deleting, it's also how you specify which record to edit or delete. This function can even be used to perform FileMaker scripts. Even though it's optional, you'll likely end up calling this method more than any other. In fact, in many instances you'll find that you need multiple AddDBParams to specify all of the criteria for an action. Let's look at some of the uses more closely.

For an FMFind action, you'll specify the search criteria using AddDBParams. Set the $name parameter to the name of the field that you want to search on. The $value parameter is where you'll place the search criteria itself. Finally, you can specify an operator for the search. If you leave this optional third parameter blank, a default operator of "begins with" will be used. Acceptable values for this parameter are the following:

'eq'—an 'equals' search
'cn'—a 'contains' search
'bw'—a 'begins with' search
'ew'—an 'ends with' search
'gt'—a 'greater than' search
'gte'—a 'greater than or equal to' search
'lt'—a 'less than' search
'lte'—a 'less than or equal to' search
'neq'—a 'not equal to' search

If you use multiple AddDBParam method calls to specify multiple search criteria, FileMaker by default will interpret your request as an "and" find. That is, it will find only records where all of the conditions hold. You can change the logical operator by adding the following call:

```
$myQuery->AddDBParam('-lop', 'or');
```

Using or as the logical operator, a find will return records where any of the conditions hold. You can only specify one logical operator (-lop) per query. Again, it's optional. If you don't include it, the default is and.

For both the FMEdit and FMDelete actions, you *must* use the AddDBParam method to specify which record you'll be editing or deleting. To do this, you'll use the "-recid" keyword as the $name and FileMaker's internal record ID as the $value, as follows:

```
$myQuery->AddDBParam('-recid', '23');
```

As an additional criterion for an FMEdit action, you can also use the AddDBParam method to specify a "-modid." Anytime you retrieve record information from the Web Companion, one of the bits of information that you'll receive back is the number of times the record has been modified. If you're editing a record and you want to be sure that the record hasn't been changed by someone else while you were viewing it on the web, you'll want to send that mod count back as part of your edit request. If the number that you send is lower than the current mod count, the edit will not be performed and an error will be returned.

The final use for the AddDBParam is for calling FileMaker scripts. Anytime you perform an action through the Web Companion, you can ask FileMaker to perform a script as well. It's as if the script rides on the coattails of the other action. One common use for this is having FileMaker print something out, usually as a PDF. For instance, you might have a form that submits a new order for a widget and then calls a Print Order script afterward. To call such a script, you'd simply include the following criterion:

```
$myQuery->AddDBParam('-script', "Print Order");
```

There are two variations of calling scripts to be aware of. If you are performing a find action and want a script to be executed before the find is performed, you can use the "-script.prefind" keyword. Similarly, if your action involves a sort, the "-script.presort" keyword will cause the script to be executed before the sort.

In Chapter 2, we discussed several reasons why you should avoid calling scripts as part of a web query. As you undoubtedly recall, the most important reason is that it can cause huge performance problems. Printing, importing, and exporting are possibly the only times that you would want to call scripts. For anything else, try to find some other solution.

AddSortParam

Syntax: AddSortParam ($field, $sortorder="")

Example:

```
$myQuery = new FX ('127.0.0.2', '80');
$myQuery->SetDBData('contacts.fp5', 'webFind', 'All');

$myQuery-> AddSortParam ('Last_Name', 'Descend');
$myQuery-> FMFindAll();
```

You hopefully are not shocked or surprised to discover that the AddSortParam is the tool you use to specify the sort order of records returned by the Web Companion. It's an optional criterion and is only useful with find and findall actions. The first parameter specifies the field to sort on; use the second parameter to indicate whether the sort should be Ascend, Descend, or Custom. If the second parameter is omitted, an ascending sort is performed by default. A Custom sort order works just as it does in FileMaker; if there's a value list attached to the specified field on the layout that you've called in SetDBParam, the field is sorted in the order of the value list entries.

You can specify multiple sort fields simply by calling the AddSortParam multiple times. The sorts are performed in the order that they appear in your code. For example:

```
$myQuery-> AddSortParam ('Last_Name');
$myQuery-> AddSortParam ('First_Name');
```

Here, the records returned from FileMaker would be sorted first by Last_Name and then by First_Name.

FMSkipRecords

Syntax: FMSkipRecords ($skipsize)

Example:

```
$myQuery->FMSkipRecords('25');
```

A skip value is useful when you want to retrieve only a subset of the records found by a query. It's a very common device in web programming. Say for instance that you have a search results page where you want to show the user the first ten records of the found set and then give him a "Next 10" button to retrieve records 11 through 20. On the query to pull back that second set, you want to skip the first ten records. The typical calculation to determine the proper skip size is:

```
(page requested - 1) * records on a page
```

So, if you displayed 15 records on a page and wanted to see the third page of results, the skip size would be (3–1) * 15 = 30.

The main purpose of limiting the set size is performance. The less data that the web server has to send back to the browser, the faster the site will run. Navigating from page to page is also generally thought to be a better user interface than scrolling through large result sets.

FMPostQuery

Syntax: FMPostQuery ($isPostQuery = true)

Example:

```
$myQuery-> FMPostQuery ();
```

When FX sends a request to the Web Companion, it uses the HTTP GET method by default. That's the same method that is used anytime you type a URL into a browser window. However, there's a 255-character limit to an HTTP GET request. For most requests, that's plenty of characters. Sometimes adding and updating records generates long query strings, depending of course on the number of fields and how much data is submitted. In these cases, you'll want to change the query method to HTTP POST by using the FMPostQuery method.

In order to send POST requests, you must configure PHP to use CURL, a library that allows PHP to communicate to a variety of servers using a variety of protocols.

Calling an Action

Now that we've looked at the various query criteria that you can set, we can finally turn to the actions themselves. Don't be surprised if the list of actions looks familiar; it should by now. They're essentially the same actions that can be performed by CDML. Only one action can be performed at a time. Once an action is performed, all of the query criteria will be reset.

Invoking any of the actions listed below triggers the action to be performed. Until the action is called, FX is just collecting bits for assembling a request. Calling one of the action methods completes the construction of the request and submits it to the Web Companion. As we've discussed, the response to your request is then parsed and put into a multidimensional array for your use.

Most of the following actions take an optional parameter of true or false to indicate whether you want FX to parse the response XML or not. By default, this parameter is true (meaning it parses the incoming XML) for every function except FMDelete(). The reason that FMDelete doesn't return data by default should be obvious; there's no data to return if the record has been deleted. For every other function, you typically want to retrieve the data returned by your request. But there are a few cases where you might want to override the default. For instance, you might want to perform a search just to get a found count without displaying the actual found data. Or you might have an add action that logs some sort of activity. If you have no intention or need to display or use the data returned by a request, consider using false—there is a small performance benefit if FX doesn't need to parse all of the incoming XML.

FMFind ($returnDataSet = true)

This is the function that you call to perform a search of a database. As discussed above, you specify the actual search criteria using the AddDBParam method.

Example:

```
$myQuery = new FX ('127.0.0.2', '80');
$myQuery->SetDBData('contacts.fp5', 'webFind', 'All')

$myQuery-> AddDBParam ('Last_Name', 'Flintstone');
$myResults = $myQuery-> FMFind();
```

The above code searches the contacts.fp5 database for all records where Last_Name is Flintstone. The response is parsed and put into the $myResults array. We discuss the structure of a result array shortly.

FMFindAll ($returnDataSet = true)

This function finds and retrieves all of the records from the database specified in the SetDBData function. Note that for any type of find, the returned data set only contains data for those fields (including related fields) that appear on the layout specified by the SetDBData function. Failure to specify a layout causes data to be returned for every field (but no related fields). If your database contains summary fields or complex calculations, performance may be severely diminished.

If you use the FMFindAll action and don't seem to be able to retrieve more than 25 records from your database, chances are that you haven't specified a third argument for the SetDBData function and the groupsize default of 25 is being used. Change it to "all" if you really want to return every record at once.

An FMFindAll action ignores any search criteria that you may have set using the AddDBParam function.

Example:

```
$myQuery = new FX ('127.0.0.2', '80');
$myQuery->SetDBData('contacts.fp5', 'webFind', 'All')

$myResults = $myQuery-> FMFindAll();
```

FMFindAny ($returnDataSet = true)

The FMFindAny function returns a single random record from a database. As with FMFind and FMFindAll, the SetDBData function determines the database and layout used for the query. Any search criteria that you may have set using the AddDBParam function are ignored.

Example:

```
$myQuery = new FX ('127.0.0.2', '80');
$myQuery->SetDBData('contacts.fp5', 'webFind')

$myResults = $myQuery-> FMFindAny();
```

FMDelete ($returnDataSet = false)

The FMDelete function deletes a record from a database. You can only delete a single record at a time; there's no Delete All function available. In order to delete a record, you must specify its record ID using a call to AddDBParam. The record ID is an internal serial number that FileMaker assigns to a record as it's created. Any time that you retrieve information about a record via the Web Companion, you receive this ID as part of the returned data. That's how you know what you should pass back when you want to delete a record. Consider the following example.

Example:

```
$request = new FX ($FMAddress, $FMPort);

$request->SetDBData('calendar.fp5, 'web', 'all');
$request->AddDBParam('Date', $myDate,'lt');

$returnedData = $request->FMFind();

foreach ($returnedData['data'] as $key=>$data) {
     $keyparts = explode (".", $key);
     $recID = $keyparts[0];

     $delRequest = new FX ($FMAddress, $FMPort);

     $delRequest->SetDBData('Database3.fp5');
     $delRequest->AddDBParam('-recid', $recID);

     $delRequest->FMDelete();
}
```

The code above begins by finding all records less than a certain date ($myDate) in a database called calendar.fp5. The foreach loop pulls the record ID out of each of the returned records and uses it as the basis for a delete request. So all records prior to the specified date are deleted from the database. We should mention that a delete loop like this is a fairly slow way to delete large sets of records. Record creation and deletion are two of the slower actions that FileMaker performs. If you ever need to do a large delete through the web, consider calling a deletion script as part of a find action.

FMEdit ($returnDataSet = true)

You use the FMEdit method to modify an existing record. Like FMDelete, FMEdit operates on a single record at a time and requires that you specify a -recid. If you have problems with deleting or editing records, the first thing you should check is whether you've specified a record ID or not.

In addition to the record ID, you also use the AddDBParam function to specify the changes that you want to make to the record. The following example shows how you might update a contact record.

Example:

```
$request = new FX ($FMAddress, $FMPort);
$request->SetDBData('contact.fp5, 'web');
$request->AddDBParam('First_name', $firstname);
$request->AddDBParam('Last_name', $lastname);
$request->AddDBParam('Address1', $address1);
$request->AddDBParam('Address2', $address2);
$request->AddDBParam('City', $city);
$request->AddDBParam('State', $state);
$request->AddDBParam('Zip', $zip);

$request->AddDBParam('-recid', $recID);

$result = $request->FMEdit();
```

You can update related records (as long as they are on the layout that you've specified) by using standard double-colon syntax. For example, you could have something like $request->AddDBParam('Customer by Contact ID::CustomerName', $customerName) as part of your update request.

FMNew ($returnDataSet = true)

The FMNew function is used to add new records to a database. You can specify initial field values using AddDBParam.

Example:

```
$request = new FX ($FMAddress, $FMPort);
$request->SetDBData('contact.fp5, 'web');
$request->AddDBParam('First_name', 'John');
$request->AddDBParam('Last_name', 'Doe');

$result = $request->FMNew();
```

The $result array that's returned by this function will contain the new record data, including the record ID that's been assigned to it.

FMView ($returnDataSet = true)

FMView is probably the least intuitive of the actions that you can perform. It really doesn't do anything at all to the database. Rather, it lets you get metainformation, such as field names, field types, and value lists. The following example shows how you might use FMView to create check boxes on the web based on a value list (called "colors") from FileMaker.

Example:

```
$request = new FX ($FMAddress, $FMPort);

$request->SetDBData('contacts.fp5', 'web');
$returnedData = $request->FMView();

$myList = $returnedData['valueLists']['colors'];

foreach ($myList as $listItem) {
     echo "<input type=\"checkbox\" name=\"color\" value=\"".
        $listItem."\">". $listItem . "<br />";
}
```

FMDBNames ($returnDataSet = true)

FMDBNames returns a list of databases that are open and shared to the Web Companion. This action is unique in that it needs no additional criteria (not even SetDBData) to work.

Example:

```
$request = new FX ($FMAddress, $FMPort);
$DBList = $request->FMDBNames();
```

FMLayoutNames ($returnDataSet = true)

FMLayoutNames returns a list of layout names from a specified database.

Example:

```
$request = new FX ($FMAddress, $FMPort);
$request->SetDBData('contacts.fp5');
$LayoutList = $request->FMLayoutNames();
```

FMDBOpen()

The FMDBOpen function allows you to have PHP open a FileMaker database. There are a few restrictions that you should be aware of. First, in order to use either the FMDBOpen or FMDBClose functions, the Web Companion must be configured to allow remote access *without a password*. See our discussion in Chapter 3 about how to configure the Web Companion to do this and about the potential security problems that this introduces. The second restriction is that the database that you want to open, or a shortcut/alias to it, must be placed in the Web directory in your FileMaker application folder.

Use the SetDBData function before calling FMDBOpen. If the database has a password, use AddDBParam (*not* SetDBPassword) to specify it. The FMDBOpen function takes no parameters and does not return anything.

Example:

```
$request = new FX ($FMAddress, $FMPort);
$request->SetDBData('contacts.fp5');
$request->AddDBParam('-password', 'foo');

$request->FMDBOpen();
```

FMDBClose()

FMDBClose is used to close a particular database. Similar to FMDB-Open, this function takes no arguments and does not return anything. The Web Companion must be configured to allow remote access without a password. Unlike FMDBOpen, you can close any open file regardless of whether it's stored in the Web folder or not.

Example:

```
$request = new FX ($FMAddress, $FMPort);
$request->SetDBData('contacts.fp5');

$request->FMDBClose();
```

The matrix below sums up which criteria can and should be used with which actions.

	Delete	Edit	Find	FindAll	FindAny	New	View	DBNames	LayoutNames	FMDBOpen	FMDBClose
SetDBData	R	R	R	R	R	R	R		R	R	R
SetDBPassword	O	O	O	O	O	O	O		O		
AddDBParam	R	R	O	O	O	O	O		O	O	
AddSortParam			O	O	O						
FMSkipRecords			O	O							
FMPostQuery	O	O	O	O	O	O	O	O	O	O	O

O = Optional R = Required

Creating Web Applications with PHP, FX, and FileMaker

In the remainder of the chapter, we use PHP and FX to construct a complete (albeit small) data-driven web application. Along the way, we focus on developing a modular site design, the anatomy of an FX result set, how to pass variables from page to page, building a log-in screen, and sessions. This is the fun part.

Let's begin by setting out the scenario for our application. Imagine that your neighbor, whom we call Fran, is the owner of a new dog walking business, and you've created a simple, relational database using FileMaker to help her keep track of scheduling and client data. Her business has become so successful that she's about to hire several walkers throughout the city, allowing her to focus on growing the business. But now Fran is worried about how her crew of walkers will get their schedules each day. "Relax," you tell her. "I'll just whip up a web interface so they can log in and review their schedule." You roll up your sleeves, put on a fresh pot of coffee, and dive right in. And we'll help a bit, too.

Now, Fran has DSL service at her home and has a spare machine that she can configure with a static IP address. She doesn't mind putting FileMaker Pro Unlimited on that machine and having it act as a host for this application. You check with the ISP that hosts her web site and are pleasantly surprised that they already have Apache and PHP all set up and ready to use on all their servers. The only setup you need to do on the web server is upload a copy of FX.php.

After you add a new Walker database to her solution, Fran's FileMaker system consists of four tables, as shown in Figure 8.4.

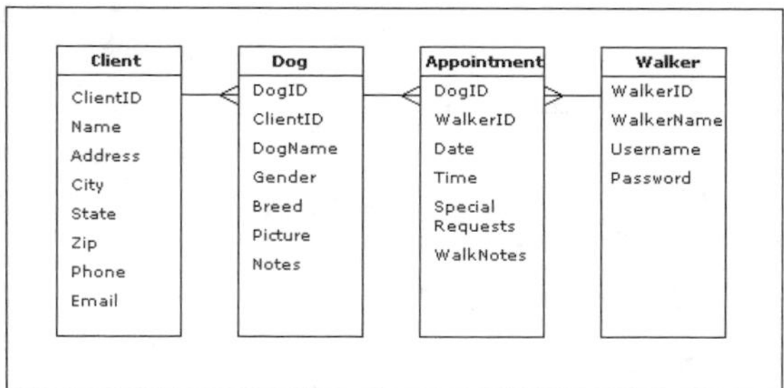

Figure 8.4

For the web site, Fran would like the walker to begin by entering his username and password. Once that's been verified, the walker should go directly to a list of his appointments for the current week. From there, he needs to be able to see detailed information about the dog and client, as well as enter post-walk notes.

Let's start with the login. That gives us an opportunity to learn how to pass variables between pages and use sessions. The first thing that the walker needs to see is a simple HTML form that prompts for a username and password. For now, then, logon.php consists of the following:

```
<html>
<head>
    <title>Log in</title>
</head>
<body>
<br /><br /><br /><br />
<form action='logon_validate.php' method='post'>
<table width='60%' border='0' align='center'>
    <tr>
        <td colspan='2' align='center'>Please enter your username
          and password to enter the site<br /><br /></td>
    </tr>
    <tr>
        <td>Username:</td>
        <td><input type='text' name='name'></td>
    </tr>
    <tr>
        <td>Password:</td>
        <td><input type='password' name='pw'></td>
    </tr>
    <tr>
        <td colspan='2' align='center'><input type='submit'
          name='submit' value='submit'></td>
    </tr>

</table>
</form>
</body>
</html>
```

Figure 8.5 shows how this would be rendered in the browser. Note that there's not a lick of PHP code on the page. The page contains a form with two input fields. When a form is submitted, the web server calls the thing specified by the form's action parameter (here logon_validate.php, which we see shortly), and it sends along all of the form's data to that thing.

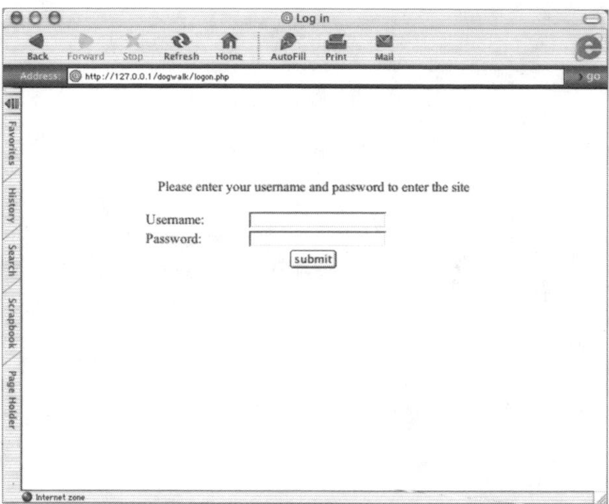

Figure 8.5

When you call a PHP page through a form or URL, PHP automatically puts any form parameters into an array called $_POST (for forms) or $_GET (for URLs). There's nothing special that you need to do either to pass or retrieve the data. On the logon_validate.php page, then, we can access the user's form entries as $_POST['name'] and $_POST['pw']. We purposefully didn't name our variables identically to the field names in the database both to keep the database schema hidden (any user can see the names of your form variables) and make it clear that we're not interacting with a database at this point.

The logon_validate page performs a query of the Walker.fp5 table. If it doesn't find a record that matches the submitted criteria, it should display a message to the user and give him another opportunity to login correctly. For this application, let's not worry about limiting the number of login attempts or anything fancy like that. At this point, logon_validate.php might look something like this:

```
<?
include ("FX.php");

$serverIP = "127.0.0.2";
$port = "591";

$query = new FX($serverIP, $port);

$query->SetDBData ('Walker.fp5', 'web');
$query->AddDBParam ('username', "==". $_POST['name']);
$query->AddDBParam ('password', "==". $_POST['pw']);
```

```
$result = $query->FMFind();

if ($result['foundCount'] == 1) {
     // successful login
     echo "will be for successful login routine.";
     exit;
} else {
     $msg = "Unsucessful login attempt.  Please try again.";
     include ("logon.php");
}

?>
```

This code uses FX to perform a find in Walker.fp5. Note that we've prepended FileMaker's exact equals operator onto the search strings. This protects against the submission of empty or truncated strings.

After sending the query to FileMaker, $result will be a multidimensional associative array with all sorts of information. One of the pieces of information is the number of records the search returned. For now, we've put a placeholder in for the successful login. If it's not successful, we set a variable to an error message and then include our original logon.php page. We don't want to echo out the error message right here because we're not at an appropriate place in an HTML stream.

In order to get that error message to display, we return to the logon.php page and add a conditional statement toward the top of the body (right above the form works well here). If there's something in the $msg variable, it is echoed to the screen, or else the page renders exactly as before. The conditional logic is as follows:

```
if ($msg) {
     echo "<center>$msg</center><br /><br />";
}
```

So much then for the unsuccessful login. A successful login is a bit more complicated to process. Once it has been determined that the user has a valid name and password, we want to start a session and jump to that walker's schedule. Sessions are powerful but complicated tools, and we certainly won't be able to discuss every nuance of them here. Essentially, a session enables you, the programmer, to store information (whatever information you want) on the server rather than having to pass everything from page to page via hidden inputs or extra URL parameters. These so-called session variables can be retrieved by a session ID that's either passed from page to page or stored as a cookie on the user's machine. If you can require that visitors to your site accept cookies, then that's probably the preferable method. For our dog walking application, we store both the walker's ID and name as session variables. That way, wherever they go after logging in, we always know who they are and that they've been authenticated.

PHP has many built-in tools for managing sessions. There are configuration settings that you can use to do things such as set the name of the session ID and determine how the data is stored on the server. There are two options for this; either the session data can be written out to a text file or it can be stored in a database. For Fran's site, let's go ahead and build a database to store the session data. It is just another FileMaker database (called session.fp5) with the following fields:

id_session - text
id_user - text
status - text
value - text
date_created - date
date_mod - date
time_created - time
time_mod - time
expiration - text

We create a table view layout called Web that has all of these fields on it, and we share the database to the Web Companion.

PHP uses functions to handle writing and reading session data. These functions are often referred to as the session handlers and are usually placed in their own document (and included as necessary). Below, we give the code for a complete FileMaker-based session handler. We put this code in a file called session_handler.php, but we won't discuss this page in much detail.

```
<?
// this page is session_handler.php

function sess_open($save_path, $session_name) {
     return true;
}

function sess_close() {
     return true;
}

function sess_read($key) {
     global $serverIP, $port, $sessLife, $sessionDB;
     $query=new FX($serverIP, $port);
     $query->SetDBData($sessionDB,'web');
```

```
    $query->AddDBParam('id_session', $key);
    $result = $query->FMFind();

    if ($result['foundCount'] > 0) {
        $recordKey = key($result['data']);
    if(($result['data'][$recordKey]['expiration'][0]*1) > time() &&
      $result['data'][$recordKey]['status'][0] == 'a') {
        return (string)($result['data'][$recordKey]['value'][0]);
    } else {
        return "exp|i:1" . $result['data'][$recordKey]
          ['value'][0];
    }

   }
    return '';
}

function sess_write($key, $val) {
    global $sessionDB, $serverIP, $port, $sessLife, $idUser;

    $expiration = time() + $sessLife;

    $query=new FX($serverIP, $port);
    $query->SetDBData($sessionDB,'web');
    $query->AddDBParam('id_session', $key);
    $query->AddDBParam('status', 'a');
    $result = $query->FMFind();

    if ($result['foundCount'] == 0) {
        $query=new FX($serverIP, $port);
        $query->SetDBData($sessionDB,'web');
        $query->AddDBParam('id_session', $key);
        $query->AddDBParam('id_user', $idUser);
        $query->AddDBParam('expiration', $expiration);
        $query->AddDBParam('value', $val);
        $query->AddDBParam('status', 'a');

        $result = $query->FMNew();
    } else {
        $recID = explode('.', key($result['data']));
        $query2 = new FX($serverIP, $port);
        $query2->SetDBData($sessionDB,'web');
        $query2->AddDBParam('-recid', $recID[0]);
        $query2->AddDBParam('expiration', $expiration);
        $query2->AddDBParam('value', $val);

        $updateResult = $query2->FMEdit();

    }
    return (string)$updateResult;
}

function sess_destroy($key) {
```

```
    global $sessionDB, $serverIP, $port;

    $query=new FX($serverIP, $port);
    $query->SetDBData($sessionDB,'web');
    $query->AddDBParam('id_session', $key);
    $result = $query->FMFind();

    $recID = explode('.', key($result['data']));

    $query2 = new FX($serverIP, $port);
    $query2->SetDBData($sessionDB,'web');
    $query2->AddDBParam('-recid', $recID[0]);
    $query2->AddDBParam('status', 'e');

    $updateResult = $query2->FMEdit();

    return (string)$updateResult;
}

function sess_gc($maxlifetime) {

    return true;
}

session_set_save_handler("sess_open", "sess_close", "sess_read",
  "sess_write", "sess_destroy", "sess_gc");
```

In order to allow this code to be as generic as possible, we've used variables to denote the IP address and port of the server, the name of the session database itself, and length of time that a session will live. Rather than specify these things over and over, it makes sense at this point to create a small file called prefs.php and put these constants in there. We then must include prefs.php on every page that we access.

```
<?
// prefs.php

// connection information

$serverIP = "127.0.0.1";          // IP address of the FileMaker Pro
                                  // Unlimited machine
$port = "591";                    // port that the Web Companion is
                                  // configured to use


// session handler variables

$sessLife = 10800;                // number of seconds til the session
                                  // expires
$sessionDB = "session.fp5";       // name of the session database

?>
```

Next, we need to edit logon_validate.php to include both the new session_handler.php and prefs.php page. After a successful login, we start a session, declare two session variables (using session_register) called $sessWalkerID and $sessWalkerName, and set them to the appropriate walker ID and name. The final change we need to make to logon_validate before it's complete is to add a redirect to the page that we build next, which is called index.php. That is the central control file for the rest of the entire application.

The finished logon_validate page looks as follows:

```
<?
include ("FX.php");
include ("prefs.php");
include ("session_handler.php");

$query = new FX($serverIP, $port);
$query->SetDBData ('Walker.fp5', 'web');

$query->AddDBParam ('username', "==". $_POST['name']);
$query->AddDBParam ('password', "==". $_POST['pw']);

$result = $query->FMFind();

if ($result['foundCount'] == 1) {
     session_set_save_handler("sess_open","sess_close","sess_read",
       "sess_write","sess_destroy","sess_gc");
     setcookie("sid");
     session_start();

     if ($exp) {
          $msg = "Your session has expired.  You must login again.";
          include_once ("logon.php");
          exit;
     }
     session_register("sessWalkerID");
     session_register("sessWalkerName");

     $recID = current($result['data']);
     $sessWalkerID = $recID['WalkerID'][0];
     $sessWalkerName = $recID['WalkerName'][0];

     echo "Logging in... one moment please";
     echo "<meta http-equiv=refresh content=\"1;url=index.php?area=
       show_schedule\">";

     exit;

} else {
     $msg = "Unsuccessful login attempt.  Please try again.";
     include ("logon.php");
```

```
}
?>
```

To thoroughly test the login and session, you should create a placeholder page for index.php. A quick, simple "hello world" will do the job just fine—anything so that you won't generate a missing file error.

We mentioned a moment ago that index.php becomes a central control file for the rest of the application. There's no reason that we couldn't call that page foo.php or anything else. For that matter, there's nothing that requires a control file at all. We've found, however, that with the exception of the logon and validation pages, it makes for a much more intuitive and easier to maintain site if you do. Just keep in mind that we're talking about programming techniques, not prescriptive rules for building web applications.

The thought behind the single page control file concept is that every form and URL in the application is sent to the control page. As part of every call, you also send one or more variables that tell the control file what documents to include. For instance, notice in our redirect from the validation page that we specified a URL of index.php?area=show_schedule. On the index.php page, then, we'll have access to a variable in the $_GET array called area, and we can use the include function to bring in a chunk of code that pertains to that area.

At the very top of the control file, you want to have a check of some sort to make sure that the user has actually gone through the login and been authenticated. If not, redirect them back to the logon page (via an expired.php page—see the demo files for an example of this). If they have been authenticated, use the include function to pull in code appropriate to the area. Remember to create hello world placeholders as you build new areas so that you can test the navigation away from one page before starting construction on another. The index.php page ends up as follows:

```
<?
include ("FX.php");
include ("prefs.php");
include ("session_handler.php");

session_set_save_handler("sess_open","sess_close","sess_read",
  "sess_write","sess_destroy","sess_gc");
session_start();

if($exp == 1 || !$_SESSION['sessWalkerID']){ // if their session
                                              // has expired
     include("expired.php");          // or they don't have a
                                      // valid session started
```

```
    exit;
}

$filename = $_GET['area'] . ".php";   // construct a filename from the
                                      // contents of the area variable

$inc = @include ($filename);          // include the file

if (!$inc){                           // error trap
    echo "Could not locate requested file for inclusion: $filename";
    exit;
}
?>
```

Not very much code for something so important, is it? The beauty of this design is that simply by feeding it a different value for $area, you can have it pull in any page that you want. By centralizing the overhead tasks (like starting the session and making sure there's a valid login), we've made it easy to troubleshoot or modify those routines.

One PHP coding detail to point out above is the @ sign in front of the include command. That sign tells PHP to suppress the display of any errors that the function may generate. By doing this, we have the opportunity to check for the error ourselves (if !$inc…), and we can display a more attractive and user-friendly error message than PHP would have provided.

Let's turn our attention now to the show_schedule.php page, which, as you recall, is supposed to retrieve all of the user's appointments for the current week. This finally gives us a good opportunity to look closely at the anatomy of the return data set that FX provides. First, though, we have to figure out what to use as query criteria. There are two approaches that we could take. One would be to have a calculation in the Appointment.fp5 database that returned the week beginning date and then have FX do a search of that field. The other would be to have PHP figure out the dates of the first and last days of the week and search on that range in the appointment date field. There's no compelling reason to use one method over the other, so let's try the latter. We need to use the PHP functions mktime(), getDate(), and Date() to do date manipulations. The mktime() function builds a timestamp (date and time combo) out of bits that you feed it. For instance, to build a timestamp representing 8:30 A.M. on Wednesday, February 19, 2003, you'd use mktime(8,30,0, 3,19,2003). We use the getDate() function to fetch the current date. This function returns an array that has elements for all of the bits that you might want. For instance, there's a wday element that tells you where a date falls within the week (0 to 6). You can also feed the getDate function a timestamp and it returns data about that date (rather than the current date). Finally, the Date() function is used for specifying the output format of a timestamp. For example, to display a date using a mm/dd/yyyy format, you'd use Date('m/d/Y'). With those three functions and a little basic math, we can construct a range string that can be passed directly to FileMaker as a search parameter. The beginning of the show_schedule page, where all of this is happening, is shown below:

```
<?
// show_schedule.php
include ("header.php")
$today = getDate();                 // gets today's date

$month = $today['mon'];             // returns the month number (ie, 2)
$year = $today['year'];             // returns the year (ie, 2003)
$dayofmonth = $today['mday'];       // returns the day of month (ie, 19)
$dayofweek = $today['wday'];        // returns the day of week
                                    // (ie, 3 = wednesday)

// build timestamps for week beginning Sunday and week ending
// Saturday

$sunofweek = mktime (0,0,0,$month,$dayofmonth - $dayofweek, $year);
$satofweek = mktime (0,0,0,$month,$dayofmonth + 6 - $dayofweek,
  $year);

$startDate = Date("m/d/Y", $sunofweek);
$endDate = Date("m/d/Y", $satofweek);

$search = $startDate . "...". $endDate; // FM search string
                                       // (ie, 2/16/2003...2/22/2003)

$query = new FX($serverIP, $port);

$query->SetDBData ('Appointment.fp5', 'web', 'all');

$query->AddDBParam ('WalkerID', $_SESSION['sessWalkerID'], 'eq');
$query->AddDBParam ('Date', $search);

$result = $query->FMFind();
```

We've put off for long enough a discussion of the structure of the data array that FX returns to you. Let's use the $result array returned by this find as a specimen for study. The structure of the returned data set is virtually the same no matter what action you run. Remember that you can always do a print_r ($result) as you're programming to see the entire result set.

Think of the returned data set as a tree structure. The highest level node contains the following:

```
[linkNext]              // URL link for next set of records
[linkPrevious]          // URL link for previous sets of records
[foundCount]            // number of records found
[fields]                // array about fields on the layout
[data]                  // array with returned data
[URL]                   // copy of the query that was sent to FM
[errorCode]             // error code.  0 means no error
[valueLists]            // array containing value lists
```

So, if you want to check after the query to see if an error has been generated, you should check $result['errorCode']. Notice that three of the nodes of this array are themselves arrays. These each deserve some discussion.

The [fields] array consists of a set of arrays that contain four pieces of data about each of the fields on the current layout (as specified by the SetDBData function). Say you had three fields on the layout used to perform an action. The fields array might look something like this:

```
[fields] => Array
        (
            [0] => Array
                (
                    [emptyok] => YES
                    [maxrepeat] => 1
                    [name] => FirstName
                    [type] => TEXT
                )
            [1] => Array
                (
                    [emptyok] => YES
                    [maxrepeat] => 1
                    [name] => YearsExperience
                    [type] => NUMBER
                )
            [2] => Array
                (
                    [emptyok] => YES
                    [maxrepeat] => 1
                    [name] => BirthDate
                    [type] => DATE
                )

        )
)
```

The [data] array is the most complex and the most useful. That's where you find the actual data returned by FileMaker. The key of the data array consists of the record ID and the modification count, separated by a period (e.g., [2.5]). Within each "record," you have another layer of keys; this time the field name is the key. Finally, the inner level of the data array is a number/value pair, where the number specifies the repetition. If you don't use repeating fields, just remember that you still have to put a [0] after the field name to grab the first repetition. As an example, then, of what an element in the data array looks like, consider the following:

```
[data] => Array
      (
          [2.5] => Array
              (
                      [First_name] => Array
              (
                           [0] =>Fred
              )
                      [Last_name] => Array
              (
                           [0] =>Flintstone
              )
      )
          [3.2] => Array
              (
                      [First_name] => Array
              (
                           [0] =>Barney
              )
                      [Last_name] => Array
              (
                           [0] =>Rubble
              )
      )
)
```

So, to actually display "Fred," you'd need to refer to $result['data']['2.5']['First_name'][0]. Usually, you'll find it helpful to set a variable to some intermediate level of this so that other calls are shorter to type. For instance, to display "Fred Flintstone," you might do this:

```
$recordData = $result['data']['2.5'];
echo $recordData['First_name'][0] . " ".$recordData['Last_
  name'][0];
```

The [valuelist] array will be populated if you've performed an FMView action. It will contain an array for each value list present on the selected layout. The key of the array is the list's name, while the list choices are the array's elements. In our earlier discussion of FMView, we showed an example of how to iterate through the [valuelist] array to create a set of check box input fields.

For our dog walking application, there are several ways that we could have PHP go through the [data] array of the returned data set. If we try a method that simply loops through the data, even in order, it may be hard to put blank placeholders for off days. It would be easier if the data were in an array with the Date field at the top node. So let's do that. We turn the returned data array inside out. It's actually pretty easy to do; just go through the data, grab the bits as they go by, and reassemble them in whatever order you prefer. The code to do this is as follows:

```
foreach ($result['data'] as $dataArray) {

     $apt_date        = $dataArray['Date'][0];
     $apt_time        = $dataArray['Time'][0];
     $apt_dogID       = $dataArray['DogID'][0];
     $apt_Status      = $dataArray['Status'][0];
     $apt_ID          = $dataArray['AppointmentID'][0];
     $dog_name        = $dataArray['Dog by DogID::DogName'][0];

     $newArray[$apt_date][$apt_time]['id']        = $apt_ID;
     $newArray[$apt_date][$apt_time]['status']    = $apt_Status;
     $newArray[$apt_date][$apt_time]['dogname']   = $dog_name;
     $newArray[$apt_date][$apt_time]['dogID']     = $apt_dogID;
}
```

After turning it around, the newArray looks something like this:

```
Array
(
    [2/17/2003] => Array
        (
            [9am] => Array
                (
                    [id] => 2
                    [status] => Complete
                    [dogname] => Tessa
                    [dogID] => 2
                )
        )
    [2/18/2003] => Array
        (
            [9am] => Array
                (
                    [id] => 1
                    [status] => Complete
                    [dogname] => Tessa
                    [dogID] => 2
                )
        )
    [2/21/2003] => Array
        (
            [3:00] => Array
                (
                    [id] => 9
                    [status] => Confirmed
                    [dogname] => Morgan
```

```
                [dogID] => 3
            )

        [9am] => Array
            (
                [id] => 3
                [status] => Confirmed
                [dogname] => Tessa
                [dogID] => 2
            )
    )
)
```

That's a much easier format to render out as a week-at-a-glance calendar. However, you probably wouldn't want to loop through this array and spit out the data. For something like a calendar, it's nice to at least have placeholders for the days without activities. A good approach is to loop through the days instead of looping through the data. Then, as your loop comes across a day, look to see if that day is a key in the $newArray. If so, it's easy to have an inner loop run through the day's events. If not, you can either just display the date and move on or, as we've done in the code below, you can put in some sort of "Nothing scheduled" message. You can see the schedule above rendered in a browser in Figure 8.6.

```
// continuation of show_schedule page ... code for rendering the
// schedule

echo "<table width=75% border=0 align=center>";
echo "<tr><td>Dog Walking Schedule for: <b>".  $_SESSION
  ['sessWalkerName']. "</b><br /><br /></td></tr>";
for ($i = 0; $i<=6; $i++){       // will loop 7 times

     $theDate = mktime(0,0,0,date("m", $sunofweek), date("d",
       $sunofweek) + $i, date("Y"));

     $dateDisplay = Date("l, F j, Y", $theDate);
     echo "<tr><td bgcolor='#666666'><font color='white'>";
     echo $dateDisplay. "</font></td></tr>";
     echo "<tr><td><table border=0 width=100%>";

     $dailyActivities = array();
     $dailyActivities = $newArray[date("n/j/Y",$theDate)];

     if (count($dailyActivities)) {
          foreach ($dailyActivities as $time=>$aptData) {
               echo "<tr><td width=20%></td><td>".$time."</td>";
               echo "<td>".$aptData['dogname']."</td>";
               echo "<td>".$aptData['status']."</td></tr>";
          }
     } else {
```

```
        echo "<tr><td width=20%></td><td>Nothing
          scheduled</td></tr>";
    }

    echo "</table><br></td></tr>";
}
echo "</table>";
```

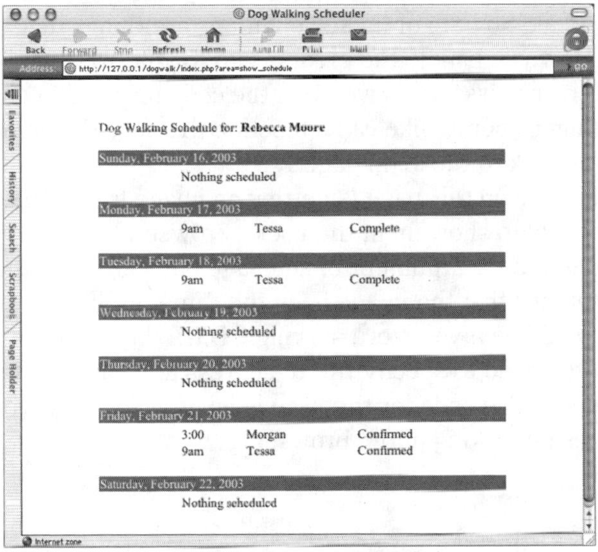

Figure 8.6

Now that we have the walker's schedule created, the remaining two tasks (seeing the dog detail and entering post-walk notes) are both simple in comparison. We tackle the dog detail first. From the weekly schedule, we want to turn the name of the dog into a hyperlink that shows the detailed dog record. If this were a FileMaker application, all you'd need is a Go To Related Record script. On the web, we just do an actual search in the related table.

Remember that we're pointing all requests to index.php for processing. Our request needs to have two pieces of information in order to be processed. First, it needs an $area. Something like $area=dog_detail should be adequate. Even though index.php is the center of the universe, you don't need to edit that page at all. Second, it must specify the dogID of the record to retrieve. To make the link, then, you need to edit the line where the dog's name is rendered out to be:

```
echo "<td><a href=\"index.php?area=dog_detail&dogID=
  ".$aptData['dogID']."\">".$aptData['dogname']."</a></td>";
```

As before, to test the link, just stub in a dog_detail.php page. Echo out the $dogID or something trivial. Once you think the link is working well, you can start to worry about building the page itself.

There are a few issues to think about on the dog_detail page. The first is error trapping. If for some reason a user gets to that page without a $dogID or with an invalid $dogID, then it's quite likely that the application will break. So both of these conditions are things that you should trap for. How you handle the errors is up to you. You could simply echo out an error message, as we do in the code below. Or you could do something elaborate like call a function that logs the error and redirects the user back to the login page.

Another challenge on this page is getting an image from a FileMaker container field to show up in the user's browser. In essence, you put the field in the src argument of an image tag. However, the resulting link assumes that the image is on the same machine as the web page (as it would be if you were serving CDML directly from FileMaker). So, you need to specify the IP address and port number of the Web Companion. The code for the page is given below; Figure 8.7 shows how it ends up looking in the browser.

```
<?

// coming here, should have a $dogID set

include ("header.php");

if (!$_GET['dogID']) {
     echo "Improper access attempt.  Go away";
     exit;
}

$query = new FX($serverIP, $port);
$query->SetDBData ('dog.fp5', 'web');
$query->AddDBParam ('dogID', $_GET['dogID']);
$result = $query->FMFind();

if (!$result['foundCount'] == 1) {
     echo "Invalid ID.  Go away";
     exit;
}

$dogInfo = current($result['data']);

echo "<table width=70% align=center>";
echo "<tr><td>Dog Detail</td>";
echo "<td align=right><a href=\"index.php?area=show_schedule\">Back
  to Schedule</a></td</tr>";
echo "</table>";
```

```
echo "<br />";
echo "<center>".$dogInfo['DogName'][0]. "</center>";
echo "<br />";

echo "<hr width=70%>";

echo "<table width=70% border=0 cellspacing=10 align=center>";
echo "<tr><td width=30% align=right>Gender:</td>";
echo "<td>".$dogInfo['Gender'][0]."</td></tr>";

echo "<tr><td width=30% align=right>Breed:</td>";
echo "<td>".$dogInfo['Breed'][0]."</td></tr>";

echo "<tr><td width=30% align=right>Notes:</td>";
echo "<td>".$dogInfo['Notes'][0]."</td></tr>";

echo "<tr><td width=30% align=right>Owner:</td>";
echo "<td>".$dogInfo['Client by ClientID::Name'][0]."</td></tr>";

echo "<tr><td width=30% align=right>Address:</td>";
echo "<td>".$dogInfo['Client by ClientID::Address'][0]."</td></tr>";

echo "<tr><td width=30% align=right>City, State, Zip:</td>";
echo "<td>".$dogInfo['Client by ClientID::City'][0]. ", ";
echo $dogInfo['Client by ClientID::State'][0]. "  ";
echo $dogInfo['Client by ClientID::Zip'][0]."</td></tr>";

echo "</table>";
echo "<hr width=70%><br />";

echo "<center><img src=\"http://$serverIP:$port/".$dogInfo
  ['Picture'][0]."\"></center>";
?>
```

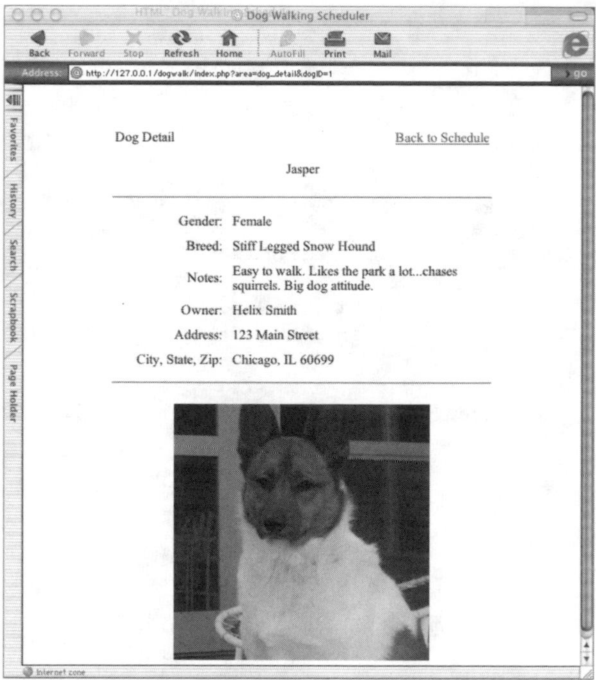

Figure 8.7

The only place to go from this page is back to the week's schedule, and that's a trivial link to create. Since the user's ID is stored as a session variable, all we need is a URL to index.php?area=show_schedule.

As a final PHP exercise, let's add one more feature to this application. Recall that Fran wanted the walker to be able to enter in notes after the walk and change the status from Confirmed to Complete. To do this, we add another link from the schedule. The link is very similar to the link to the dog_detail, except we want to go to a walk_notes area this time, and instead of dogID, we need to know the AppointmentID (we're just calling it ID for brevity). Creating the link requires only the addition of one line of code to the show_schedule.php page:

```
echo "<td><a href=\"index.php?area=walk_notes&ID=". $aptData
  ['id']."\">Walk Notes</a></td></tr>";
```

Rendering the walk_notes page is similar in some ways to what we needed to do on the dog_detail page: We need to find the record and echo out everything that we know about it. The big difference is that there's editable information on this page. When rendering the page, that difference only means that we need a form, some input fields, and a button. The tricky part is figuring what to do when that form is actually submitted. Should the user end up back on the schedule page, or should the form submission leave them on the walk_notes page? This is important because it determines where the update logic will live. We just checked with Fran, and she said that she'd like the walk notes page to have a Save and a Cancel button, both of which take the user back to the schedule.

Let's look at the code for the walk_notes page. Note especially the logic in the middle for determining which status should be selected. We didn't pull the value list from the database since it's a static list, but we would have used the same sort of logic if we had loop through the list items, build up the HTML text for all of the choices, and the one that's currently selected (as determined by comparison to the record value) gets marked as selected. Figure 8.8 shows the completed page.


```
<?
// walk_notes.php
// coming here, should have an AppointmentID ($ID)

include ("header.php");

if (!$_GET['ID']) {
     echo "Improper access attempt.  Go away";
     exit;
}

$query = new FX($serverIP, $port);
$query->SetDBData ('Appointment.fp5', 'web');
$query->AddDBParam ('AppointmentID', $_GET['ID']);
$result = $query->FMFind();

if (!$result['foundCount'] == 1) {     // you can perhaps handle the
                                       // error more tactfully...
     echo "Invalid ID.  Go away";
     exit;
}
$recKey = key ($result['data']);
$keyParts = explode (".", $recKey);
$recID = $keyParts[0];

$appInfo = current($result['data']);

echo "<form action=\"index.php?area=show_schedule\" method=
  \"post\">";
echo "<input type=\"hidden\" name=\"rec\" value=\"$recID\">";

echo "<table width=70% align=center>";
echo "<tr><td>Walk Notes</td>";
echo "</tr></table>";

echo "<hr width=70%>";
```

```
echo "<table width=70% border=0 cellspacing=10 align=center>";
echo "<tr><td width=30% align=right>Dog:</td>";
echo "<td>".$appInfo['Dog by DogID::DogName'][0]."</td></tr>";

echo "<tr><td width=30% align=right>Walker:</td>";
echo "<td>".$appInfo['Walker by WalkerID::WalkerName']
  [0]."</td></tr>";

echo "<tr><td width=30% align=right>Date:</td>";
echo "<td>".$appInfo['Date'][0]."</td></tr>";

echo "<tr><td width=30% align=right>Time:</td>";
echo "<td>".$appInfo['Time'][0]."</td></tr>";

$choices = array("Confirmed", "Canceled", "Complete");
foreach ($choices as $myChoice) {
     if ($appInfo['Status'][0] == $myChoice) {
          $selected = "selected";
     } else {
          $selected = "";
     }
     $options .= "<option value=\"". $myChoice. "\" $selected>".
       $myChoice. "</option>\n";
}

echo "<tr><td width=30% align=right>Status:</td>";
echo "<td><select name=\"status\"><option>$options";

echo "</select></td></tr>";
echo "<tr><td width=30% align=right>Notes:</td>";
echo "<td><textarea name=\"notes\" cols=50 rows=6>".$appInfo
  ['WalkNotes'][0]."</textarea></td></tr>";

echo "</table>";
echo "<hr width=70%><br />";

echo "<table width=40% align=center>";
echo "<tr><td align=center><input type=\"Submit\" name=\"Action\"
  value=\"Cancel\"></td>";
echo "<td align=center><input type=\"Submit\" name=\"Action\"
  value=\"Submit\"></td></tr>";
echo "</table>";

?>
```

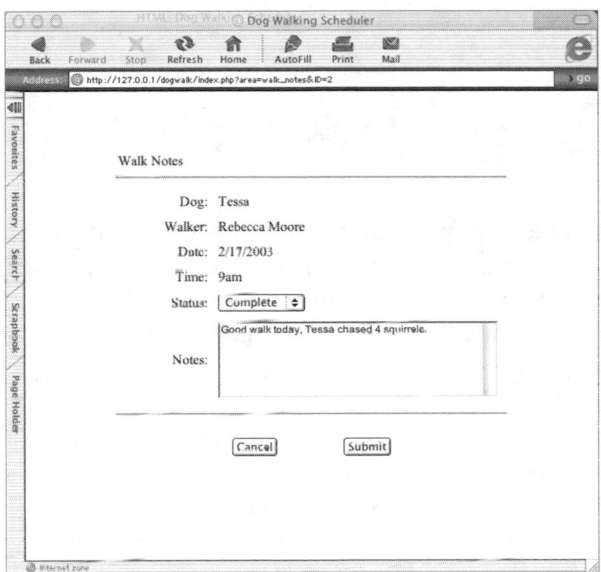

Figure 8.8

Notice in the code that we've already specified the return to the schedule as part of the form action, regardless of which button the user selects. We now need to add some logic to the top of the show_schedule page to check the incoming form parameters for something called "Action" with a value of "Submit." It's important that the test is done at the top of the page so that when the search is performed afterward, it picks up the latest changes that you may have just made. Also, don't forget that to edit a record, you must have its record ID. That's why we parsed the ID out in the code above and created a hidden input field. It will be sent back to the show_schedule page with the rest of the form parameters.

The logic that we need to add to show_schedule is fairly straightforward: If the user submitted something, then update the record; if not, don't. As code, it would look something like this:

```
if ($_POST['Action'] == 'Submit') {   // means they've submitted from
                                      // walk note page
     $update = new FX($serverIP, $port);

     $update->SetDBData ('Appointment.fp5', 'web');
     $update->AddDBParam ('Status', $_POST['status']);
     $update->AddDBParam ('WalkNotes', $_POST['notes']);
```

```
        $update->AddDBParam ('-recid', $_POST['rec']);
        $updateResult = $update->FMEdit();

        if ($updateResult['ErrorCode'] != 0) {
            echo "There was a problem updating the walk notes.";
        }
}
```

Our dog walking schedule application is now functionally complete. The single-page architecture may take some getting used to, but hopefully you can at least appreciate the efficiency and simplicity of it. For any additional functionality that we want to add later on, we just need to figure out what "area" it belongs in and what input parameters it needs to be fed.

Another nice thing about this architecture is that it scales very well. For a large solution, you'll find it helpful to have another variable besides $area. We commonly use $sub as a second variable, and that allows us to group pages by functional areas. For instance, within an "area" of "contacts," there might be "sub" pages to find, add, edit, or delete contacts. Then, for your filename, use a concatenation of the area and sub (contacts_find.php or contacts_add.php).

Summary

PHP is a fast, popular, free, and easy-to-learn web development environment. We covered four main areas in this chapter. First, we gave you a sense of what PHP is and how it compares with other web development tools. Second, we presented an overview of the PHP programming syntax and a brief tutorial of how variables, arrays, functions, and objects are represented and manipulated by PHP. We then investigated how PHP can be used to talk to FileMaker's Web Companion via XML. The FX class greatly simplifies hooking PHP to FileMaker. Finally, we built an entire web application using PHP, FX, and FileMaker.

FileMaker and Web Services: Learning about XML Import

By now you might have heard of the concept of a *web service*. Like other subjects connected with XML and the web, the idea of web services has been at the center of a great deal of discussion and a certain amount of hype. So what exactly is a web service?

Web services build on the universality of XML. Remember that one of the most important features of XML is that it breaks down the wall of proprietary data formats. Web services are a way to use XML (among other tools) as an all-purpose language for communication between different computers doing different things.

It might be best to start with an example. Let's go back to Blue Horizon Bison Breeders again. Researchers have told BHBB that the online reports of herd activity that the new web site provides are extremely useful. The problem is that these reports still present the data visually, marked up with HTML. These researchers would like a way to get their hands on the raw data, and these web pages don't do that. The researchers can resort to workarounds, such as downloading the HTML pages and running a bunch of "screen scraper" parsing processes to extract the herd information again, but this is not only tedious to program, it's very fragile. If anything in the HTML changes, the parsing routines will probably break. The researchers don't really want to head down that path. They'd rather find some way to send a request to the BHBB servers and get the data back in some unvarnished form.

How about XML? Yes, an XML data feed would be perfect, the researchers say. That would allow them to apply their own XSL transformations to the data (say, into tab-delimited text or whatever other format their analysis tools require). Since the Web Companion can publish data in XML, nothing could be easier. BHBB can simply tell the researchers the appropriate URLs to use to extract the XML data—something like:

```
http://services.bhbb.com/FMPro?-db=Herd&-format=-fmp_xml&-findall
```

Once BHBB lets its clients know about this URL, they are providing a web service—a facility that works over the existing web protocols (HTTP) to distribute information. That's all there is to it. It's up to BHBB to decide which data they want to publish and how they want to grant or restrict access to it, but the idea is always the same; a researcher submits a specially formatted URL and gets back a stream of XML data.

Web services are not limited to returning data from a database. The command you send to a remote server could in fact be a complicated set of instructions to do something. The remote server could take action based on the commands that you sent it and return a response telling you the status of your request. Consider the following transaction. You send this URL to a remote server:

```
http://mytrade.stockloss.com/traderApp?symbol=TXX&action=buy&
  maxPrice=55.6&shares=100&account=10019298381&passKey=A908DF82348F
```

...and you get back the following reply:

```
<?xml version="1.0" encoding="UTF-8" ?>
<trade>
     <symbol>TXX</symbol>
     <shares>100</shares>
     <action>buy</action>
     <tradePrice>55.125</tradePrice>
     <tradeStatus>Complete</tradeStatus>
</trade>
```

Apparently, you just sent a command to your stockbroker's server, asking it to buy 100 shares of TXX stock at a price not to exceed \$55.60. The server has responded with an XML message confirming what you asked for and letting you know the trade was completed for \$55.125 per share. The common thread here is that, once again, we are using familiar, standardized protocols for both the request and the response. The request is a simple URL, and the response is sent back over HTTP in the form of XML. It may be that you never need to read or see the XML response directly. The trading software that you use may invisibly translate it back into the proper feedback, possibly in some graphical environment. The important thing is that another wall is being broken down here. Probably in the past, your stockbroker's computers used some proprietary networking protocol, thus vastly limiting the number of other computers that could possibly send it requests or interact with it. If we use a standard protocol (HTTP) instead and send our messages in a standard format (XML), suddenly everything is wide open. If you want to interact with the trading systems at Stockloss.com, suddenly all you need is to be able to send and receive requests over HTTP and maybe parse some XML. (You probably also need to pay Stockloss a fee for access to their servers.)

This idea of sending messages in a standard format over a standard protocol is at the heart of the idea of web services. If you can send and receive web requests and read XML, you can publish or consume web services, regardless of your operating system or hardware or that of the remote machines with which you interact.

Working with a Real Web Service

Let's look at some real-life examples. One company that has been something of a pioneer in opening its databases to the world via web services is Amazon.com. If you go to http://www.amazon.com/webservices, you'll see instructions there for downloading their developer's kit and getting a free "developer's token" that lets you have access to their web services. The token is what you really need—this gets sent with each request you submit to make sure you're an authorized user. We suggest that you go ahead and download the kit and apply for the token; it should arrive in your e-mail in a few minutes.

Note: As of publication, you did not actually need to submit a valid value for the developer's token, but it would probably be courteous to apply and use your own token anyway.

Once you've got your Amazon developer's token, open up an XML-aware web browser and send this URL, replacing the XXXXXXXXXX with your own developer's token:

```
http://xml.amazon.com/onca/xml2?t=webservices-20&dev-t=
  XXXXXXXXXX&KeywordSearch=american%20indians&mode=books&type=
  lite&page=&f=xml
```

You're performing a book search on Amazon for books matching the keywords "american indians." Before long, your XML-aware browser should show you several screenfuls of XML that tell you about the results of your search. We've chosen Amazon's "lightweight" data format (that's the type=lite parameter that you sent). Feel free to experiment with the heavy form by sending type=heavy. In my case the search retrieved 7507 titles. Of course, I didn't get the XML data for all of those at once. Amazon sent them to me in "pages" of ten books each. If I want to see books 11-20, I can send page=2 instead.

This is all very well, but what good does this do me in FileMaker? Well, as of FileMaker 6, you can import this data directly back into FileMaker. You can create new records in a database using this information or just use it to update an existing database. If you were a book publisher, for example, and you had your book database in FileMaker, you could use FileMaker 6's XML Import to add the Amazon price and the Amazon sales rank to your database for each book.

That sounds almost too good to be true. FileMaker can read any XML data from anywhere and turn it into FileMaker records? Well, no, not quite. There is one catch: In order for FileMaker to import the data, it needs to be in one of the two FileMaker XML grammars that we looked at earlier. In particular, it needs to be in the FMPXML grammar. The way that we get it there, as you might guess, is to transform it using a stylesheet. Here's what that process looks like:

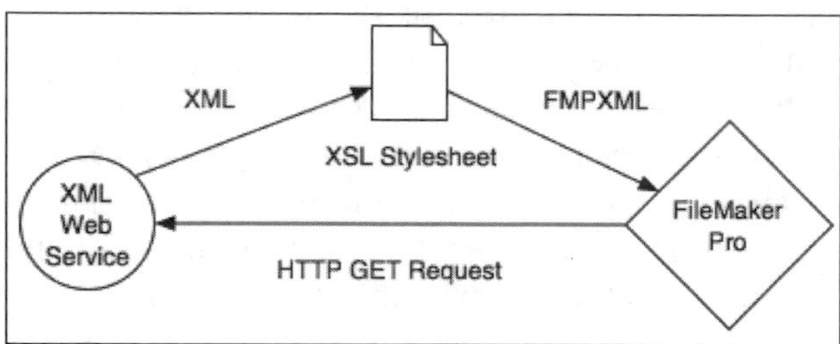

Figure 9.1

So let's look at the data that we just got from Amazon and then look at what we need to turn it into in order for FileMaker to read it. Here's a partial sample of the Amazon XML:

```
<?xml version="1.0"?>
<ProductInfo xmlns:xsi="http://www.w3.org/2001/XMLSchema-instance"
  xsi:noNamespaceSchemaLocation="http://xml.amazon.com/schemas2/
  dev-lite.xsd">
     <TotalResults>7571</TotalResults>
     <Details url="http://www.amazon.com/exec/obidos/redirect?tag=
       webservices-20%26creative=XXXXXXXXXX%26camp=2025%26link_
       code=xm2%26path=ASIN/0684818868">
          <Asin>0684818868</Asin>
          <ProductName>Lies My Teacher Told Me: Everything Your
            American History Textbook Got Wrong</ProductName>
          <Catalog>Book</Catalog>
          <Authors>
               <Author>James W. Loewen</Author>
          </Authors>
          <ReleaseDate>September, 1996</ReleaseDate>
```

```
        <Manufacturer>Touchstone Books</Manufacturer>
        <ImageUrlSmall>http://images.amazon.com/images/P/
          0684818868.01.THUMBZZZ.jpg</ImageUrlSmall>
        <ImageUrlMedium>http://images.amazon.com/images/P/
          0684818868.01.MZZZZZZZ.jpg</ImageUrlMedium>
        <ImageUrlLarge>http://images.amazon.com/images/P/
          0684818868.01.LZZZZZZZ.jpg</ImageUrlLarge>
        <ListPrice>$15.00</ListPrice>
        <OurPrice>$10.50</OurPrice>
        <UsedPrice>$5.00</UsedPrice>
</Details>
<Details url="http://www.amazon.com/exec/obidos/redirect?tag=
  webservices-20%26creative=XXXXXXXXXX%26camp=2025%26link_code=
  xm2%26path=ASIN/0969297939">
        <Asin>0969297939</Asin>
        <ProductName>Learning by Designing Pacific Northwest Coast
          Native Indian Art, vol.1</ProductName>
        <Catalog>Book</Catalog>
        <Authors>
              <Author>Jim Gilbert</Author>
              <Author>Karin Clark</Author>
        </Authors>
        <ReleaseDate>27 November, 1999</ReleaseDate>
        <Manufacturer>Raven Publishing</Manufacturer>
        <ImageUrlSmall>http://images.amazon.com/images/P/096929793
          9.01.THUMBZZZ.jpg</ImageUrlSmall>
        <ImageUrlMedium>http://images.amazon.com/images/P/
          0969297939.01.MZZZZZZZ.jpg</ImageUrlMedium>
        <ImageUrlLarge>http://images.amazon.com/images/P/
          0969297939.01.LZZZZZZZ.jpg</ImageUrlLarge>
        <ListPrice>$27.95</ListPrice>
        <OurPrice>$27.95</OurPrice>
</Details>
```

Overall, the Amazon XML format consists of a root element called ProductInfo, which contains one TotalResults element (giving the total found count for your query) and then a number of Details elements, which each contain data on an individual title. Right now Amazon is handing us ten of these Details records per request, so as not to overwhelm its servers. The Details element itself is pretty uncomplicated; the only thing that we need to note is that the Authors element can contain multiple authors, which is an issue we need to resolve as far as importing that data into FileMaker.

Now we need to figure out how that data should look to appease FileMaker's XML Import capability. The best thing to do here is cheat. We're going to build a simple FileMaker database that contains the fields we're interested in, put a little sample data into it, perform an XML Export using the FMPXML grammar, and see what we get.

Here's our database structure:

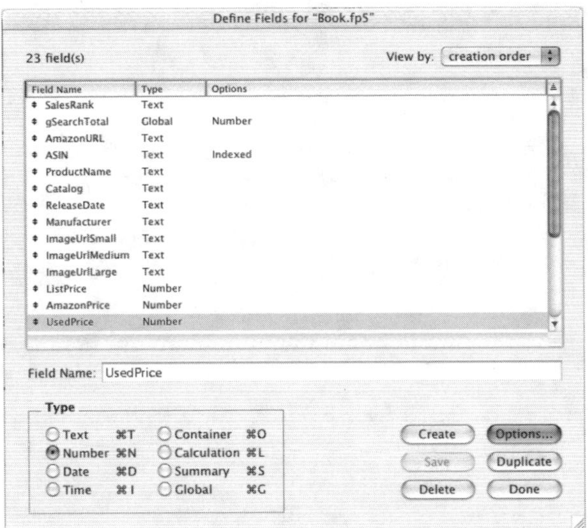

Figure 9.2

We've included some fields that are part of the "heavy," rather than the "light," Amazon format. For now, just ignore these fields.

Let's go ahead and put in one record's worth of sample data, and then export that data in XML format using the FMPXML grammar to a file called AmazonLiteFormatExport.xml. Here's how the export looks:

```
<?xml version="1.0" encoding="UTF-8" ?>
<fmpxmlresult xmlns="http://www.filemaker.com/fmpxmlresult">
     <errorcode>0</errorcode>
     <product build="08/09/2002" name="FileMaker Pro" version=
       "6.0v3" />
     <database dateformat="M/d/yyyy" layout="" name="Book.fp5"
       records="1" timeformat="h:mm:ss a" />
     <metadata>
          <field emptyok="YES" maxrepeat="1" name="ASIN" type=
            "TEXT" />
          <field emptyok="YES" maxrepeat="1" name="ProductName"
            type="TEXT" />
          <field emptyok="YES" maxrepeat="1" name="Catalog"
            type="TEXT" />
          <field emptyok="YES" maxrepeat="1" name="ReleaseDate"
            type="TEXT" />
          <field emptyok="YES" maxrepeat="1" name="Manufacturer"
            type="TEXT" />
          <field emptyok="YES" maxrepeat="1" name="ImageUrlSmall"
            type="TEXT" />
          <field emptyok="YES" maxrepeat="1" name="ImageUrlMedium"
            type="TEXT" />
          <field emptyok="YES" maxrepeat="1" name="ImageUrlLarge"
```

```
            type="TEXT" />
          <field emptyok="YES" maxrepeat="1" name="ListPrice"
            type="NUMBER" />
          <field emptyok="YES" maxrepeat="1" name="AmazonPrice"
            type="NUMBER" />
          <field emptyok="YES" maxrepeat="1" name="UsedPrice"
            type="NUMBER" />
     </metadata>
     <resultset found="1">
          <row modid="4" recordid="12">
               <col>
                    <data>0684818868</data>
               </col>
               <col>
                    <data>Lies My Teacher Told Me: Everything Your
                      American History Textbook Got Wrong</data>
               </col>
               <col>
                    <data>Book</data>
               </col>
               <col>
                    <data>September, 1996</data>
               </col>
               <col>
                    <data>Touchstone Books</data>
               </col>
               <col>
                    <data>http://images.amazon.com/images/P/
                      0684818868.01.THUMBZZZ.jpg</data>
               </col>
               <col>
                    <data>http://images.amazon.com/images/P/
                      0684818868.01.MZZZZZZZ.jpg</data>
               </col>
               <col>
                    <data>http://images.amazon.com/images/P/
                      0684818868.01.LZZZZZZZ.jpg</data>
               </col>
               <col>
                    <data>15</data>
               </col>
               <col>
                    <data>10.5</data>
               </col>
               <col>
                    <data>5</data>
               </col>
          </row>
     </resultset>
</fmpxmlresult>
```

So, as we understand it, if we can transform the incoming Amazon XML into data in the above format, FileMaker should be able to import it. Well, we're battle-scarred XSL veterans by now, and we know how to do that. Let's think about the general strategy, though, before starting to code up the XSL. The FMPXML grammar begins with a lot of header-like information, which is the database metadata. So we need to arrange to output all of that at the top of the document. The FMPXML grammar contains a <resultset>, which contains one or more instances of a <ROW>.

Well, for one-time output, we probably want to write a template that matches on the incoming XML's root element. The FMPXML <ROW> element matches up to the Amazon XML <Details> element, so we presumably want a template that matches the <Details> element and then output a <ROW> in its place. Or we could use <xsl:for-each> to loop through the available <Details> records.

That sounds like enough of a plan, so let's dive in and take a cut at the stylesheet:

```
<?xml version="1.0" encoding="UTF-8"?>
<xsl:stylesheet xmlns:xsl="http://www.w3.org/1999/XSL/Transform"
  version="1.0">
<xsl:template match="ProductInfo">
          <FMPXMLRESULT xmlns="http://www.filemaker.com/
            fmpxmlresult">
               <ERRORCODE>0</ERRORCODE>
               <PRODUCT BUILD="" NAME="" VERSION=""/>
               <DATABASE DATEFORMAT="M/d/yyyy" LAYOUT="" NAME=""
                 RECORDS="10" TIMEFORMAT="h:mm:ss a"/>
               <METADATA>
                    <FIELD EMPTYOK="YES" MAXREPEAT="1"
                      NAME="AmazonURL" TYPE="TEXT" />
                    <FIELD EMPTYOK="YES" MAXREPEAT="1" NAME="ASIN"
                      TYPE="TEXT" />
                    <FIELD EMPTYOK="YES" MAXREPEAT="1"
                      NAME="ProductName" TYPE="TEXT" />
                    <FIELD EMPTYOK="YES" MAXREPEAT="1"
                      NAME="Catalog" TYPE="TEXT" />
                    <FIELD EMPTYOK="YES" MAXREPEAT="1"
                      NAME="ReleaseDate" TYPE="TEXT" />
                    <FIELD EMPTYOK="YES" MAXREPEAT="1"
                      NAME="Manufacturer" TYPE="TEXT" />
                    <FIELD EMPTYOK="YES" MAXREPEAT="1"
                      NAME="ImageUrlSmall" TYPE="TEXT" />
                    <FIELD EMPTYOK="YES" MAXREPEAT="1"
                      NAME="ImageUrlMedium" TYPE="TEXT" />
                    <FIELD EMPTYOK="YES" MAXREPEAT="1"
                      NAME="ImageUrlLarge" TYPE="TEXT" />
                    <FIELD EMPTYOK="YES" MAXREPEAT="1"
                      NAME="ListPrice" TYPE="NUMBER" />
                    <FIELD EMPTYOK="YES" MAXREPEAT="1"
                      NAME="AmazonPrice" TYPE="NUMBER" />
                    <FIELD EMPTYOK="YES" MAXREPEAT="1"
                      NAME="UsedPrice" TYPE="NUMBER" />
```

```
                </METADATA>
                <RESULTSET>
                        <xsl:attribute name="FOUND"><xsl:value-of
                          select="/ProductInfo/TotalResults"/>
                          </xsl:attribute>
                        <xsl:for-each select="Details">
                                <ROW>
                                        <xsl:attribute name="MODID">0
                                          </xsl:attribute>
                                        <xsl:attribute name="RECORDID">0
                                          </xsl:attribute>
                                             <COL><DATA><xsl:value-of select=
                                              "@url"/></DATA></COL>
                                             <COL><DATA><xsl:value-of select=
                                              "Asin"/></DATA></COL>
                                             <COL><DATA><xsl:value-of select=
                                              "ProductName"/></DATA></COL>
                                             <COL><DATA><xsl:value-of select=
                                              "Catalog"/></DATA></COL>
                                             <COL><DATA><xsl:value-of select=
                                              "ReleaseDate"/></DATA></COL>
                                             <COL><DATA><xsl:value-of select=
                                              "Manufacturer"/></DATA></COL>
                                             <COL><DATA><xsl:value-of select=
                                              "ImageUrlSmall"/></DATA></COL>
                                             <COL><DATA><xsl:value-of select=
                                              "ImageUrlMedium"/></DATA></COL>
                                             <COL><DATA><xsl:value-of select=
                                              "ImageUrlLarge"/></DATA></COL>
                                             <COL><DATA><xsl:value-of select=
                                              "ListPrice"/></DATA></COL>
                                             <COL><DATA><xsl:value-of select=
                                              "OurPrice"/></DATA></COL>
                                             <COL><DATA><xsl:value-of select=
                                              "UsedPrice"/></DATA></COL>
                                </ROW>
                        </xsl:for-each>
                </RESULTSET>
        </FMPXMLRESULT>
    </xsl:template>
</xsl:stylesheet>
```

We've chosen to write this stylesheet with just one template that matches on <ProductInfo>. Inside this template, we first output all of the components of the <METADATA> elements. We then start up the <RESULTSET> element. To gather up all of the <Details> elements in the Amazon XML, we use <xsl:for-each>. Since our context is the <ProductInfo> node, <xsl:for-each select="Details"> tells the XSL processor to loop through all <Details> nodes that are children of the <ProductInfo> node, which is exactly what we want. Finally, for each <ROW>, we output a ModID and a RecordID of 0 and then output a <COL><DATA>...</COL></DATA> tagset for each field that we're interested in.

One small note concerns the field that we're calling AmazonURL. The data we want to bring into that field lives in the <Details> element in the url attribute. So an opening <Details> tag looks like this:

```
<Details url="http://www.amazon.com/exec/obidos/redirect?tag=
  webservices-20%26creative=XXXXXXXXXX%26camp=2025%26link_code=
  xm2%26path=ASIN/0684818868">
```

We need to fetch the url attribute, so our XPath expression reads 'select = "@url" '. This translates as "fetch an attribute of the current node called url." In this context, the current node is always a <Details> node, so this expression pulls the URL from the current <Details> node.

Once the stylesheet is complete, we need to set up the import routine in FileMaker. Save the stylesheet as AmazonLite.xsl. Select File>Import Records, and choose XML as the import type. Use the following for the source URL, remembering to use your own developer token in place of the XXXXXXX.

```
http://xml.amazon.com/onca/xml2?t=webservices-20&dev-t=XXXXXXX&
  KeywordSearch=american%20indians&mode=books&type=lite&page=
  1&f=xml
```

Then specify AmazonLite.xsl. Go ahead with the import, and you get the familiar FileMaker Import dialog. If all is well with the stylesheet, you should see a set of field names on the left that correspond to the ones that we defined in the <METADATA> section of our stylesheet. Proceed with the import, and ten new records should be created in our Books database.

This stylesheet should work well enough, but it does leave a few questions unanswered. Suppose we want to know the total number of records that our query returned? Right now we can only see and fetch them in groups of ten. If we learn what the total number was, how can we fetch *all* of them? First let's try to get the total record count and do something with it.

This number is available in the Amazon XML as <TotalResults>, a child of <ProductInfo>. We'd like to bring it into a global field. We've defined such a field in our FileMaker database already, so we just need to tweak our stylesheet to bring that information back from Amazon. If we add this row to the <METADATA> section of the stylesheet:

```
<FIELD EMPTYOK="YES" MAXREPEAT="1" NAME="gSearchTotal" TYPE=
  "NUMBER" />
```

...and this row to the <ROW> section of the stylesheet:

```
<COL><DATA><xsl:value-of select="../TotalResults"/></DATA></COL>
```

...that should do the job. Repeat the import with this new stylesheet, and the total found count should be stored in our gSearchTotal field. (We got about 7500 records the last time we tried this.)

Now, on to the more challenging part. We want to import some user-defined number of these records, instead of just ten. Before proceeding, we should say that we're showing the following technique by way of illustration. Be aware, though, that the reason web service providers "throttle" the amount of data returned is to keep the load on their servers reasonable. To fetch all 7500 records, we would have to run 750 consecutive requests against the server, which is potentially abusive. Use this technique carefully.

In the case of the Amazon XML, the returned record sets are governed by the page parameter that we pass as part of the URL. Somehow we need to submit the same URL repeatedly, varying just the page parameter. FileMaker gives us a good way to do this. If we drive our XML import by a script, we get an additional option that the menu-driven version doesn't give us: We can draw our source URL from a field. This means that we can define a calculation that returns different URLs based on different circumstances. What we want to do is set a global page counter and then set up a calculation that uses the current value of that page counter to generate the right URL. Then we submit that URL multiple times to fetch as many pages as we want.

Let's add a few fields to our Books database. We can add gRecordsToFetch, which is a value that the user can manipulate to decide how many records to bring back. We can define gPagesToFetch, which is just the number of HTTP requests that we need to fetch the specified number of pages. We can also define CalculatedAmazonURL, which dynamically generates the right URL based on which page we currently need to fetch. CalculatedAmazonURL looks like this:

```
"http://xml.amazon.com/onca/xml2?t=webservices-20&dev-t=
  XXXXXXXXXXXX&KeywordSearch=american%20indians&mode=books&type=
  lite&page=" & gCurrentPage & "&f=xml"
```

(So elsewhere, you should substitute in your own developer token.) We also need to add two scripts to make this work. One, which we call Import Amazon Lite Data from Calc, does an XML Import using CalculatedAmazonURL as the URL for the data source. We can add a master script that calculates the total number of necessary page fetches and then runs a loop to fetch each new page in sequence:

```
Fetch Specified Record Count

Show All Records
Delete All Records [ No dialog ]
Set Field [ gPagesToFetch, ( Int( gRecordsToFetch/10 ) ) ]
Set Field [ gCurrentPage, 1 ]
Loop
     Exit Loop If [ gCurrentPage > gPagesToFetch ]
     Perform Script [ "Import Amazon Lite Data From Calc" ]
       [ Sub-scripts ]
     Set Field [ gCurrentPage, 1 + gCurrentPage ]
End Loop
# "To break out of found set from last import"
Show All Records
```

With that, we can display a menu of possible record counts to the user: 10, 20, 50, 100, 500, up to whatever we like. Since we're now fetching the total found count into a global field, we can even add an "All" option. This would require a little extra work in the Fetch script and could lead to some very lengthy processing times for large record counts.

Processing the Author Data

One other unexplored item is the author information. Author data comes with each record, but it's a compound element; one instance of the <Authors> element can contain one or several <Author> elements. How should we handle this? Well, first we should decide how we want to store it in FileMaker. There are three clear choices—store the authors in a repeating field, store them in a single flat text field (perhaps with a comma delimiter), or store them in a separate, related file.

If we want to store them in a repeating field, we're out of luck. FileMaker actually exports all the repetitions of a repeating field as multiple <DATA> instances within a single <COL> element. But when you try to import such a file back into FileMaker, only the first repetition is populated.

Storing the authors in a separate, related file sounds like the most correct thing to do. But since we don't have unique keys for these authors, we're potentially going to get multiple records per individual author (so we're certainly not cutting out any redundancy that way). For now, let's go for the option of turning the authors into a comma-delimited list. Here's what the stylesheet looks like:

```
<?xml version="1.0" encoding="UTF-8"?>
<xsl:stylesheet xmlns:xsl="http://www.w3.org/1999/XSL/Transform"
  version="1.0">
```

```
<xsl:template match="ProductInfo">
     <FMPXMLRESULT xmlns="http://www.filemaker.com/
       fmpxmlresult">
          <ERRORCODE>0</ERRORCODE>
          <PRODUCT BUILD="" NAME="" VERSION=""/>
          <DATABASE DATEFORMAT="M/d/yyyy" LAYOUT="" NAME=""
            RECORDS="10" TIMEFORMAT="h:mm:ss a"/>
          <METADATA>
               <FIELD EMPTYOK="YES" MAXREPEAT="1" NAME=
                 "AmazonURL" TYPE="TEXT" />
               <FIELD EMPTYOK="YES" MAXREPEAT="1" NAME="ASIN"
                 TYPE="TEXT" />
               <FIELD EMPTYOK="YES" MAXREPEAT="1" NAME=
                 "ProductName" TYPE="TEXT" />
               <FIELD EMPTYOK="YES" MAXREPEAT="1" NAME=
                 "Catalog" TYPE="TEXT" />
               <FIELD EMPTYOK="YES" MAXREPEAT="1" NAME=
                 "ReleaseDate" TYPE="TEXT" />
               <FIELD EMPTYOK="YES" MAXREPEAT="1" NAME=
                 "Manufacturer" TYPE="TEXT" />
               <FIELD EMPTYOK="YES" MAXREPEAT="1" NAME=
                 "ImageUrlSmall" TYPE="TEXT" />
               <FIELD EMPTYOK="YES" MAXREPEAT="1" NAME=
                 "ImageUrlMedium" TYPE="TEXT" />
               <FIELD EMPTYOK="YES" MAXREPEAT="1" NAME=
                 "ImageUrlLarge" TYPE="TEXT" />
               <FIELD EMPTYOK="YES" MAXREPEAT="1" NAME=
                 "ListPrice" TYPE="NUMBER" />
               <FIELD EMPTYOK="YES" MAXREPEAT="1" NAME=
                 "AmazonPrice" TYPE="NUMBER" />
               <FIELD EMPTYOK="YES" MAXREPEAT="1" NAME=
                 "UsedPrice" TYPE="NUMBER" />
               <FIELD EMPTYOK="YES" MAXREPEAT="1" NAME=
                 "gSearchTotal" TYPE="NUMBER" />
               <FIELD EMPTYOK="YES" MAXREPEAT="1" NAME=
                 "Author" TYPE="TEXT" />
          </METADATA>
          <RESULTSET>
               <xsl:attribute name="FOUND"><xsl:value-of
                 select="/ProductInfo/TotalResults"/>
                 </xsl:attribute>
               <xsl:for-each select="Details">
                    <ROW >
                         <xsl:attribute name="MODID">0
                           </xsl:attribute>
                         <xsl:attribute name="RECORDID">0
                           </xsl:attribute>
                              <COL><DATA><xsl:value-of select=
                               "@url"/></DATA></COL>
                              <COL><DATA><xsl:value-of select=
                               "Asin"/></DATA></COL>
                              <COL><DATA><xsl:value-of select=
                               "ProductName"/></DATA></COL>
                              <COL><DATA><xsl:value-of select=
```

```
                                "Catalog"/></DATA></COL>
                              <COL><DATA><xsl:value-of select=
                                "ReleaseDate"/></DATA></COL>
                              <COL><DATA><xsl:value-of select=
                                "Manufacturer"/></DATA></COL>
                              <COL><DATA><xsl:value-of select=
                                "ImageUrlSmall"/></DATA></COL>
                              <COL><DATA><xsl:value-of select=
                                "ImageUrlMedium"/></DATA></COL>
                              <COL><DATA><xsl:value-of select=
                                "ImageUrlLarge"/></DATA></COL>
                              <COL><DATA><xsl:value-of select=
                                "ListPrice"/></DATA></COL>
                              <COL><DATA><xsl:value-of select=
                                "OurPrice"/></DATA></COL>
                              <COL><DATA><xsl:value-of select=
                                "UsedPrice"/></DATA></COL>
                              <COL><DATA><xsl:value-of select=
                                "../TotalResults"/></DATA></COL>
                              <COL><DATA>
                                  <xsl:variable name=
                                   "authorCount" select=
                                   "count(Authors/Author)"/>
                                  <xsl:for-each select=
                                   "Authors/Author">
                                      <xsl:value-of select=
                                       "."/>
                                      <xsl:if test=
                                       "position() &lt;
                                       $authorCount">
                                          <xsl:text>,
                                           </xsl:text>
                                      </xsl:if>
                                  </xsl:for-each></DATA>
                              </COL>
                    </ROW>
                </xsl:for-each>
            </RESULTSET>
        </FMPXMLRESULT>
</xsl:template>
</xsl:stylesheet>
```

So we've added a field called Author to the <METADATA> section. Corresponding to that new field in the part of the stylesheet that generates the <ROW> element, we have a more complicated statement than we had for other fields. We first declare a variable called authorCount using <xsl:variable>. The authorCount variable stores the total number of authors for this book. We then use <xsl:for-each> to loop through the authors, and for each one, we output the content of the given <Author> element. We then need to decide whether to output a comma-space pair after the name. We do so only if the current author isn't the last of the bunch. We use the XPath position() function to decide where the current <Author> is in its set and compare that position to the authorCount. If it's less, we output the comma-space (using xsl:text), and if not, we don't. Note that we have to express the less-than operator by writing "<." This is the XML entity for the less-than symbol, and we have to use it because the symbol itself is reserved for starting XML tags.

So now we've devised a way to import differing numbers of records, and we've found out how to bring the author data in as well. Let's move on to some refinements intended to make the whole thing quicker and more usable.

Optimizing the XML Import

So far, we've been using XML Import to browse an online data repository. But as a browsing tool, our little application isn't too efficient. For example, it fetches a lot of data about each book, even if the user never wants to look at that book closely. We can probably speed things up a bit (and lower the penalty for those big record fetches) if we fetch a little bit of information at first and then fetch all the details if and only if the user requests a closer look at a particular book. (We can't actually control how much data Amazon sends us, but we can control how much of it we import.)

Here's our new strategy. Initially we import just the author, title, and list price for each book. We display these in a list view with a button that the user can click to view the detailed information for each book. Each book record has a flag field, initially set to 0, indicating whether we've fetched full details for the record or not. If we haven't fetched them, we fetch the detail for just that one record, take the user to a detail screen, and change the flag field to 1 to indicate that we've fetched the full detail. We update the current record by selecting a match field and using FileMaker's option to update matching records on import.

We need a couple of new fields. One, called FlagGotDetails, is a number field where 0 means that no details have been fetched yet and 1 means they have been. We also need a field to produce a calculated URL that fetches data for just the one record that we're interested in. That URL should look like this:

```
http://xml.amazon.com/onca/xml2?t=webservices-20&dev-t=
  XXXXXXXXX&AsinSearch=0671600419&mode=books&type=lite&page=1&f=xml
```

This URL searches by ASIN (equivalent to the book's ISBN, so it's a unique identifier for the book). Our calculated field inserts the correct ASIN for whatever record we're on. The field definition looks like this:

```
"http://xml.amazon.com/onca/xml2?t=webservices-20&dev-t=
  aasdasdasda&AsinSearch=" & ASIN & "&mode=books&type=
  lite&page=1&f=xml"
```

With these new fields in hand, we also need a couple of new scripts. One script brings in just the information that we need for the list view, while the other fetches details for one record. Here's the list import script:

```
Import Amazon Lite Data For List

Show All Records
Delete All Records [ No dialog ]
Import Records [ XML (from http):
"http://xml.amazon.com/onca/xml2?t=webservices-20&dev-t=
  XXXXXXXXXXXXXXX&KeywordSearch=american%20indians&mode=
  books&type=lite&page=2&f=xml"; XSL (from file):
  "AmazonLiteList.xsl";
  Import Order: ASIN(Text), ProductName(Text), AmazonPrice(Number),
  Authors(Text) ] [ Restore import order, No dialog ]
```

We're taking a few shortcuts in this script. We're automatically deleting all records and starting fresh. We're still hard-coding all the search parameters, such as keyword and page. Consider it a challenge to improve it on your own. For now, let's stick with our simple version.

We import four fields: ASIN, Product Name, Amazon Price, and Authors. We transform the incoming data using a new stylesheet called AmazonLiteList.xsl, which looks like this:

```
<?xml version="1.0" encoding="UTF-8"?>
<xsl:stylesheet xmlns:xsl="http://www.w3.org/1999/XSL/Transform"
  version="1.0">
<xsl:template match="ProductInfo">
     <FMPXMLRESULT xmlns="http://www.filemaker.com/
       fmpxmlresult">
          <ERRORCODE>0</ERRORCODE>
          <PRODUCT BUILD="" NAME="" VERSION=""/>
          <DATABASE DATEFORMAT="M/d/yyyy" LAYOUT="" NAME=""
            RECORDS="10" TIMEFORMAT="h:mm:ss a"/>
          <METADATA>
               <FIELD EMPTYOK="YES" MAXREPEAT="1" NAME="Asin"
                 TYPE="TEXT" />
               <FIELD EMPTYOK="YES" MAXREPEAT="1" NAME=
                 "ProductName" TYPE="TEXT" />
               <FIELD EMPTYOK="YES" MAXREPEAT="1" NAME=
                 "AmazonPrice" TYPE="NUMBER" />
               <FIELD EMPTYOK="YES" MAXREPEAT="1" NAME=
```

```
                "Author" TYPE="TEXT" />
        </METADATA>
        <RESULTSET>
            <xsl:attribute name="FOUND"><xsl:value-of
              select="/ProductInfo/TotalResults"/>
              </xsl:attribute>
            <xsl:for-each select="Details">
                <ROW >
                    <xsl:attribute name="MODID">0
                      </xsl:attribute>
                    <xsl:attribute name="RECORDID">0
                      </xsl:attribute>
                        <COL><DATA><xsl:value-of
                          select="Asin"/></DATA></COL>
                        <COL><DATA><xsl:value-of
                          select="ProductName"/></DATA></COL>
                        <COL><DATA><xsl:value-of
                          select="OurPrice"/></DATA></COL>
                        <COL><DATA>
                            <xsl:variable name=
                              "authorCount" select=
                              "count(Authors/Author)"/>
                            <xsl:for-each select=
                              "Authors/Author">
                                <xsl:value-of select="."/>
                                <xsl:if test=
                                  "position() &lt;
                                  $authorCount">
                                      <xsl:text>,
                                      </xsl:text>
                                </xsl:if>
                            </xsl:for-each></DATA>
                        </COL>
                </ROW>
            </xsl:for-each>
        </RESULTSET>
    </FMPXMLRESULT>
</xsl:template>
</xsl:stylesheet>
```

This pulls just the few fields that we need out of the incoming XML. We then take the user to a List View Layout and let her look at the titles. From there, clicking on any row in the list view triggers a new script:

```
View Detail

If [ FlagGotDetails = 0 ]
     Perform Script [ "Import One" ] [ Sub-scripts ]
End If
Go to Layout [ View Detail ]
Toggle Status Area [ Hide ]
Import One
```

Chapter 9

```
Import Records [ XML (from field): "CalculatedAsinSearchURL"; XSL
  (from file): "Amazonlite2.xsl"; Import Order:
  AmazonURL(Text), ASIN(Text), ProductName(Text), Catalog(Text),
  ReleaseDate(Text), Manufacturer(Text), ImageUrlSmall(Text),
  ImageUrlMedium(Text), ImageUrlLarge(Text), ListPrice(Number),
  AmazonPrice(Number), UsedPrice(Number), gSearchTotal(Number),
  Authors(Text) ]
[ Restore import order, No dialog ]
Set Field [ FlagGotDetails , 1 ]
Show All Records
```

The View Detail script checks the FlagGotDetails field, and if it's 0, it calls the Import One script to fetch the full data set for the given record. The new import command uses the CalculatedASINSearch-URL field and imports using the Update Matching Records option with ASIN set as the match field.

This kind of "lazy fetch" technique is typical of many client-server computing. It's a bit less effective here because Amazon always sends us the same data, but it's still an important technique to be aware of.

So What Can I Do with Web Services?

Now we understand the basics of FileMaker's XML Import. Let's summarize. FileMaker 6 and above can import data from an XML data source. That data source can be a file, or a resource accessible over a network via HTTP. The URL for the network resource can either come from a hard-coded value or a FileMaker field. When we import, FileMaker fetches the source XML, either by reading a file that we specified or by issuing an HTTP GET request for the URL that we specified (we see later on why it's important that FileMaker accesses URLs via the GET method only).

Once FileMaker has the XML in hand (so to speak), it can then transform it using an XSL stylesheet that we specify. This step is necessary only if the source XML is not already in the FMPXML grammar. If it is, we can import it directly, but if not, the import would fail, and we'd need to transform it to FMPXML with a stylesheet. We can specify the stylesheet by pointing to a particular file. We can also (and this is something that we haven't discussed so far) access the stylesheet via HTTP, either through a hard-coded URL or one taken from a field. (The field-based options for XML data source and XSL stylesheet are only available when you are scripting the import.) If you are writing a solution for many users, you do not need to have copies of all of your stylesheets that are local to each user's machine or accessible via some common network volume; you can simply put them up on a web server, in your building or in Patagonia, and access them that way.

We understand how XML Import works, but what good is it? We've all been exposed to techno-hype, and we've heard all the fancy speeches that begin with "Well, you could...." You could pull stock quotes (still everyone's favorite example, for some reason) from Yahoo and display them in your accounting system. You could pull weather data from a satellite for your travel agency system. But I'm tired of hearing about what I *could* do. I want to know what I *can* do. That boils down to one of two things: You can consume someone else's web service or you can write your own.

Finding Web Services

By now there are many web services out there that do everything from the aforementioned stock quoting and mortgage calculation to more esoteric applications. There are several things that we, as FileMaker developers, need to know about these:

- They're not always easy to find (or maybe they're *too* easy).
- They tend to cost money.
- FileMaker can't necessarily use all of them.

To the first point, there is not necessarily any central repository of information about web services. There are a number of web sites that index and catalog web services (see http://www.xmethods.com for an example or search for "Web Services Directory" on your favorite Internet search engine).

To the second point, web services are just that; they're services, usually distributing some kind of information—information that somebody owns. Most places (Amazon is an exception) don't open their databases to outside queries for free. Once you find one you want to use, you may have to purchase an access code or enter into some kind of subscription agreement in order to use it. Fortunately, FileMaker has entered into an arrangement with ServiceObjects, a provider of web services, whereby FileMaker users can experiment with ServiceObjects' web services. See http://www.filemaker.com/xml for details and http://www.serviceobjects.com/products/default.asp for an overview of ServiceObjects' offerings. But in general, expect many web services to cost something.

To the third point, FileMaker is currently limited to fetching XML from a web service via an HTTP GET operation. But many, if not most, of today's web services use more complex models, such as

XML-RPC and SOAP. We look more at these later on, but one key point about these models is that they expect their requests as an HTTP POST, which FileMaker cannot deliver yet.

None of this is intended to be discouraging. There are plenty of good web services available directly to FileMaker (some at no charge, some with a fee). Hit the Internet and take a look at what's out there. Just be aware that when you see web services that require XML-RPC or SOAP, you won't be able to use those directly. In the section that follows we show you how to create a middleware layer that lets you access these web services as well.

Writing Your Own

Write my own web service? What does that mean? Why would I want to do it? Well, here's where web services get interesting. Web services use standard languages and protocols: XML, HTTP, TCP/IP. With the right programming, they can be used to link together many different computing environments doing many different things. FileMaker, for example, can provide web services (by spitting XML out of the Web Companion) or consume them (as we've just seen). To the environments on the other end of these transactions, no one knows whether it's talking to FileMaker, SAP, Oracle, or a very powerful new toaster. Likewise, when it consumes a web service, FileMaker doesn't need to know what's on the other end. All that matters is the information. Very powerful applications are possible with this kind of abstraction. But let's start small.

Writing a Time Server

Have you, as a FileMaker developer, ever been bedeviled by the difference between server time and client time? Let's say that you timestamp your records with the date and time of their creation, and your users often need this data for auditing or reconciliation of some kind. But every time a user's local date and time settings get out of whack, the creation times in the system are wrong. Sasha's Mac battery died and all of her charts from last week show a creation date of 1954. Worse, even when all the desktops are kept clean and in sync, if your application spans time zones, you have an even less tractable problem. Since FileMaker reckons time based on the individual client desktop, not on the server, it's very easy to get bad timestamp data.

What we need is a way to have a central timekeeping server that keeps time on a unified clock. When we create a new record, we first fetch the date and time from that server and use them to timestamp the new record. Well, suppose there were a timekeeping web service. All it needs to do is hand back a date and a time in XML format. We'd use a stylesheet to transform it into the mandatory FMPXML grammar and pull the data into a couple of global fields before creating the new record.

That all sounds good, but how do we write this time server? Any middleware language that can send XML over HTTP will do. For our purposes, we show how to do this in PHP. Our strategy is to write a PHP page that returns the current date and time, according to the PHP server, in some XML format. Here's how that page will look:

```
TimeService.php:

<?
/*
 * This page returns current server date and time in a generic XML
   format
 */

header ("Content-type: text/xml"); // signal that we're sending XML
echo '<?xml version="1.0"?>';
$serverTime = time(); // get and hold current server time
 ?>

<TimeService>
     <ServerDate><? echo date( "m/d/Y", $serverTime);
       ?></ServerDate>
     <ServerTime><? echo date( "H:i:s", $serverTime);
       ?></ServerTime>
</TimeService>
```

We begin by using PHP's header function to send an HTTP header that declares we're sending XML. This is not mandatory for import into FileMaker, but it does help in other areas. For example, this lets Internet Explorer display the page as XML rather than HTML, which helps us in troubleshooting.

We then send the opening XML declaration and grab the current time. Down below, we're outputting straight XML except inside the ServerDate and ServerTime elements. There we use PHP to format the current server time, first as month/day/four-digit year and then as military hours:minutes:seconds.

Here's how the output would look:

```
<?xml version="1.0"?>
<TimeService>
     <ServerDate>01/05/2003</ServerDate>
     <ServerTime>12:06:15</ServerTime>
</TimeService>
```

We can now import this into FileMaker, transforming it on the way. Wait a minute, you say. Couldn't we just have the TimeService.php page produce its output in the FMPXML form? Then we wouldn't have to write a stylesheet to transform it. Let's save some work!

Well, yes, we could do that. But it would fly in the face of one of the most important principles of computing—the principle of sufficient abstraction. The point about web services is that anyone can use them. Maybe our TimeService page will be hit by FileMaker. But maybe later some Access users will need it too. The XML service should be platform- and tool-agnostic, so it should not be tailored to FileMaker. It wouldn't actually hurt anything to do that, of course. Others could just write stylesheets to transform the FMPXML into whatever form they needed. The data would still be intact. All the same, we're going to use the two-step method because it's the right thing to do.

This means that we need a stylesheet to transform this generic TimeService XML into FMPXML. Here's how it looks.

```
TimeService.xsl:
<?xml version="1.0" encoding="UTF-8"?>
<xsl:stylesheet xmlns:xsl="http://www.w3.org/1999/XSL/Transform"
  version="1.0">
<xsl:template match="TimeService">
          <FMPXMLRESULT xmlns="http://www.filemaker.com/
            fmpxmlresult">
               <ERRORCODE>0</ERRORCODE>
               <PRODUCT BUILD="" NAME="" VERSION=""/>
               <DATABASE DATEFORMAT="M/d/yyyy" LAYOUT="" NAME=""
                 RECORDS="1" TIMEFORMAT="h:mm:ss a"/>
               <METADATA>
                    <FIELD EMPTYOK="YES" MAXREPEAT="1" NAME=
                      "gServerDate" TYPE="DATE" />
                    <FIELD EMPTYOK="YES" MAXREPEAT="1" NAME=
                      "gServerTime" TYPE="TIME" />
                    <FIELD EMPTYOK="YES" MAXREPEAT="1" NAME=
                      "Constant" TYPE="NUMBER" />
               </METADATA>
               <RESULTSET>
                    <xsl:attribute name="FOUND">1</xsl:attribute>
                    <ROW >
                         <xsl:attribute name="MODID">0
                           </xsl:attribute>
                         <xsl:attribute name="RECORDID">0
                           </xsl:attribute>
                         <COL><DATA><xsl:value-of select=
                           "ServerDate"/></DATA></COL>
                         <COL><DATA><xsl:value-of select=
                           "ServerTime"/></DATA></COL>
                         <COL><DATA>1</DATA></COL>
                    </ROW>
```

```
                </RESULTSET>
            </FMPXMLRESULT>
        </xsl:template>
</xsl:stylesheet>
```

We want to import the ServerDate and ServerTime content into two FileMaker global fields called gServerDate and gServerTime. That's pretty much all the above stylesheet does. The only oddity is the addition of a field called Constant. On the FileMaker side, we've defined a typical constant field as a calculation with a value of 1. In the stylesheet, we include this field in the metadata and also supply it a constant value of 1.

The reason for doing this is that, left to itself, the XML import behaves like any other import and creates new records. We don't want that—we just want it to populate two globals. So, rather than have it create new records, we have it "update matching records." We're populating globals, so it doesn't matter which record it updates. We use the constant field as a match field when we define the import. That way, the globals get populated but no new records get created. (Actually, since our goal is to create a new record with a server-based timestamp, we could probably allow the import to create a new record and save some work. But in other cases, we might truly want to just fetch globals, so it's good to practice this technique here.)

With this stylesheet in hand, the rest is easy. We define a script to perform the import, matching the server date and time up to the correct globals, choosing the option Update Matching Records, and using the Constant field for the match. We add two fields to the database called CreationDate and CreationTime. We make these auto-enter fields; CreationDate auto-enters gServerDate, and CreationTime auto-enters gServerTime.

Finally, we write a New Record script. It calls the time-import script to set the globals with the current server date and time and creates a new record where the auto-entry options fire and bring in the creation date and time from the globals. (Note that this will only work in environments where record creation is scripted.)

There you have it. To make this work well, you would put the TimeService.xsl stylesheet up on a web server somewhere as well and end up with a transparent central time server that would guarantee consistent creation times across all records. For a production environment, you'd need some error checking. You'd want to set Error Capture on in the XML import script and test for errors after the import. If an error was found, you could either try again up to some maximum number of attempts or fall back right away to local desktop time, possibly marking a flag field to indicate client vs. server time. As with most production code, the error checking could easily be more work than the core logic itself.

Other Kinds of Web Services

Web services are just one manifestation of a widespread trend toward *distributed computing*. The idea behind distributed computing is that it can be very beneficial to decouple certain kinds of functionality from one another. Let's say that you're working on a system that needs to do calculations of mortgage loans. The functionality for amortizing a loan is very well understood, and thousands of systems can do it. But if you're building software from scratch, you may need to reimplement this functionality yourself. Or, if you're working in a development environment, such as FileMaker, you'll be constrained by whether that environment offers the needed functionality or not.

In a distributed computing environment, we're going to try to abstract that functionality out and have it live someplace on its own, not embedded in any application. Applications that need that functionality can send a request to the mortgage service and get back the data that they need. They don't need to embed this functionality inside themselves; they just need to know where to find it and how to use it. Ideally, these services don't need to be any particular place—just accessible over a network somehow.

There are many flavors of distributed computing already in play. If you've run across acronyms such as CORBA, DCOM, Java-RMI, Sun-RPC, and the like, these all refer to different distributed computing technologies. Web services are yet another form of distributed computing, one that runs over HTTP and uses XML as its data format. With web services, as with any other kind of distributed computing, we can, in effect, "outsource" certain tasks in the event that our own software or environment doesn't or can't perform those tasks.

Let's return to PHP. PHP offers many capabilities that can't be found inside of FileMaker. One way to unlock that functionality for use with FileMaker is to write a PHP-based web service that lets FileMaker exchange data with PHP. Let's say that we want to do some sort of password encryption inside of FileMaker of the kind that Unix systems do. In this scenario, we never store a user's password inside the system. Instead, we store what's called a *hash equivalent* (or just *hash*) of the password, which we get by running a particular hash function on the password. This isn't really encryption—the password can never be recovered from the hashed value. But it can be used for comparison, since the same password should always hash to the same value.

FileMaker doesn't have a built-in hashing algorithm. But PHP does! Why not write a small web service to hash up FileMaker passwords? That way, we can patch the security hole inherent in storing the user's actual password in a database. (Note that this would only apply to a custom security system that you would write yourself; it has nothing to do with FileMaker's built-in password security, nor do we mean to imply that the built-in FileMaker security has a vulnerability in this regard.)

This service is different from the last one, since we need to pass some data in from FileMaker and let PHP act on it. What we'd like to do is send a URL that looks something like this:

```
http://my.host.com/pw_hash.php?input=shangri_la
```

...and then get back some XML that looks like this:

```
<xml version="1.0">
<PWHash>
     <Input>shangri_la</Input>
     <Output>aaf271f04dbe72c4412f3b23d9fee21e</Output>
</PWHash>
```

Here we are sending a password, "shangri_la," to the server for hashing and getting back XML with the original password (for confirmation) plus the hashed output, "aaf271f04dbe72c4412f3b23d9fee21e." We can now apply a stylesheet, as usual, and bring it back into FileMaker.

This looks a lot like our last example. Let's look at the PHP code for the web service first:

```
<?
/* pw_hash.php
 * This page accepts a text string and returns the MD5 hash in XML
   format
 * The incoming text string must be called input in the HTTP request
 */

header ("Content-type: text/xml"); // signal that we're sending XML
echo '<?xml version="1.0"?>';
$output = md5( $input ); // get the hash of the input
 ?>

<PWHash>
     <Input><? echo $input;  ?></Input>
     <Output><? echo $output;  ?></Output>
</PWHash>
```

This page simply calls PHP's md5 function on the input and sends the result back. (MD5 happens to be the name of the hashing algorithm that PHP is using.)

When we hit that page with the URL http://my.host.com/PWHash.php?input=hasdrubal, here's what we get back in XML:

```
<?xml version="1.0"?>
<PWHash>
     <Input>hasdrubal</Input>
     <Output>feda91b2282169b09977a6717368edb4</Output>
</PWHash>
```

We then need a stylesheet to bring that back into FMPXML and into FileMaker:

```
PWHash.xsl:
<?xml version="1.0" encoding="UTF-8"?>
<xsl:stylesheet xmlns:xsl="http://www.w3.org/1999/XSL/Transform"
  version="1.0">
<xsl:template match="PWHash">
          <FMPXMLRESULT xmlns="http://www.filemaker.com/
            fmpxmlresult">
               <ERRORCODE>0</ERRORCODE>
               <PRODUCT BUILD="" NAME="" VERSION=""/>
               <DATABASE DATEFORMAT="M/d/yyyy" LAYOUT="" NAME=""
                 RECORDS="1" TIMEFORMAT="h:mm:ss a"/>
               <METADATA>
                    <FIELD EMPTYOK="YES" MAXREPEAT="1" NAME=
                      "Password" TYPE="TEXT" />
                    <FIELD EMPTYOK="YES" MAXREPEAT="1" NAME=
                      "HashMD5" TYPE="TEXT" />
               </METADATA>
               <RESULTSET>
                    <xsl:attribute name="FOUND">1</xsl:attribute>
                    <ROW >
                         <xsl:attribute name="MODID">0
                           </xsl:attribute>
                         <xsl:attribute name="RECORDID">0
                           </xsl:attribute>
                         <COL><DATA><xsl:value-of select=
                           "Input"/></DATA></COL>
                         <COL><DATA><xsl:value-of select=
                           "Output"/></DATA></COL>
                    </ROW>
               </RESULTSET>
          </FMPXMLRESULT>
     </xsl:template>
</xsl:stylesheet>
```

In our FileMaker database, we have fields called Password and HashMD5. We also have a calculated field called HashRequestURL, which looks like this:

```
"http://agamemnon.fmpro.com/slane/WebServices/PWHash.php?input="
  & Password
```

So it builds a URL and passes the current record's Password field along in the HTTP "input" parameter. PWHash.php expects to receive a parameter called input, and that's what it processes to return the hash.

From here, we need to only write a simple script that fetches XML from the URL specified by HashRequestURL (so we use the option to fetch the URL from a field). We apply the PWHash.xsl stylesheet to it, and when importing, we update matching records with Password as the match field. (This is actually an inferior technique because it assumes that the password is unique. It would be better to have FileMaker generate a serial number for each record. We could then send that along with the password and have the PHP page ship it straight back to us. We could then use that unique key as the match field.)

You can now use these hashes for password validation. Every time a user sets or updates her password, we can fetch the hashed value from the web service and store it in her record. Her security can never be breached; the system doesn't store her password, only the hash, and the hash cannot easily be used to reconstruct the password. Whenever the user logs in, you would fetch the hash of whatever password she typed and compare it to the stored hash value of her password. You'd need to extend our example a bit to make all these things happen, but the work is straightforward.

FileMaker and SOAP

FileMaker and what? Apparently, we've veered into the topic of cleaning liquids. Well no, not quite. We are not talking about soap, but SOAP, yet another acronym, which stands for Simple Object Access Protocol. Reams of ink have been spilled on this topic, as with most of our other buzzwords. We'll try to boil it down for you. SOAP is one of a number of technologies that are being touted as ways to send messages between computers using standard protocols, such as TCP/IP and XML. Think of SOAP as a standard for defining how web services look and act using XML. It's a standard that provides some additional structure to messages that pass between computers, written in some form of XML. Although the SOAP standard doesn't mandate that SOAP messages pass over HTTP, this is a common transport mechanism.

SOAP messages are XML messages with a standard structure. If it helps to think of them as documents rather than messages, that's fine. What we mean by "message" is that what's important about these chunks of XML is not that they're stored on a disk as files but that they're sent and received as part of a communication between computers. They could be stored as files, but it's more likely that they're composed dynamically, passed back and forth, and never saved.

Here's a sample SOAP message:

```
<soap:Envelope xmlns:soap="http://schemas.xmlsoap.org/soap/envelope"
  soap:encodingStyle="http://schemas.xmlsoap.org/soap/encoding/">
     <soap:Header>
          <fm:version xmlns:fm="http://www.fmpro.com/xml/
            Header">6.0v2</fm:version>
     </soap:Header>
     <soap:Body>
          <pw:GetPasswordHash xmlns:pw="http://www.fmpro.com/xml/
            password_hash">
               <pw:clearText xmlns:pw="http://www.fmpro.com/xml/
                 password_hash">myUnhashedPassword</pw:clearText>
          </pw:GetPasswordHash>
     </soap:Body>
</soap:Envelope>
```

The first thing that we notice about this message is that it's XML. The root element is something called an Envelope, and inside the Envelope are a Header and Body. All of these elements are in the soap: namespace; SOAP makes heavy use of XML namespaces. (Namespaces, remember, are an additional level of specification you can use in an XML document to prevent conflicting element names. If we just called something Envelope, there could be other Envelope definitions out there, but when we put in the soap namespace and call it soap:Envelope, the chances of conflict go way down.)

The Header has one element in the fm namespace called fm:version. The Body seems to encapsulate something like a function call. There's an element called GetPasswordHash, and then inside it is an element called clearText. In fact, that's exactly what this SOAP message does—it sends a function call to a remote server, calling a function named GetPasswordHash and passing it a parameter named clearText that contains the password to be hashed.

That's fine, but where's the link with FileMaker? Many web services these days are based on SOAP. Rather than a straight HTTP GET request like the ones FileMaker sends to perform XML Import, they expect to receive a formatted XML message that follows the SOAP protocol. Once they receive it, they send back a SOAP-formatted message in response. The SOAP return message is XML, so in theory FileMaker could import it the way we've already done in this chapter. The catch here is that although FileMaker could handle a SOAP message if it got one back, it doesn't have the means to send the SOAP request in the first place. Why? There are many reasons, but the simplest is that FileMaker sends its XML Import requests via the HTTP GET method, and SOAP requests are sent inside an HTTP POST request, which FileMaker can't send at the moment.

So what do we do? Give up on the large and growing number of web services that are written as SOAP services? Wait for FileMaker to add SOAP capabilities? None of the above. Like many such integration problems, this one can be solved by writing something in middleware. Assuming that we're using PHP, we need to write a PHP web service that can take an XML Import request from FileMaker, turn it into a full-blown SOAP request, hand off the SOAP request to a remote server, and get the SOAP return message back. Then, depending on the circumstances, it can either send its own XML message back to FileMaker or just hand the SOAP message off as is and let FileMaker work with that. We've already written a couple of small web services for FileMaker in PHP. This one is a little bigger, but the theory is the same.

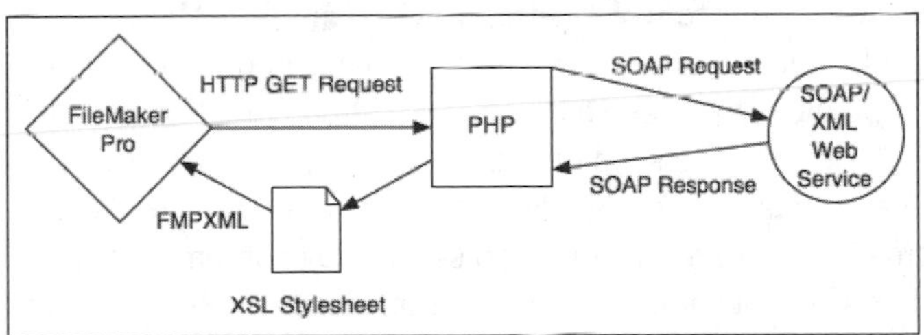

Figure 9.3

So, suppose that we've found a web service that we really want to use with FileMaker, but it's only available over SOAP. Let's say that we want to consume some web services from Google, the massive Internet search engine. Like Amazon, Google exposes its search capabilities as a web service. Unlike Amazon, it doesn't make them available via HTTP GET—only over SOAP.

Google suggests that you download their developer's kit and requires that you register for a key code, just as Amazon did. The developer kit download can be found at http://www.google.com/apis/, along with instructions for signing up to receive a token. If you want to follow along and build these or similar examples, we suggest that you grab the developer's kit and sign up for a token before proceeding. At the time of publication, there was no fee for signing up.

We actually need several pieces of software in order to make this work. No surprise there; we need to write or tap into a piece of middleware with fairly significant features. To make our job easier (*much* easier), we can download and install a PHP library that helps us work with SOAP web services. The one we use is called NuSOAP, available at http://dietrich.ganx4.com/nusoap/.

NuSOAP is a pure PHP library. This means that rather than being a core part of PHP, it is a set of source code files written in the PHP language, just like FX/PHP. To use it, we need to do more or less what we did with FX: Download the files, unpack them, and install them where PHP can see and use them. You can download the latest version of NuSOAP by following the links at http://dietrich.ganx4.com/. Once you unpack it, you should have a single (large) file called nusoap.php. Put it somewhere in your PHP include path, or if you haven't quite got your head around the concept of include paths yet, put it in the directory where you'll be building your SOAP services for FileMaker.

There's a lot to know about SOAP, and it would be hard, or rather impossible, for us to cover this complex topic in the context of this book. But we can give you a brief overview of the concepts that you need to know in order to work with NuSOAP and FileMaker.

If you take a look at the developer kit that you downloaded from Google (if you did), you'll see a document called GoogleSearch.wsdl. We show it below for the sake of convenience. The .wsdl at the end of the filename stands for Web Services Definition Language. Documents in this format (and others) attempt to solve the problem of how to specify what kinds of commands and parameters a web service can respond to. In the earlier example with Amazon's XML, we had to read the Amazon documentation in order to find out how to format and populate a URL that would get us back some XML from Amazon. That's fine for us, but it's not very easy for a computer. WSDL and similar protocols are intended to be machine-readable descriptions of what a web service can do. If you've ever programmed in a language that uses header files, you are familiar with this concept. Header files tell the computer, for example, the name of all the individual functions in a code library. With the header file, it's easy to know what the library can do. Without it, you have to guess or read code examples.

WSDL and similar technologies try to solve this problem. A WSDL document describes a web service. Let's look at Google's:

```
<?xml version="1.0"?>

<!-- WSDL description of the Google Web APIs.
     The Google Web APIs are in beta release. All interfaces are
     subject to change as we refine and extend our APIs. Please see
     the terms of use for more information. -->

<!-- Revision 2002-08-16 -->

<definitions name="GoogleSearch"
             targetNamespace="urn:GoogleSearch"
             xmlns:typens="urn:GoogleSearch"
             xmlns:xsd="http://www.w3.org/2001/XMLSchema"
             xmlns:soap="http://schemas.xmlsoap.org/wsdl/soap/"
             xmlns:soapenc="http://schemas.xmlsoap.org/soap/
               encoding/"
             xmlns:wsdl="http://schemas.xmlsoap.org/wsdl/"
             xmlns="http://schemas.xmlsoap.org/wsdl/">

  <!-- Types for search - result elements, directory categories -->

  <types>
    <xsd:schema xmlns="http://www.w3.org/2001/XMLSchema"
                targetNamespace="urn:GoogleSearch">

      <xsd:complexType name="GoogleSearchResult">
        <xsd:all>
          <xsd:element name="documentFiltering" type="xsd:boolean"/>
          <xsd:element name="searchComments"    type="xsd:string"/>
          <xsd:element name="estimatedTotalResultsCount"
                                                type="xsd:int"/>
          <xsd:element name="estimateIsExact"   type="xsd:boolean"/>
          <xsd:element name="resultElements"    type="typens:
                                                ResultElementArray"/>
          <xsd:element name="searchQuery"       type="xsd:string"/>
          <xsd:element name="startIndex"        type="xsd:int"/>
          <xsd:element name="endIndex"          type="xsd:int"/>
          <xsd:element name="searchTips"        type="xsd:string"/>
          <xsd:element name="directoryCategories"  type="typens:
                                            DirectoryCategoryArray"/>
          <xsd:element name="searchTime"        type="xsd:double"/>
        </xsd:all>
      </xsd:complexType>

      <xsd:complexType name="ResultElement">
        <xsd:all>
          <xsd:element name="summary" type="xsd:string"/>
          <xsd:element name="URL" type="xsd:string"/>
          <xsd:element name="snippet" type="xsd:string"/>
          <xsd:element name="title" type="xsd:string"/>
```

Chapter 9

```
        <xsd:element name="cachedSize" type="xsd:string"/>
        <xsd:element name="relatedInformationPresent"
          type="xsd:boolean"/>
        <xsd:element name="hostName" type="xsd:string"/>
        <xsd:element name="directoryCategory" type=
          "typens:DirectoryCategory"/>
        <xsd:element name="directoryTitle" type="xsd:string"/>
      </xsd:all>
    </xsd:complexType>

    <xsd:complexType name="ResultElementArray">
      <xsd:complexContent>
        <xsd:restriction base="soapenc:Array">
           <xsd:attribute ref="soapenc:arrayType" wsdl:arrayType=
             "typens:ResultElement[]"/>
        </xsd:restriction>
      </xsd:complexContent>
    </xsd:complexType>

    <xsd:complexType name="DirectoryCategoryArray">
      <xsd:complexContent>
        <xsd:restriction base="soapenc:Array">
           <xsd:attribute ref="soapenc:arrayType" wsdl:arrayType=
             "typens:DirectoryCategory[]"/>
        </xsd:restriction>
      </xsd:complexContent>
    </xsd:complexType>

    <xsd:complexType name="DirectoryCategory">
      <xsd:all>
        <xsd:element name="fullViewableName" type="xsd:string"/>
        <xsd:element name="specialEncoding" type="xsd:string"/>
      </xsd:all>
    </xsd:complexType>

  </xsd:schema>
</types>

<!-- Messages for Google Web APIs - cached page, search,
  spelling. -->

<message name="doGetCachedPage">
  <part name="key"             type="xsd:string"/>
  <part name="url"             type="xsd:string"/>
</message>

<message name="doGetCachedPageResponse">
  <part name="return"          type="xsd:base64Binary"/>
</message>

<message name="doSpellingSuggestion">
  <part name="key"             type="xsd:string"/>
  <part name="phrase"          type="xsd:string"/>
```

```
</message>

<message name="doSpellingSuggestionResponse">
  <part name="return"          type="xsd:string"/>
</message>

<!--note, ie and oe are ignored by server; all traffic is UTF-8.-->

<message name="doGoogleSearch">
  <part name="key"             type="xsd:string"/>
  <part name="q"               type="xsd:string"/>
  <part name="start"           type="xsd:int"/>
  <part name="maxResults"      type="xsd:int"/>
  <part name="filter"          type="xsd:boolean"/>
  <part name="restrict"        type="xsd:string"/>
  <part name="safeSearch"      type="xsd:boolean"/>
  <part name="lr"              type="xsd:string"/>
  <part name="ie"              type="xsd:string"/>
  <part name="oe"              type="xsd:string"/>
</message>

<message name="doGoogleSearchResponse">
  <part name="return"          type="typens:GoogleSearchResult"/>
</message>

<!--Port for Google Web APIs, "GoogleSearch"-->

<portType name="GoogleSearchPort">

  <operation name="doGetCachedPage">
    <input message="typens:doGetCachedPage"/>
    <output message="typens:doGetCachedPageResponse"/>
  </operation>

  <operation name="doSpellingSuggestion">
    <input message="typens:doSpellingSuggestion"/>
    <output message="typens:doSpellingSuggestionResponse"/>
  </operation>

  <operation name="doGoogleSearch">
    <input message="typens:doGoogleSearch"/>
    <output message="typens:doGoogleSearchResponse"/>
  </operation>

</portType>


<!--Binding for Google Web APIs - RPC, SOAP over HTTP-->

<binding name="GoogleSearchBinding" type="typens:GoogleSearchPort">
  <soap:binding style="rpc"
              transport="http://schemas.xmlsoap.org/soap/http"/>
```

```
  <operation name="doGetCachedPage">
    <soap:operation soapAction="urn:GoogleSearchAction"/>
    <input>
      <soap:body use="encoded"
                 namespace="urn:GoogleSearch"
                 encodingStyle="http://schemas.xmlsoap.org/soap/
                   encoding/"/>
    </input>
    <output>
      <soap:body use="encoded"
                 namespace="urn:GoogleSearch"
                 encodingStyle="http://schemas.xmlsoap.org/soap/
                   encoding/"/>
    </output>
  </operation>

  <operation name="doSpellingSuggestion">
    <soap:operation soapAction="urn:GoogleSearchAction"/>
    <input>
      <soap:body use="encoded"
                 namespace="urn:GoogleSearch"
                 encodingStyle="http://schemas.xmlsoap.org/soap/
                   encoding/"/>
    </input>
    <output>
      <soap:body use="encoded"
                 namespace="urn:GoogleSearch"
                 encodingStyle="http://schemas.xmlsoap.org/soap/
                   encoding/"/>
    </output>
  </operation>

  <operation name="doGoogleSearch">
    <soap:operation soapAction="urn:GoogleSearchAction"/>
    <input>
      <soap:body use="encoded"
                 namespace="urn:GoogleSearch"
                 encodingStyle="http://schemas.xmlsoap.org/soap/
                   encoding/"/>
    </input>
    <output>
      <soap:body use="encoded"
                 namespace="urn:GoogleSearch"
                 encodingStyle="http://schemas.xmlsoap.org/soap/
                   encoding/"/>
    </output>
  </operation>
</binding>

<!--Endpoint for Google Web APIs-->
<service name="GoogleSearchService">
  <port name="GoogleSearchPort" binding="typens:
    GoogleSearchBinding">
    <soap:address location="http://api.google.com/search/beta2"/>
```

```
    </port>
  </service>

</definitions>
```

That's quite a headful, but we don't need to understand it all. We're not going to write WSDL files, since you only need to do this if you're providing a web service. From here on, we're not even going to read them. The NuSOAP library can do some pretty neat things if it has access to the WSDL definitions for a web service, things that make our life very easy. So glance over the above, before forgetting it and moving on.

The WSDL file has many elements, but the most interesting to us consist of message definitions. Think of a message like a function call: It has a name, and it takes parameters. The WSDL file tells us what these are. For example:


```
<message name="doGoogleSearch">
    <part name="key"            type="xsd:string"/>
    <part name="q"              type="xsd:string"/>
    <part name="start"          type="xsd:int"/>
    <part name="maxResults"     type="xsd:int"/>
    <part name="filter"         type="xsd:boolean"/>
    <part name="restrict"       type="xsd:string"/>
    <part name="safeSearch"     type="xsd:boolean"/>
    <part name="lr"             type="xsd:string"/>
    <part name="ie"             type="xsd:string"/>
    <part name="oe"             type="xsd:string"/>
  </message>
```

Here's the definition for a message/function, one we're actually going to call in a bit. It's called doGoogleSearch and has no fewer than ten parameters. This definition tells us the message name and the names and data types of each parameter. The type information is important to any intermediate library, like NuSOAP, that needs to translate a stream of XML into native data types in some language (in this case, PHP).

So the WSDL file, among other things, defines the format and input types of all the messages the service listens to. Also, in the <service> element, it points to a URL. This URL is the address of the actual web service and tells us where to send the request.

That's about all we need to know about WSDL. The point to make for our purposes is that these files can make it very easy to work with web services via NuSOAP. Let's leave FileMaker out of the picture for the moment and look at a PHP page that uses NuSOAP to make a Google query via SOAP. We show you the entire code here first and then walk through it:

```
<?

require_once( 'nusoap.php' );

// make a new SOAP client using the Google WSDL file ...
$s = new soapclient('http://api.google.com/GoogleSearch.wsdl',
  'wsdl');
// and create a proxy class that we can call directly
$p = $s->getProxy();

// set up the parameters for a call to Google's doGoogleSearch method

$key = 'qw2rrPVQFHLsLQQ3IeUPnRm5mWSayn4o';
$query = 'Native American Languages';
$start = 0;
$maxResults = 10;
$filter = '';
$restrict = '';
$safeSearch= '';
$lr = 'lang-en';
$ie = '';
$oe = '';

// call the function on our proxy with the specified values
$result = $p->doGoogleSearch( $key,
                              $query,
                              $start,
                              $maxResults,
                              $filter,
                              $restrict,
                              $safeSearch,
                              $lr,
                              $ie,
                              $oe );

// now that we have the result, the following code is devoted to
   outputting some XML

header ("Content-type: text/xml"); // signal that we're sending XML
echo '<?xml version="1.0"?>';
?>

<GoogleResults>
    <documentFiltering><? echo $result['documentFiltering'];
      ?></documentFiltering>
    <estimatedTotalResultsCount><? echo
      $result['estimatedTotalResultsCount'];
      ?></estimatedTotalResultsCount>
    <directoryCategories><? echo $result['directoryCategories'];
      ?></directoryCategories>
    <searchTime><? echo $result['searchTime']; ?></searchTime>
    <resultElements>
    <?
        $elements = $result['resultElements'];
```

```
        for ( $i = 0; $i < $maxResults; $i++) {
            $currentResult = $elements[$i]; ?>
        <resultElement>
            <cachedSize><? echo $currentResult['cachedSize'];
              ?></cachedSize>
            <hostName><? echo $currentResult['hostName'];
              ?></hostName>
            <snippet><? echo htmlspecialchars
              ($currentResult['snippet']); ?></snippet>
            <directoryCategory>
                <specialEncoding><? echo $currentResult
                  ['directoryCategory']['specialEncoding'];
                  ?></specialEncoding>
                <fullViewableName><? echo $currentResult
                  ['directoryCategory']['fullViewableName'];
                  ?></fullViewableName>
            </directoryCategory>
            <relatedInformationPresent><? echo $currentResult
              ['relatedInformationPresent'];
              ?></relatedInformationPresent>
            <directoryTitle><? echo $currentResult
              ['directoryTitle']; ?></directoryTitle>
            <summary><? echo $currentResult['summary'];
              ?></summary>
            <URL><? echo $currentResult['URL']; ?></URL>
            <title><? echo $currentResult['title']; ?></title>
        </resultElement>
    <?    }
    ?>
    </resultElements>
</GoogleResults>
```

This code is even simpler than it looks since about half of it is devoted to outputting the XML that we're eventually sending back to FileMaker. Though the SOAP message does come back in an XML format, the NuSOAP library transparently converts the returned data into PHP native data types, such as arrays. Thus, somewhat inconveniently, we need to recompose the data into XML so that FileMaker can import it.

In any case, we start off by importing the NuSOAP library:

```
require_once( 'nusoap.php' );
```

We then make a new instance of the soapclient class. In doing this, we're going to hand it the web address of the Google WSDL file and specify that this is a WSDL file, not an actual web service. (The WSDL file, remember, contains the URL of the actual web service.)

```
// make a new SOAP client using the Google WSDL file ...
$s = new soapclient('http://api.google.com/GoogleSearch.wsdl',
  'wsdl');
```

Now we have a soap client object called $s. It's kind of hard to do justice to the neatness and convenience of what happens next.

```
// and create a proxy class that we can call directly
$p = $s->getProxy();
```

We call the client's getProxy() method, which returns an object that has all of the Google web service functions as methods. The WSDL file tells us that Google supports messages such as doGoogleSearch() and doSpellingSuggestion(). Well, our new proxy object, $p, actually supports the very same function calls. Since it was built with Google's WSDL file, it transparently converts calls on itself to calls on the Google web service. It listens for the response, receives it, parses it into PHP data types, and hands the result back to us. Once we've built the proxy object, we don't need to worry about Google at all. The proxy handles all the communications.

Once we've got our proxy, we can now set up and call our search function:

```
$key = 'qw2rrPVQFHLsLQQ3IeUPnRm5mWSayn4o';
$query = 'Native American Languages';
$start = 0;
$maxResults = 10;
$filter = '';
$restrict = '';
$safeSearch= '';
$lr = 'lang-en';
$ie = '';
$oe = '';

// call the function on our proxy with the specified values
$result = $p->doGoogleSearch( $key,
                              $query,
                              $start,
                              $maxResults,
                              $filter,
                              $restrict,
                              $safeSearch,
                              $lr,
                              $ie,
                              $oe );
```

The proxy, again, handles all the details of talking to Google; it learned how to do this from the WSDL file, and that's all we need to know. When we call the proxy's doGoogleSearch function, it relays the call to Google, gets the data back, and builds a PHP array out of it. The rest of our code above just parses out that array and sends it back in a generic XML format of our own definition. To get that data back into FileMaker, of course, we need to write a stylesheet that transforms the generic XML into FMPXML. As before, we can have PHP output FMPXML directly, rather than going through the transform phase, but we feel strongly that this would be bad abstraction and bad design.

Our PHP page above, by the way, is not quite ready to go. Right now it's hard-coding all the function parameters, especially the query string. But we want to be able to send those from FileMaker, so we need to rewrite the page to accept parameters in the HTTP request. We can do that easily by changing our function call setup to look like this:

```
/// set up the parameters for a call to Google's doGoogleSearch
    method
// first figure out which request array to use, $_GET or $_POST
$method = $_SERVER['REQUEST_METHOD'];
$requestArrayName = "_$method";
$requestArray = $$requestArrayName;

if ( $requestArray['useDefault'] == true ) { // set default
  parameters if instructed
      $key = 'qw2rrPVQFHLsLQQ3IeUPnRm5mWSayn4o';
      $query = 'Native American Languages';
      $start = 0;
      $maxResults = 10;
      $filter = '';
      $restrict = '';
      $safeSearch= '';
      $lr = 'lang-en';
      $ie = '';
      $oe = '';
} else {
      $key = $requestArray['key'];
      $query = $requestArray['query'];
      $start = $requestArray['start'];
      $maxResults = $requestArray['maxResults'];
      $filter = $requestArray['filter'];
      $restrict = $requestArray['restrict'];
      $safeSearch= $requestArray['safeSearch'];
      $lr = $requestArray['lr'];
      $ie = ''; // these last two params are deprecated by Google so
        no need to worry about them
      $oe = '';
}
```

We need to be able to inspect the name-value pairs that were sent to our page. In PHP, the more secure way to do this is to use the different request arrays that PHP provides. Prior to PHP 4.1, these were called $HTTP_GET_VARS and $HTTP_POST_VARS, while in PHP 4.1 and above, though the old names still work, the names $_GET and $_POST are preferred and behave in a more convenient fashion. Here we assume that the PHP version is at least 4.1 and do a little work with the $_SERVER['REQUEST_METHOD'] value to figure out if our page was accessed via POST or GET to set the arrays up accordingly.

If you've been reading closely, you'll point out that FileMaker's XML Import only works via GET, so why do we need to provide for POST requests here? We give the same answer here that we do to the question of why we don't generate FMPXML in our pages but insist on creating generic XML and transforming it: The fewer assumptions that you make about how your code is going to be used, the easier a time you have later on. If we do it this way now, if FileMaker ever supports a POST flavor of the XML Import, we're already prepared.

What we've done up above is configured our page to look for an incoming parameter called useDefault. If that's set to true, we don't look at the incoming parameters any more; we just use the default data hard-coded in the page. We decided to leave those defaults in place and control them with a flag because it makes testing easier. In order to test this page, we don't need to drive it by some outside request that specifies all parameters; we can just hit it with a parameter of useDefault=true and test it with data that we know gives a good result. But if we leave useDefault out of the request or set it to false, the page will try to use parameters from the incoming request.

So now we have two jobs remaining: Set up a FileMaker database that can send a query to our SOAP-enabled PHP page, and write a stylesheet that can transform the XML output. Both of these tasks are going to be very similar to the way we set up our database and stylesheet for the Amazon query. After all, it's all the same to FileMaker; in one case it talks directly to Amazon and in another it talks to an intermediate PHP layer, but in each case it's gathering up user input, formatting a URL that's intended to retrieve some XML, transforming the XML, and importing it.

For our FileMaker database, we want a way for a user to enter a query, perform a search, and see the results. We define the following fields:

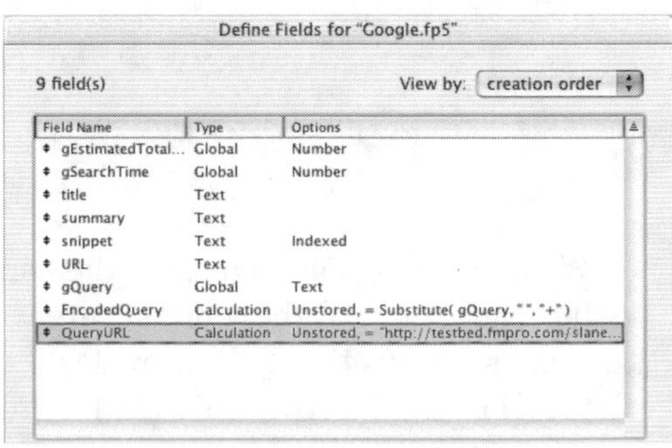

Figure 9.4

We set up a search screen with a single global field into which a user can type a query. We make an auxiliary field called EncodedQuery to transform any spaces in the query into the + symbol, which is one acceptable way of encoding whitespace so that it can be sent as part of a URL. (In fact, this is a fairly minimal form of URL encoding, and in a production system we'd want to be more thorough; there are a number of other characters that we would need to trap for and encode as well.) We also have the usual calculation field that assembles the final URL based on the user's input. Here it looks like this:

```
"http://testbed.fmpro.com/slane/WebServices/GoogleSOAP.php?key=
  XXXXXXXXXXXXXXX&query=" & EncodedQuery & "&start=0&maxResults=
  10&lr=lang-en&filter=&restrict=&safeSearch="
```

As usual, you would need to replace the host name by your own host name and the XXXXX sequence with your actual Google developer code. We provide the user with a simple search screen that looks like this:

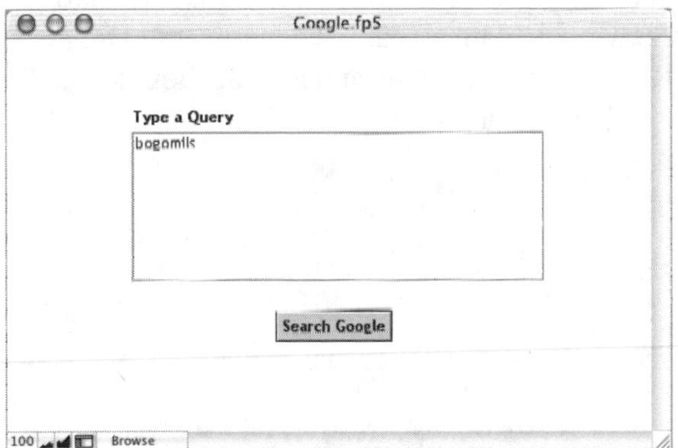

Figure 9.5

Once the search is run and the XML is imported, we take them to a results list that looks like the following:

Figure 9.6

All that remains is to write the XSL stylesheet that transforms the generic XML output of GoogleSOAP.php into FileMaker's native FMPXML. From the Google data stream, we just want to select the title, summary, URL, and snippet fields and format them for the user. The stylesheet should be familiar by now:

```
<?xml version="1.0" encoding="UTF-8"?>
<xsl:stylesheet xmlns:xsl="http://www.w3.org/1999/XSL/Transform"
  version="1.0">
<xsl:template match="GoogleResults">
          <FMPXMLRESULT xmlns="http://www.filemaker.com/
            fmpxmlresult">
               <ERRORCODE>0</ERRORCODE>
               <PRODUCT BUILD="" NAME="" VERSION=""/>
               <DATABASE DATEFORMAT="M/d/yyyy" LAYOUT="" NAME=""
                 RECORDS="10" TIMEFORMAT="h:mm:ss a"/>
               <METADATA>
                    <FIELD EMPTYOK="YES" MAXREPEAT="1" NAME=
                      "gEstimatedTotalResults" TYPE="NUMBER" />
                    <FIELD EMPTYOK="YES" MAXREPEAT="1" NAME=
                      "gSearchTime" TYPE="NUMBER" />
                    <FIELD EMPTYOK="YES" MAXREPEAT="1" NAME="title"
                      TYPE="TEXT" />
                    <FIELD EMPTYOK="YES" MAXREPEAT="1" NAME=
                      "summary" TYPE="TEXT" />
                    <FIELD EMPTYOK="YES" MAXREPEAT="1" NAME=
                      "snippet" TYPE="TEXT" />
                    <FIELD EMPTYOK="YES" MAXREPEAT="1" NAME="URL"
                      TYPE="TEXT" />
               </METADATA>
               <RESULTSET>
                    <xsl:attribute name="FOUND"><xsl:value-of
                      select="/GoogleResults/maxResults"/>
```

```
                </xsl:attribute>
              <xsl:for-each select="/GoogleResults/
                resultElements/resultElement">
                  <ROW >
                        <xsl:attribute name="MODID">0
                          </xsl:attribute>
                        <xsl:attribute name="RECORDID">0
                          </xsl:attribute>
                        <COL><DATA><xsl:value-of select=
                          "../estimatedTotalResultsCount"/>
                          </DATA></COL>
                        <COL><DATA><xsl:value-of select=
                          "../searchTime"/></DATA></COL>
                        <COL><DATA><xsl:value-of select=
                          "title"/></DATA></COL>
                        <COL><DATA><xsl:value-of select=
                          "summary"/></DATA></COL>
                        <COL><DATA><xsl:value-of select=
                          "snippet"/></DATA></COL>
                        <COL><DATA><xsl:value-of select=
                          "URL"/></DATA></COL>
                  </ROW>
              </xsl:for-each>
          </RESULTSET>
      </FMPXMLRESULT>
  </xsl:template>
</xsl:stylesheet>
```

As we saw with the Amazon example, there's much more that we can do to improve the user experience with a tool like this. We can vary the number of results fetched, we can give the user an easy way to fetch the next ten results, and so forth. That's all fairly routine FileMaker programming for us at this point though, so let's move on.

SOAP Wrap-up

We've learned that, although FileMaker doesn't natively have the capability to converse directly with SOAP-based web services, it's relatively straightforward to build a middleware layer that can mediate between these types of web services and FileMaker. If working with the NuSOAP library and writing a chunk of PHP seemed like a lot of work, well, in one way, it is. On the other hand, think of the amazing feat of computing that we just performed. In more or less the blink of an eye, our routines query Google's internal servers, come back with a pile of data, pull it through many networks, protocols, and database languages, and bring it back to a FileMaker user. Without XML, this would be fiendishly difficult; the remote data source would probably have to open its databases directly to you, set up some security that limited your queries, and you'd still need to set up some kind of

SQL/ODBC query, configure local drivers, and so forth. But XML does what many modern software technologies do—take tasks that used to be really, really difficult and turn them into tasks that are merely annoying. That's quite a feat.

So, with some PHP in the middle, FileMaker can be a first-class web services citizen, fully able to converse with all those SOAP-based web services out there. If you hear someone belittling FileMaker because it's not "SOAP-capable," you know what to tell them. Actually, if that person is insistent and a little fiendish, she'll press the point. "Ah, but FileMaker can't publish its *own* data over SOAP, right?" she'll say. Well, a little thought will show that that's not true either. The PHP NuSOAP library lets us write both SOAP *clients* that go and get data from SOAP sources and also SOAP *servers*, which can publish data in a SOAP format. So the answer here again is that, with some PHP in the middle, FileMaker can be a SOAP-based web service in its own right. We're not going to work through all the code here, one reason being that we'd need a SOAP-based client in order to test the results. We're just going to mention the possibility. To accomplish this, you'd write a SOAP server in PHP using NuSOAP, and any functions supported by the server that need FileMaker data would have custom code written in FX to go and fetch that data. To help possible client applications know what services we would offer, we'd write or publish a file in WSDL or a similar protocol and publish that on the web as well. This would be a fairly involved application, but we've already worked with all the required tools.

Web Services Push

So far, all of our examples in this chapter have dealt with bringing data into FileMaker. After all, the feature that underlies FileMaker's ability to consume web services is called XML Import, right? All the same, the benefits of this feature extend well beyond just bringing data from the web into FileMaker. They can be used equally as well to push data out of FileMaker to, well, just about anywhere. Let's say, for example, that we're dealing with a student information system. Staff in the admissions office follow prospects through the whole admissions cycle using a FileMaker database. When a prospect accepts an offer and is admitted, there needs to be a new student record created in the big iron mainframe that runs the campus-wide student database that everyone else uses. Typically, this means some kind of double entry.

Or we could try to find a way for FileMaker to insert the data directly in the mainframe.

If the server is ODBC- or JDBC-capable, we could try to do this directly from the FileMaker desktop, using the built-in SQL capabilities or a plug-in that adds JDBC capabilities. But this puts us back in the realm of drivers, desktop operating systems, and multiple client configurations. We want something easier. It still depends on what interfaces the mainframe makes available, but let's say for the sake of argument that the server is an IBM mainframe running OS/400 and IBM's DB2 database software. As it happens, PHP has a library that lets it talk to DB2 database servers. FileMaker would have to jump through some serious hoops to talk directly to a DB2 server. Using HTTP and PHP, it has to jump through one rather small one.

Here's the strategy: We want to make some kind of HTTP request from FileMaker to a PHP-based web page that instructs PHP to send FileMaker data off to the DB2 server. We don't actually need to send the student record data directly to PHP via the HTTP request. In fact, it's probably not even a good idea to try; data sent via an HTTP GET, which is FileMaker's request method, can easily get cut off along the way if the resulting URL is too long. There are no hard and fast rules for when and at what point the cutoff will happen, but it can happen. What we want to do instead is send a short request to PHP that tells it which FileMaker record to query for and ship off to the mainframe. Consider the following short URL:


```
http://www.exchanger.local-university.edu/AdmissionsPush.php?
  prospectID=A12DE70
```

If we use that as our URL for an XML Import operation, the target page (AdmissionsPush.php) receives the specified value for prospectID and is able to do something with it. Specifically, it should pull that record from FileMaker (possibly using FX), read the resulting data, format a database request to DB2, send it off, and report the results back to FileMaker in an XML format. So the only XML that FileMaker is actually going to import here is a message from the PHP middleware layer letting FileMaker know how things went. This really isn't an import at all; it's a multi-tier, multi-database transaction with HTTP and XML as the messaging protocol.

Let's look at a PHP page that could act as the middleware for a transaction like this. For our example, since we don't have any OS/400 mainframes lying around to test on, we're going to pretend that we have a group of archaeologists who record their finds in FileMaker but ultimately want to push them into a museum database that's based on the open-source SQL database server PostgreSQL. The museum possibly chose PostgreSQL over FileMaker for the back end because they need to store tens of millions of records or because they need to perform extremely complex queries across multiple physical locations. Whatever the reason, we want to be able to originate and work with data in FileMaker but ultimately store it in the SQL back end. Here's a diagram of the architecture that we need:

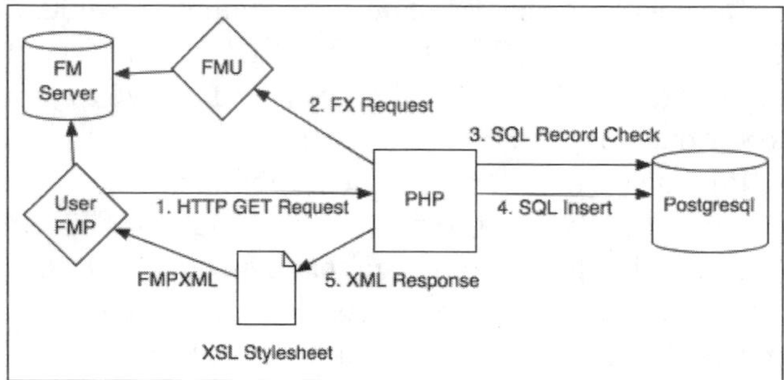

Figure 9.7

We have, of course, a full-fledged FileMaker client-server setup with an instance of FileMaker Server and however many FileMaker clients that we need. One of those clients is FileMaker Pro Unlimited for communicating with our middleware layer. We also have our PHP layer, with one or more pages that know how to exchange data between FileMaker and PostgreSQL. Finally, we have our PostgreSQL server all the way on the back end. The transaction that we're trying to set up looks like this: Starting from a record in FileMaker, we perform an XML Import that sends the record's designation code to a PHP page. That PHP page does the heavy lifting; it fetches the full record from FileMaker and tries to pass the data over to SQL via native PHP calls. At the end, PHP sends an XML-formatted message back to FileMaker to report on how the transaction went.

First, let's take a quick look at our FileMaker database. It has six fields that capture data about artifacts and some utility fields:

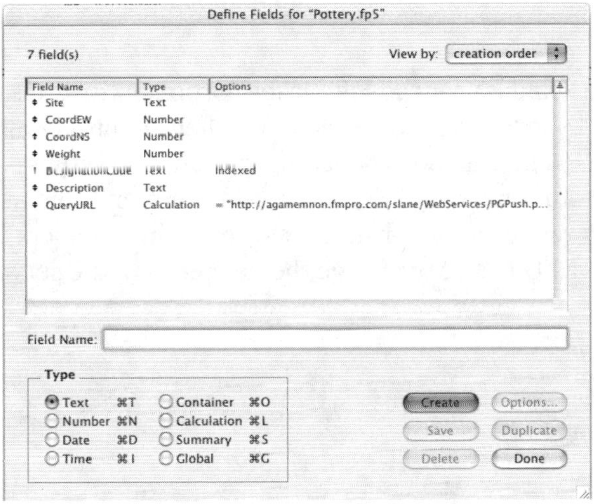

Figure 9.8

The "update" script sends an XML Import request that looks like this:

```
http://hosts.museum.org/slane/WebServices/PGPush.php?designation=
  AR456GQ
```

Naturally, the import is hooked up to the stylesheet that transforms the XML from the PHP page back into something that FileMaker can import. But the bulk of the logic for this transaction lives in the PHP page, so let's walk through it step by step and see what it does. One note about this code is that we've tried to be more rigorous with our error handling this time. Multi-tier transactions like this have a host of possible failure points, and without solid error handling, problems can be a nightmare to debug. Hopefully, this offers a look at what a more production-level error-handling scheme would look like:

```
<?

/* Page to pull data from FileMaker and insert in PostgreSQL database
   table
 *
 */

require_once( 'FX.php' );

// database variables
$fmDataServer =  '209.242.196.70';
$fmDataPort = 1080;
$fmDatabase = 'Pottery.fp5';
$fmLayout = 'Web';
```

```
$sqlDatabase = "webservices";
$sqlTable = "pottery";
```

We're going to be using FX for the FileMaker portion of the transaction, so we begin by including the FX code. We then set up a number of variables that hold information about our two database setups—one in FileMaker, the other in PostgreSQL. It's always better to put such "magic" values in variables (or constants, as we see in a moment), since it makes it vastly easier to change them when, say, the server IP changes.

```
// error constants
define ( 'ERROR_NO_ERROR', 0 );
define ( 'ERROR_NO_DESIGNATION', -10 );
define ( 'ERROR_FM_ERROR', -11 );
define ( 'ERROR_PG_CONNECT', -12 );
define ( 'ERROR_PG_QUERY', -13 );
define ( 'ERROR_NO_SUCH_FM_RECORD', -14 );

$resultCode = ERROR_NO_ERROR;

// first figure out which request array to use, $_GET or $_POST
$method = $_SERVER['REQUEST_METHOD'];
$requestArrayName = "_$method";
$requestArray = $$requestArrayName;
```

We next set up a number of constants to support our error-handling scheme. Constants are values in a computer program that are never allowed to change. Defining these values as constants here, rather than variables, can give us certain advantages (primarily that we can use these values inside PHP functions without doing any extra work).

Once the error codes are set up, we start by initializing our result code to a status that shows no error yet. Then we use the same code that we've seen earlier to decide whether to look in the GET variable array or the POST array for incoming variables.

```
$primaryKey = $requestArray['designation'];

if (  $primaryKey == '' ) {
      $resultCode = ERROR_NO_DESIGNATION;
} else {
      // query FileMaker for the record whose designation we were sent
      $fmpConnection = new FX( $fmDataServer, $fmDataPort );
      $fmpConnection->setDBData( $fmDatabase, $fmLayout );
      $fmpConnection->addDBParam( "DesignationCode", $primaryKey );
      $fmReturn = $fmpConnection->FMFind();
      //print_r($fmReturn);
      if ( $fmReturn['errorCode'] != 0 ) { // got a FileMaker Error
                                           // of some kind
            $resultCode = ERROR_FM_ERROR;
```

Next we delve into the data sent to the page and extract the "designation" parameter. This is the primary key of the FileMaker record, and we need it for a number of operations. If we don't find it, we set the resultCode to an error code. Execution effectively stops there, since all the rest of the code is inside an else clause. So this is our strategy when looking for errors: We test for them inside of if-else constructs, and if we find one, we don't go on with the regular code flow. The effect of this is to skip straight to the end of the program if we find an error. We see later on what we do when we get there.

If we do have a primary key, the next thing we do is set up an FX connection to our databases. We need to point FX to a FileMaker Pro Unlimited instance that has access to the database file or files that we're working with. It's very important, by the way, that you not point FX straight back to one of the FileMaker clients that initiate this transaction. If so, that client makes an XML request and waits to hear back from the PHP page, but the PHP page, before returning any XML, tries to make an XML request against the very same FileMaker client that's still waiting to hear back from it. The two requests deadlock and you will likely have to shut down your copy of FileMaker by force.

So we set up a new instance of the FX class, point it to our database and layout, and ask it to perform a search action for the primary key that was sent to the page. This way, we fetch back all the other record data associated with that record. At the end, we check to see whether the operation generated a FileMaker error, and if so, we stop the main execution of the program.

```
} else { // no error looking for the record in FileMaker
     $foundCount = $fmReturn['foundCount'];
     if ( $foundCount == 0 ) { // no FMP record corresponds to
                                // the primary key that was sent
          $resultCode = ERROR_NO_SUCH_FM_RECORD;
     } else {
          $dataArray = $fmReturn['data'];
          foreach( $dataArray as $id_mod=>$recordData ) {
               $site = $recordData['Site'][0];
               $coordEW = $recordData['CoordEW'][0];
               $coordNS = $recordData['CoordNS'][0];
               $weight = $recordData['Weight'][0];
               $designationCode = $recordData
                 ['DesignationCode'][0];
               $description = $recordData['Description'][0];
               //echo ( "$site, $coordEW, $coordNS, $weight,
                 $designationCode, $description" );
          } // we're not checking for more than one found
            // record, which perhaps we should
```

Chapter 9

Assuming that there was no serious FileMaker error in making the search request, we next check the FileMaker found count. If it's 0, this is again a problem, since it means we were sent a designation code that doesn't match anything in the database. So again we would error out here with still another different error code. If we pass that test, though, we can delve into the data returned by FX and pick out all the record fields that we need. Then we can go ahead and try to move the data into the SQL database, as we see in the following code.

```
          // set up connection to PostgreSQL database
          $pgConnectionString = "dbname=$sqlDatabase user=
            PostgreSQL";
          $pgConnection = @pg_connect( $pgConnectionString );
          if ( $pgConnection == false ) { // got some error
                                   // connecting to postgres
               $resultCode = ERROR_PG_CONNECT;
          } else {
               // first check to see if this record is already
               // in the SQL database
               $sqlStmt = "SELECT * FROM $sqlTable WHERE
                 designation_code='$designationCode'";
               $queryResult = @pg_exec( $pgConnection,
                 $sqlStmt );
               if ( $queryResult == false ) { // some query
                                            // error
                    $resultCode = ERROR_PG_QUERY;
                    $resultMessage = pg_errormessage(
                      $pgConnection );
               } else { // we got some result from the database
                    $pgFoundCount = pg_numrows(
                      $queryResult );
                    if ( $pgFoundCount == 0 ) { // the record
                                   // was not already in the db
                         $sqlStmt = "INSERT INTO $sqlTable
                           VALUES ( '$site', $coordEW,
                           $coordNS, $weight,
                           '$designationCode',
                           '$description' )";
                    } else {
                         $sqlStmt = "UPDATE $sqlTable set
                           site='$site', coord_ew=$coordEW,
                           coord_ns=$coordNS, weight=$weight,
                           description='$description' WHERE
                           designation_code=
                           '$designationCode'";
                    }
                    $queryResult = @pg_exec( $pgConnection,
                      $sqlStmt );
                    if ( $queryResult == false ) { // some
                                             // query error
                         $resultCode = ERROR_PG_QUERY;
                         $resultMessage = pg_errormessage
```

```
                            ( $pgConnection );
                    }
                }
            }
        }
    }
}
```

If we successfully fetched the FileMaker record, we now need to work on the PostgreSQL side of things. Our logic is similar: First try to connect to the PostgreSQL server, and error out if we can't. Then things get a little trickier; we want to know if the record has already been added to PostgreSQL, since the SQL is different for an update than for adding a record. So we need to run a query that tells us if the record already exists there. If that query has a problem, we error out (monotonous, eh?). Then, we generate an SQL statement. Depending on whether the record was already stored in PostgreSQL, we create either an SQL INSERT statement or an SQL UPDATE statement using the data values from the FileMaker record. Once we have our statement, we try to execute it against the server. If we fail, well, you know.

By now, we've either done all the work we came to do or found an error of some kind. So all that remains is to check the error code and then generate our XML response. Here's how it looks:

```
switch( $resultCode ) {
    case ERROR_NO_DESIGNATION:
        $errorMsg = "No designation code was sent so the request
          could not be processed.";
        break;
    case ERROR_NO_SUCH_FM_RECORD:
        $errorMsg = "No FileMaker record matching the specified
          designation could be found.";
        break;
    case ERROR_FM_ERROR:
        $errorMsg = "A FileMaker error occurred: FileMaker
          error #" . $fmReturn['errorCode'];
        break;
    case ERROR_PG_CONNECT:
        $errorMsg = "A connection to the Postgres database could
          not be established.";
        break;
    case ERROR_PG_QUERY:
        $errorMsg = "An error occurred processing the Postgres
          query. Database said: $resultMessage";
        break;
    case ERROR_NO_ERROR:
        $errorMsg = "The Postgres database was successfully
          updated!";
        break;
```

```
}

header ("Content-type: text/xml"); // signal that we're sending XML
echo '<?xml version="1.0"?>';
?>

<PGPushResult>
     <resultCode><? echo $resultCode; ?></resultCode>
     <resultMessage><? echo $errorMsg; ?></resultMessage>
     <designationCode><? echo $primaryKey; ?></designationCode>
</PGPushResult>
```

We set up an error message based on the value of the $resultCode variable (which includes the code for no error). Once we have that, we send the result code, the result message, and the original primary key back to FileMaker as our XML response. Here's the simple stylesheet that we use to transform it:

```
<?xml version="1.0" encoding="UTF-8"?>
<xsl:stylesheet xmlns:xsl="http://www.w3.org/1999/XSL/Transform"
  version="1.0">
<xsl:template match="PGPushResult">
          <FMPXMLRESULT xmlns="http://www.filemaker.com/
            fmpxmlresult">
               <ERRORCODE>0</ERRORCODE>
               <PRODUCT BUILD="" NAME="" VERSION=""/>
               <DATABASE DATEFORMAT="M/d/yyyy" LAYOUT="" NAME=""
                 RECORDS="1" TIMEFORMAT="h:mm:ss a"/>
               <METADATA>
                    <FIELD EMPTYOK="YES" MAXREPEAT="1" NAME=
                      "gResultCode" TYPE="NUMBER" />
                    <FIELD EMPTYOK="YES" MAXREPEAT="1" NAME=
                      "gResultMessage" TYPE="TEXT" />
                    <FIELD EMPTYOK="YES" MAXREPEAT="1" NAME=
                      "DesignationCode" TYPE="TEXT" />
               </METADATA>
               <RESULTSET>
                    <xsl:attribute name="FOUND">1</xsl:attribute>
                    <ROW >
                         <xsl:attribute name="MODID">0
                           </xsl:attribute>
                         <xsl:attribute name="RECORDID">0
                           </xsl:attribute>
                         <COL><DATA><xsl:value-of select=
                           "resultCode"/></DATA></COL>
                         <COL><DATA><xsl:value-of select=
                           "resultMessage"/></DATA></COL>
                         <COL><DATA><xsl:value-of select=
                           "designationCode"/></DATA></COL>
                    </ROW>
               </RESULTSET>
          </FMPXMLRESULT>
```

```
    </xsl:template>
</xsl:stylesheet>
```

This is just one example of the kind of multi-tier, multi-database logic we could create using FileMaker's XML Import capability. There's a host of other possibilities as well. Let's say that you're building a FileMaker system for a large vendor of starches and cleaning products. They use FileMaker to handle their ordering, but all of their customer data is stored in a large Oracle database. FileMaker doesn't need to originate or change any customer information. You just need to make certain that the FileMaker system always has a full and accurate customer list that reflects what's contained in Oracle. We need some way to refresh the customer data from Oracle into FileMaker—either on a regular basis or on demand.

Of course, we can go through the various two-tier client-server permutations that we've talked about before—Oracle drivers on the desktop, and so forth. But by now, you know a better answer. Have FileMaker send an HTTP command to a PHP middleware layer; that in turn holds all the logic for querying Oracle, formatting the results as XML, and sending them back to FileMaker. FileMaker's update script would simply delete all the current customer records, send an XML Import request to a PHP page, and get back all the customer records in XML format.

If you let your imagination roam a little bit, you can probably see that these techniques could even be used for building synchronization solutions, where data is kept in synch between FileMaker and PostgreSQL, FileMaker and Oracle, or even FileMaker and FileMaker.

It should be said that FileMaker, Inc. has been careful to state that they're not positioning the XML Import capability as a replacement for client-server technologies. It's not necessarily meant to be used to build, for example, an Oracle or a PostgreSQL client. But that's more or less exactly what we've sketched out how to do here. FileMaker Inc. doesn't say that the technology *can't* be used this way or that it shouldn't—merely that multi-tier applications like this are not the primary use that they had in mind for this new tool. But we feel obliged to point out all of the possible cool applications and what we've tried to do here.

Summary

In our opinion, XML Import is one of the coolest and most significant new FileMaker features in a long time. In this chapter we've seen a host of possible uses for this capability. We can bring in data from web services around the world using plain old HTTP GET. With the help of a relatively thin, SOAP-aware layer of middleware written in PHP, we can consume SOAP-based web services as well. Using the same middleware layer we could, if we so desired, broadcast FileMaker data to SOAP clients. We can even turn the XML Import capability into a pretty capable multi-tier, multi-platform messaging base for exchanging data between FileMaker and other database platforms with nary a whiff of an ODBC driver. If the madness took us, we could probably use this technology to put together a pretty compelling synchronization solution as well.

Lastly, we also saw how we could use PHP (or indeed, any similar middleware language) to write our own web services to add capabilities like unified time service and password hashing to FileMaker. If you need a capability that FileMaker doesn't have, try to code it up in FileMaker or look for a plug-in that does what you need and install it everywhere. Or you could write it once in some middleware language and put it out there as a web service for FileMaker or anyone else to use. Maybe there's a great Java library that you can buy that performs some complex operations tailored to a vertical market. Buy the library, wrap it in a web service (with PHP, for example, which can talk to Java, or via a Java servlet, if you know how to write the same). Now have FileMaker talk to your new web services layer, and you have a whole new library of functionality waiting to be tapped. Hopefully, these examples and possibilities have made the reasons for our excitement clear.

Appendix

CDML Reference Guide

Notes:

1) CDML tags, parameters and values, unless otherwise specified, are not case sensitive.

2) Because of formatting constraints, many long commands appear to have returns in them. In general, avoid having returns within any CDML tag or URL. The text may soft wrap in your text editor, but don't put in hard returns.

Request Parameters

CDML command parameters are sent with a request, either as part of a URL (GET method) or as part of an HTML form (POST method). They are distinguished by being prefixed by a hyphen. Within the command parameters is also the important subgroup of the action parameters.

Action Parameters

A CDML request, whether by URL (GET) or form (POST), must have one and only one action parameter. We call it an action parameter because it tells the CDML engine what one database action to perform in the course of the request. An action parameter may be any one of the following:

Database Close **-DBClose**

Description: -DBClose is a tag that allows you to close a database on a FileMaker Pro host machine from a remote browser. It will look to the -db parameter for the name of the database to close and at the URL to determine which host to work with. The database host must have

Remote Administration enabled (in the Web Companion configuration settings under Application Preferences) in order for this command to work. For security purposes it is strongly advised that you apply a password to the Remote Administration capability so that unauthorized users can't send a -DBClose command to your Web Companion and start shutting down databases.

Example: In an embedded URL:

```
http://thehost.com/FMPro?-db=Employees.fp5&-format=
  aFormatFile.html&-DBClose
```

To execute the same command using a form:

```
<form action="FMPro" method="post">
     <input type="hidden" name="-DB" value="Employees.fp5">
     <input type="hidden" name="-format" value=" aFormatFile.html">
     <input type="submit" name="-DBClose" value="Close Employees
       Database">
</form>
```

Note that the -format parameter is required, even though -DBClose doesn't use it.

Database Open -DBOpen

Description: -DBOpen is a tag that allows you to open a database on a FileMaker Pro host machine from a remote browser. It will look to the -db parameter for the name of the database to close and at the URL to determine which host to work with. The database host must have Remote Administration enabled (in the Web Companion configuration settings under Application Preferences) in order for this command to work. In addition, the database to be opened must be in the host's Web folder.

Example: In an embedded URL:

```
http://thehost.com/FMPro?-db=Employees.fp5&-format=
  aFormatFile.html&-DBOpen
```

To execute the same command using a form:

```
<form action="FMPro" method="post">
     <input type="hidden" name="-DB" value= "Employees.fp5">
     <input type="hidden" name="-format" value=" aFormatFile.html">
     <input type="submit" name="-DBOpen" value="Open Employees
       Database">
</form>
```

Note that the -format parameter is required, even though -DBOpen doesn't use it.

Delete Record -Delete

Description: -Delete is an action tag that will delete the record specified by the -RecID tag. In order to use this function, a user must have delete privileges for the file. Using JavaScript, it's possible to include a confirmation dialog to a Delete action (see below for an example). Only one record at a time can be deleted from the web. It would be possible, however, to script deletion of multiple records.

Example: In an embedded URL:

```
<a href="FMPro?-DB=classes.fp5&-Format=DeleteReply.html&-RecID=
  [FMP-CurrentRecID]&-Delete>Delete this record</a>
```

Note: This embedded URL contains a replacement tag, [FMP-CurrentRecID], which means that the current format file would need to be dynamically generated. Only if the RecID is literally specified can the -Delete action occur on a static page.

To delete a record using a form:

```
<form action="FMPro" method="post">
      <input type="hidden" name="-DB" value="classes.fp5">
      <input type="hidden" name="-Format" value="DeleteReply.html">
      <input type="hidden" name="-RecID" value="[FMP-CurrentRecID]">
      <input type="submit" name="-Delete" value="Delete this record">
</form>
```

To add a JavaScript confirmation to a delete action:

1. Change the <head> section of your HTML document to include the following:

```
<head>
<script language="javascript">
<!-- begin to hide script contents from old browsers

function DeleteConfirmation()
{
      return confirm('Are you sure you wish to delete this record?');
}
// end hiding script from old browsers -->
</script>
</head>
```

2. Change your submit button so that it invokes the DeleteConfirmation function when it is clicked:

```
<input type="submit" name="-Delete" value="Delete this record"
  onclick="return DeleteConfirmation()">
```

Remember that JavaScript is case sensitive, so be careful naming and invoking your functions! The same JavaScript could function as a confirmation for any action, such as a Duplicate or Update, with only trivial modifications.

Duplicate Record -Dup

Description: The -Dup action duplicates the record specified by the -RecID tag. In order to use this function, a user must have record creation privileges for the file.

Example: In an embedded URL:

```
<a href="FMPro?-DB=classes.fp5&-Format=DuplicateReply.html&-RecID=
   [FMP-CurrentRecID]&-Dup">Duplicate this record</a>
```

Note: This embedded URL contains a replacement tag, [FMP-CurrentRecID], which means that the current format file would need to be dynamically generated. Only if the RecID is literally specified can the -Duplicate action occur on a static page.

To duplicate a record using a form:

```
<form action="FMPro" method="post">
     <input type="hidden" name="-DB" value="classes.fp5">
     <input type="hidden" name="-Format" value="DupReply.html">
     <input type="hidden" name="-RecID" value="[FMP-CurrentRecID]">
     <input type="submit" name="-Dup" value="Duplicate this record">
</form>
```

Note: The form in the example above contains only one submit button, but keep in mind that forms can contain multiple submit buttons. Only one, of course, can be selected by the user. For instance, this means that from the same form you can give the user the option to Edit, Duplicate, or Delete the record currently being displayed. Unfortunately, you can specify only one format file as the response file. Using the [FMP-CurrentAction] tag on that response file will let you customize it based on the action that the user selected.

Edit Record -Edit

Description: The -Edit action tag is used to change the record in a database specified by the -RecID tag. Only one record at a time can be updated from the web. To use this function, the user must have edit privileges for the database being called. When performing an edit, you must also specify the fields to update. This is done through name-value pairs in embedded URLs and user input fields in forms.

Often, edits will be done from some sort of Detail page. Instead of creating a separate HTML file that serves as an Edit reply page, try using the Detail page as its own response page. This way, a user edits a record and immediately sees the results of the update and has the option to make additional modifications.

The most frequent cause of errors using the -Edit tag is forgetting to specify the -RecID. Also, take care never to attempt to update calculation fields, as this will also trigger errors.

Example: In an embedded URL:

```
<a href="FMPro?-DB=parts.fp5&-Lay=WebEdit&-Format=Detail.html&-RecID=
  [FMP-CurrentRecID]&part_status=Out+Of+Stock&-Edit">Flag as Out of
  Stock</a>
```

Note: As many fields as necessary can be updated in an embedded URL. Remember to change any spaces in the text into plus signs (+) or into %20.

Using a form:

```
<form action="FMPro" method="post">
     <input type="hidden" name="-DB" value="parts.fp5">
     <input type="hidden" name="-Lay" value="WebEdit">
     <input type="hidden" name="-Format" value="Detail.html">
     <input type="hidden" name="-RecID" value="[FMP-CurrentRecID]">

     Part Number: [FMP-Field:part_number]
     Description: <input type="text" name="description" value=
       "[FMP-Field: description]">
     Status: <input type="text" name="part_status" value="[FMP-Field:
       part_status]">

     <input type="submit" name="-Edit" value="Update this Record">

</form>
```

This would create a form that displays the part number (non-updateable), description, and status. The description and status could be changed by the user.

Find All Records — -FindAll

Description: The -FindAll action will find all records of a specified database. A user must have browse permission to use this tag. It's generally a good idea to use the -Max tag when returning large sets of records, both to achieve better performance and to avoid out-of-memory errors. If the -Max tag is not specified, the default value of 25 records will be used. Use -Max=All to return the entire found set all at

Appendix

once. Any name-value pairs specified will be ignored by the -FindAll action, so there is no problem having a form with buttons to perform both a Find (using name-value pairs) and a FindAll.

As with all Finds, you will get better performance if you specifiy a layout using the -Lay tag.

Since -FindAll is a fairly innocuous action, it's often specified as the action when you simply want to send mail or perform a script. Both of these features require some sort of action to occur.

Example: In an embedded URL:

```
<a href="FMPro?-DB=Contact.fp5&-Lay=WebSearch&-Format=hitlist.html&-
  Max=20&-SortField=Last_Name&-FindAll">Find All Contacts</a>
```

In a form:

```
<form action="FMPro" method="post">
     <input type="hidden" name="-DB" value="Contact.fp5">
     <input type="hidden" name="-Lay" value="WebSearch">
     <input type="hidden" name="-Format" value="hitlist.html">
     <input type="hidden" name="-Max" value="20">
     <input type="hidden" name="-SortField" value="Last_Name">
     <input type="submit" name="-FindAll" value="Find All Contacts">
</form>
```

Find Any Record — -FindAny

Description: -FindAny will find a single random record in the specified database. As with all Find actions, a user must have browse privileges to use this function. Since only a single record will be returned, it is unnecessary to specify -Max or -SortField as you might for other Finds.

Example: In an embedded URL:

```
<a href="FMPro?-DB=Cards.fp5&-Lay=WebSearch&-Format=detail.html&
  -FindAny">Pick a Card, Any Card.</a>
```

In a form:

```
<form action="FMPro" method="post">
     <input type="hidden" name="-DB" value="Cards.fp5">
     <input type="hidden" name="-Lay" value="WebSearch">
     <input type="hidden" name="-Format" value="detail.html">
     <input type="submit" name="-FindAny" value="Find All Contacts">
</form>
```

Find Record -Find

Description: The -Find tag is used to query a specified database based on a certain set of criteria. These criteria can either be completely predefined (as in an embedded URL) or based on a user's input (as in a form). A user must have Browse privileges in order to perform a Find.

As with all actions, a -Find involves two separate but complementary HTML files—one to specify the parameters of the search and the other to display the results of the search (often called a hit list). A form or URL is required on the search page itself but not on the response page. Any replacement tags used on the response page (such as [FMP-CurrentFoundCount] or [FMP-Field]) will be determined by the database specified on the search page.

For better performance, use the -Max tag to specify the number of records that should be returned at a time. Also, use the -Lay tag to specify on which layout the query should be performed. Any fields involved in your find or that you intend to display on the response page, must appear on the specified layout. Unless an error response page is specified using the -Error tag, a generic "No Records Found" response will be generated if no records match the search criteria.

Finally, keep in mind that your search page can be either static or dynamic. Dynamic pages allow you to use replacement tags and, more importantly, value lists generated by the database on your form.

Example: In an embedded URL:

```
<a href="FMPro?-DB=Compact_Disc.fp5&-Lay=SearchMe&-Format=
  hitlist.html&-Error=Error.html&-Max=15&-SortField=Artist&Category=
  Classical&Status=On+Hand&-Find">Click here for Classical Music
  selections.</a>
```

In a form (on a dynamic search page):

```
<form action="FMPro" method="post">
     <input type="hidden" name="-DB" value="Compact_Disc.fp5">
     <input type="hidden" name="-Lay" value="SearchMe">
     <input type="hidden" name="-Format" value="hitlist.html">
     <input type="hidden" name="-Error" value="error.html">
     <input type="hidden" name="Status" value="On Hand">
     Category:
     <select name="Category">
          <option>
          [FMP-ValueList: Category]
          <option value="[FMP-ValueListItem]">[FMP-ValueListItem]
          [/FMP-ValueList]
     </select>
```

```
    <input type="submit" name="-Find" value="Find CDs">
</form>
```

The above form would allow the user to select a category from a pull-down menu generated by a value list in FileMaker. An additional search criteria for Status=On Hand is hard-coded as a hidden input field.

Display Image -Img

Description: -Img is a command that returns an image from a database. In general, there's no need to use this command directly; instead use the [FMP-Image] tag to retrieve an image.

Using the -Img command, images can be retrieved from a FileMaker database in two ways. The first is to specify a value for -DB, a record ID (using -RecID), and a field name. The second is to specify a value for -DB and an "image key." An image key is specified using the [FMP-Field] tag. See below for examples.

Example: Link to a page containing an image:

```
<a href="FMPro?-DB=db.fp5&-RecID=11&pictures=&-Img">
  Display the picture from record ID 11 and field name "pictures"</a>
```

Display an image in a page by ID and field:

```
<img src="FMPro?-DB=db.fp5&-RecID=[FMP-CurrentRecID]&pictures=&-Img">
```

Display an image in a page by image key:

```
<img src="FMPro?-DB=db.fp5&key=[FMP-Field:pictures,url]&-Img">
```

Display an image the recommended way:

```
<img src="[FMP-Image:pictures]">
```

New Record -New

Description: -New is an action tag that is used to add records to a database. Data for the new record can be specified by name-value pairs. A user must have create permission in order to use this function.

Example: As an embedded URL:

```
<a href="FMPro?-DB=Event.fp5&-Lay=WebAdd&-Format=AddReply.html&
  EventType=Track&-New">Create a new Track Event</a>
```

To do the same in a form:

```
<form action="FMPro" method="post">
     <input type="hidden" name="-DB" value="Event.fp5">
     <input type="hidden" name="-Lay" value="WebAdd">
     <input type="hidden" name="-Format" value="AddReply.html">

     Event Type: <input type="text" name="EventType">
     <input type="submit" name="-New" value="Add Event">
</form>
```

View Form -View

Description: The -View action allows you to process a format file without interacting directly with the database. It's most frequently used as a link to a search or add page that needs to include data drawn from FileMaker, such as a set of value lists. Additionally, the -View action is often used in conjunction with sending e-mail, and is also one of the principal ways of kicking off a page where most of the work is done with inline actions.

Example: A link to a search page can be made either through a plain file reference or through the -View action, which enables the use of replacement tags and value lists from the database.

As a plain file reference, the link would be:

```
<a href="search.html">Search the database</a>
```

Using the -View action would result in an embedded URL similar to the following:

```
<a href="FMPro?-DB=products.fp5&-Format=search.html&-View">
  Search the database</a>
```

In a form:

```
<form action="FMPro" method="post">
     <input type="hidden" name="-DB" value="products.fp5">
     <input type="hidden" name="-Format" value="search.html">
     <input type="submit" name="-View" value="Search the database">
</form>
```

Other Request Parameters

Like the database action parameters, the following request parameters can all be passed via a form or URL and are all distinguished by the prefix of a hyphen. These parameters can all be added to a request in addition to the action parameter. In some cases, a request could contain numerous of these additional parameters; a request with the -Find action parameter might, for example, also include the -LOP, -Max, and -Skip parameters to control the search, while an e-mail command might contain as many as eight additional parameters. The following section details the use of these parameters and what other parameters they can combine with, if any.

Blind Carbon Copy for E-mail — -MailBCC

See E-mail

Carbon Copy for E-mail — -MailCC

See E-mail

Database Name — -DB

Description: The -DB tag is perhaps the most used CDML tag, since all actions require that you specify which database to process. By convention, it is the first name-value pair specified in embedded URLs and the first hidden input field in a form.

The name of the database and any extension needs to be specified—but not the path. The database must simply be open and in Browse mode. In fact, it's a good idea to keep your databases anywhere except your Web folder.

Example: In an embedded URL:

```
<a href="FMPro?-DB=inventory.fp5&-Format=Search.html&-View>Click
  here to go to the search page</a>
```

To do the same using a form:

```
<form action="FMPro" method="post">
     <input type="hidden" name="-DB" value="inventory.fp5">
     <input type="hidden" name="-Format" value="Search.html">
     <input type="submit" name="-View" value="Click here to go to
       search page">
</form>
```

E-mail

To Address for Mail	**-MailTo**
From Address for Mail	**-MailFrom**
Subject for Mail	**-MailSub**
Host for Mail	**-MailHost**
Format Field for Mail	**-MailFmtField**
Format File for Mail	**-MailFormat**
Blind Carbon Copy for E-mail	**-MailBCC**
Carbon Copy for E-mail	**-MailCC**

Description: FileMaker has the ability to automatically send e-mail after a CDML action has taken place. All of the tags above, with the exception of -MailBCC and -MailCC, are required to send mail. Moreover, the tags must have values.

-MailTo	The e-mail address of the recipient of the e-mail
-MailFrom	The e-mail address to use as the sender for the e-mail
-MailSub	The subject of the mail message
-MailHost	The SMTP server to use for sending the mail
MailFmtField	Name of a field containing the name of a text file to use as the body of the mail message
-MailFormat	Name of a text file to use as the body of the mail message
-MailBCC	(Optional) E-mail address to receive a blind carbon copy of the message
-MailCC	(Optional) E-mail address to receive a carbon copy of the message

Multiple values can be specified for the -MailTo, -MailCC, and -MailBCC by adding additional input fields. The value for each tag can either be hard-coded or it can be specified as a replacement tag.

Note: No error message is generated if the e-mail message is either malformed or missing data. The web log in the web directory is the only way that you can tell if there was an error.

Example: In any sort of shopping cart solution, you'd likely want to send an e-mail confirmation to your customers after they place an order. Let's say that the user has filled out and submitted an order form (which included customer information such as e-mail address), and you've specified OrderConfirm.html as the reponse file. Add the following HTML form to the OrderConfirm file. The -MailCC tag is used to notify you that an order has been placed.

```
<form action="FMPro" method="post">
     <input type="hidden" name="-DB" value="order.html">
     <input type="hidden" name="-Format" value="thanks.html">
     <input type="hidden" name="-MailTo" value="[FMP-Field:
       Customer::E-mail]">
     <input type="hidden" name="-MailCC" value=
       "bobcmc@mindspring.com">
     <input type="hidden" name="-MailFrom" value=
       "bobcmc@mindspring.com">
     <input type="hidden" name="-MailSub" value="Order Confirmation">
     <input type="hidden" name="-MailHost" value="SMTP.Company.COM">
     <input type="hidden" name="-MailFormat" value="email.txt">
Please confirm the following order items:
[FMP-Portal:  OrderItems]
     Quantity:    [FMP-Field: OrderItems::Quantity]
     Description: [FMP-Field: OrderItems::Quantity]
     Unit Price:  [FMP-Field: OrderItems::Quantity]
[/FMP-Portal]

     <input type="submit" name="-View" value="Confirmed">
</form>
```

The format file email.txt is a plain text file, but it can contain CDML tags like any other format file. In this example, that file might be something like the following:

```
     Dear [FMP-Field:  Customer::First Name]
     Thank you for your order!
     The following items will be shipped to you via [FMP-Field:
       Shipping Method].
     [FMP-Portal:  OrderItems]
          Quantity:  [FMP-Field: OrderItems::Quantity]
          Description:  [FMP-Field: OrderItems::Quantity]
          Unit Price:  [FMP-Field: OrderItems::Quantity]
     [/FMP-Portal]
     Please call us if you have any problems with your order.
     Thanks and come again soon!
```

Error Format Field -ErrorFmtField

Description: This tag is used to indicate the name of a field that contains the HTML that will be returned in the event of an error in a database action. Rather than direct the user to a new page (which would entail using the -Error tag), you may opt instead to pull the error response HTML from a page in the database instead.

Example: In an embedded URL:

```
<a href="FMPro?-DB=Employee.fp5&-Lay=WebSearch&-Format=
  hitlist.html&-ErrorFmtField=error_response&Status=Full+Time&
  -Find">Find Full Time Employees</a>
```

To specify an Error reply page in a form:

```
<form action="FMPro" method="post">
      <input type="hidden" name="-DB" value="Employee.fp5">
      <input type="hidden" name="-Lay" value="WebSearch">
      <input type="hidden" name="-Format" value="hitlist.html">
      <input type="hidden" name="-Error" value="error.html">

      Employment Status?: <input type="text" name="Status">
      <input type="submit" name="-Find" value="Find">
</form>
```

Error Number -ErrNum

Description: This parameter is used to indicate a range of FileMaker Pro error codes that will trigger the use of any special error page indicated by the -Error or -ErrorFmtField parameters. If you only want your error pages or error code to be used in the event of certain FileMaker errors, you can use this parameter to limit the range of error codes that will trigger your custom error handling. You may specify a single code or a range of codes, and you can use the -ErrNum parameter multiple times to specify multiple different error ranges.

Any error not specified in the -ErrNum tags (if -ErrNum is being used) will be caught by the Web Companion's default error-handling pages. You cannot use -ErrNum with multiple instances of -Error or -ErrorFmtField to specify different custom error pages for different error codes or error code ranges.

Example: In an embedded URL:

```
<a href="FMPro?-DB=Employee.fp5&-Lay=WebSearch&-ErrNum=500-509&
  -Format=hitlist.html&-ErrorFmtField=custom_error_response&Status=
  Full+Time&-Find">Find Full Time Employees</a>
```

Error Response -Error

Description: This tag is used to specify a format file to use in the event of an error during processing of an action. If no such file is specified, FileMaker will display a generic error message. Using Error reply files allows you to give more information to the user about how to fix the error, and it keeps the overall "look and feel" of your site intact. It doesn't matter where you put the -Error tag within your URL or form.

The path to use for the Error reply file is relative not to the Web folder but rather to the current file. So if your Error reply file is in the same directory as your Search file, then you shouldn't re-specify the directory name—just put the name of the file.

If you prefer to use paths that are relative to the Web folder, just change the path of the FMPro action to /FMPro or ../FMPro.

Example: In an embedded URL:

```
<a href="FMPro?-DB=Employee.fp5&-Lay=WebSearch&-Format=hitlist.html&
  -Error=error.html&Status=Full+Time&-Find">Find Full Time
  Employees</a>
```

To specify an Error reply page in a form:

```
<form action="FMPro" method="post">
     <input type="hidden" name="-DB" value="Employee.fp5">
     <input type="hidden" name="-Lay" value="WebSearch">
     <input type="hidden" name="-Format" value="hitlist.html">
     <input type="hidden" name="-Error" value="error.html">

     Employment Status?: <input type="text" name="Status">
     <input type="submit" name="-Find" value="Find">
</form>
```

Format Field -FmtField

Description: This parameter is used to indicate the name of a field that contains the HTML that will be used as the "format page" for a given database action. Rather than direct the user to a new page (which would entail using the -Format tag), you may opt instead to pull the response HTML from a field in the database instead.

Example: In an embedded URL:

```
<a href="FMPro?-DB=Employee.fp5&-Lay=WebSearch&-Format=hitlist.html&
  -ErrorFmtField=error_response&-FmtField=custom_format_field&Status=
  Full+Time&-Find">Find Full Time Employees</a>
```

Format Field for Mail **-MailFmtField**

See E-mail

Format File **-Format**

Description: The -Format tag is used to specify the HTML document that should be used as the response for the current action. It's a mandatory part of any embedded URL or form.

If the response document is in a directory other than the one containing the current document, you may need to include a path to the document (relative to the location of the current document). For instance, say you have a folder inside your Web folder called TimeTrack, which contains most of your HTML documents for your site. You have a subdirectory inside this folder called Admin, and you want to specify a document in this folder as your response to a search from a document in the parent directory. For this, you'd use -Format=Admin/SearchReply.html.

It's a little trickier to specify a format file in a directory above the current working directory. Let's say that you have a generic error page at the root level of your Web folder, and you want to use that no matter what subdirectory you're in. In this case, change the path to the CGI as specified in the action tag to "../FMPro," and then make all paths relative to the root directory. Your error page would then be simply -Format=Error.html, while your pages in subdirectories would be -Format=TimeTrack/SearchReply.html.

Example: In an embedded URL:

```
<a href="FMPro?-DB=TimeLog.fp5&-Lay=WebSearch&-Format=search.html&
  -View">Go to the Seach Page</a>
```

In a form:

```
<form action="FMPro" method="post">
     <input type="hidden" name="-DB" value="TimeLog.fp5">
     <input type="hidden" name="-Lay" value="WebSearch">
     <input type="hidden" name="-Format" value="search.html">
     <input type="submit" name="-View" value="Go to the Search Page">
</form>
```

Appendix

Format File for Mail **-MailFormat**

See E-mail

From Address for Mail **-MailFrom**

See E-mail

Host for Mail **-MailHost**

See E-mail

Layout Name **-Lay**

Description: The -Lay tag specifies the name of the layout that the current action should reference as it processes the user's request. In most cases, it's an optional tag, but for performance reasons, it should be specified whenever possible.

If the -Lay tag is not used, FileMaker uses what's known as Layout 0, which contains all the fields in the database. Actions such as Finds and Edits will run significantly faster if they are performed on a layout that only contains the fields that are pertinent for that specific action. Referencing related fields and portals requires the use of the -Lay tag and the presence of the referenced fields on the specified layout.

Additionally, the layout is used to specify value lists for the field and specify the number of repetitions available for repeating fields.

Example: In an embedded URL:

```
<a href="FMPro?-DB=activity.fp5&-Lay=WebSearch&-Format=
  Hitlist.html&-FindAll>List All Activities</a>
```

To do the same using a form:

```
<form action="FMPro" method="post">
     <input type="hidden" name="-DB" value="activity.fp5">
     <input type="hidden" name="-Lay" value="WebSearch">
     <input type="hidden" name="-Format" value="hitlist.html">
     <input type="submit" name="-FindAll" value="List All
       Activities">
</form>
```

Logical Operator -LOP

Description: Searches on the web will be either AND searches or OR searches; the default is the AND search. For instance, if you have two input fields on your search form (one for First Name and Last Name), searching for "Fred" in First Name AND "Flintstone" in Last Name will return records where both criteria are true. An OR search will return records that match either criteria. It can be tricky, since the OR search returns these records *and* those records.

The logical operator should not be confused with the search operator, which is a field-level comparison, such as First Name "begins with" Fred. The logical operator can be specified anywhere in the form and is usually either a hidden input field or a user-selectable value list.

FileMaker users are accustomed to performing multiple find requests; the logical operator OR can be used to achieve similar results through the web. For example, to search an activity file for all "calls" and "meetings," create two input fields with the same name (see the example below for the correct syntax). FileMaker will create a find request for each input field on the form for which the user types or selects data. Alternatively, a user can type multiple requests into a single input field, separated by spaces. As long as the logical operator is OR, FileMaker will create find requests for each word entered. This is also how multiple requests can be created using embedded URLs.

At this time, it's not possible to perform complex finds (such as "active calls" and "active meetings") because that would involve using two logical operators. To test and troubleshoot searches, activate FileMaker after submitting a web search and do a Modify Last Find (Cmd-R/Ctrl-R).

Example: In an embedded URL:

```
<a href="FMPro?-DB=activity&-Lay=WebSearch&-Format=hitlist.html&type=
  calls+meeting&-LOP=or&-Find">Search for Calls and meetings.</a>
```

Find some records using a form action:

```
<form action="FMPro" method="post">
     <input type="hidden" name="-DB" value="activity.fp5">
     <input type="hidden" name="-Lay" value="web">
     <input type="hidden" name="-Format" value="hitlist.html">
     <input type="hidden" name="-LOP" value="OR">
     Enter Search Criteria below.<br>
```

```
    Activity Type<input type="text" size=12 name="type">
    Activity Type<input type="text" size=12 name="type">
    <input type="submit" name="-Find" value="Find">
</form>
```

Max Records **-Max**

Description: The -Max tag is used to set the maximum number of records to display per page on the search reply page. The -Max tag belongs on the search page rather than the search reply page. If omitted, a default of 25 is used. To return all records in the set rather than break the set into chunks, set -Max to "all."

The maximum that the -Max tag can be set to is 2147483647. On the reply page, [FMP-CurrentMax] can be used to display the value that was used for the search.

Example: As an embedded URL:

```
<a href="FMPro?-DB=Employee.fp5&-Lay=WebSearch&-Format=EmpList.html
  &-Max=15&-FindAll">Employee List</a>
```

In a form:

```
<form action="FMPro" method="post">
    <input type="hidden" name="-DB" value="Employee">
    <input type="hidden" name="-Lay" value="WebSearch">
    <input type="hidden" name="-Format" value="EmpList.html">
    <input type="hidden" name="-Max" value="15">
    <input type="submit" name="-FindAll" value="Find All Employees">
</form>
```

Modification ID **-ModID**

Current Modification ID **[FMP-CurrentModID]**

Description: The modification ID parameter and its associated tag, [FMP-CurrentModID], were introduced in order to deal with the difficulties of record locking on the web—or, more exactly, with the lack of record locking. In regular FileMaker Pro, if you attempt to edit a record that another user is already editing, FileMaker will warn you that the record is in use and prevent you from modifying it until the other user has released it. The web was never designed for client-server database use, so there is nothing built into HTTP that helps overcome this. If two of your web users opt to edit the same record at the same time, they may do so. If the first one submits some changes, they will get written back to the database. When the second one submits his changes, they will overwrite the first user's changes, leaving neither of them any the wiser about what has happened.

FileMaker Pro keeps track internally of a "modified ID" that is guaranteed to change every time a record is modified. In general, the technique for using this ID is to inspect the ID whenever a user "checks out" a record for editing (for example, by bringing up a web page that allows her to edit the record) and then inspect the ID again when changes are submitted to the record. If the two ModIDs don't match, this indicates that someone else has modified the record between the time the current user "checked out" the record and the time she submitted it.

To overcome this problem, you may add the -ModID parameter to an -Edit request in CDML. You then supply a ModID that the record's own ModID needs to match (typically this would be whatever the record's ModID was at the time it was fetched). If the two IDs don't match, the -Edit action will fail.

Example: In a form:

```
<!-- Make sure, when updating the country, that no one else changed
  it -->

<FORM ACTION="FMPro" METHOD="POST">
  <INPUT TYPE="HIDDEN" NAME="-DB" VALUE="contacts.fp5">
  <INPUT TYPE="HIDDEN" NAME="-Format" VALUE="results.html">
  <INPUT TYPE="HIDDEN" NAME="-RecID" VALUE="[FMP-CurrentRecID]">
  <INPUT TYPE="HIDDEN" NAME="-ModID" VALUE="[FMP-CurrentModID]">
  <INPUT TYPE="TEXT" NAME="Country">
  <INPUT TYPE="SUBMIT" NAME="-Edit" VALUE="Edit This Record">
</FORM>
```

Operator -Op

Description: The -Op tag specifies the find operator to use when searching for records. An -Op can be specified for each field in a find request; the operator should be inserted directly before the field that it affects. The default operator is "begins with."

There are short values and long values for each operator. Either can be used.

Short	Long
eq	equals
neq	not equals
cn	contains

bw	begins with
ew	ends with
gt	greater than
gte	greater than or equals
lt	less than
lte	less than or equals

Example: In an embedded URL:

```
<a href="FMPro?-db=Members.fp5&-Lay=Search&-Format=Hitlist.html&
  -Op=gte&Days_Overdue=90&-Op=gt&Amount_Due=0&-Find">Find Members
  over 90 days overdue</a>
```

To do the same in a form:

```
form action="FMPro" method="post">
     <input type="hidden" name="-DB" value="Members.fp5">
     <input type="hidden" name="-Lay" value="Search">
     <input type="hidden" name="-Format" value="Hitlist.html">

     <input type="hidden" name="-Op" value="gte">
     Days Overdue: <input type="text" name="Days_Overdue" value="90">
     <input type="hidden" name="-Op" value="gt">
     Days Overdue: <input type="text" name="Amount_Due" value="0">

     <input type="submit" name="-Find" value="Find Members >
</form>
```

The choice of operator can be left to the user as well. To create a hard-coded selection list of operators, use the following syntax:

```
Operator: <select name="-Op">
          <option>Begins with
          <option>Equals
          <option>Not Equals
          <option>Contains
          </select>
```

Perform Script **-Script**

Perform Script Before Find **-Script.PreFind**

Perform Script Before Sort **-Script.PreSort**

Description: The -Script tags specify a script to run during the processing of an action. There are three options as to what order the action and scripts take place:

-Script	Script executes after finding and sorting the records

-Script.PreSort	Script executes after finding the records but before sorting
-Script.PreFind	Script executes prior to both the find and sort

Only scripts that are in the database specified by the -DB tag can be executed. If execution of a script causes the found set to change, the new found set is the one that is returned to the user.

The reply format file will not be generated until all scripts have finished. Multiple scripts can be specified simply by putting multiple tags on the same page. They will be executed in the order that they appear in the HTML document.

Scripts should be used sparingly (when at all) in web-based solutions. This is particularly the case in heavy traffic sites. Since FileMaker is not multithreaded, no other requests will be processed while a script is running.

Example: In an embedded URL:

```
<a href="FMPro?-DB=Registration.fp5&-Format=menu.html&
  -Script.Prefind=Export+Registrants&-FindAll">Export this set of
  registrants</a>
```

When clicked, this link would run the Export Registrants script in the Registrants database, perform a find all in same, and return the user to the menu.html page.

The following form specifies a script to run every time a new record is added to a database:

```
<form action="FMPro" method="post">
     <input type="hidden" name="-DB" value="Purchase_Order.fp5">
     <input type="hidden" name="-Lay" value="WebAdd">
     <input type="hidden" name="-Format" value="AddReply.html">
     <input type="hidden" name="-Script" value="Verify Data">

     .... user inputs

     <input type="submit" name="-New" value="Submit this PO Request">
</form>
```

Record ID **-RecID**

Description: The -RecID tag specifies the record to be used for certain actions. It points not to a field in the database, but rather to FileMaker's internal serial number for records. -RecID is a required tag for updating, duplicating, and deleting records.

Normally, the -RecID will be set to the [FMP-CurrentRecID], which is a replacement tag that returns this internal serial number.

Example: In an embedded URL:

```
<a href="FMPro?-DB=OrderItem.fp5&-Format=OrderDetail.html&
  -RecID=[FMP-CurrentRecID]&-Delete">Delete this item</a>
```

To do the same in a form:

```
form action="FMPro" method="post">
     <input type="hidden" name="-DB" value="OrderItem.fp5">
     <input type="hidden" name="-Format" value="OrderDetail.html">
     <input type="hidden" name="-RecID" value="[FMP-CurrentRecID]">
     <input type="submit" name="-Delete" value="Delete this item">
</form>
```

Skip Records -Skip

Description: The -Skip tag is used to indicate how many records to skip when performing a search. It's most often used in conjunction with the -Max tag to jump forward or backward through a found set. The -Skip value must be between 0 (the default) and 214749367 (the maximum number of records in a FileMaker database), or it can be "All." When the value is "All," or if the value exceeds the number of records in the found set, the last record is displayed. Skipping records does not change the found set nor the active record in FileMaker.

-Skip is specified on the search page as either an embedded URL or as an input tag in a form. Most often it will be a hidden tag, though it can certainly be turned into a user selection. The order of the tags in either case is not relevant.

The Link Forward and Link Previous tags are shortcuts for skipping records while browsing through a found set.

Example: As an embedded URL:

```
<a href="FMPro?-DB=Employee.fp5&-Lay=WebSearch&-Format=
  SearchReply.html&-Max=20&-Skip=40&-SortField=EmpID&-FindAll">Goto
  Page 3 of Employee List</a>
```

This would create a hyperlink that would perform a FindAll action in the Employee.fp5 database, sort the records by EmpID, skip the first 40 records in the found set, and then return a set of the next 20 records.

To do the same in a form:

```
<form action="FMPro" method="post">
     <input type="hidden" name="-DB" value="Employee.fp5">
     <input type="hidden" name="-Lay" value="WebSearch">
     <input type="hidden" name="-Format" value="SearchReply.html">
     <input type="hidden" name="-Skip" value="40">
     <input type="hidden" name="-Max" value="20">
     <input type="hidden" name="-SortField" value="EmpID">
     <input type="submit" name="-FindAll" value="Goto Page 3 of
       Employee List">
</form>
```

Sort Field **-SortField**

Sort Order **-SortOrder**

Description: -SortField and -SortOrder are used on search pages to specify the sort to perform on the resulting set of records. -SortOrder is optional and defaults to Ascending. Additionally, multiple sort fields can be specified—they are processed in the order they occur in the HTML. The -SortOrder tag must come immediately after the -SortField that it modifies.

-SortOrder can be defined as Ascending, Descending, or Custom according to a value list. Custom sorts either use the value list associated with the field on the layout, or the value list to be used can be specified by name, like Custom=StatusList.

Example: In an embedded URL:

```
<a href="FMPro?-DB=movies.fp5&-Lay=WebSearch&-Format=
  hitlist.html&-SortField=Title&-SortOrder=Ascend&-FindAll">Find All,
  sort by Title.</a>
```

In a form:

```
<form action="FMPro" method="post">
     <input type="hidden" name="-DB" value="movies.fp5">
     <input type="hidden" name="-Format" value="hitlist.html">

     <input type="hidden" name="-SortField" value="Date">
     <input type="hidden" name="-SortOrder" value="Descending">

     <input type="hidden" name="-SortField" value="Title">
     <input type="hidden" name="-SortOrder" value="Ascending">

     <input type="submit" name="-FindAll" value="Sort by Color">
</form>
```

Subject for Mail **-MailSub**

See E-mail

To Address for E-mail **-MailTo**

See E-mail

Token **-Token**

Description: A token is nothing more than a temporary variable that you can use to pass data from one format file to another without storing it in the database. Unlike cookies, tokens don't require the consent of the user to store; they are stored by the CGI and don't persist from visit to visit to a site.

Tokens are set using the -Token tag, and they are retrieved using the [FMP-CurrentToken] tag. To continue to pass along a token stored on a previous page, include a hidden input (or name-value pair) that sets -Token=[FMP-CurrentToken]. The value of a token can also be used as an argument in conditional statements.

A token will typically be set to the value of a field from a database, a user-entered value, or a record ID (using [FMP-CurrentRecID]). The maximum length for a token is 255 characters.

One common use of tokens is to store the order ID in a shopping cart solution. Typically, a new record will be created as a user enters the site. On the first response page, a token will be set to the [FMP-CurrentRecID] or the [Field: Order ID]. For further examples of this implementation of tokens, refer to the example shopping cart solution that comes with FileMaker.

Example: In an embedded URL:

```
<a href="FMPro?-DB=OrderItems.fp5&-Lay=Web&-Format=ItemList.html&
  -Token=[Field: OrderID]&OrderID=[Field: OrderID]&-Find">Go to
  Related Records</a>
```

This code would be used to "jump" to a set of related records and could be used on a detail or hit list page. In this case, assume that you're in an Order database and you want a link to display the related records as a hit list. The URL above will perform a find in the related database for order items with the current OrderID, and it sets the OrderID into a token so that on a later page there is something that you can use to find the correct order again. Since the user might want to delete order items, relying on the OrderID of the order items is unreliable.

To do the same with a form:

```
<form action="FMPro" method="post">
     <input type="hidden" name="-DB" value="OrderItems.fp5">
     <input type="hidden" name="-Lay" value="Web">
     <input type="hidden" name="-Format" value="ItemList.html">
     <input type="hidden" name="-Token" value="[Field: OrderID]">
     <input type="hidden" name="OrderID" value="[Field: OrderID]">
     <input type="submit" name="-Find" value="Go to Related Records">
</form>
```

Replacement Tags

Client Address [FMP-ClientAddress]

Description: [FMP-ClientAddress] is a replacement tag that returns the current user's domain address if domain name lookups are enabled in the web server or the user's IP address if it's not. When used in conditional statements, the syntax changes slightly to just ClientAddress.

Example: As a replacement tag:

```
Client Address is: [FMP-ClientAddress]
```

...would return:

```
Client Address is: fmpro.com
```

In a conditional statement:

```
[FMP-If:  ClientAddress .eq. fmpro.com]
     <p>Only users from the fmpro.com domain can access this
       site.</p>
[/FMP-If]
```

Client IP Address [FMP-ClientIP]

Description: [FMP-ClientIP] is a replacement tag that returns the current user's IP address. In a conditional statement, the syntax is simply ClientIP. Wildcards can be used for sections of the IP address, and multiple IPs can be specified, separated by commas.

Example: As a replacement tag:

```
Client IP is: [FMP-ClientIP]
```

...would return:

```
Client IP is:  248.231.25.84
```

In a conditional statement:

```
[FMP-If:  ClientIP .eq. 248.231.*, 248.230.*]
     <p>You must be from either the 231 or 230 subnet. Hi there!</p>
[/FMP-If]
```

Client Password [FMP-ClientPassword]

Description: When you implement security, users will be prompted by HTTP basic authentication to enter a username and password. [FMP-ClientPassword] is a replacement tag that returns the user's entry. It's probably most useful in conditional statements, where its syntax is ClientPassword.

Example: As a replacement tag:

```
The Password you entered is: [FMP-ClientPassword]
```

...would return:

```
The Password you entered is: abracadabra
```

In a conditional statement:

```
[FMP-If:  ClientPassword .neq. abracadabra]
     <p>You haven't entered the secret password correctly.</p>
[FMP-Else]
     <p>Welcome!</p>
[/FMP-If]
```

Client Type [FMP-ClientType]

Description: [FMP-ClientType] returns information about the type of browser being used to view your page. Again, it's not terribly useful as a straight replacement tag, but consider using it in conditional statements to customize your site for certain browsers or platforms. In conditional statements, the syntax is ClientType.

The following are examples of what is returned for different types of browsers:

- Mozilla 1.3 (Mac)—Mozilla/5.0 (Macintosh; U; PPC Mac OS X; en-US; rv:1.3a)
- Mozilla 1.3 (PC)—Mozilla/5.0 (Windows; U; Windows NT 5.1; en-US; rv:1.3)

- Netscape 4.76 (Mac)—Mozilla/4.76 (Macintosh; I; PPC)
- Netscape 4.76 (Windows)—Mozilla/4.76 [en] (Win98; U; Windows NT 5.0)
- Netscape 7 (Mac)—Mozilla/5.0 (Macintosh; U; PPC Mac OS X; en-US; rv:1.0.1)
- Netscape 7 (PC)—Mozilla/5.0 (Windows; U; Windows NT 5.1; en-US; rv:1.0rc2)
- Explorer 5.22 (Mac)—Mozilla/4.0 (compatible; MSIE 5.22; Mac_PowerPC)
- Explorer 5.5 (PC)—Mozilla/4.0 (compatible; MSIE 5.5; AOL 8.0; Windows NT 5.0)
- Explorer 6 (PC)—Mozilla/4.0 (compatible; MSIE 6.0; Windows NT 5.0; T312461)

For an exhaustive list of browser name strings, see http://www.pgts.com.au/pgtsj/pgtsj0208c.html.

Example: As a replacement tag:

```
Your browser type is: [FMP-ClientType]
```

...would return:

```
Your browser type is: Mozilla/3.0 (Macintosh; I; PPC)
```

In conditional statements, since the exact string that gets returned differs slightly from version to version, using the contains operator (.cn.) is likely a more useful comparison than an equals operator.

```
[FMP-IF:  ClientType  .cn. Mac]
     <p>You're using a Mac</p>
[FMP-Else]
     [FMP-IF:  ClientType .cn. Win]
          <p>You're using a Windows machine, n'est ce pas?</p>
     [/FMP-IF]
[/FMP-IF]
```

Client User Name [FMP-ClientUserName]

Description: Similar to the [FMP-ClientPassword] tag, [FMP-ClientUserName] returns the name that the user entered if he was prompted by HTTP basic authentication. The syntax in conditional statements is ClientUserName.

Example: As a replacement tag:

```
Your Username is: [FMP-ClientUserName]
```

...would return:

```
Your Username is: Fred
```

In a conditional statement:

```
[FMP-If:  ClientUserName .eq. Fred]
     <p>Howdy Fred!  This section is just for you!</p>
[/FMP-If]
```

Content MIME Type [FMP-ContentMIMEType]

Syntax: [FMP-ContentMIMEType: *Mime Type*]

Description: MIME stands for Multipurpose Internet Mail Extension; it specifies information about the type of document being transmitted. Now referred to as Internet Media Types, MIME extensions allow documents to contain things like character sets other than ASCII, images, audio or video messages, or even binary files.

When an HTTP Server sends information to a client, it includes the MIME type in the header to inform the client what type of data will be following the header. The client then uses this information to determine how to handle the incoming data and whether it needs to find a movie player or image viewer. The client's browser stores these mappings. With Netscape, for instance, go to General Preferences> Helpers to see how the browser is configured to handle MIME encoded documents.

The [FMP-ContentMimeType] tag allows the MIME type of a document to be specified. The default MIME type is text/html. Even though this is a replacement tag, nothing will be actually substituted.

Example: [FMP-ContentMIMEType: text/plain]

Cookie [FMP-Cookie]

Description: [FMP-Cookie: COOKIE_NAME] is used to retrieve the value of cookies set in the user's browser. (See [FMP-SetCookie] for a complete description of the function and use of cookies.) When used in conditional statements, the syntax is CurrentCookie:COOKIE_NAME. Both [FMP-Cookie] and [FMP-SetCookie] are replacement tags and as such can only be used on dynamic format files. Keep this in mind if you're thinking about setting or retrieving cookies from your default page, which is generally a static page.

Example: To set the date of a person's visit to your site into the cookie LastVisitDate and subsequently retrieve this value, you would need to do the following:

1. Create an unstored calculation (date result) in your database called CurrentDate.

```
CurrentDate=Status(CurrentDate)
```

2. Set the cookie at some point during the user's visit. The Expires parameter can be set to anything you wish.

```
[FMP-SetCookie: LastVisitDate=FMP-Field:CurrentDate, Expires=200000]
```

3. Use the [FMP-Cookie] tag to retrieve the cookie during the user's next visit.

```
<p>The last day you visited our site was [FMP-Cookie:
  LastVisitDate]</p>
```

This would be returned to the user as:

```
The last day you visited our site was 6/6/98.
```

Current Action **[FMP-CurrentAction]**

Syntax: [FMP-CurrentAction: Encoding]

The Encoding parameter is optional and can either be:

- HTML (default)—Performs HTML encoding
- Display—Displays the results in the language specified in the configuration of the Web Companion

Description: [FMP-CurrentAction] will be replaced by the name of the action that was performed to arrive at the current page. For instance, if you were to place this tag on a search reply page, it would return "find." Often, there will be multiple ways of getting to a page, and this tag allows you to customize the page, depending on the route taken.

The syntax in conditional statements is CurrentAction.

Example: As a replacement tag:

```
The Action you did to get here was: [FMP-ClientAction]
```

...would return:

```
The Action you did to get here was: edit
```

If you change the configuration of the Web Companion to use German then:

```
The Action you did to get here was: [FMP-ClientAction: Display]
```

Appendix

...would return:

```
The Action you did to get here was: Suchen
```

In a conditional statement:

```
[FMP-If:  ClientAction .eq. edit]
     <p>The database has been updated. Thank you!</p>
     [FMP-If:  ClientAction .eq. find]
          <p>Here is the record you requested.</p>
     [/FMP-If]
[/FMP-If]
```

Current Database [FMP-CurrentDatabase]

Description: [FMP-CurrentDatabase] is a replacement tag that returns the name of the database that was processed to return the current page. It's most helpful during the development of a site to help track down errors. The syntax in conditional statements is CurrentDatabase.

Example: As a replacement tag:

```
You just did a find in the [FMP-CurrentDatabase] database
```

...would return:

```
You just did a find in the Employee.fp5 database
```

In a conditional statement:

```
[FMP-If:  CurrentDatabase .neq. Employee.fp5]
     <p>Something's wrong.  The find used the wrong database!</p>
[/FMP-If]
```

Current Date [FMP-CurrentDate]

Syntax: [FMP-CurrentDate: Format]

Format is optional and can either be Short (default), Abbrev, or Long:

- Short—Short date format (6/1/98)
- Abbrev—Abbreviated date format (Mon, Jun 1, 1998)
- Long—Full date format (Monday, June 1, 1998)

Description: [FMP-CurrentDate] returns the current date as set on the web server. This tag is often used in conditional statements, where its syntax is CurrentDate, to customize a site for particular days, like the fourth of July or New Year's Eve. The date can be specified in any of the above formats in conditional statements.

Example: As a replacement tag:

```
Today is [FMP-CurrentDate: Long]
```

...would return:

```
Today is Monday, June 1, 1998
```

In a conditional statement:

```
[FMP-If: CurrentDate .cn. 7/4]
     <p>Happy 4th of July!</p>
[/FMP-If]
```

Current Day **[FMP-CurrentDay]**

Syntax: [FMP-CurrentDay: Format]

Format is optional and can either be Short (default) or Long:

- Short—Short day name (Mon)
- Long—Full day format (Monday)

Description: [FMP-CurrentDay] returns the name of the current day of the week, as set on the web server. Similar to the [FMP-CurrentDate] tag, it's often found in conditional statements, where its syntax is CurrentDay, to dynamically modify a web page.

Example: As a replacement tag:

```
Today is [FMP-CurrentDay: Long]
```

...would return:

```
Today is Monday
```

In a conditional statement:

```
[FMP-If: CurrentDay .eq. Friday]
     <p>Don't forget to get your timecards in by the end of the
       day!</p>
[/FMP-If]
```

Current Error **[FMP-CurrentError]**

Description: [FMP-CurrentError] returns the error number for the current action. The error numbers are the same as those returned by the Status(CurrentError) function in FileMaker. Usually, this tag is on a custom error reply page to give the user more information ab what went wrong. The error reply page can be specified in the se arguments using the -Error tag. Without this, a default error dialog will be displayed to the user.

CurrentError can also be used in conditional statements. If there was no error during the action, [FMP-CurrentError] will return 0. There is no tag that returns the description of the error.

The list of error codes is below. Codes 100-105 and 500-509 are among the most often encountered by web users.

-1	Unknown error
0	No error
1	User cancelled action
2	Memory error
3	Command is unavailable (for example, wrong operating system, wrong mode, etc.)
4	Command is unknown
5	Command is invalid (for example, a Set Field script step does not have a calculation specified)
100	File is missing
101	Record is missing
102	Field is missing
103	Relation is missing
104	Script is missing
105	Layout is missing
200	Record access is denied
201	Field cannot be modified
202	Field access is denied
203	No records in file to print or password doesn't allow print access
204	No access to field(s) in sort order
205	Cannot create new records; import will overwrite existing data
300	The file is locked or in use
301	Record is in use by another user
302	Script definitions are in use by another user
303	Paper size is in use by another user
304	Password definitions are in use by another user
305	Relationship or value list definitions are locked by another user

400	Find criteria is empty
401	No records match the request
402	Not a match field for a lookup
403	Exceeding maximum record limit for demo
404	Sort order is invalid
405	Number of records specified exceeds number of records that can be omitted
406	Replace/Reserialize criteria is invalid
407	One or both key fields are missing (invalid relation)
408	Specified field has inappropriate data type for this operation
409	Import order is invalid
410	Export order is invalid
411	Cannot perform delete because related records cannot be deleted
412	Wrong version of FileMaker Pro used to recover file
500	Date value does not meet validation entry options
501	Time value does not meet validation entry options
502	Number value does not meet validation entry options
503	Value in field does not meet range validation entry options
504	Value in field does not meet unique value validation entry options
505	Value in field failed existing value validation test
506	Value in field is not a member value of the validation entry option value list
507	Value in field failed calculation test of validation entry option
508	Value in field failed query value test of validation entry option
509	Field requires a valid value
510	Related value is empty or unavailable
600	Print error has occurred
601	Combined header and footer exceed one page
602	Body doesn't fit on a page for current column setup
603	Print connection lost
700	File is of the wrong file type for import
701	Data Access Manager can't find database extension file

702	The Data Access Manager was unable to open the session
703	The Data Access Manager was unable to open the session; try later
704	Data Access Manager failed when sending a query
705	Data Access Manager failed when executing a query
706	EPSF file has no preview image
707	Graphic translator cannot be found
708	Can't import the file or need color computer to import file
709	QuickTime movie import failed
710	Unable to update QuickTime file reference because the database is read-only
711	Import translator cannot be found
712	XTND version is incompatible
713	Couldn't initialize the XTND system
714	Insufficient password privileges do not allow the operation
800	Unable to create file on disk
801	Unable to create temporary file on System disk
802	Unable to open file
803	File is single user or host cannot be found
804	File cannot be opened as read-only in its current state
805	File is damaged; use Recover command
806	File cannot be opened with this version of FileMaker Pro
807	File is not a FileMaker Pro file or is severely damaged
808	Cannot open file because of damaged access privileges
809	Disk/volume is full
810	Disk/volume is locked
811	Temporary file cannot be opened as FileMaker Pro file
812	Cannot open the file because it exceeds host capacity
813	Record Synchronization error on network
814	File(s) cannot be opened because maximum number is open
815	Couldn't open lookup file
816	Unable to convert file
900	General spelling engine error
901	Main spelling dictionary not installed
902	Could not launch the Help system

903 Command cannot be used in a shared file

Example: As a replacement tag:

```
The error number is:  [FMP-CurrentError]
```

...would return:

```
The error number is:  501
```

In a conditional statement:

```
[FMP-If: CurrentError .gte. 500]
     [FMP-If: CurrentError .lte. 509]
          <p>One of your entries failed validation. Click Back on
            your browser and check your entry.</p>
     [/FMP-If]
[/FMP-If]
```

Current Find **[FMP-CurrentFind]**

Find Field Item **[FMP-FindFieldItem]**

Find Operator Item **[FMP-FindOpItem]**

Find Value Item **[FMP-FindValueItem]**

Syntax:

```
[FMP-CurrentFind]
     [FMP-FindFieldItem] [FMP-FindOpItem] [FMP-FindValueItem]
[/FMP-CurrentFind]
```

Description: Everything between the [FMP-CurrentFind] and [/FMP-CurrentFind] tags is repeated for each find criterion that was part of the find request that created the current page.

[FMP-FindFieldItem] returns the name of the field used in the find request. If a search was performed on a related field, the name of the field will include the relationship (e.g., Contact::First Name)

[FMP-FindOpItem] returns the find operator used for the search. The find operator is linked to a specific find field. This tag returns the long description of the operator (e.g., equals) as opposed to the short version (e.g, eq). The default find operator is begins with.

[FMP-FindValueItem] returns the value that was specified for the search. Like the find operator, it is linked to a specific Find Field Item

Example:

```
The find you just performed was: <br>
[FMP-CurrentFind]
     <li>[FMP-FindFieldItem] [FMP-FindOpItem][FMP-FindValueItem]<br>
[/FMP-CurrentFind]
```

...would return:

```
The find you just performed was:
• Last Name begins with Smith
• Color equals Blue
```

Current Format File **[FMP-CurrentFormat]**

Description: [FMP-CurrentFormat] will return the name and relative path of the current format file. Path will be relative to the Web folder. As with any replacement tag, keep in mind that this tag can only be used on a dynamic format file.

Example:

```
<p>Current file: <b>[FMP-CurrentFormat]</b>
```

...would return:

```
Current file: tracker/results.html
```

Current Found Count **[FMP-CurrentFoundCount]**

Description: Similar to the status function of the same name, [FMP-CurrentFoundCount] will return the number of records in the found set. In conditional statements, its syntax is CurrentFoundCount. The value is determined after the previous action has taken place, so when it's placed on a search reply page, it will equal the number of records found by the search.

Example: As a replacement tag:

```
Your search found [FMP-CurrentFoundCount] records.
```

...would return:

```
Your search found 244 records.
```

In a conditional statement:

```
[FMP-If: CurrentFoundCount .gt. 1]
     <p>Your search found multiple records.</p>
[/FMP-If]
```

Current Layout **[FMP-CurrentLayout]**

Description: As its name suggests, the [FMP-CurrentLayout] tag can be used to display or test for the name of the layout used during the processing of the current page. Like the [FMP-CurrentDatabase] tag, its main use is for troubleshooting as you're constructing a site.

Example: As a replacement tag:

```
The action was performed using the [FMP-CurrentLayout] layout.
```

...would return:

```
The action was performed using the AllFields layout.
```

In a conditional statement:

```
[FMP-If: CurrentLayout .ne. AllFields]
     <p>The action didn't use the AllFields layout. Something's
       amiss!</p>
[/FMP-If]
```

Current Logical Operator **[FMP-CurrentLOP]**

Description: [FMP-CurrentLOP] will return the logical operator that was used to generate the current page. It will either be AND or OR.

Example:

```
<p>The search was performed using the <b>[FMP-CurrentLOP]</b>
  operator.
```

...would return:

```
The search was performed using the AND operator.
```

Current Max **[FMP-CurrentMax]**

Description: This tag can be used on search reply pages to display the maximum records returned variable (see -Max) that was specified on the search that generated the current page. If no value was explicitly set on the search page, [FMP-CurrentMax] will return the default -Max, which is 25.

If -Max was set to All on the search page, Current Max will retu 2147483647, which is the maximum number of records in a FileMa database. You can test for this value and return a more user-frien reply by the following:

```
[FMP-If: CurrentMax .eq. 2147483647]
     <p>All found records are being displayed.
[fmp-else]
     <p>Records displayed in [FMP-CurrentMax] record sets.
[/FMP-If]
```

Example: On a search page, if you have the following in your form:

```
<input type="hidden" name="-Max" value="15">
```

Then on the reply page, [FMP-CurrentMax] can be used as follows:

```
<p>Click below to see the next [FMP-CurrentMax] records.
```

This would return:

```
Click below to see the next 15 records.
```

Current Modification ID [FMP-CurrentModID]

See the description for the -ModID command parameter.

Current Portal Number [FMP-CurrentPortalRowNumber]

Description: Used inside the [FMP-Portal]...[/FMP-Portal] tag pair, [FMP-CurrentPortalRowNumber] outputs the number of the current portal row being processed.

Example:

```
<!-- Add row number in front of each portal row -->
   [FMP-Portal:lineitems]
     [FMP-CurrentPortalRowNumber]: [FMP-Field:lineitems::name]<br>
   [/FMP-Portal]

<!-- After processing it could look like:
    1:  Red
-->
```

Current Record Count [FMP-CurrentRecordCount]

Description: [FMP-CurrentRecordCount] returns the total number of records of a database. More specifically, it returns the record count from the database that was acted upon to arrive at the current page. Current Record Count can also be used in conditional statements.

Example: As a replacement tag:

```
Your search found [FMP-CurrentFoundCount] records out of
  [FMP-CurrentRecordCount] in the database.
```

...would return:

```
Your search found 244 records out of 894 in the database.
```

In a conditional statement:

```
[FMP-If: CurrentRecordCount .eq. 1000]
     <p>Congratulations!  You've placed the 1000th order and win a
       lovely prize.</p>
[/FMP-If]
```

Current Record ID [FMP-CurrentRecID]

Description: [FMP-CurrentRecID] represents a unique ID number assigned by FileMaker to each record. The number itself is meaningless with respect to the data in the database. It's the behind-the-scenes identification for a record. Don't get this tag confused with any serialized ID fields that you may have in your database.

It's also a very important and useful CDML tag. You can display its value as a straight replacement, but more often, [FMP-CurrentRecID] will be used as an argument in a search string as a way to link to a particular record without having to rely on the primary key of the database.

The [FMP-CurrentRecID] tag will be used almost every time you want to update, duplicate, or delete a record from the database. The -RecID tag, which is required for all of these actions, will usually be set to [FMP-CurrentRecID].

Example: In an embedded URL:

```
<a href="FMPro?-DB=contact.fp5&-Format=DeleteReply.fp5&
  -RecID=[FMP-CurrentRecID]&-Delete">Delete this Contact</a>
```

On a form:

```
<form action="FMPro" method="post">
     <input type="hidden" name="-DB" value="contact.fp5">
     <input type="hidden" name="-Format" value="DeleteReply.html">
     <input type="hidden" name="-RecID" value="[FMP-CurrentRecID]">
     <input type="submit" name="-Delete" value="Delete this Contact"
</form>
```

Current Record Number [FMP-CurrentRecordNumber]

Description: [FMP-CurrentRecordNumber] returns the current record's position within the found set. It cannot be used in conditional statements.

Example:

```
Displaying record [FMP-CurrentRecordNumber] of [FMP-
  CurrentFoundCount] records found.
```

...would return:

```
Displaying record 5 of 24 records shown.
```

Current Repeat Number [FMP-CurrentRepeatNumber]

Description: Used inside the [FMP-Repeating]...[/FMP-Repeating] tag pair, [FMP-CurrentRepeatNumber] outputs the number of the current portal row being processed.

Example:

```
<!-- Add a number in front of each repetition -->
   [FMP-Repeating: extensions]
     [FMP-CurrentRepeatNumber]: [FMP-RepeatingItem]<br>
   [/FMP-Repeating]


<!-- After processing it could look like:
  3:  Green
-->
```

Current Skip Setting [FMP-CurrentSkip]

Description: [FMP-CurrentSkip] returns the -Skip value that was used to generate the current page. If -Skip was set to all or a number greater than the size of the found set, then [FMP-CurrentSkip] will be one less than the current found count.

This tag can be used as the value argument for the -Skip of subsequent searches. It can also be used in conditional statements, where its syntax is simply CurrentSkip.

Example: As a replacement tag:

```
Records skipped: [FMP-CurrentSkip]
```

...would return:

```
Records skipped:  100
```

As an argument for -Skip in an embedded URL:

```
<a href="FMPro?-DB=Employee.fp5&-Lay=WebSearch&-Format=
  SearchReply.html&-Max=20&-Skip=[FMP-CurrentSkip]&-SortField=
  EmpID&-FindAll">Go to Next Page</a>
```

As an argument for -Skip in a form:

```
<input type="hidden" name="-Skip" value="[FMP-CurrentSkip]">
```

In a conditional statement:

```
[FMP-If:  CurrentSkip .eq. 0]
     <p>This is the first page of data
[/FMP-If]
```

Current Sort Order **[FMP-CurrentSort]**

Sort Field Item **[FMP-SortFieldItem]**

Sort Order Item **[FMP-SortOrderItem]**

Description: These tags are used on search reply pages to indicate what sort criteria were used to process the current page. [FMP-CurrentSort] is a looping tag, which means that it requires a closing tag. Everything between the opening and closing tag is repeated for each sort criteria. [FMP-SortFieldItem] and [FMP-SortOrderItem] are replaced with the appropriate values, as defined on the search page.

Example:

```
Sort criteria:<br>
[FMP-CurrentSort]
     <li>Field: [FMP-SortFieldItem], Order: [FMP-SortOrderItem]
[/FMP-CurrentSort]
```

...would return:

```
Sort criteria:
• Field: Activity Date, Order: descend
• Field: Type, Order: ascend
```

Current Time **[FMP-CurrentTime]**

Description: [FMP-CurrentTime] returns the current time (as set by the server, not the client) in either a short or long format. It can be used in conditional statements—with the syntax CurrentTime—to make a page more personalized, depending on the time of day.

- Short (default)—7:36 PM
- Long—7:36:24 PM

Example: As a replacement tag:

```
<p>The current time is [FMP-CurrentTime, long]
```

...would return:

```
The current time is 6:34:26 PM
```

In a conditional statement:

```
[FMP-If: CurrentTime .lt. 12:00 PM]
     <p>Good Morning!
[/FMP-Else]
     [FMP-If: CurrentTime .lt. 5:00 PM]
          <p>Good Afternoon!
     [/FMP-Else]
          <p>Good Evening!
     [/FMP-If]
[/FMP-If]
```

Current Token **[FMP-CurrentToken]**

Description: [FMP-CurrentToken] returns the value of the token as set during the previous action. If no token was set as a parameter for that action, [FMP-CurrentToken] will be blank. It can also be used as the left-hand argument in conditional statements where its syntax is CurrentToken.

Example: As a replacement tag:

```
<p>The token passed was: [FMP-CurrentToken]
```

...would return:

```
The token passed was: fred
```

To continue to pass a previously set token set to the next page, set the -Token tag to [FMP-CurrentToken]. This must be done to retrieve the token value on the following page.

```
<input type="hidden" name="-Token" value="[FMP-CurrentToken]">
```

The same holds true for embedded URLs:

```
<a href="FMPro?-DB=products&-Format=detail.html&-Token=
  [FMP-CurrentToken]&ProductID=23&-Search>Click here to go to the
  search page</a>
```

CurrentToken can also be tested in conditional statements. The following example tests if the token is empty, which can be useful for troubleshooting errors.

```
[FMP-If: CurrentToken .eq.]
No token has been set. What happened?
[/FMP-If]
```

Else If **[FMP-ElseIf]**

See [FMP-If]

Field **[FMP-Field]**

Description: This tag will be replaced with the value from the appropriate field from the database used to generate the current page. It can also be used as either argument in conditional statements.

Syntax: [FMP-Field: Field_Name, Encoding]

If a layout was specified by the -Lay tag on the previous page, then the field must be present on that layout. Related fields can also be displayed, but the -Lay tag is required.

Encoding can be:

- Raw—No encoding is performed. Use if your fields contain HTML.
- URL—URL encoding; should be used when field names are used in URLs, such as anchors and images
- HTML (default)—Performs standard HTML encoding
- Break—Performs standard HTML encoding and replaces soft returns with breaks (<br>)

Example: [FMP-Field] is used extensively as a replacement tag in generating hit lists of records returned. The following is an example of table that would be found on a search reply page.

Appendix

```
<table border=1 align=center>
	<tr>
		<th>First Name</th>
		<th>Last Name</th>
		<th>Phone Number</th>
	</tr>
[FMP-Record]
	<tr>
		<td>[FMP-Field: first_name]</td>
		<td>[FMP-Field: last_name]</td>
		<td>[FMP-Field: phone_number]</td>
	</tr>
[/FMP-Record]
</table>
```

In an embedded URL:

```
<a href="FMPro?-DB=Employee.fp5&-Lay=WebSearch&-Format=Detail&Last_
  Name=[FMP-Field: Last_Name, URL]&-Find">Find [FMP-Field:Last
  Name]</a>
```

In a form, the [FMP-Field] tag will generally be used both to populate the value of input fields with data and as a straight replacement tag.

```
<form action="FMPro" method="post">
	<input type="hidden" name="-DB" value="Employee.fp5">
	<input type="hidden" name="-Lay" value="WebSearch">
	<input type="hidden" name="-Format" value="Detail.html">

	Employee ID:  [FMP-Field: EmpID]
	<input type="text" name="first_name" value="[FMP-Field:
	  first_name">
	<input type="text" name="last_name" value="[FMP-Field:
	  last_name">
	<input type="text" name="phone_number" value="[FMP-Field:
	  phone_number">

	<input type="submit" name="-Edit" value="Update this Record">
</form>
```

In conditional statements:

```
[FMP-If:  Field:authorization_level .eq. administration]
	<p>Click <a href="secretadmin.html>here</a> to get to the secret
	  admin page!
[/FMP-If]


[FMP-If: Field:HomeTeamScore .gt. Field:AwayTeamScore]
	<p>We won!
[FMP-Else]
	[FMP-If: Field:HomeTeamScore .eq. Field:AwayTeamScore]
		<p>It was a tie
	[FMP-Else]
		<p>We Lost. Drat
```

```
    [/FMP-If]
[/FMP-If]
```

Field Name [FMP-FieldName]

See [FMP-LayoutFields]

Find Field Item [FMP-FindFieldItem]

See [FMP-CurrentFind]

Find Operator Item [FMP-FindOpItem]

See [FMP-CurrentFind]

Find Value Item [FMP-FindValueItem]

See [FMP-CurrentFind]

Header [FMP-Header]

Description: [FMP-Header] can be used to specify the HTTP header information for a document. It is a replacement tag (so it can only be used on pages that are responses of CDML actions), and it requires a closing tag, [/FMP-Header]. The tag can be placed anywhere in a document.

The header of an HTTP action can specify such things as the type of data being transferred, authorizations, cache instructions, and encoding mechanisms. If you need to learn more about specific header actions, there are many resources on the web. The Web Developer's Virtual Library at http://WDVL.com is a good place to start.

The most common use of the [FMP-Header] tag is to create what is often referred to as a header redirect, which allows you to perform multiple CDML actions. That is, the first action calls a page that consists only of a header redirect, and the header redirect performs a second action that specifies its own response page. An example of this is given in a moment.

Another interesting use of the [FMP-Header] tag, also demonstrated here, is to add a command to refresh a document after a certai time interval. This could be used to cause a session to "time out" af a period of inactivity. Also, the refresh can be used to create the fee a chat room in CDML, where the page being refreshed performs a search for the latest entries to the chat.

Finally, many header attributes can also be set using META HTTP-EQUIV tags. For instance, the META tag for refreshing a page every five seconds would be:

```
<META HTTP-EQUIV="Refresh" Content = "5">
```

...and the META tag for not allowing caching of a page would be:

```
<META HTTP-EQUIV="Pragma" Content = "no-cahce">
```

META tags must appear between the <HEAD> and </HEAD> portion of your HTML document.

Example: To perform a simple header redirect, create a document called redirect.html that contains only the text below. Then, reference redirect.html as the format response file (or error response file).

```
[FMP-Header]
     HTTP/1.0 302
     Location: http://www.fmpro.com
[/FMP-Header]
```

Similarly, Location can contain an embedded URL, which would allow you to perform additional database actions. For instance, in a shopping cart solution, you might want to be able to update an item and then return a list of all items in the shopping cart. In the update file, you would set the -Token equal to the Order Number and specify the -Format file as redirect.html, which would be similar to the following:

```
[FMP-Header]
     HTTP/1.0 302
     Location: FMPro?-db=OrderItems.fp5&-Lay=Shop&-Format=
       shoppingcart.html&OrderNumber=[FMP-CurrentToken]&-find
[/FMP-Header]
```

In the example below, a Refresh attribute is set in [FMP-Header], which would cause a client who has been inactive for more than five minutes to be taken back to the default page of the site.

```
[FMP-Header]
     HTTP/1.0 302
     Refresh: 5;URL=http://www.fmpro.com
[/FMP-Header]
```

If **[FMP-If]**

Else If **[FMP-ElseIf]**

Description: The [FMP-If] tag, along with the optional [FMP-Else] tag, allows you to enable or disable the display of different HTML based on conditions that you specify. Its syntax is as follows:

```
[FMP-If: LeftSide operator RightSide ]
     ...HTML if condition is true...
[FMP-ElseIf]
     ...HTML if condition is false...
     [/FMP-If]
```

The [FMP-If] tag contains a logical *test,* expressed as *LeftSide operator RightSide*. Descriptions of these items are as follows.

Left side: The following tags can be used on the left side of an [FMP-If] test. Note that many of these are based on CDML replacement tags, but the syntax is quite different. This is CDML's *intratag syntax*, meaning that when you, in effect, use a tag inside another tag, the syntax changes.

Boolean comparisons
CanDelete—Do password privileges allow for deleting records?
CanEdit—Do password privileges allow for editing records?
CanNew—Do password privileges allow creation of new records?
IsSorted—Is the database currently sorted?

Numeric comparisons
CurrentError—Returns the current error number. See the entry for [FMP-CurrentError] for possible values.
CurrentFoundCount—Returns how many records are in the found set
CurrentMax—Returns the current -Max value, which describes how many records should be shown
Current ModID—Returns the current ModID for the current database record (if applicable)
Current RecID—Returns the current RecID for the current database record (if applicable)
CurrentRecordCount—Returns how many records are in the database
CurrentRecordNumber—Returns the current record number

Appendix

CurrentSkip—Returns how many records were skipped to the beginning of the range
RangeEnd—Returns the record number of the last record in the range
RangeSize—Returns the number of records that were actually shown in the range
RangeStart—Returns the record number of the first record in the range

Text comparisons
ClientPassword—Returns the client's password
ClientType—Returns the type of browser the web user is using
ClientUsername—Returns the client's username as typed in by the web user in the authentication dialog box
CurrentAction—Returns the current action (e.g., Delete, New)
CurrentCookie: Cookie Name—Returns the value of the named cookie
CurrentDatabase—Returns the current database name
CurrentFormat—Returns the name of the current format file
CurrentLayout—Returns the current layout name
CurrentToken—Returns the current token value

Text or numeric comparisons depending on field type
Field: Field Name—Name of a field to compare with

Value list comparisons
ValueListItem—Returns the current value list item

Date/time comparisons
CurrentDate—Returns the current date in short format
CurrentDay—Returns the current day name in short format
CurrentTime—Returns the current time in short format

Address comparisons
ClientAddress—Returns the domain address
ClientIP—Returns the IP address

Operators: The operator specifies how the left side and the right side should be compared. Unlike operators in many programming languages, the CDML operators are not single symbols but short strings of text, as follows:

.eq—equals
.neq—not equal to
.gt—greater than

.gte—greater than or equal to
.lt—less than
.lte—less than or equal to
.cn—contains
.ncn—does not contain

Right side: In CDML, you're relatively constrained as to what you can compare things *to*. Further, the choices depend on the data type of the left side of the test. Here are the possibilities:

Boolean comparisons (only with .eq. and .neq. operators)
False
True

Numeric comparisons (only with eq, neq, gt, gte, lt, lte)
Field: Field Name—Name of a field to compare with (should be a number)
Literal Numeric Value—A number

Text comparisons (all operators allowed)
Field: Field Name—Name of a field to compare with
Literal Value—Any literal text that does not contain a] character (right square bracket)

Value list comparisons (all operators, except for Checked, which can only use eq)
Checked—Used with .eq. to test if the value list item should be checked
Field: Field Name—Name of a field to compare with
Literal Value—Any literal text that does not contain a] character (right square bracket)

Date/time comparisons (only with eq, neq, gt, gte, lt, lte)
Literal Value—Proper date, day, or time literal in current OS's format

Address comparisons (only with eq)
List of Literal Value—List of address or IP numbers with wildcards if wanted, separated by commas

Notes about literal values:

- If specifying a literal value, FileMaker Pro treats everything from the end of the operator to the closing right square bracket (minus leading and trailing blanks) as the comparison value.

Appendix

- Don't enclose literal values in quotes. If you include quotes, they're treated as part of the comparison value.
- Literal values are not case sensitive and can include spaces within text or number values.

Examples: Show information on the current found set:

```
[FMP-If:  CurrentFoundCount .eq. 0 ]
   Sorry, no records were found!
[FMP-Else]
   [FMP-CurrentFoundCount] records were found
[/FMP-If]
```

Check whether the user is permitted to delete records:

```
[FMP-If: CurrentAction .eq. Delete]
   [FMP-If: CanDelete .eq. False]
     Sorry, you do not have sufficient privileges to delete this
       record!
   [/FMP-If]
[/FMP-If]
```

Customize a greeting based on the user's address:

```
[FMP-If: ClientAddress .eq. users.home.cx]
   Welcome, Christmas Island user!
[/FMP-If]
```

Image [FMP-Image]

Description: This tag is the preferred means to display a picture from a FileMaker container field. When processed, this tag is replaced with a URL pointing to the specified image.

Syntax: [FMP-Image: *Field name*]

Examples: Display a picture:

```
<img src="[FMP-Image: illustration]">
```

Link to a picture:

```
<a href="[FMP-Image: illustration]">Click to view the image</a>
```

Include [FMP-Include]

Syntax: [FMP-Include: Filename]

Description: The [FMP-Include] tag allows a site to be built in a modular fashion by specifying a file to insert into the current document. For instance, if there is a header or navigation bar that needs to appear on multiple pages, that code can be moved to its own file and substituted with an Include tag reference. Updating sites becomes much easier, since the code is changed in one location and cascades automatically to all files that reference it.

The file that is included doesn't need to be a complete HTML document. Similarly, the included file can be inserted anywhere in the current document, even as header information.

The path to the included file is relative to the current document, so if they are in the same subdirectory, no path should be necessary. If the path of the action has been changed (to ../FMPro, for instance), then the path to the file will need to be specified.

Example: Specify general page information, such as background color or logos, as includes. Modifying the one included document will immediately update the whole site. The include file (let's call it header.txt) might look something like this:

```
<BODY bgcolor="#FFFFFF">
<CENTER>
<IMG SRC="MainLogo.gif">
```

Then, incorporate this into all of your pages by using an Include tag. Note that in this example, the <BODY> tag is in the header file and should therefore be omitted from any pages that include it.

```
<HTML>
<HEAD>
<TITLE>Search Page</TITLE>
</HEAD>

    [FMP-Include: header.txt]

// the rest of the page

</BODY>
</HTML>
```

Include Field **[FMP-IncludeField]**

Description: Though similar to [FMP-Include], this tag includes HTML taken from the specified database field, as opposed to the contents of a named file.

Syntax: [FMP-IncludeField: *FieldName*]

Examples:

```
[FMP-If: CurrentTime .lt. 12:00:00]
   [FMP-Include: Morning_HTML]
[FMP-Else]
   [FMP-Include: Evening_HTML]
[/FMP-If]
```

Inline Action **[FMP-InlineAction]**

Description: [FMP-InlineAction] allows for the processing of multiple database actions within a single target page (format file) rather than the "classic" CDML programming technique, which only allows one database action per page (specified by the action parameter in the URL or the HTML form that caused the page to load).

Each [FMP-InlineAction] tag has its own set of parameters, which are the same as the parameters that we would pass to CDML via a URL or a form. This means that we need at least a database name, a format file, and a database action, but optionally also a layout name and any of the other possible command parameters. The syntax of these differs from both the URL and the form syntax; instead, it uses the CDML *intratag syntax* that we've seen before.

Inside the inline tag pair, all replacement tags will function in the context of the current inline action. If the inline action were a search, for example, any [FMP-Record] or [FMP-Field] tags would refer to whatever found set resulted from the inline search. Outside the inline tag pair, the original page context would be in effect again.

Syntax: [FMP-InlineAction: *intratag command parameters*]

Examples: List all invoices for the current customer:

```
[FMP-InlineAction: -db=Invoice.fp5, -lay=Web, customer_id={field:
  customer_id}, -find]
   [FMP-Field: invoice_date] [FMP-Field: invoice_amount]
[/FMP-InlineAction]
```

Log record edits in an audit trail database (this inline would be present on any page that loaded after a successful edit action):

```
[FMP-InlineAction: -db=audit_trail.fp5, -lay=web, time=
  "{CurrentTime}", date="{CurrentDate}", record_id = {CurrentRecID},
  browser="{ClientType}", ip="{ClientIP}", -new]
[/FMP-InlineRequest]
```

Send a mail message after a subscription application:

```
[FMP-InlineAction: -db=application.fp5, -mailto={field:applicant_
  email}, -mailfrom=webserver@host.edu,
 -mailsub=Application Confirmation, -mailhost=mail.nexus.be,
   -mailformat=newuser.txt, -view]
[/FMP-InlineAction]
```

Layout Fields **[FMP-LayoutFields]**

Field Name **[FMP-FieldName]**

Description: These tags are used to display a list of all the fields on a certain layout. Any text between the [FMP-LayoutFields] and [/FMP-LayoutFields] tags will be repeated for every field on the layout specified during the preceding action. [FMP-FieldName], when placed between these tags, is replaced with the name of the current field.

Any related fields on a layout will also be returned, but a layout must be specified. If no layout has been specified, then all fields in the database will be returned (in creation order). Field names of related fields do not include the name of the relationship. Related fields contained in portals will not be returned by the [FMP-LayoutFields] tag. Instead, the name of the portal's relationship is returned.

The order in which fields are listed is based on their position on the specified layout; they are ordered from topmost field to bottommost field.

Two uses of these tags are to provide dynamic pop-up lists for users to choose sort fields and create search pages where the user can select the field to find from a pop-up list. The latter of these is demonstrated below.

Example: To get a simple list of all the fields on a given layout:

```
[FMP-LayoutFields]
     Field:  [FMP-FieldName]<br>
[/FMP-LayoutFields]
```

Following is an entire HTML document that allows a user to select the field he wishes to search on from a pop-up generated by the [FMP-LayoutFields] tags. This page needs to be dynamically generated so that the CGI can query the database for the list of field names. It is the name of the input field itself that needs to be changed, which requires the use of JavaScript.

```
<html>
<head>

 <script language="JavaScript">
 <!--Hide JavaScript from older browsers-->

 function Finder() {

 with (document.myForm.foo) {
      for (j=0 ; j<options.length ; j++) {
           if (options[j].selected == true) {
                document.myForm.elements[0].name=options[j].text;
           }
      }
  }
      document.myForm.elements[0].value=document.myForm.foobar.value;
      document.myForm.foobar.value="";
      document.myForm.foo.options[0].selected=true;

 }
 <!-- Ending Hiding -->
 </script>

 </head>
<body><center>
<form name="myForm" action="fmpro" method="post">

<input type="hidden" name="" value="">

<input type="hidden" name="-db" value="Contact.fp5">
<input type="hidden" name="-lay" value="web">
<input type="hidden" name="-format" value="reply.html">
<input type="hidden" name="-error" value="error.html">
In the Field: <select name="foo">
                <option>
           [FMP-LayoutFields]
                <option>[FMP-FieldName]
           [/FMP-LayoutFields]
      </select>
Find records that begin with: <input type="text" name="foobar"
  value="">
<br><br>
<input type="submit" name="-Find" value="Search" onClick="Finder()">
<br>
</form>
</body>
</html>
```

When processed, the page above will present the user with a form containing two input fields. The first, called "foo" here, will be a pop-up menu with a blank option at the top as the default, followed by a list of all the fields on the web layout of the Contact.fp5 database. For instance, the list might contain First Name, Last Name, and Favorite

Color. The second, called "foobar" here, will contain the value that the user wants to search for. After filling these in, the user clicks the Search button.

At this point, the onClick event handler kicks in and runs the JavaScript function "Finder." The function does four things:

1. It loops through all the options in the pull-down menu to find the selected one. When it finds it, it sets the name of the first form element to that value. The first form element is a hidden text field, which is actually the one that will be passed to the CGI for performing the search.
2. It sets the value of the first form element to the value of foobar.
3. The value of foobar is cleared so that it won't show up as a search request.
4. The first blank option is selected for foo, again, so that this won't show up as a search request.

The names foo and foobar can be anything; they don't need to be fields in the database. They are simply temporary input fields where the user can enter his selections. When users submit the form, JavaScript compiles the name and value to search for.

It would be easy to extend this example to allow the user to "dynamically" specify multiple search criteria or select find operators other than "begins with."

Link [FMP-Link]

Description: [FMP-Link] gives you a convenient way to reuse some or all of the command parameters that a particular page was invoked with. For example, let's say that you are producing an online catalog, where users can select a record from a hit list and view the record details. Rather than have them go back and forth to the hit list each time they want a new record detail, put Next and Previous buttons on the detail screen that will take them directly to the next or previous detail. To do this, you'd like to "reuse" most of their search parameters, possibly only changing a -Skip value or a record ID.

[FMP-Link] by default will regenerate the current page's URL in its entirety. You can also hand [FMP-Link] a series of character codes that will tell it which components of the URL to leave out. You can then add your own parameters to the resulting URL. For example, th code "r" will instruct CDML to leave out the format file section of t URL, while the code "a" will cause it to omit the action section. So command [FMP-Link: ra] will regenerate the current page's URL, minus the format file and action parameters. Here's a full list of possible character codes. They can be used in any order.

d—Omit database section of the URL
r—Omit format file section of the URL
l—Omit layout section of the URL
s—Omit sort criteria section of the URL
f—Omit find criteria section of the URL
m—Omit max section of the URL
k—Omit skip section of the URL
t—Omit token section of the URL
a—Omit action section of the URL

Syntax: [FMP-Link: *character codes*]

Examples: Reload a hit list page with a different sort order (this could be applied to each of the column headers in a hit list to allow the user to click a column head and resort by that column):

```
<a href="[FMP-Link:s]&-sortOrder=LastName">Last Name</a>
```

Link First **[FMP-LinkFirst]**

Link Last **[FMP-LinkLast]**

Link Next **[FMP-LinkNext]**

Link Previous **[FMP-LinkPrevious]**

Description: The link tags are used for navigation between sets of records on a search reply page. Returning large found sets of records to the web can be time consuming, so splitting the set into more manageable chunks using the -Max tag during the search is usually advisable. Then, the various link tags are used on the reply page to navigate to the first, last, next, or previous chunk of records.

When a search results in a found set smaller than the size designated by the -Max tag, the Web Companion is smart enough to know not to display the links. Similarly, Link Previous and Link First won't appear on the first page of data, nor will Link Last or Link Next appear on the last page of data.

The Link tags all require a closing tag. Any text (or images) between the tags becomes the hyperlink to the next page. FileMaker will actually perform a new search each time the user clicks one of the links, but it will figure out how many records to skip to display the proper set of data. The smaller the set, the quicker the search. All search and sort criteria will be identical for each subsequent search.

Another potential use of the Link tags is to navigate from record to record within a found set. To do this, simply set the -Max tag to 1 (so no more than one record will ever be displayed at a time) and then use the Link Previous and Link Next tags to move from record to record.

Example:

```
[FMP-LinkFirst]First set of records[/FMP-LinkFirst]
[FMP-LinkPrevious]Previous set of records[/FMP-LinkPrevious]
[FMP-LinkNext]Next set of records[/FMP-LinkNext]
[FMP-LinkLast]Last set of records[/FMP-LinkLast]
```

Link to a Record ID [FMP-LinkRecID]

Syntax: [FMP-LinkRecID: Format=*Pathname*, Layout=*Layout Name*]

Description: [FMP-LinkRecID] is a replacement tag that returns an embedded URL that points to a specific record in the database. Its main use is as a shortcut for putting a detail link on a hit list page. The same embedded URL that might be constructed manually is constructed entirely by the LinkRecID.

The Format and Layout parameters are optional. If they are not specified, they will default to those used to generate the current page.

The LinkRecID restores any find and sort criteria that were used to arrive at the current page, even though they will be largely superfluous because of the inclusion of the RecID in the search.

Example: In a hit list, use [FMP-LinkRecID] to provide a link to more detailed information about any given record.

```
<table border=1>
    <tr>
        <th>First Name</th>
        <th>Last Name</th>
        <th> </th>
    </tr>
[FMP-Record]
    <tr>
        <td>[FMP-Field: First_Name]</td>
        <td>[FMP-Field: Last_Name]</td>
        <td><a href="[FMP-LinkRecID: Format=detail.html, Layout=
           WebSearch]More Info</a></td>
    </tr>
[/FMP-Record]
</table>
```

Appendix

After processing, the HTML source returned to the user would look something like the following. The search performed to get to the hit list, Last_Name begins with "Fred," returned two records—one for Fred Flintstone and one for Fred Smith.

```
<table border=1>
<tr>
     <th>First Name</th>
     <th>Last Name</th>
     <th>Last Name</th>
</tr>

<tr>
     <td>Fred</td>
     <td>Flintstone</td>
     <td><a href="FMPro?-db=contact.fp5&-format=reply.html&-lay=
       web&First%5fName=fred&-recid=1&-find">More Info</a></td>
</tr>

<tr>
     <td>Fred</td>
     <td>Smith</td>
     <td><a href="FMPro?-db=contact.fp5&-format=reply.html&-lay=
       web&First%5fName=fred&-recid=6&-find">More Info</a></td>
</tr>
</table>
```

Log [FMP-Log]

Description: You can use the [FMP-Log] tag to write information into a log file. This can be useful for diagnostic or debugging purposes. For this capability to be enabled, you'll need to select the check box that says Information Log File in the Web Companion configuration dialog.

Syntax: [FMP-Log: *some text to be written to the log*]

Example: [FMP-Log: The welcome page was accessed at {Current-Time} from IP Address {Client IP}]

Option [FMP-Option]

Description: The [FMP-Option] tag provides a quick and easy way to dynamically access the contents of a value list for use in a selection list. All of the values in the list are replaced by <option>Value. This tag will usually be placed between <select name="FieldName"> and </select> tags.

Keep in mind that in order to display value lists derived from the database, the page must be dynamically generated (likely by the -View action).

Syntax: [FMP-Option: Field Name, List= Value List Name]

The first parameter, Field Name, specifies the name of the field that the value list is associated with.

The second parameter, Value List Name, is optional. If omitted, the default is to use the value list specified for that field on the layout defined by the preceding -Lay tag.

Example: To create a value list for a selection field:

```
Favorite Color: <select name="Favorite_Color"><option>[FMP-Option:
  Favorite_Color, List=Colors]</select>
```

The extra <option> tag creates a blank entry at the top of the selection list. It isn't required, but if omitted, the first value of the value list will be the default value.

Portal [FMP-Portal]

Description: The Portal tag allows you to display multiple related records, like you would with a portal in FileMaker Pro. You must specify a layout using the -Lay tag on the previous format file, and any related fields that you want to display must be on that layout. There doesn't need to be an actual portal on the layout. Having the related fields there is all that's needed.

Everything between the begin and end portal tags will be repeated for each related record. It is not possible to update portal records.

Syntax:

```
[FMP-Portal: Relationship_Name]
     ...some HTML
[/FMP-Portal]
```

Example: Imagine that you have an Employee file with a related Equipment file that contains information about hardware issued to that employee. On the Employee detail page, you'd like to place a portal displaying the related equipment. You've come to the detail page through a search and subsequent detail link.

```
<center>
<h3>Equipment Log for:  <b>[FMP-Field: Employee_Full_Name]</b></h3>

<table border=1>
```

```
    <tr>
        <th>Model</th>
        <th>Description</th>
    </tr>
[FMP-Portal:  Equipment_by_Employee_ID]
    <tr>
        <td>[FMP-Field: Equipment_by_Employee_ID::Model]</td>
        <td>[FMP-Field: Equipment_by_Employee_ID::
          Description]</td>
    </tr>
[/FMP-Portal]
</table>
```

Range End **[FMP-RangeEnd]**

Range Size **[FMP-RangeSize]**

Range Start **[FMP-RangeStart]**

Description: The Range tags are substitution tags that will display the First and Last record numbers of a found set. They are used in close conjunction with the Link and Max tags. [FMP-RangeStart] is the first record number, and [FMP-RangeEnd] is the last. [FMP-Range Size] indicates how many records are in the found set. In most cases, [FMP-RangeSize] will always be the same as the value of [FMP-CurrentMax], with the exception of partial pages where RangeSize will be the actual number of records shown (whereas [FMP-CurrentMax] is still the chunk size).

Example:

```
<p>Displaying records [FMP-RangeStart] through [FMP-RangeEnd] of
  [FMP-CurrentFoundCount] records found.<br>
([FMP-RangeSize] records displayed)<br>
```

...would return:

```
Displaying records 16 through 30 of 1835 records found
(15 records displayed)
```

Record **[FMP-Record]**

Description: Everything between the [FMP-Record] and [/FMP-Record] tags will be repeated for each record in the found set. Anytime you want to create a list of records (usually as the result of a search), you'll need the [FMP-Record] tag. If a -Max tag has been specified as part of the search, only that number of records will be displayed at any one time. If a -Skip tag has been specified, the search will return records beginning at the value of the -Skip tag, plus one. See the entries for -Max and -Skip for more information.

Example: After a successful search, the user will likely be taken to a hit list of found records. The HTML below uses the [FMP-Record] tag to format a table of search results.

```
<table border=1>
<tr><th>Employee ID</th>
<th>Last Name</th>
<th>First Name</th>
<th>Phone Number</th></tr>
[FMP-Record]
     <tr><td>[Field: Emp ID]</td>
     <td>[Field: Last_Name ID]</td>
     <td>[Field: First_Name]</td>
     <td>[Field:Phone Number]</td></tr>
[/FMP-Record]
```

Repeating **[FMP-Repeating]**

Repeating Item **[FMP-RepeatingItem]**

Syntax: [FMP-Repeating: FieldName]...[FMP-RepeatingItem]... [/FMP-Repeating]

Description: The [FMP-Repeating] tag is used to display and update data stored in a repeating field within a FileMaker Pro database. Everything between the [FMP-Repeating] and [/FMP-Repeating] tags will be repeated the number of times that the repeat is defined to display on the layout specified during the proceding action. The actual data contained in the repeating field is obtained by the [FMP-RepeatingItem] tag.

To add data to repeating fields in new records, however, does not require the repeating tags. Instead, use multiple instances of <input type="text" name="FieldName"> on your form, one for each repetition that you want to set.

Example: Say that you have a repeating field called Keywords, which was defined to display five occurrences on the preceding layout. Now, to simply display the contents of the field on a response page, the following HTML could be used:

```
Keyword List: <br>[FMP-Repeating: Keywords]
                     [FMP-RepeatingItem]<br>
                  [/FMP-Repeating]
```

To be able to update this same field would require the use of <input> tags:

```
Keyword List: <br>[FMP-Repeating: Keywords]
                     <input type="text" name="Keywords" value="[FMP-
                       RepeatingItem]">
                     [/FMP-Repeating]
```

The HTML above would need to be part of a <form> to display and update properly.

Set Cookie [FMP-SetCookie]

Description: Cookies are used by server-side connections (like CGIs) to store and retrieve information on the client side of the connection. They can significantly extend the capabilities of web-based applications.

Cookies are stored by the user's web browser and are sent to the server during subsequent visits to a site. Therefore, to set cookies, a user must have a browser that supports this feature (older versions of browsers may not), and it must be enabled.

Cookies can be used to store information like a user's client ID, the number of times he's visited your site, and information about his purchasing habits, shipping preference, and so on. To modify an existing cookie, simply set it again with the same path and name parameters as when it was originally set.

[FMP-SetCookie] is a replacement tag (and therefore can only be used in dynamic format files), but it returns nothing as its value.

If you need more information on cookies than what is presented here, check out http://home.netscape.com/newsref/std/cookie_spec.html or one of the dozens of other sites that offer definitions and examples of cookies.

Syntax: [FMP-SetCookie: CookieName=CookieValue, Expires=Minutes, Domain=DomainName, Path=Pathname]

Expires, Domain, and Path are optional parameters and can appear in any order within the tag.

Parameter descriptions:

<u>CookieName</u>: The name of the cookie that you want set. It can either be straight text or set to the value of a field using Field: FieldName. The name of the cookie can be anything you want; it doesn't have to be

the name of a field in your database. CookieName must be fewer than 1,024 characters.

<u>CookieValue</u>: The value assigned to the cookie. It can either be straight text or set to the value of a field using Field: FieldName. CookieValue must be fewer than 1,024 characters.

<u>Expires</u>: The number of minutes until the cookie expires. If this parameter is not specified, the cookie will expire at the end of the user's current session.

<u>Domain</u>: Defines the valid domain to which the browser will pass the cookie. This ensures that only applications on the specified domain can access the cookie value. If there is a tail match, the cookie goes through path matching to see if it should be sent. Tail matching means that the domain ".fred.com" would match "pudding.fred.com" and "www.fred.com." The domain is required to have at least two periods in it to prevent it from being set to something like ".com." Only hosts within the specified domain can set a cookie for that domain. The default value of the domain is the host name of the server that generated the cookie response. Finally, the domain must be fewer than 256 characters.

<u>Path</u>: The path attribute specifies the subset of URLs in a domain for which the coookie is valid. A cookie first must pass domain matching, and then the pathname of the URL is compared with the path attribute. If there is a match, the cookie is considered valid and passed to the server. The path "/fred" would match "/fred/wilma" and "/fredflintstone." If the path is not specified, it will default to the path to FileMaker Pro. Path must be fewer than 256 characters.

The length of the entire SetCookie tag must be less than 2,048 characters.

Example: As an example, say that you're selling gourmet food on the web and wanted to capture the type of food that a customer ordered so that you could automatically display those items during any subsequent visit in the next six months. The user has filled out and submitted an order form in the format file order.html and is then taken to the format file orderreply.html. To set the cookie, the following would need to be added to the reply page:

```
<p>Thank you for your order. A cookie has been set on your local
  browser so that the next time you visit our site, we'll immediately
  take you to a listing of our [FMP-Field: FoodType].</p>
[FMP-SetCookie: FavoriteFood=Field: FoodType, Expires=259200]
```

To retrieve the cookie during the user's next visit, the [FMP-Cookie] tag would be used.

```
[FMP-If: CurrentCookie:FavoriteFood .neq.]
     <p>Welcome back!  Click  <a href="FMPro?-DB=products.fp5-Lay=
       WebSearch&-Format=hitlist.html&FoodType=[FMP-Cookie:
       FavoriteFood]&-Max=10&-Find">here</a> to see our currently
       available [FMP-Cookie: FavoriteFood].</p>
[/FMP-If]
```

The conditional statement used is a Boolean comparison and simply tests to see if the specified cookie is not empty. If not, the user would see the following:

```
Welcome back! Click here to see our currently available Mushrooms.
```

Sort Field Item **[FMP-SortFieldItem]**

See [FMP-CurrentSort]

Sort Order Item **[FMP-SortOrderItem]**

See [FMP-CurrentSort]

Value List **[FMP-ValueList]**

Value List Checked **[FMP-ValueListChecked]**

Value List Item **[FMP-ValueListItem]**

Syntax: [FMP-ValueList: Field Name, List=List Name]

Description: These tags are used to create radio buttons or check boxes based on a value list from a database. Everything between the [FMP-ValueList] and [/FMP-ValueList] tags will be repeated for each member of the specified value list. The [FMP-ValueListItem] tag, when placed between these tags, will be replaced with the names of the value list items. Similarly, the [FMP-ValueListChecked] tag will return either "selected" or nothing, depending on the contents of the specified record.

List=Listname is an optional parameter. It is not required as long as the field is formatted to use a value list on the layout that was specified during the preceding action. For clarity, however, it's good practice to always specify the list name explicitly.

The syntax of radio buttons and check boxes may differ slightly, depending on what type of format file they are contained in. It doesn't make any sense, for instance, to use the [FMP-ValueListChecked] field on a search or add page, as there is no data available to evaluate yet. It hurts nothing to include it, but it is completely superfluous. Keep in mind also that search and add pages need to be dynamically generated in order to use value lists stored in the database.

Example: In any of the following examples, substitute type="radio" for type="checkbox" to change the format of the value list. The syntax otherwise is identical.

To create a check box data entry field on a dynamic search or add page:

```
[FMP-ValueList: Favorite_Color, List=Color]
     <input type="checkbox" name="Favorite_Color" value="[FMP-
       ValueListItem]">[FMP-ValueListItem]<br>
[/FMP-ValueList]
```

The <br> tag at the end of the second line will cause a line break between values. Omitting it will cause the value list to be displayed on one line horizontally.

On a response page, include [FMP-ValueListChecked] at the end of the input tag to display the data already selected.

```
[FMP-ValueList: Favorite_Color, List=Color]
     <input type="checkbox" name="Favorite_Color" value=
       "[FMP-ValueListItem]" [FMP-ValueListChecked]>
       [FMP-ValueListItem]<br>
[/FMP-ValueList]
```

After the page is processed by the CGI, the source that's passed back to the user would look something like the following. Note especially how [FMP-ValueListChecked] is interpreted.

```
<input type="checkbox" name="Favorite_Color" value="Black" >Black<br>
<input type="checkbox" name="Favorite_Color" value="Blue" >Blue<br>
<input type="checkbox" name="Favorite_Color" value="Green"
  checked>Green<br>
<input type="checkbox" name="Favorite_Color" value="Pink" >Pink<br>
<input type="checkbox" name="Favorite_Color" value="Red" >Red<br>
<input type="checkbox" name="Favorite_Color" value="White"
  checked>White<br>
```

Value Name Item **[FMP-ValueNameItem]**

Value Names **[FMP-ValueNames]**

Syntax: [FMP-ValueNames]...[FMP-ValueNameItem]...
[/FMP-ValueNames]

Description: Anything between the [FMP-ValueNames] and [/FMP-ValueNames] tags will be repeated for each value list in the database that was specified during the preceding action. [FMP-ValueNameItem] will be replaced with the names of the value lists.

Example: The primary use of these tags would be to give a user a selection list on a search page for defining a -SortOrder based on a custom value list.

```
<select name="-SortOrder">
     <option>Ascending
     <option>Descending
     [FMP-ValueNames]
          <option value="Custom=[FMP-ValueNameItem]">
            [FMP-ValueNameItem]
     [/FMP-ValueNames]
</select>

<select name="-SortOrder">
     <option>Ascending
     <option>Descending
     <option value="Custom=StatusList">Colors
     <option value="Custom=Color">Sizes
</select>
```

Index

About the Companion Files

All of the code samples and database files mentioned in the book are available for download at http://www.wordware.com/files/fmweb and http://www.moyergroup.com/webbook/. The files are grouped by chapter and, in the case of code samples, identified by page number. The files consist of FileMaker database files and text files containing source code. The downloads are available in a variety of commonly used archive formats.

Any errata or updates to the book will also be downloadable from these sites.